A Skeleton
in God's Closet

A Skeleton
in God's Closet

A Novel

Paul L. Maier

Thomas Nelson
Since 1798

NASHVILLE   DALLAS   MEXICO CITY   RIO DE JANEIRO

Published in Nashville, TN, by Thomas Nelson. Thomas Nelson is a registered trademark of Thomas Nelson, Inc.

Thomas Nelson, Inc. titles may be purchased in bulk for educational, business, fundraising, or sales promotional use. For information, please email SpecialMarkets@ThomasNelson.com.

Publisher's Note: This novel is a work of fiction. Most characters, plot, and incidents are either products of the author's imagination or used fictitiously. Most characters are fictional, and any similarity to people living or dead is purely coincidental.

Library of Congress Cataloging-in-Publication Data

Maier, Paul L.
    A skeleton in God's closet / Paul L. Maier
        p. cm.
    ISBN-10: 1-5955-4002-4 (Rpkg)
    ISBN-13: 9781-5955-4002-7 (Rpkg)
    ISBN-10: 0-8407-7721-3 (hc)
    ISBN-13: 978-0-8407-7721-8 (hc)
    1. Christian antiquities—Collection and preservation—Fiction.
    2. Excavations (Archaeology)—Israel—Fiction. I. Title
PS3563.A382S54 1994
813'.54—dc20   93—28203

Printed in the United States of America

07 08 09 10 11 RRD 10 9 8 7 6

To my colleagues
at Western Michigan University

Other Books by Paul L. Maier

Fiction

Pontius Pilate
The Flames of Rome
More Than a Skeleton
The Constantine Codex

Nonfiction

A Man Spoke, a World Listened
The Best of Walter A. Maier (ed.)
Josephus: The Jewish War (ed., with G. Cornfeld)
Josephus: The Essential Works (ed., trans.)
In the Fullness of Time
Eusebius: The Church History (ed., trans.)
The First Christmas
The Da Vinci Code—Fact or Fiction?
(with Hank Hanegraaff)

For Children

The Very First Christmas
The Very First Easter
The Very First Christians
Martin Luther—A Man Who Changed the World
The Real Story of Creation
The Real Story of the Flood
The Real Story of the Exodus

PREFACE

While most characters in this book are fictitious, several authentic personalities do appear. So that they might not be thought to endorse everything in this novel, I have not sought their permission. All are famous enough to be "in the public domain," and will, I trust, find their portrayal in these pages both appropriate and congenial. The reader, however, should know that the dialogue I supply for them is mine and not theirs.

When *A Skeleton in God's Closet* was first published in 1994, I had named the successor to Pope John Paul II as Benedict XVI. But in April 2005, Cardinal Joseph Ratzinger chose this very name for his pontificate. The reader is urged to distinguish between the two Benedicts: one imagined, the other authentic.

Special appreciation is due Professors Douglas J. Donahue, Stephen M. Ferguson, Nancy L. Lapp, Walter A. Maier III, and, in particular, Walter E. Rast and Dr. Robert H. Hume for technical assistance. A grateful word also goes to Opal Ellis, Connie Erickson, Linda Gaertner, David H. Scott, and David Stout for their advice and care in dealing with the manuscript.

P.L.M.
Western Michigan University
August 1, 1993

PROLOGUE

The archaeological discovery threatened to tear Western Civilization off its hinges. One out of every three people on earth was affected—some 2,000,000,000 whose lives were suddenly, brutally wrenched out of joint. It was like waking up one morning to find that a week had ten days, that there were forty-three minutes in each hour, or that one counted "1, 2, 8, 4, 5" and— maddeningly—no one else thought anything amiss.

The earth yielded its great secret only grudgingly, and the trowel that turned the world would not find its mark until summer. Now it was still spring in the life of Jonathan Weber, Professor of Near Eastern Studies at Harvard University. Had he known that it would be *his* hand on the trowel, he might have passed up his sabbatical that June.

ONE

Sabbatical: (def.) A year of absence for study, rest, or travel granted some college or university professors every seven years.

The greatest of the academic perks," Jonathan Weber often called it, though he himself had been too busy to take a sabbatical in recent years. A cascade of scholarly articles and books had flowed from "the Busiest Pen in the East," as *Time* once portrayed Weber. If university professors were supposed to "publish or perish," Weber was clearly courting immortality.

His major work, *Jesus of Nazareth*, had appeared the previous fall, just in time to catch the Christmas market. A book of vast—though surprisingly readable—erudition, the 580-page tome was expected to "bomb" in the trade and sell only to the scholarly world. But the bomb detonated unexpectedly in the general market, and the months since had cluttered Weber's quiet, scholarly life with media interviews and appearances, accolades and controversies. A few of his faculty colleagues groused openly that popularity tainted scholarship—and perhaps scholars.

Never mind, Weber mused. At the close of the semester in June he would skirt the snares of success and flee the classroom. The sabbatical would be his salvation and Austin Balfour Jennings his savior. Months earlier, Jennings, the internationally famed senior archaeologist at the British School in Jerusalem, had all but demanded Weber's presence in Israel with the playful lines:

> You seem to have retained at least *some* of the lessons I taught you at Oxford back in your Rhodes Scholar days, dear fellow, as witness your recent publications. But what about *field* experience? Yes, I know you spent a summer with Rast, digging that fabulous cemetery near the Dead Sea. But that's nothing compared to what

we're uncovering at Rama. You'd best join us this summer and get your fingernails dirty for a *worthy* cause. There's a good chap. . . .

Rama was the prophet Samuel's hometown, and although Jennings had failed so far in his quest to discover the grave of the prophet himself, he had unearthed some artifacts "of possibly *spectacular* importance," he wrote, adding, "You *must* come share the excitement!"

Such language was hardly vintage Jennings, Weber reflected, since his Oxford mentor despised sensationalism. A master of understatement, the unflappable Briton would likely have yawned on the foredeck of Columbus's ship as land came into view. Weber tried to pry out further details, coaxing by correspondence, but to no avail. Jennings would tell him only in person, only in Israel, and only at the dig itself.

On the blessed ninth day of June, Jonathan Weber had graded his exams, processed his seminar papers, and marched with the faculty in the commencement procession through Harvard Yard. It was a rite of passage for Weber, too, since his sabbatical year, including the summers straddling it, would extend for the next fifteen months. At his home that night in suburban Weston, he set no alarm and planned to sleep as late into Sunday morning as a pampered teenager.

The phone's ringing was penetrating, persistent, and altogether brutal. "Un*god*ly hour!" Weber muttered, as he yanked the receiver to his ear and emitted something that passed for "Hello."

"This is the Vatican City operator. Is Dr. Jonathan Weber there?"

"Speaking—"

"One moment, please, for Dr. Sullivan."

Almost before his sleepy neurons could respond, Weber heard—indecently loud for such a distance—the voice of his roommate in graduate school.

"*Hello, Jon!* Hope I didn't call too early."

"Hi, Kevin! No, it's all right." But why lie? He added, "Though it *is* bloody *5:45 AM!*"

"Oh, but it's going on *noon* here in Rome. Beautiful day, by the way!"

"So, what would the Reverend Kevin F. X. Sullivan, Ph.D., S.J., have on his mind besides the weather? Oh, sorry, sport. I'm finally waking up. Good to hear the likes of you!"

"How's your book on Jesus doing?"

"Inching up 'The List,' believe it or not. *Why*, I don't know."

"Congratulations! By the way, Mondadori has just published you in Italian—*Gesu di Nazareth.*"

"*Really?* I'd no idea it would be out this soon!" Now Weber was fully awake; authors have endless interest in their published progeny.

"I understand you're digging this summer in Israel, Jon?"

"Right. With Jennings at Rama."

"When do you leave?"

"Next Thursday."

"That soon? Glad I caught you! Jon, I have a *big* favor to ask—"

"Shoot."

"Could you arrange to stop off at Rome en route?"

"Why? I'm flying direct to Tel Aviv."

"It's *extremely* important, Jon."

"Such as?"

"Well, I can't tell you over the phone. Trust me."

Déjà vu, thought Jon. *First Jennings and now Sullivan—Come over here on blind faith. The inscrutable East!* Then he replied, "Unless it's earthshaking, Kev, I'd really like to fly direct. Perhaps on the return—"

"Jon, we *need* you to stop in! And yes, it may indeed be 'earth-shaking'!"

"Who's 'we'?"

"Ah, the Holy Father and I."

"Oh, sure! Then I fly on to Moscow for a reception at the Kremlin, right?"

"No. I'm *not kidding*, Jon. This is very serious."

Weber paused for several moments, then asked, "Why me?"

"Remember how you advised us on the Shroud business—the way you coordinated the scientific testing?"

Weber thought back to the days of John Paul II and how he had convinced the Vatican to have the supposed burial cloths of Jesus—the Shroud of Turin—tested for age via carbon 14. "But we proved the Shroud a *forgery,* Kevin," he resumed.

"Never mind. Honesty's the name of the game."

"How much time would you need?"

"Just a day. Longer, if you let me show you around Rome."

"No, another time. OK, Kev. I'll switch to Alitalia and stop off at the Eternal City. Phone you my arrival details shortly."

"*Thanks,* Jon! See you soon! *Ciao!*"

The night before his now-earlier flight to Rome, Weber crossed out all the items on his "must-do" checklist except one phone call, which he now made to his parents in Hannibal, Missouri. After two rings, his mother came on the line: "Pastor Weber's residence."

"Isn't it *Mrs.* Weber's residence too?" asked Jon.

"Who . . . who's this?"

"I represent the Boston chapter of Women's Lib—"

"Jonathan! Oh, Jon, it's you. Erhard! Get on the other phone! It's Jonathan. Oh, Jon, we're *so* proud of you! Several of the ladies at church have bought your new book, and—"

"*Several?*" thundered the clerical voice of the Reverend Erhard Weber at the other phone. "The St. Louis Post-Dispatch has had you on top of the best-seller list for several weeks now. Congratulations, son!"

"Well, it's not that big a deal, but thanks, Dad. Anyhow, my sabbatical is under way, and I wanted to call you before flying overseas tomorrow. I'll be stopping off at Rome on the way to Israel."

"Why Rome?" his mother wondered. "We knew about Israel, but—"

"Well, among other things, the pope wants to have a chat with me." That was the line he had wanted to drop on that Missouri Lutheran parsonage ever since Sullivan had called him.

"Well, that's fine, son," his father replied. "But why? You're not turning Catholic, are you?"

Jon laughed. "No, I'll give you a full report later on. But Mom, *don't* send me a packet of Protestant tracts to give to the pope, okay?"

"*Heh, heh!*" his father chuckled. "Trudi would do just that! *Heh, heh!*"

"Well, I have to run. You have my address in Israel?"

"Sure."

"Jonathan," his mother interposed, "I . . . I only wish Andrea were going with you—"

"Don't, Mother. Not now. But we'll say in touch. Take care!"

Although they were calling his flight, Jon zigzagged through a phalanx of travelers at Boston's Logan Airport and reached a newsstand, where he bought a *New York Times* before hurrying onto the Alitalia 747. Swinging into his seat, he flipped to the "Books" section of the *Times* and broke into a low smile. His own three-column photograph smiled back at him in an "Author's Portrait" feature with caption: "Jonathan P. Weber, Reginald R. Dillon Professor of Near Eastern Studies at Harvard University and author of *Jesus of Nazareth*."

"LIFE OF JESUS TOPS LIST" was the header of the story that followed, but Jon suddenly abandoned his reading and folded the paper. A silver-haired dowager sitting to his right had been looking over his shoulder and was starting to compare real and still life.

Once airborne, however, he twisted away from her gaze, unfolded the paper, and continued reading the article surreptitiously, as if it were hard-core pornography. He winced a bit at the irreverent first line of the piece:

> "Jesus!" is both the title of the new number one best-seller and also the reaction of the publishing industry to what may well be *the* trade phenomenon of the season. Lives of Christ are nothing new in the book business—an estimated 20,000 titles have been published across the world in this century alone—and it is commonplace that more books have been written about Jesus than any other figure in history.
>
> What, then, distinguishes Weber's work? The critical jury is still out, but an early consensus points to the way he has supplemented the biblical account with fresh evidence from a wide array of ancient disciplines, ranging from Babylonian astronomy to Roman

provincial law. His portrayal also cuts across denominational lines. Endorsements have arrived from evangelicals, mainline Protestants, Roman Catholics, and even . . .

Well, not quite, Jon mused. *The Fundamentalists don't like parts of it, of course, but some of them would probably criticize God's own arrangements in heaven!* He returned to the article:

The result may be *the* definitive life of Jesus for this generation. And all this from a very *un*professorial-looking scholar of comparatively tender years. (The man is only 43.) No beard etches his jawline, no gray speckles his dark blond thatch. Weber is medium tall, and carries a spare but solid frame, well-equipped for the archaeology he plans to pursue this summer in Israel. His steel-blue eyes and square-cut chin remind some of Robert Redford.

"Bloody nonsense!" Jon muttered, stuffing the *Times* into the seat pouch in front of him. The verbal fare was getting a little rich for his blood and could lead to fat in the head. No one knew his limitations better than himself.

When the woman next to him fell asleep, however, he returned to the article. The story now focused on the ancient languages he had mastered—Aramaic (the tongue Jesus and his disciples actually spoke), Hebrew, Greek, and Latin, as well as the modern research languages. Biographical details carried him from student days at Harvard to Oxford, and then on to his doctorate in Semitics at Johns Hopkins, before returning full-circle to teach at Harvard. *But the ICO hadn't been given enough credit,* Jon thought.

The ICO had been his dream—the Institute of Christian Origins. It was an academic talent pool that held quarterly symposia at which some of the world's finest scholars contributed their latest findings as to how Christianity was launched in the first century. Membership in the ICO was "by invitation only," and its roster included intellectual blue bloods who were delighted to have their scholarship reflected—with due credit—in Jon's new book.

The ICO had been funded by Philadelphia philanthropist J. S. Nickel, the chain-store prince and devout layman who, in the fiscal sense, had made it all possible. Jon hoped everyone would understand that dedicating his book to "Joshua Scruggs Nickel and all my colleagues at the Institute of Christian Origins" was a debt repaid.

Dinner aboard the 747 offered pasticcio, prosciutto, and melon as appetizers, with tortellini as the pasta course. Only an Italian gourmet could decipher the courses that followed, each served up with choice vintages from the vineyards of Italy. Jon thought the dessert a little showy, if not risky—flames shooting up from the "Vesuvio Surprise." A strolling violinist in Tarantella costume accompanied the after-dinner brandy. Clearly Alitalia was going all-out for its new direct flight to Rome.

Jon doused the overhead light and tried to sleep several hours before the too-early Atlantic dawn intercepted the plane somewhere over Ireland. His mind, however, would not disengage. He felt a strange interplay, a curious volley between two quite contrary moods—elation over the current success, yet also a relentless pain over the loss that had gnawed a gaping hole in his life. What should have been the glad late springtime of his career could not be shared with the one who had mattered most to him.

Why? Again he asked himself the nagging query raised ever since Job. In his younger, more religious days, he had asked it of God. But God had not replied.

Andrea *deserved* to share his success, he reminded himself. She was such a great part of it all. The album of his sleepless mind opened again to the July he'd spent at Heidelberg during his Oxford days. The first snapshot showed an exquisite, petite blonde caressing a book in the university library—north German or Scandinavian, he had opined at the time. The next zoomed in on the girl at a party in the Roter Ochsen, hoisting a stein of suds and blowing them in his face when he doubted that she was a Fulbright from Virginia! (She'd refused to speak English, and her German was *so* good.) A gallery of photographs followed, progressive enlargements of an outrageously rapid romance.

It was all straight out of Sigmund Romberg, *The Student Prince* revisited. Germans might call it *schmaltz,* but every syllable of the old university song had applied to Andrea and himself in spades:

Ich hab' mein Herz in Heidelberg verloren
auf einer lauen Sommer Nacht . . .

English could never convey the mood: "I lost my heart in Heidelberg on a mild summer night . . ."

He proposed to her on one of those nights, blazing with stars, as they stood at the parapets of the great castle overlooking the Neckar River. She hesitated, worried over the mad pace of their courtship, but then wrapped her arms around him and murmured, "A year from now I'd feel exactly the same way. *Yes,* Jon! I want to be your wife with all my heart!"

As if timed for the event, half the skyrockets in Germany seemed to explode over the valley below in one of the *Schlossbeleuchtungen* or castle illumination/fireworks displays Heidelberg offered each summer. "Now, *that* is music to suit the occasion!" said Jon, enclosing the lithe, willowy figure in an embrace of exuberant joy.

When they married and moved to Baltimore and Cambridge, the promise of happiness was easily fulfilled in fact. Andrea proved versatile in her roles as housewife, colleague, and critic, equally at home in the kitchen or the study. She also wanted to become a mother, but they waited until the ICO had been launched. Then, in November, Andrea happily announced her pregnancy, and they celebrated by spending Christmas as a second honeymoon in Davos, Switzerland.

Both were excellent skiers, but neither had ever skied Davos. Blizzards in early December had blanketed the Alps with an unusually heavy base, and during breakfast on the final morning of their holiday, Jon and Andrea had heard the echoing booms of cannon setting off controlled avalanches before the lifts started up. A warming wind from the southeast proved this a wise precaution, but someone had overlooked a bulbous snow mass looming over a hidden run on the expert course.

Jon twisted in his seat on the jet, his stomach taut, his hands gripping the armrests like two vises, trying desperately to warp the past into a different channel, a new vector in which he and Andrea would simply have left Davos after breakfast and taken the next plane home. He even constructed a fresh scenario of the time since then, tableaus that featured Andrea at her vital best, and now sleeping on his shoulder in the adjacent seat.

But no. *Blast* the inexorable past! Curses on history for its inevitability! He and Andrea were determined to conquer the expert run before leaving Davos. Just as they skied around a steep, brutal curve, the sodden snow mass parted from its frozen base and started to grind, then thunder its way down upon them. Jon, who was some distance behind Andrea, shouted, *"AVALANCHE!"* with every rarified breath in his lungs as he took refuge under a crag. But while he looked on helplessly, his precious Andrea was swept off the trail and buried under forty-five feet of snow. To no avail the shouts of *"Lavina! Lavina!—*Avalanche! Avalanche!" that rattled across the valley and brought helicopters, rescue teams, dogs, long probing poles. Too late, Andrea's uninjured but lifeless body was located and dug out. Three hours of hypothermia had killed her. And their tiny offspring-to-be.

It was now almost a year and a half since the disaster, months in which Jon had driven himself maniacally to finish his book, both as a memorial to her and because hard work tended to blunt grief. And yet, when the completed manuscript was to be dedicated, he could not, for some reason, bring himself to write *in memoriam* after Andrea's name. He decided to write someday on love and dedicate that book to her instead.

Just before finally falling asleep, he wondered if there had been a deeper reason for *not* dedicating a book with so religious a theme to his beloved. Perhaps ire at a God who "guards and protects us from all evil," as Luther explained The Creed, yet who must have been fast asleep that early Alpine morning? Or even nonexistent?

But no; a girl like Andrea easily proved that God did exist.

TWO

"*Attenzione i prego! Tutti passagieri . . .*"

"Attention, please! All passengers should fasten their seat belts for landing." The voice of a flight attendant filled the cabin speakers first in Italian, and then English. Jon stretched himself awake, reset his watch from 2:30 AM Massachusetts time to 8:30 AM Italian time, and looked out the window. Creamy clusters of clouds were parting to reveal the lazy green snake of the Tiber River below, beset on both sides by the brick and stone and marble that were Rome.

This was not his first visit to the Eternal City, yet each approach to Rome seemed to quicken the pulse. Not to pay the city homage was to play the barbarian. St. Paul in chains had stopped along the Appian Way to gather in her wonders. Later on, a Saxon monk named Luther knelt down on the highway at his first glimpse of "Holy Rome," as did hordes of pilgrims before and since. The plane banked over a satin Mediterranean, descended across the ruins of Ostia Antica, and glided onto the runway at Leonardo da Vinci Airport.

Just after Jon cleared passport control, a familiar voice penetrated the announcement chimes and cacophony of the terminal, "*Benvenuto, Jonathan!*"

Jon turned to see waving arms and a smiling face that pried some happy memories out of the past. "Hello, Kevin!"

Nattily attired in summer clerical grays, Sullivan gave Jon the sort of hug that might have crushed the rib cage of a lesser man. The Irish are enthusiastic about anything they undertake—even airport welcomes—and the dark-haired, ruddy-faced Sullivan hardly seemed the Jesuit prodigy who had the ear of Curia power brokers, including Pope Benedict XVI.

11

vin," said Jon, "you're *some* far cry from the haggard
to hoist beers with in Baltimore! Still teaching at the
?"

d—"
your commentary on First and Second Maccabees

ng along. You certainly stay well informed, Jon!"
ur ICO operation in Cambridge. We have spies every-

ge in hand, they bantered their way out of the terminal
o a waiting limousine. Jon looked at the long, black
es fluttering yellow-and-white Vatican pennants atop each
and smiled. "*Some* transportation you've arranged, Kev!
u sure this isn't some kind of Palm Sunday entry into the
City with a Calvary lurking at the weekend?"
w, you hit upon our plan," said Sullivan, raising his palms in
dismay. "Yes, it's all a Jesuit plot—kidnap one of the world's
t Protestant minds and then bend it to Rome's bidding!"
he ten-mile trip into the city was a festival of reunion, both
arsing memories from Johns Hopkins days. Since then,
livan had continued his graduate studies in Rome, where an
dress he delivered at a Jesuit conclave had intrigued the Father
General, who soon had Kevin taking the Fourth Vow and becoming a Jesuit himself.

Before reaching Rome, however, Jon started to probe the *why*
of his visit. Kevin first swore him to secrecy and then led off, "Let's
talk about how Mark's Gospel ends in the New Testament."

Jon thought for a moment, then responded, "You mean the
abrupt ending at 16:8 in the great uncial manuscripts? The
ephobounto gar in the *Codex Sinaiticus* and the *Vaticanus?*"

"Exactly."

The two could speak openly, even if their driver knew
English—which he did not—since the conversation would have
sounded like Outer Mongolian to him. In fact, however, Sullivan
was verging on one of the thorniest problems in biblical scholarship—the fact that two of the earliest and most important Greek
manuscripts of Mark's Gospel do *not* contain the crucial verses

9 through 20 in the last chapter, which report Jesus's resurrection appearances. One of these manuscripts, the *Codex Sinaiticus*, was discovered at Mount Sinai; and the other, the *Codex Vaticanus*, at the Vatican Library. Jon's reference to *ephobounto gar* was not a lapse in brain function, but the last two Greek words in these manuscripts describing the reaction of the women at Jesus's empty tomb, "for they were afraid."

"*Ephobounto gar!*" Jon repeated. "What a way to end the Easter story!"

"*If* indeed it ended there. No wonder the other manuscripts and papyri add verses 9 through 20!"

"Yes, but those verses hardly seem part of the original. So, again, what shakes, Kevin? How am I involved?"

Sullivan was silent for some moments. Then he replied, "This involves the *Codex Vaticanus.*"

"And . . . ?"

At that moment, the Mercedes was skirting the west bank of the Tiber and now turned sharply into Vatican City. "That's all for now, Jon," said Sullivan. "We're putting you up at one of our VIP apartments, okay?"

"Fine, but give me *some* idea what's going on!"

"Well, think of how we involved you last time. Now it's something similar, though maybe in reverse. But here are your digs. Settle in, and I'll pick you up for lunch at noon. And I hope you don't have too much jet lag, Jon; our visit with the Holy Father is at 3:30 PM this afternoon. Can you handle it?"

"No problem. *If*, that is, you give me a refresher course in protocol over lunch."

"Not to worry! You'll find Benedict congenial. He's quite a scholar, you know, really keeps up theologically. He even read your *Jesus*—in *English*, no less—before it came out in Italian!"

Benedict XVI—Bishop of Rome, Vicar of Jesus Christ, Supreme Pontiff of the Universal Church, Patriarch of the West, Sovereign of Vatican City, and Servant of the Servants of God—was the sort who would have winced had his official titles (and there were more) been formally announced. Like his saintly predecessor,

John XXIII, and the engaging John Paul II, the 265th incumbent of Peter's chair was determined to maintain a broad outreach to the world while charming it in the process. However, unlike his immediate predecessor, Benedict was a traditional Italian once again, but with a very *un*traditional openness on some of the thorny issues pricking the consciences of Catholics across the world. Jon had been delighted to find that *this* pope, at last, was encouraging fresh discussion on such matters as birth control, Holy Communion for divorced Catholics, and the role of women in the church. Some thought Benedict XVI—the former Ricardo Cardinal Albergo, Archbishop of Naples—might even review the issue of clerical celibacy.

It was exactly 3:30 PM when Kevin Sullivan brought Jon inside the Apostolic Palace, up to the papal apartments, and introduced him to the spiritual leader of a billion faithful. The face of the late-middle-aged pontiff bloomed with a warm smile as he extended his right hand. A simple white cassock, caped at the shoulders, and white skullcap sufficed the pope this day, as on so many other days. The linen was tailored perfectly to his five-foot, ten-inch frame and only marginally rotund girth.

"I bid you welcome, Professor Weber, in the name of our sovereign Lord." The papal English was flawless, though garnished with a delightful Italian accent.

"*Io sono molto onorato di incontrarla, Sua Santita,*" replied Jon, hoping the Italian for "I'm very honored to meet you, Your Holiness" was correct. Then he quickly added, "But since your English is clearly superior to my Italian, let—"

"Oh, I doubt that. But let me add my appreciation for your *Gesu di Nazareth.* Your pages combine scholarship with faith, or at least strong respect for faith. You have not abandoned the one for the other, as happens so often."

Jon reddened a bit at the accolade, but Benedict immediately put him at ease by adding, "And to think a *Lutheran* could have accomplished this!"

They both chuckled and went on to a variety of topics as they sat down to espresso in the private reception room. Asked about his plans in Israel, Jon told of the Jennings dig at Rama.

"You mean the Rama of Samuel? Ramathaim in Ephraim?"

"Yes indeed, but I'm astonished that you—"

"Oh, I'm a—how do you say it?—a 'dirt archaeologist' at heart. I almost took up the spade instead of the staff. Finding paths into the past is such a luxury, finding them for the future such a burden!"

The pope now glanced pointedly at Sullivan, who picked up his cue and said, "*Santissimo Padre,* I've briefed Professor Weber on the problem in Mark's Gospel and that the *Codex Vaticanus* may be involved, but I've told him nothing more."

Benedict nodded. "And the matter of confidentiality?"

Jon interposed, "I shall respect it categorically, Your Holiness."

"Fine. Then, shall we go?"

They walked through a series of ornate corridors until they reached the great wooden doors of the Biblioteca Apostolica Vaticana, the illustrious Vatican Library. The curator of the restricted archives met them at the entrance hall, a grizzle-bearded Dominican who bowed to the pope and conducted them to the guarded sanctum where the *Vaticanus* was stored. Then he left the chamber, locking the door after him.

The *Vaticanus* stood open on a desk, its leaves covered with a large black cloth to prevent light deterioration of the precious manuscript. Sullivan carefully removed the cloth, and said, almost in a tone of reverence, "It's open to Mark 16, Jon."

Approaching the *Codex,* Jon reflected on the rare privilege that was his. For four hundred years until the modern era, the *Vaticanus* had been virtually inaccessible to the world. He peered down and admired the fine vellum of the open leaves, each a little less than a foot square. He was amazed at the clarity of the beautiful uncial lettering in capitals, three columns to the page. Instantly he saw where the Gospel of Mark ended at verse eight, and the last two words were indeed *ephobounto gar:* "for they were afraid."

"Look, gentlemen, at how much space follows the end of Mark before Luke begins," commented Jon. He was too engrossed to notice a possible slip in etiquette in using collective address for the pope, but no one in the room cared. In that place, respect for a document from the fourth century reigned supreme.

"It's almost as if the scribe left a space after Mark in case 'the lost ending' ever did turn up somewhere," Jon continued. "It could then have been written in."

"It's possible," Sullivan admitted, then exchanged glances with the pope that had some obscure meaning, Jon assumed. Sullivan now went to the corner of the chamber, wheeled over a large apparatus, and plugged it in.

"Ultraviolet?" asked Jon. "Hasn't UV already been used on the *Vaticanus?*"

"Not this sort. It's the latest—laser-assisted—for a very pure and intense beam." Then he drew the curtains, turned off the overhead lights, and turned the machine on.

"Now take a look, Jon. You'll soon understand the reason for all this cloak-and-dagger routine."

Jon bent over the manuscript. Squinting a bit, he now saw the vague outlines of some ghostly, chalky lettering appear *after* Mark's concluding verse. Slowly, haltingly, he tried to make it out—no easy task, since the Greek left no spaces between words but ran them alltogetherlikethis.

In the hush of the chamber, Jon now read aloud, "HO . . . DE . . . TO . . . SOMA . . . IESOU . . . ANELAYMPHTHAY."

No one said anything, until Jon translated aloud to himself, "'*But the body of Jesus . . . was taken.*' Or 'taken back . . . retrieved.' Removed? . . . *Good heavens!*" Jon whispered, reaching down to the table to steady himself. If the meaning *were* 'removed' or 'stolen,' it would place a dagger at the very heart of Christianity. It was the oldest pagan explanation for what happened to Jesus's body on Easter Sunday morning.

"But the same verb form, *anelaymphthay,*" said the pope, "is used for Jesus's ascension, in the meaning 'taken up'."

"True." Again Jon peered down at the lettering, and said, "The uncials certainly look like they came from the same hand as the rest of the text. Have you taken photographs and checked that out, Kevin?"

"Yes. So far it looks like the same scribe."

"But *why* the eradication? Who deleted the line, and why?"

"Who knows? Someone, obviously, who feared that the verb

could be interpreted as 'stolen,' which would undermine Jesus's resurrection."

"And that could be anyone who had access to the *Vaticanus* for the past . . . how many centuries has it been here?"

The pope smiled and said, "Unfortunately, we don't know that either. The first Vatican Library Catalogue was published in 1475, and it lists the *Vaticanus*. We have no idea when or how it came to the Vatican. It could even date back to Constantine."

Jon cupped his chin in hand and paced the chamber in thought. Then he asked, "Who else knows about this?"

"You're looking at the only two in this world," Sullivan replied, with a wan smile. "The *Vaticanus* had never been given a good examination under strong ultraviolet, and I started with the New Testament three weeks ago. I got no further than Mark 16."

"For obvious reasons," said Jon. "Well, I'm honored that you both have trusted me with word of this discovery, though I do wonder why *I* am so privileged."

Sullivan explained, "Your advice on the Shroud proved to be the best *modus operandi* the Vatican could have pursued some years ago, Jon. We've already told you that. Now we wonder if you couldn't design a similar strategy for us regarding that eradicated line. For example, are there any scientific tests that could determine *how* that line was erased? *When* this might have happened? Or, *far* more importantly, if the original line was genuine? Or a forgery?"

Jon smiled wryly at the incredible complexity of the request. His hands wrestled each other, and he paced a tight circle around the desk on which the *Vaticanus* lay. Finally he answered, "The chemistry exists that could identify the eradication agent—*if* it happened in recent centuries. But going after the *original* writing?" He shook his head. "I doubt if there's any technology that could handle that."

For some moments, a silence—palpable, almost embarrassing—hung over the room. Finally the pope asked, "Do you have any recommendations, Professor Weber?"

Jon nodded. "I'll draw up a written agenda," he said. "For your eyes only, of course. Just off the top of my head, I'd suggest that you complete your ultraviolet scan of the entire *Vaticanus*, Kevin, and check if there are any other eradications. Then do the same with the *Codex Sinaiticus* in London, to see if there's a parallel eradication at the end of Mark. I can grease the rails for you on that—I know the keeper of manuscripts at the British Museum. Meanwhile I'll work on the problem with some of the scientists we assembled for the Shroud project. Don't worry, I won't identify the manuscript or give them the slightest hint at what we've got here."

Benedict XVI and Sullivan both nodded approvingly. "I'll also do a word study on *anelaymphthay* and see how it's used through the New Testament," Sullivan added.

"Yes . . . good, Kevin! That's *most* important."

Sullivan moved the apparatus aside and once again shrouded the *Vaticanus* in black cloth. Then he summoned the curator, and they returned to the papal apartments.

At the door, Benedict turned, smiled at Jon, and said, "I thank you for your advice, good professor—or, as I would now prefer to call you—good *friend*. I would like to remain in touch with you on this . . . and perhaps other matters."

"Nothing would please me more, *Santissimo Padre*."

"No, no—'*amico mio!*' Then it's *addio, caro professore*."

"*Arrivederci . . . e grazie, Sua Santita!*"

That evening, Jon was sitting with Kevin at an outdoor café just across from the ancient Roman Forum. It was Campari and soda for the Romanized Kevin, but Nastro Azzurro beer for the Germanic Jon, who was still aglow over his instant rapport with the Bishop of Rome.

"It's a little surrealistic, Kevin. I enter the papal apartments as a curiosity from abroad, and emerge as . . . as a friend?"

"Not to burst your bubble, good buddy, but that's Benedict's style. Here we are, only a year into his pontificate, and already we can see how we lucked out with that man. Some of the other *papabile* were, frankly, dreadful. Several hadn't had a new thought since their ordination. Others shouldn't have been ordained in the first place! And here we're graced with a good scholar, a warm personality, and a really able administrator. Makes one think the Holy Spirit *does* guide those conclaves!"

"If you had to point to any weakness in the man, what would it be?" Jon probed.

Kevin hesitated a bit, and then replied, "Well, it may be one of his credits that's the weakness—his trust in people. Trust can get misplaced around here. Like any agency on earth, we have our share of scoundrels, too, and some of them are in high places."

Kevin stopped just at the point Jon wished he'd continue. A friendly nudge, perhaps?

"Scoundrels in high places? Discuss and clarify," Jon teased. "This question is worth twenty-five points."

"Ever the pedagogue!" Kevin laughed. "Well, scoundrels in any outfit come in various shapes and sizes. I'm not so worried about the yo-yos in charge of Vatican finances. All they did was lose millions of church dollars in the Sindona scandal and other delightful enterprises. No, I'm more concerned about our doctrinaire oracles on the extreme right or left who are putting such pressure on Benedict. On the one hand, we have the Holy Office types with twitching nostrils who can sniff out heresy at a hundred kilometers. They're trying to drag the Church, kicking and screaming, back into the sixteenth century. The Latin mass? Of course! Just so it's medieval Latin!"

Jon laughed. "And the left?"

"Well, some of our boys are so far out they think the German higher critics a band of reactionaries! You know the sort: Jesus *may* have been born, but certainly not in Bethlehem. A few of Jesus's sayings in the Gospels *may* be his own, but not many. The miracles are myths. Jesus died, of course, since humans have a habit of doing that. But forget about any resurrection, afterlife, heaven, or anything else. Oh, I'll admit, we don't have many of those in the Vatican, but the *political* liberals are back again in force. 'Liberation Theology' not only lives, but it's 'the one hope of the Church'—Jesus and Marx, walking hand-in-hand into the great beyond. Never mind that communism collapsed in eastern Europe and Russia."

"It's all due to your marvelously wide canopy, Kevin. You Catholics stretch one vast umbrella over every extreme. We Protestants prefer division and subdivision into church bodies accommodating *every* conceivable viewpoint . . . But where, on the theological scale, do you place Benedict XVI?"

"Clearly, he's more moderate than John Paul II—not so incredibly narrow on birth control, for example—but he's still something of a centrist who's trying to hold the Church together. But you watch—both fringe right and fringe left will be tugging at him."

They now shifted to a technical discussion of the potentially staggering implications of the new line in Mark's Gospel, which lasted another hour. But that theological exchange was expressed *sotto voce:* no need to panic the Christian public just yet.

"Another beer?" Sullivan offered.

"I don't think so, Kev. Jet lag has me in its clutches. But thanks—I think!—for a rare and extraordinary day, friend!"

THREE

The next afternoon, Jon's El Al jet touched down softly at Lod, as if respecting land that was holy, and disgorged its passengers onto the tarmac at Ben Gurion Airport. After the usual intense security screening (*They forgot to check my armpits and groin,* thought Jon), he spotted the towering, lanky figure of Austin Balfour Jennings waving his orange sun hat.

It had been some years since he had seen his Oxford mentor, but recognition was no problem for Jon or anyone else. Once "A.B.J." walked into your life, he left a dominating imprint on the memory cells. At age sixty-three he was not merely hairless but imperially bald, in the Yul Brynner tradition. Americans who had dug under Jennings called him, depending on their generation, Daddy Warbucks or Mr. Clean—though always reverently. Ruddy, tanned skin stretched across his lofty, oval dome, then dropped past eyes of livid turquoise onto a triangular landmark of a nose. A double row of yellowish incisors, stained from pipe tobacco, had parted in a great smile.

"Welcome to *Eretz Israel,* Jonathan!" he said, squeezing Jon's hand in greeting. "Your baggage should have an easier time getting cleared than you did. We have a friend in customs. Otherwise, it's a frightful bore."

"Honored that you came personally, Austin! You surely could have sent one of your staff."

"Wouldn't *think* of it. Good flight?"

"Fine. Ah, my luggage."

"Off we go. My car's in front."

With Jerusalem a scant hour's drive eastward and upward from the airport, there was no time for the slightest lull in conversation.

Jon fired a volley of questions about the dig, and Jennings was eager to brief him.

"Once again, how'd you ever discover the site, Austin?" Jon inquired.

"Well, 'twasn't I but Sir Lloyd Kensington who first identified Rama back in the early sixties, and a *splendid* piece of sleuthing that was! He was bent on finding the Rama that was Samuel's hometown, but the name of the place has a *maddening* number of variations—Rama, Ramah, Ramatha, Ramathem, Ramathaim, Haramathaim, Arimathaim. And in the Gospels, of course, it shows up as Arimathea, Joseph's hometown. To add to the confusion, there are several other Ramas in the Bible—"

"Isn't there one on the outskirts of Jerusalem?"

"Quite right, my boy. But Kensington finally solved the matter by taking his clue directly from the *first chapter* of 1 Samuel. Here, see if you can find it." Jennings reached into the back seat, extracted a Hebrew Bible, and handed it to Jon. "Start reading at the first verse."

Thumbing to the spot, Jon read aloud: "'*Whyhee ish echad min haramathaim*—'"

"That'll do. Now translate."

"There was a certain man from Ramathaim . . ."

"Righto! The 'man,' of course, was Samuel's father. Now look down farther and tell me what that place is called in verse 19."

Jon's finger ran down the page, then stopped. "Ramah," he replied.

"Correct. Now since *rama* means 'height,' Kensington assumed that the author of 1 Samuel was trying to distinguish *which* of the same-named 'High Towns' he had in mind by using a *dual* the first time he named the place—Ramathaim, *which could be rendered,* 'the Rama with the two heights'."

"Oho! So Kensington scouted out all the twin peaks in Ephraim until—"

"Precisely! Until he found a pair near Bethel. There was an interesting tel here in a saddle between two heights which the Arabs—too good to be true—called *er-Ram.* He started digging, oh, back in 1963. I joined him during the third summer there."

"But how did you get positive identification? I mean, that the site actually *was* Ramathaim?"

"We uncovered a Maccabean cemetery, and several of the tombstones have names with '*of Ramathaim*' as suffix." Jennings paused, smiled, and continued, "And it's bloody good that we did, because Kensington collapsed at the dig and died toward the close of our next season. That way he could die a happy man!"

By now they were well into the foothills of Judea. The grades grew steeper and Jennings had to shift down his Peugeot. "See why it's always '*up* to Jerusalem,' Jonathan?"

"Right! But tell me what you've uncovered at Rama so far." Nothing pleased an archaeologist more than talking about his discoveries, Jon knew.

Jennings's eyes seemed to sparkle, and his commanding visage softened into a mellow smile. Stretching his arms against the steering wheel, he replied, "Well, Kensington started with the eastern half of Rama and eventually exposed much of it. Having this fixation on Samuel, of course, he favored the Late Bronze era."

"Around 1200 BC on?"

Jennings nodded. "He found the spirits of Samuel or Saul or David hovering over every other stone there, I think. *Beastly* of me to say this, but I'm afraid he rather hurried through the Roman and Hellenistic levels to get down to his 'hobby' stratum. Anyway, Rama reached its apex in the Herodian and first-century period, so *that's* the level that should have been favored throughout. In any case, we've been working on the western half of Rama—the part Kensington barely touched—and it's been *fascinating* in the extreme."

Jon wondered how much longer Jennings would play cat-and-mouse with him. *What in blue* blazes *did you discover of such* 'spectacular' *importance?* he felt like shouting. But he restrained himself and asked, "But again, what have you found, Austin?"

"Ah, dear me . . . I haven't really answered you, have I? Well, after Kensington died, the dig was shut down until I finally got back here four years ago. First, of course, we dug a survey trench across the midsection and got down to a very nice Middle Bronze IIc stratum, where we hit bedrock."

"Which means the site was settled no earlier than 1700 BC?"

"Probably 1600."

"If that's the earliest stratum, what's the latest?"

"Aside from negligible medieval and Arab artifacts near the surface, Rama seems to have terminated late in the first century . . . most probably during the Jewish war with Rome in AD 66. A rubble layer at that point shows the Romans must have leveled the place on their way to Jerusalem."

"What's the latest coinage at the destruction stratum, *if* you found any?"

"So far, it's a silver denarius minted under Claudius, datable to AD 53. Well, no, Clive Brampton, my second-in-command, found a Turkish pound piece from the 1890s, but that 'spook' must have intruded, somehow."

The steep hills of undulant reddish brown soil, gently forested with pine and cypress, suddenly gave way to the stark white limestone of Jerusalem. *Few cities on earth loom into sight so swiftly as Jerusalem,* thought Jon, *and none form so fascinating a foil for the deep azure of the late afternoon sky.*

Jennings, however, was unimpressed. "Those skyscrapers are spoiling the lines of the city, Jonathan. 'Next year in Jerusalem!' by all means, because after that it'll be ruined! The Hilton, the Plaza, the Ramada Renaissance, the Hyatt Regency are all making a 'permanent pilgrimage' here, it seems! But welcome back to *al-Quds,* as the Arabs called it—*'the Holy'.*"

They drove across the northern rim of Jerusalem, then turned left on the Nablus Road, the main highway northward out of the city. Jennings now rattled off a list of the major structures and artifacts discovered in each of the strata at Rama. The stone foundations of houses, streets, and shops of the western town during the Roman period had been exposed. Each level, apparently, had delivered more than its quota of beads and jewelry, tools, lamps, figurines, seals, and weapons, in addition to the pottery that dated the strata.

Fascinating finds, Jon mused, but none was enough to lure him halfway around the world. It was time to play "prod the professor." Shifting his muscular frame in the cramped Peugeot, he faced Jennings directly and said, "Well, Austin, you've liberated an impressive collection from Mother Earth. But which of these finds did you write me about? Which has 'possibly *spectacular* importance'?"

"'None of the above,' as you Yanks put it," he chuckled. "You'll find out soon enough." He now handed Jon a list of the twenty names of the Rama archaeological staff, giving a brief commentary on each.

"Who's this Shannon Jennings?" Jon inquired. "A relative?"

"My shrewish stepmother from Ireland, of course, in charge of security! The obnoxious old witch rides her broom around the dig to—" Jennings stopped when he noticed no smile on Jon's face, and asked, "You *were* spoofing, weren't you? Don't you really remember my daughter, Shannon, from your Oxford days?"

"Oh . . . oh, of course. How stupid of me! But she was only a little schoolgirl back in—"

"But since then, she took the oh-so-predictable route of growing up." Jennings yawned. "She keeps the journal for our dig."

Jon thought back to his Rhodes Scholar days. Snippets of recollection pieced themselves together into a mosaic of memory—his awe at being invited to tea at the home of *the* Austin Balfour Jennings shortly after his arrival at Oxford, his embarrassment at inquiring about Mrs. Jennings, only to learn she had died shortly after her daughter was born . . . and the smallish six-year-old girl who would never be able to remember her mother, and who asked him endless questions about America.

"Well, here's Ramallah, Jonathan."

"The dig staff stays here?"

Jennings nodded. "At the *Fanduq al-Kebir,* which means 'The Big Inn,' if you recall your Arabic." He drove to the eastern edge of the town and stopped in front of a three-story structure of aging buff-colored limestone and windows flanked by faded green shutters.

"*Our* name for the place is 'The Grand Hotel,'" Jennings observed, in jest. "But you won't find it in *Fodor's Guide*. Still, it's the best Ramallah has to offer us. We commute by bus to the dig each day, and be glad we're close enough to civilization that we don't have to sleep in tents!"

"When do we start out in the morning?" asked Jon, after a late supper with Jennings, his hand beginning to itch for the smooth wooden handle of a trowel.

"Frightful of me to have to tell you this, dear fellow, but we can only work in the cool of the morning. Breakfast is at 5:30 AM, and our bus leaves for the dig at 6:15."

"That late? I was ready to start by starlight!" Jon was almost half serious.

Jennings smiled. "Good that you overcame your jet lag back in Italy! But no, we don't go for nocturnal archaeology! In any case, it's really *smashing* to have you aboard, Jonathan!"

"I look forward to returning to your tutelage, *mon precepteur!*"

Just before retiring, Jon opened the shutters of his room and looked eastward across the barren hills. A three-quarters moon was floating upward from the Jordan Valley, dusting the slumbering countryside with a blanket of luminous chalk.

The land . . . the Holy Land . . . the Bloody Land . . . the Land of Death—and Life . . . The Land woven so closely into the beliefs of Jew, Christian, and Muslim that no one seemed to know where the earth stopped and dogma started . . . the Land of the One God.

The heavens . . . the moon and the stars—the same luminaries, but in a different context . . . the warm and fragrant breeze wafting up from the Jordan Valley . . . the supernal beauty of the night . . . the Sky of the One God.

And Andrea . . . the missing piece in his panorama. He could still see the tiny freckles on her nose, and the way her eyes glowed whenever he held her. Jon clenched his fist.

The mournful howl of a jackal echoed across the hills. To the scientist, the haunting counterpoint was a mere biological performance. But to the Arabs who had lived there for centuries, it was the call of Destiny.

FOUR

The dig's bus, an old British Leyland, groaned its way six miles into the hill country northeast of Ramallah and wheezed to a stop at the Rama site, just as the rising sun painted a widening band of lambent gold across the twin hilltops. Before allowing anyone to grab a pick, trowel, brush, pan, or notebook, Jennings gathered his task force around a lofty cypress and introduced them to the newest member of the dig. A contingent of thirty-five students and volunteers from seven countries, along with a corps of local Arab laborers formed the basic work detail. The students and volunteers—some of them retirees—did most of the actual excavating, while the Arabs hauled away the spoil in wheelbarrows.

Jennings now presented his senior staff members. "This is my second-in-command, Clive Brampton, from the University of Manchester—but we'll forgive him for that! Clive's been with the dig ever since I took it over. I inherited him from Kathleen Kenyon."

The natty Welshman had a medium build and nicely chiseled features. His long, luxuriant, dark hair seemed to compensate for Jennings's baldness. Holding out a cordial hand, he said, "Welcome, Professor Weber! I think you'll find my library well supplied with your articles and monographs."

"And mine with your field reports from Jericho, Dr. Brampton."

"Clive."

"Jon."

Jennings resumed, "And this is Naomi Sharon, our ceramicist. She's a *sabra*, no less!"

A sultry, native-born Israeli beauty with velvet brown eyes, Naomi quickly responded, "No, *not* a relative of Ariel Sharon, thank God! *Shalom*, Professor Weber." Skin deeply tanned and figure nicely turned, *Naomi hardly seems the scholarly sort,* thought Jon. The dig crew likely found it pleasant to discuss pottery with her.

"And this Bohemian sort with frizzled beard who looks like a starving artist *is* one in fact, though hardly starving. Meet Richard Cromwell from the University of Chicago, our artist and photographer."

"Dick," he advised. "Delighted to meet you, Professor Weber!"

"Please, all of you, it's 'Jon.' Consider me just another student getting field experience."

"Achmed Sa'ad here was born in Ramallah," Jennings resumed, gesturing toward a figure wearing a red-and-white Hashemite *keffiyeh* over his head. "He's our liaison with the Arab workmen, which easily makes him the most valuable member of our dig!"

Sa'ad's dark brown visage was illumined by perfect white teeth as he smiled his welcome. Bowing gracefully with arms swept wide, he said, "I bid you welcome, Professor Weber, in the name of Allah the All-Merciful!"

Jennings went on to introduce the staff geologist, the architect, the botanist, zoologist, and the anthropologist. "I'm sure you'll all get much better acquainted shortly," Jennings concluded. "Now it's off to work, everyone! As Nelson said just before Trafalgar, 'England expects every man to do his duty!' So does Jennings! Every woman too!"

He brought Jon inside the headquarters tent and showed him a series of site maps from the Kensington campaigns on. Each new overlay showed an ever-enlarging excavation area. Jon studied the current chart carefully, then pointed to the western half of the map and asked, "This is the Hellenistic town?"

"Yes. And Herodian-Roman . . ."

"Seems as though you've exposed most of it."

"Not really. But look closely now, Jonathan: Do you notice anything . . . anything *unusual*, shall we say?"

Jon scrutinized the map, and the anomaly soon snared his attention. There, at the northwestern edge of the excavations, was a structure that seemed to dwarf the others—a near-labyrinth of ten rooms opening onto a central court in the Greco-Roman style. "What *is* that, Austin?" he asked. "A mansion?"

Jennings nodded. "Quite the largest town house in the entire site. And it may be a villa or estate, too, since we've not excavated it entirely, as you can see." Jennings pointed to the line where all drawing stopped abruptly, indicating undisturbed earth beyond. "This bears out Flinders Petrie's claim that the wealthy always built at the northwest sector of towns so as to be upwind from the dust and stench of the city. Prevailing winds here are northwesterlies."

Jennings now reached over, planted his index finger firmly inside the sketch of the town house, and said, "*Here's* where we found them, Jonathan, in the kitchen."

"Found what?"

"What you've been asking about in your letters. And the drive up here."

"You mean the discoveries 'of possibly *spectacular* importance'?"

Jennings beamed like a boy with a new toy who couldn't wait to show his friends. "Follow me, Jonathan."

They walked over to a large shed of corrugated metal. Jennings unlocked it and took Jon through a rustic museum tour of shelved artifacts—utensils, measuring bowls, oil lamps, jewelry, and tools. "Some of these were discovered in that town house," he said. "This gold ring, for example. From the ceramics, Naomi dates the house materials to the Herodian-Roman era."

At a far corner of the shed, Jennings pulled a throw rug aside, opened a storage cache beneath the floor, and extracted a box. He set it on a work table, lifted the lid, and said, "*Voilà*, Jonathan! Here's what I promised you. Have at it."

With extreme care, Jon lifted a reddish buff ceramic object out of the cotton surrounding it and examined it closely. "It's . . . it's a *jar handle*, isn't it?" he said.

"That it is, my boy. Here, use this magnifying glass. Look closely."

Jon unleashed a broad smile and said, "There's a *seal* imprint! And in Hebrew or Aramaic."

"Right you are, lad. Read it."

Slowly, Jon read aloud: "'*Le Yosef B'Asher.*' Well, the *beth* [B] must be an abbreviation for '*ben*' if Hebrew, or, more probably '*bar*' if Aramaic, so it's, well, literally, '*to Joseph, son of Asher.*' And meaning, of course, '*Belonging to Joseph, son of Asher*'."

"True, Jonathan. But so far, dear fellow, you've told us no more than we already knew. Now play the Aramaic epigrapher for us and give us a dating on the basis of the script. There's a good chap."

"But that's obvious." Jon smiled. "The lettering's . . . oh . . . I'd call it textbook semicursive of the late Hellenistic—early Roman period, about first century BC to first century AD."

"Aha!" Jennings was beaming again. "But now tell me what you make of *this.*" He returned to the subterranean cache and this time extracted a box containing a jar handle of fired darker clay, its lower end still attached to part of the amphora. "We also discovered this one in the kitchen of that town house."

"Another seal!" said Jon. "Incredible, it's *Greek!*" then he read: "*Eimi tou Iosafe*" and translated, "*I am [the property] of Joseph.*" He set the handle down and looked at Jennings in astonishment. "Bilingualism out here in the boondocks?"

"Nothing unique, dear fellow—Greek was a mark of high culture in that era, particularly among wealthy Jews. But do you understand my . . . excitement over these handles?"

For the life of him, Jon could not. Important? Of course they were, in that *any* ancient writing was important. But *spectacular?* Hardly!

"Think, Jonathan, *think!*" Jennings persisted.

Jon seemed to return to his Oxford days and Jennings's first questions to him in class, which he had answered rather miserably. Would they *ever* get beyond a professor-student relationship?

"Think, man!" Jennings urged, mercilessly. "Work with the names."

"All right: Joseph, son of Asher . . . Joseph, son of Asher, of Rama . . . Joseph, son of Asher, of Ramathaim . . . Joseph . . . *Oh, good heavens!* Not . . . not Joseph of *Arimathea?*"

Jennings was beaming again. "Isn't it at least *possible*, Jonathan?

The location's right. The stratum fits. The Gospels say that the Joseph who gave his tomb for Jesus's burial was 'a wealthy man from Arimathea.'"

Jon steadied himself against the table, deep in thought. Suddenly he broke into a grin and said, "Yes, it's possible! The New Testament doesn't mention the father of Joseph of Arimathea, so 'Asher' isn't ruled out. . . . Austin, I tell you true: if this *does* turn out to be Joseph of Arimathea's villa, you'll have made archaeological history! *Now* I can understand the 'of possibly *spectacular* importance' bit!"

"But I think we ought to stress the *'possibly'* at this point, Jonathan. Only Clive Brampton knows what we've found, and he's keeping the matter confidential, as must you."

"Of course. Actually, we have no proof whatever that this *is* the same Joseph." Jon scratched his head for several moments, then added. "Though we *can* firmly conclude that *someone* named Joseph had rather impressive real estate here two thousand years ago!"

When they returned to the headquarters tent, Jennings said, "Now, my erstwhile student, I'm assigning your homework for the rest of the day—our log here. Read through it, all eight notebooks meticulously recorded by my daughter, Shannon."

"I thought you said she was aboard this dig. I didn't see her this morning, did I?"

"No. She's in Jerusalem, getting supplies. But carry on, Jonathan. Pleasant reading!" With that, he planted his orange sun cap squarely over his bald dome and stalked outside to wage his continuing campaign into the past.

Jon read without interruption until 11:00 AM when the dig staff stopped for a light lunch of cheese, tomatoes, olives, cucumbers, and peanut-butter sandwiches. Throughout the meal Jon fired queries at Jennings in a losing attempt to master the history of the excavation in one day. But Jennings cheerfully indulged him. "You'd best hurry back to the books," he advised, over one last cup of tea. "We leave by 2:00 PM. Too beastly hot to dig after that."

Near that hour, however, Jon had gotten no further than

Volume 4 when a dark-haired girl in white shirt and shorts walked in and looked startled.

"Oh . . . hello," she said. "You're . . . reading my journal?"

"*Io non parlo inglese, carissima,*" he jested in Italian. "*Sono Italiano—*"

She looked at him quizzically, and said, "But you seem to have no trouble *reading* English!"

"I surrender!" Jon laughed. "You must be Shannon Jennings. Please tell me you are."

"Yes—"

"And I'm Jon Weber, just catching up on the past here at—"

"*Oh!* Professor Weber!" Now her frown melted into a warm smile. "Welcome to our dig!" She extended her hand.

"I'm really disappointed you didn't remember me, Shannon," he said, feigning a pout. "We chatted endlessly at Oxford when you were a six-year-old!"

She laughed easily. "That *was* twenty years ago!"

The girl was a slender, smallish, Irish colleen, whose flowing dark hair cascaded over tanned bare shoulders onto her cutaway tank top shirt, which bore the slogan, in blue: "I DIG" on the top line, and an elevated "RAMA" on the next. Her pert nose, bright sapphire eyes, and rose-petal lips made for a pixie face that innocently called attention to its natural loveliness. *Thank goodness, you took after your mother and not your father in the looks department,* thought Jon.

"I hope everything's clear to you in the journals," she said.

Catching himself, Jon broke off staring and replied, "Everything except the correlation code for the artifacts. For example, what does 'III, 4, 067' mean?"

"Where? Show me." She leaned over him, her hair brushing against his cheek. He felt tiny electric pulses, even tactile shock. *Ease off, man!* he scolded himself, silently. *You nearly changed her diapers years ago.*

"Oh . . . that means Third Season, fourth sector, artifact registration number 67. You'll find it catalogued exactly that way in the shed."

"Oh. Obviously. Thanks!"

"Not at all. Catch you later." With that, she breezed out of the tent.

Now properly oriented, Jon was back to reading the log when he heard the squeal of brakes. Peering outside, he saw a man opening a car door labeled "Israel Antiquities Authority" in Hebrew and English. The man looked about for some moments and then called, "Shannawn! O Shannawn!"

Jon walked outside and said, "She's up at the excavations with her father. I'm Jon Weber from the U.S. I've just joined the dig."

"Oh . . . welcome to *Eretz Israel,* Dr. Weber," he said. "I'm Gideon Ben-Yaakov."

"Honored to meet you, Dr. Ben-Yaakov."

"Gideon, if you please. Will you be staying with the dig for some time?"

"I hope to be here for the rest of the season."

"Excellent, excellent!" he said, in flawless, though accented, English. "I know we'll have a chance to get better acquainted."

A dashing figure in his middle thirties, Ben-Yaakov had ash-blond hair, bleached by the Israeli sun, as well as the obligatory tan. A thin gold chain circled his neck, and his clothes that afternoon were hardly field expedition khaki: form-fitting white pants, blue silk shirt, and shoes by Gucci.

"Ah, *there* you are, my little *shiksa!*" Ben-Yaakov exclaimed. He took Shannon in his arms and kissed her. She giggled coyly, and then drove off with him.

Jennings strode inside the headquarters tent, tossing his hat onto the desk. "Did you meet Shannon and Ben-Yaakov, Jonathan?" he inquired.

"Just now."

"Yes, I saw them driving off. I'm not really discouraging that romance," Jennings admitted, with a wicked grin. "Shannon's my secret weapon to keep the Israel Antiquities Authority happy! He's director, you know."

Two days later, Jennings inquired, "Ready to get your hands dirty, Jonathan? You now have all the background—"

"Today's the day!"

"Where do you want to work?"

Jon unleashed a broad smile. "At the town house, I think. I always go for the main attraction!"

"Ah yes, 'The Villa of the Joseph Jar Handles,' as it will doubtless be styled in the future. Good! But Jonathan, don't feel that you have to take trowel in hand and actually excavate. Just help me supervise."

"*Bad* suggestion, honored Director! I intend to start at the bottom, or rather, work *toward* the bottom!"

"Well, as you wish. Have a jolly good dig!" Jennings turned and was off to another sector.

Clive Brampton was in charge of the five-meter-square section being excavated at the rear of the villa. "We're now uncovering the back of the residence," he explained to Jon. "We've just exposed a *mikvah* here. Want to pitch in?"

"A purification bath? Splendid!"

At long last, Jon's trowel embedded itself into the dust of the past, as it would for days and weeks to follow. He recalled quickly enough that archaeology, for all its glamour, meant *work*, much of it tedious, if not outright boring. In many ways, but to a different scale, the dig resembled a gigantic anthill, where its swarming residents were busy reducing rather than building. After picks and shovels removed the overburden, small, pointed trowels were the weapons of choice in attacking each stratum for artifacts of any kind—what man had put there, not nature. Each layer was sifted for *any* item other than the earth itself, in strata that began with surface grasses, dipped down into the Islamic period (back to the 600s AD), then the Byzantine below that (back to AD 323), the Roman below that (back to 63 BC), the Hellenistic below that (back to 300 BC), and on down through Late, Middle, and Early Iron periods, and finally the Late and Middle Bronze eras to bedrock.

Not that all of Rama would be scraped away and a vast pit of orange-white limestone bedrock left in its place. Jennings and Brampton were using the "balk" method of excavation, pioneered by the British archaeological greats, Sir Mortimer Wheeler and Dame Kathleen Kenyon. Some vertical balks or columns of absolutely untouched material would be left standing in each excavated section to demonstrate the original composition of the strata.

A given stratum, however, could also be "favored," that is, larger areas cleared away to expose the principal structures of the site at its historical high point. At Pompeii, for example, that point was August of AD 79, just before Mount Vesuvius buried it under tons of volcanic ash. Archaeologists never tore below the magnificent ruins of the city at that date for the Bronze Age village beneath it. At Rama, the western town of the Roman era was to be preserved as much as possible, Jennings insisted.

Over lunch, Jon kept an eye on the excavation "frontier line" and asked Jennings, "How far do you plan to go beyond this?"

"Right up to the escarpment over there." He pointed to a small cliffside rise that was part of the western hill.

"What's that hole or opening, oh, about a third of the way up the escarpment?"

"Where? Oh, there. It's a cavern tomb with loculi—all empty. Probably empty for centuries. Grave robbers did their nasty work long ago."

"Care if I have a look?"

"Help yourself."

Jon left the table, walked over to the escarpment, and peered inside the cavern. Crawling through the opening, he glanced about the dank interior. Once his eyes had adjusted to the darkness, he saw a series of oblong, giant cigar-shaped cavities cut into the rock facing the entrance chamber, receptacles for the dead. These were the loculi, but all of them were empty. Crawling back outside, he took a deep breath of fresh air as his eyes constricted again in the bright sunshine. He returned to Jennings and said, "I hope there's a special hell for grave robbers!"

After lunch, Jon continued scraping dirt away from the small purification bath that was coming to light at the villa, filling buckets with spoil. He was about to trundle these off to the dump pile when a small hand slapped him lightly on the wrist.

"Not on your life!" said Shannon Jennings, who somehow

managed to scowl and smile at the same time. "This stuff has to be *sifted* first!"

"Oh, of course!" Jon muttered, sheepishly. "How . . . stupid of me."

"Common mistake. Not to worry."

"I'll learn in time, Shannon. But aren't you supposed to be minding the books?"

"I also mind the new help," she replied with a chuckle, as she scampered off to supervise the Arab work detail. Shannon seemed to know all the workers by name, and each smiled as she chatted with them. Jon liked the sparkle in her uninhibited style. To hear her spouting good Arabic was impressive enough, but to see that the linguist was an extremely winsome lass in white shorts . . .

A hand touched his shoulder and a voice said, "Don't even *think* about that one!"

"Oh, it's you, Dick," said Jon. "Yes, I know all about the Israel Antiquities Authority!" He hoped Cromwell wouldn't notice the flush in his cheeks. "I was just . . . intrigued by that cavern in the escarpment over there." Fortunately, it was in the same direction.

Rather than ponder the ethics of half-truths, Jon quickly hauled the spoil buckets over to a screen and sifted for any tiny item, such as a bead or scarab, that would otherwise have been lost. Only what fell through the sieve went to the dump pile. Anything fashioned by humankind he dusted off with a brush and put into plastic sacks, along with a card indicating sector and stratum. The sacks then went to the flotation tank crew, who hovered over an oblong, water-filled trough, where the botanist was both cleaning the artifacts and also "floating" the soil clinging to them, separating out the seeds and fruit-pits that would open the menu on ancient diets.

All the while, the orange hat of Austin Balfour Jennings could be seen moving from one sector to the next, as he issued directives, answered questions, offered advice. Though the director did little physical work, his tongue was in constant motion:

"No, no, no! That's only a lump of soil. Throw it away!"

"Yes, yes, yes! Save that! It's not trash, it's a *potsherd!*"

"A little more aggressive with that trowel, Natalie! You're just picking away at dirt. You'll know when you come to something important. *Dig in!* There's a good girl!"

"You were going to throw *that* away? Look at it again. It's a faience bead. Now check carefully. There may well be others there. . . ."

Late the next morning, Jennings looked over Jon's shoulder to check his progress. Jon, of course, had hoped to make a brilliant discovery within hours of taking trowel in hand, but his efforts had only laid bare the small bath others had discovered.

"Well, lad, you do acceptable work," Jennings commented. "There *may* be some hope for you in this field. But really, now, wouldn't you rather help me supervise?"

"I'll earn my way, Austin."

"Spoken like a worthy chap!"

Just then, a cavalcade of cars rolled to a stop below the dig. All doors seemed to open simultaneously, and a procession of bearded, black-hatted figures moved solemnly toward the excavations. Filing onto the upper perimeter, they pointed to the escarpment and chanted in a ghastly unison: "*ASSUR! ASSUR! LA'ASOT ET ZEH! ASSUR! ASSUR!*"

"It's the bloody, blinking Hasidim," Jennings snarled, "the superorthodox fanatics!"

"*Weird* sight!" exclaimed Jon. It was indeed. With temperatures above ninety degrees, these guardians of orthodoxy had sallied forth in fur-lined, broad-brimmed hats and long-coated suits in solid black—atavistic throwbacks to their ancestors' days in the cold ghettos of northern Europe. Their faces were fringed with lengthy beards, while their hair dangled in carefully curled forelocks down each side. Now they were shaking their fists at the excavators, screaming again, "*ASSUR! ASSUR! LA'ASOT ET ZEH! ASSUR! ASSUR!*"

Then their spokesman, a pale, scholarly sort who seemed to know that an Englishman was in charge of the dig, lifted a piping voice in translation: "*Forbidden! Forbidden! It is forbidden to do this!*" Again he pointed, with the others, to the escarpment tomb.

"The idiots think we've discovered *bodies!*" Jennings hissed.

"They don't want the dead disturbed in any way. . . . *LO!*" he cried in Hebrew. "*REIK!*" ("No! It's empty!")

To no avail. The chanting continued. Jennings summoned Naomi Sharon and said, "Go over and explain to them that we've *not* found any bodies there, that the cavern's been empty for centuries . . . grave robbers, et cetera!"

Naomi scampered across the dig and climbed up to the spokesman, who averted his eyes from her shorts and shapely bare legs. Five minutes of animated Hebrew dialogue failed to convince him, for Naomi returned and said, "They don't believe you. They think you're hiding the bodies."

The Hasidim now stooped down to pick up stones and hurl them at the excavators. But they were out of range, except for Dick Cromwell, who caught a rock squarely on his shin. It drew blood. In a rage, he picked it up, threw it back at them, and yelled, "I'll show you dorks the art of stoning!"

The rock sent a fur cap twirling off the head of one of the leaders. A low, ugly howl growled up from the group. Jon looked apprehensively at Jennings and commented, "Might we say, 'the situation is deteriorating'?"

"It certainly is," said Shannon. "Got any ideas, Jon? These *yukshis* could close down our dig!"

Jon walked up to an ancient rabbi who seemed to be one of the leaders of the demonstration. Nodding in courtesy, he said, "*Shalom aleichem. Bo itti, bevakashah, ten li leharot lecha et hakevarim.*" Then, in case his biblical Hebrew proved inadequate, he turned to the Hasidic scholar who had spoken English and said, slowly, "Peace be with you. Come with me, please, and let me show you the tombs."

The aged rabbi studied Jon suspiciously for several moments. Then he turned to his followers with some instructions, nodded to the other Hasid, and they both followed Jon to the escarpment as the rest looked on in stunned silence. Jon crawled inside the cavern, helping them do likewise. Then he scraped his finger along the floor of each loculus, showing the dust of time clinging to his finger. "*Reik! Ein anashim metim kan!*" he said, with emphatic sincerity, then reiterated in English, "Empty! There are no dead people here."

Returning outside, the two Hasidim seemed satisfied. "*Ken,*" the rabbis said, nodding. "*Reik.*"

"Yes," the other Hasid agreed. "Empty."

Within minutes, the demonstration evaporated.

FIVE

It was while taking the Hasidim through the cavern that Jon first noticed it. Spring rains had eroded a small gully next to the escarpment at the rim of the dig site, washing away some of the soil along its base. A flat, gray-white stone was now partially exposed, which Jon would not have noticed were it not for the top of a neighboring stone of the same shape and color butted against it in the same plane. Somehow, the fit seemed a shade too perfect for nature.

Jon forgot all about the stones until the midmorning break the next day. While sipping a cup of Turkish coffee, he chanced to look across to the escarpment and then recalled the anomaly he thought he saw. Draining the cup, he walked over to the slope and began troweling into the cliffside next to the gray-white stones. There was nothing of interest to their right, but after some troweling on the left-hand side, *another* flat stone started coming to light in the same plane, again tightly abutting its neighbor. And the surface of this one showed pick marks. It had been hewn! Jon stood up, cupping chin in hand. "Mother Nature had very little to do with *this*," he muttered.

Grabbing a hand pick from the toolshed, he returned to the cliff and started removing the dirt more efficiently. Burrowing deeper, he noticed that the stones were partially joined to each other with some sort of mortar. Now he swung the pick like some crazed zealot, relishing, at last, the thrill of archaeology—liberating something unanticipated and unknown from the shroud of earth and letting it take on new life.

Darn! Jon suddenly thought. *I forgot to ask Jennings for permission!* Hurrying over to the director, he admitted rather sheepishly that he had sinned. *"Mea maxima culpa,"* he confessed. "First, I abandoned my post here. Second, I opened up a new sector without your approval. Come and see."

"Those are mortal sins, Jonathan, not venial," Jennings replied, with a smirk. "But before we excommunicate you, let's see what you have."

Jon led him over to the site. Jennings knelt down and ran his hand along the exposed stonework. Then he stood up and surveyed the whole face of the escarpment, waving off flies with his hat. Now he crouched down again and studied the hewn stone very carefully. Finally he said, "Oh, oh, oh, laddie! You *have* brought something to light here, haven't you?"

"But what could it be? Looks like a retaining wall . . . maybe to brace up the cliff? That *is* mortar of some sort, isn't it?" He pointed to one of the joints.

"Clay mortar," Jennings nodded. "We've found it all over the dig. Now, what I want you to do is this: keep removing the overburden to the left here—switch to a brush when you get close to the facing—and keep at it until the structure stops. Then call me, all right?"

"Fine."

But Jon called him back sooner than expected, because the hewn rock, once fully exposed, proved to be the end of the stonework. Jon was crestfallen: a structure three stones wide was nothing to write home about.

"Not to worry," Jennings advised. "Now you must dig *down*— carefully, of course—and see if there's any more stone."

"Then I'm forgiven, good master, for my transgressions?"

"Possibly." Jennings chuckled. "But go and sin no more!"

At the end of the day's digging, Jon had, to his surprise, uncovered two more courses of stone beneath the original series. The row just below it was four stones long, the one beneath it five, and all rocks were a similar gray-white limestone. When Jennings stopped by again, his face was cut by a vast grin.

"If this progression continues," said Jon, "the wall should eventually reach the Mediterranean!"

"I doubt it'll get much wider."

"Aha! You know what this is, then?"

"Well . . . no."

"You think you *may* know what it is?"

"Perhaps."

"What is it?"

"And spoil your fun? Never! Discover for yourself, dear fellow!"

Weekday evenings of the campaign were devoted to reviewing the day's finds in a secluded conference room at the hotel in Ramallah. For the benefit of the students, Jennings or Brampton would also give illustrated slide lectures on "The Archaeology of Palestine," as Jennings preferred to call it, from his pre-Israeli years of working the dust of the "Holy Land."

"Why can't he say, 'The Archaeology of *Israel'?*" Jon overheard Gideon Ben-Yaakov ask Shannon Jennings in the darkened room, as her father held forth with slides from a previous dig.

"Don't get paranoid, Gideon," she replied, in more than a whisper. "And don't give me any Jewish rot on that score! Dad's been politically neutral ever since 1948. He likes Israelis, but he bloody well likes Arabs too!"

"Fine, fine!" he replied, holding up his hands.

Here and on other occasions Jon found Shannon nothing if not candid—a Gaelic firebrand who seemed to have arrived via virgin-birth from her sainted Irish mother, Jennings having played the Joseph-like role of mere foster father in an updated parallel to the Nativity. Shannon spoke her mind on any occasion in less-than-Oxonian accents and prided herself on her ability to tell a man off in five languages.

Ben-Yaakov, clearly, tolerated her tongue because he adored the rest of her. He showed up at Rama much more frequently than at the twelve other digs taking place that summer in Israel, for reasons that were at least transparent. Jon assumed it was only a matter of time before they announced their engagement.

When day's work was done and the lecture sessions over, there seemed to be some pairing off also among the students and younger staff. Clive Brampton appeared to spend more than a professional amount of time with Naomi Sharon, and their conversations likely went beyond ceramic chronology, Jon assumed. Photographer Dick Cromwell had a favorite assistant, Natalie Pomeroy, a striking blonde from Oregon, and she often had a curious flush to her cheeks when they emerged from the darkroom after developing the day's photographs. Anthropologist Noel Nottingham, who was newly divorced from his wife in Cambridge (England), was doubtless delighted to explain comparative anatomy to the well-endowed Regina Bandicoot from the outback of Australia. Just possibly there was more demonstration than explanation in those sessions, according to dig gossip.

In bed that night, Jon smiled at his own poignant memories of the volatility possible when past mixes with present, and the romance of archaeology takes on dimensions of another sort. For years, though, he had wondered if romance would *ever* put in an appearance in his own life. It had taken him such an age to "discover" women, he reflected, thanks to his growing up in the Hannibal parsonage. It had meant a happy youth, to be sure, but one well-fenced-off from any temptations of the flesh. Only rarely had he gone to high-school dances, not because his parents had anything against dancing, but there was a conservative faction in the church they did not wish to offend. PKs—pastors' kids—were supposed to serve as "examples to the youth," his mother insisted. This left Jon two choices—go along with the scheme, or rebel. He had gone along, perhaps because he was an only child and struggled to live up to his parents' expectations. They had wanted more children, but none ever came.

While at Harvard, he had dated girls from Radcliffe and nearly fell in love with a Cliffie from the Long Island Hamptons. Jon turned in bed with an embarrassed grin as he thought of Pamela. On one of their dates at Crane's Beach near Ipswich, as they huddled together on a blanket behind a secluded sand dune, she tried to make it easy for Jon by assuring him that she had brought along a condom in case he had forgotten. In one instant, his whole universe shattered. He had been *so* sure that the lovely Pamela, fresh as the first flower of spring, had fallen for him and him alone. He tried to recover, but his clumsy efforts to probe her past helped not at all. She found his preference for virginity in a woman "old hat," "medievalist," and altogether unrealistic. He finally asked about the number of lovers she had had and was promptly told to go straight to the destination he had been warned against ever since Sunday school. They never dated again.

Later, when his roommates pumped the information out of him, their comments were quite the same as Pamela's: he was a Neanderthal who had missed out on the sexual revolution. *Was he some kind of social misfit?* he wondered at the time. *A freak? A Puritan pietist? One who let his faith become a joy-killer?*

Plunging into his studies at Harvard and then Johns Hopkins, Jon had given women a wide berth for a time. Books became his first and only love, an all-encompassing intellectual mistress that demanded all of his time.

Until Andrea stepped so surprisingly into his life at Heidelberg, and he learned for the first time about the principal entrée in life's feast: love. The appetizers had been saucy and piquant, promising much, but Andrea had shown him the main course. They had spent their honeymoon summer digging together in Israel at Caesarea-on-the-Sea. Their hot, sweaty efforts each day were rewarded by swims in the Mediterranean at sundown or hikes up to Mount Carmel. *Those were the magnificent, the carefree, the salad days,* Jon reflected in reverie, and what happened on the night of July 14 that summer he would remember beyond memory itself.

French students in the dig were celebrating Bastille Day, and they broke out several cases of wine for the others partying with them in a late-night soirée on the Mediterranean beach. Near midnight, one of them yelled, "*Allons nager!*" and a chorus of "*D'accord! . . . Oui! . . . Bonne idée!*" responded. "Let's go sweeming," a French girl explained to Jon and Andrea, who hardly needed the translation. In a trice, the young people had shed their shirts and jeans and had dived into the Mediterranean *au naturel.*

"Oh, oh," Andrea had worried. "This doesn't look good, Jon."

"You figure a beach bacchanal's in the making?"

"Could be. Let's go."

That was typical of Andrea and her stringently conservative Southern upbringing, Jon recalled. Few would have guessed she was still a virgin at marriage, but she was. To be sure, she had previously permitted Jon some exquisite intimacies, but never ultimacies.

Now, however, their honeymoon gloriously vanquished most restraints. They left the beach party and walked northward along the shore toward the ancient Roman aqueduct, rejoicing in the grandeur of a star-saturated canopy of sky over their heads, a warm wind from Cyprus caressing them, and the Mediterranean swarming with millions of tiny luminous particles of some kind. Jon stooped down to feel the wash of a wave at his feet.

"Water's *deliciously* warm, Andrea. Let's *do* go for a swim."

"I don't have my swimsuit."

"Neither do I. But so what? Nobody's around."

"No. We shouldn't."

"Yes. We should."

She stooped down to feel the final ebb of a spent wave. "It *is* warm . . ."

"It's *magnificent!*"

"Promise not to look until I'm submerged?"

"We're *married*, Andrea!"

"I know. Still . . . promise?"

"Okay," he said, smiling at her shyness.

"Breaking promises is dangerous in the Holy Land!" she laughed, as she peeled off her clothes and hurried into the water.

The swim was merely exhilarating, but it became glorious when they brushed against each other in the water—innocently at first, but then with gathering intention. The Mediterranean served as a cloak of modesty, shielding and yet fostering their intimacy. Slowly, he put his arms around her, and they trembled at the tactile shock of joy as she touched his chest, while their lips and mouths found the seawater a piquant garnish for the rich taste of one another.

Hurrying onto the beach, they clasped each other in exuberance, tumbling down onto the sand in a manic quest for oneness. The rising thrill . . . the love that was building to its ultimate expression . . . the gentle caresses . . . the sands and waves celebrating with them . . . the tender nuzzling of one another . . . the incredible crescendo to the rarest of raptures . . . the serenity of the denouement . . . the oneness they pledged for eternity . . .

Jon buried his face in the pillow and whispered, "I *miss* you, Andrea! You'll never—*ever*—know how much!"

Six

Achmed Sa'ad's seventeen-year-old son, Ibrahim, now assisted Jon at the stonework he was excavating, and progress was rapid. Another course of fitted rock was uncovered, but this row had an oblong stone bridging a pronounced recess below it. Next, they uncovered three smaller courses on each side, flanking the indentation, which Jon measured at about two feet square. It was time to summon the master.

"*Aha!*" Jennings chortled with glee, rubbing his hands together. "Just as I thought! Have you gone inside yet?"

"What do you mean 'inside'?"

Both knew that the two questions were idle chitchat designed to conceal their excitement. Jon knew the oblong stone looked for all the world like a lintel, and Jennings could plainly see that the threshold—if it were that—had not been penetrated.

Jon broke the silence. "It *does* look like a small doorway, doesn't it, Austin? But to what? Another sepulcher, like the one above?"

"Or even a treasure trove?!" Jennings winked. "It could be a natural cliffside cavern that was converted into some sort of storage chamber simply by walling in the front. And I find *any* of those possibilities . . . just fabulous," Jennings murmured.

Jon wiped his forehead in a surge of elation. Then he noticed that even young Ibrahim was standing tall, drenched in the pride of accomplishment. Jon threw an arm across his shoulders and said, "*Kwais! Kwais! Shukran, shukran!*" ("Good, good, my friend! Thank you, thank you!")

But Ibrahim replied in very acceptable English, "And I am thanking you, *Sayyed* Weber, for letting me work with you."

"Wait a moment and don't touch anything," Jennings advised.

He returned minutes later with a camera, a small prybar, two flashlights, and a black-and-white-banded meter stick that he placed against the now fully exposed stonework. After taking a series of photographs, he handed Jon the prybar and said, "Now wedge out those four stones beneath the lintel."

The stones proved to be only a foot thick, and Jon pried them apart without much difficulty. Beyond question, it was a passageway. When he had hauled the last stone aside, he looked up to Jennings and said, "You first, Austin; it's your dig."

"No. It's your discovery, Jonathan. But first, we'd best make sure the air inside is good. Ibrahim, run to the supply shed and fetch us a candle, some tape, and some matches. There's a good lad . . ."

They managed only small talk while Ibrahim was gone, both refusing to ventilate their excitement. When he returned, Jennings taped the candle onto the end of the meter stick, lit it, and poked it through the dark threshold as far as he could reach. "If the flame goes out, it's not safe to go inside until we give the cavern a complete airing."

They waited two minutes. "Flame's still burning," Jennings said. "I doubt that this place was hermetically sealed." Then he stood up and said, "But I also made my first mistake in over thirty years in the field." He winked at Jon to show that he was not really a pompous ass. "I should've used our air pump. If a goodly collection of methane had been inside there, I do believe I would quite have exploded your find—if not myself as well!"

"I've always said you were a blasted good archaeologist, Austin."

"*Do* spare me the bad humor! Now grab a torch and climb inside."

"After what you just said, I much prefer our American term: *flashlight*."

"But do come out immediately if the air smells bad, or if you feel dizzy."

Jon hunkered down on all fours, crawled through the opening, and turned on his flashlight. He saw little but smelled much. The odor was overpowering, an unholy mixture of dank, musty dungeon, mixed with rotting cistern, essence of primordial swamp, and bat guano. He coughed, retched, and backed out of the cavern.

Sitting ruefully in front of his find, Jon said, "The place smells as if the whole Chinese army hung its socks here after Mao's Thousand-Mile March!"

"I dare say, Jonathan. It's likely worse than a Turkish toilet! Let's give it more time to air out."

Fifteen minutes had passed when Jon said, "I can't wait. I've *got* to go back inside."

He crawled through the passageway again. "The air seems more tolerable," he reported. "Or maybe my nose just died." While his eyes adjusted to the darkness, he combed the interior with his flashlight. "It's not hewn, Austin," he called back. "It's a natural cavern. At this point I see nothing artificial. It's just high enough to stand—*if* you're a hunchback or a dwarf!"

When Jennings heard nothing for several minutes, he called, "What else do you see?"

"Many wonderful things!"

"What?!"

"Only spoofing! That's what Carter said the first time he saw all the gold in King Tut's tomb. No, all I see is an empty cavern."

"Well, I'm coming in, now that my stalking horse seems to be surviving. See why I let you go in first?"

Chuckling, Jon pointed his flashlight toward the passageway to illuminate Jennings's path. As the taller of the two, Jennings found it easier to explore the cavern on his knees than to go about stoop-shouldered as did Jon. Sniffing the air, he said, "Not that bad, Jonathan, not that bad. I've smelled worse."

"Sure, now that I've aired it out for you."

Slowly, Jennings circled the cavern with his flashlight, muttering such unintelligibles as "Hmmmm," "Umm-hmmmm," "Well, now," "Hmmmpf," and "My, my!" He spent an inordinate amount of time examining the walls of the cavern, gently tapping them with his mallet and listening closely. He did the same between rocky outcroppings on the floor. Finally he halted his search and said, "It's closing time, Jonathan. Ah, let's keep this confidential for the moment. I'll have a word with Ibrahim about that also. . . . But I'm canceling my lecture for this evening, because you and I have *much* to discuss."

Jon found two letters waiting for him at the hotel, one from his parents in Hannibal, the other embossed with the triple crown and papal keys of Vatican City. Kevin Sullivan's letter concluded:

> *Yesterday, I completed my UV scan of the entire Vaticanus. No other eradications appear in the entire Codex. I did detect some points at which the scribe had corrected himself, but these had been known for years.*
>
> *Next Monday I fly to London, where I'll examine the Sinaiticus, thanks to your kindness in clearing the way at the British Museum. I await final approval from the Holy Father for your testing proposal.*
>
> *Carry on, Jon! I only wish I were getting my fingernails dirty too! All the best!*
>
> *Kevin*

And I only wish I *knew how to get a proper handle on that Markan ending,* Jon mused. *That new line could be a sputtering bombshell!*

After dinner, Jennings came up to his room with a bottle of sherry and two glasses. "I know," he apologized, "it's supposed to be sherry *before* dinner, among civilized English, and port *after.* But we exist here under *dire* privations!"

"Not to worry, dear Austin," responded Jon, in a contrived Oxonian accent. "Frightfully glad you were able to fetch *any* sort of spirituous beverage!"

"Good effort, Jonathan. With a little tutelage, you might even learn to communicate in a civil manner. But to the point at hand. Did you find anything *strange* about what we uncovered today?"

"Not really. Except for the walled-in opening, every inch of that cavern looked like a natural grotto to me. There are hundreds like it all over Israel and Jordan, aren't there?"

"To be sure. But you're losing the forest for the trees. Once again, which piece doesn't fit the puzzle? What is *the* master anomaly?"

"The threshold, the stonework, of course."

"Exactly. But why, pray tell, would anyone wall in an empty cavern?"

"Masonry practice? No, I'll get serious. Clearly something of value *had* at one time been inside that cavern, but it must have fallen prey to robbers centuries ago."

Jennings wrinkled his brow, then began the ritual of lighting his pipe. Meticulously, he poured an aromatic blend into the bowl, tamped the tobacco exactly to his specifications, lit it with a great sweep of his hand, and then sucked the mixture into life, filling the room with bluish clouds of smoke. Only then did he respond, "That's a quite proper hypothesis, Jonathan. But you've overlooked the anomaly inside the anomaly."

Jon pondered for a time, then shrugged his shoulders and said, "I . . . just don't see it."

"Why, then, would treasure thieves or grave robbers have bothered to replace those four stones so carefully at the threshold?"

"Of course! They replaced them to disguise the theft."

"That's your American mind at work, Jonathan. Near Eastern grave robbers aren't so sophisticated. I can't think of a single cavern or tomb in Palestine that was robbed and then occluded again."

Jon stroked his cheek in thought, then quaffed the remaining sherry in his glass and poured another for Jennings and himself. "Well, then, we have a quite fascinating mystery on our hands. Can you solve it?"

"I have some thoughts on the matter. But I'd like to hear yours first."

Jon paused some moments, then said, "I can think of three alternatives. One, some grave robber long ago *was* sophisticated; two, something remains hidden inside the cavern that we missed; or three, we'll never know."

"Quite right. I incline to the second, and let me tell you why. To ward off grave robbery, the ancients sometimes made secret burials and then camouflaged their tombs. Several such have been discovered in the so-called Tombs of the Sanhedrin in north

Jerusalem. That's why I tapped the walls of the cavern: I was searching for hidden loculi. But I heard nothing hollow, nothing suspicious."

"And that, of course, was why the Egyptian pharaohs abandoned pyramids for their hidden tombs in the Valley of the Kings. We must have overlooked something, Austin. That was just a 'once-over' this afternoon. . . . But why are you keeping our find confidential?"

"Can you imagine fifty-five curious people squeezing into that cavern?"

"Oh, obviously."

Jennings held his glass high. "To the morrow!" he toasted.

The clink of their glasses was answered by the haunting yowl of a jackal.

The next morning, they brought thin probing rods, hammers, and metal detectors along with them to the cavern. A careful sweep of the sides, ceiling, and floor of the grotto set up no howl in the electronic detectors, even with sensitive settings. Then they began a systematic tapping of the walls of the cavern, inserting probing rods wherever there seemed to be a suspicious echo, crease, or recess. Every surface, however, appeared to be solid virgin bedrock.

Returning after lunch, Jennings sighed, "Well, it's the floor . . . or nothing." They were now illuminating the grotto with a Coleman gas pressure lantern set into a niche on the far wall. Jon squatted down and studied the base of the cavern for some moments. Then he said, "Austin, do you see what I see?"

"Rock, dirt, debris, guano . . ."

"No, look at those rocky outcroppings. They show up everywhere *except* in this center area here." He traced a large rectangle with his flashlight. Emitting a low whistle, he asked, "*So!* Do we finally have a 'diggable' area here?"

"Good show, Jonathan! Let's find out."

Both set to work with hand picks, loosening the composite of dirt and guano, and handing buckets of the material out to Ibrahim. By closing time, they had dug eleven inches into the floor, uncovering an area that clearly was not part of bedrock.

"Well, we have our work cut out for us again tomorrow, Austin," said Jon, wiping his brow.

Jon sat across from Shannon at dinner that night. Their conversation drifted to an inevitable topic for that quarter of the world—Israel versus the Arabs.

"Will there *ever* be real peace?" he wondered.

"The Israel-PLO accords are a great first step," she replied, as she peeled a Jaffa orange. "But the extremists keep the pot boiling. And you can't believe the wild variety of pressure groups on both sides."

"Such as?"

"Well, among the Palestinians it's Hamas that makes the PLO or Fatah look tame. Hamas are the 'true believers,' mind you, the Muslim fundamentalists who reject any talks with Israel because they oppose the very existence of a Jewish state."

"What about the Israeli factions?" asked Jon. "They have extremists too. There's that wonderful Jewish adage, 'two Jews, three opinions.'"

"They run from the *Gush Emunim*—who want to plant the Star of David flag in Damascus, if possible—to some of the orthodox groups who *oppose* the State of Israel."

"Who *what?* Jews opposing Israel?"

"True. Take the *Neturei Karta.* They're rigorously orthodox Jews who think the State of Israel is a *violation* of God's will."

"Oh, that group!" he now recalled. "Aren't they the ones who think it was God who willed Jewish exile from Israel in the first place? And the exile will end only when the Messiah comes?"

"That's the group. Some of them even claim the Nazi Holocaust happened as divine punishment for Zionist thinking even *before* the State of Israel was founded in 1948."

"Beyond belief!"

Shannon smiled and nodded. "Nobody pays them *that* much attention, but they're part of the crazy-quilt that's Israel today."

Jon squirmed a bit in his chair. He had moved into a frustration zone. Shannon was an engaging, obviously attractive, and delightfully lively woman, with a first-class intellect to boot. With such a woman one could fall in love. With such a woman, one could also fall into hopeless frustration—she was too young for him . . . and too spoken for. He had to get back on track with their conversation.

"So, Shannon," he finally managed. "Back to my original question: Will there *ever* be peace around here?"

A wistful smirk crossed her face. Then she nodded and said, "Of course."

"When, then?"

"When Messiah comes."

Three blasts of a horn pierced the quiet of evening.

"Oh, oh, have to go," she said. "Gideon gets impatient if I don't hop to."

The next morning, Jon and Jennings gently hammered probing rods into their shallow pit inside the cavern. Both encountered something solid at a distance of twelve and thirteen inches respectively.

Their digging was now impassioned. Neither said anything as they excavated on their knees with small half-spades, handing bucket after bucket of spoil out to Ibrahim. The lantern kept hissing its brightness into a grotto that had not seen light for ages.

"I've bottomed onto something," said Jon.

"Then switch to your trowel. Be careful not to scrape our target, whatever it may be."

Several minutes passed when Jennings said, "I've reached it too."

An hour more of the most meticulous excavation laid bare a two-meter angular slab of grayish limestone, less than a meter wide, peaked at the center line, with sides sloping at a four-to-one ratio and horned at the corners.

"Good heavens!" Jennings whispered in exclamation. "You know what we have here?"

"Yes, beyond any debate. It's the lid of a sarcophagus!"

At lunch they could barely disguise the mood roaring through them. Again Jennings had urged silence until their discovery was complete. One exception, however, was Dick Cromwell, whom he now assigned to the cliffside cavern with all his camera equipment.

The rest of the afternoon saw a lightning storm of electronic flashes in the grotto as Cromwell recorded their progress at every stage in liberating the sides of the stone coffin.

That task went rapidly, since there was far less bulk to remove. At 2 PM, they sent a message that the bus should leave without them, and they would drive back in the dig's Land Rover instead. Some phases of excavation did not brook interruption of any kind.

By late afternoon, the sides of the sarcophagus were fully exposed. They stood two-and-a-half feet high, and were of the same limestone as the lid. Attractive rosettes had been cut into both of the long sides of the sarcophagus, and small seven-branch candlesticks into the two ends, the *menorah* symbol.

But it was not the art that transfixed the three as they knelt before the stone coffin at the most awesome moment of their professional lives. It was the inscription. Jon had uncovered the first lettering in midafternoon, but left it enshrined in dirt caking until the sides had been fully cleared. Then he had taken a camel's-hair brush and gently dusted off the inscription. It had two-inch lettering, it was in two languages, and it would evoke the first flourish from the trumpets of destiny:

ΕΝΘΑΔΕΚΙΤΕ
ΙѠϹΗΦΑΡΙΜΑΘΑΙΟϹΥΙΟϹ
ΑϹΗΡΒΟΥΛΕΥΤΗϹ

םולש הננבל וניבונ

"That's Greek on top and Hebrew at the bottom, isn't it?" Cromwell wondered.

"Well . . . Aramaic, the later cousin to Hebrew," Jon explained.

"But what does it say?"

Jon pointed out each syllable with his index finger as he said, "*Here . . . lies . . . Joseph of Arimathea . . . son of Asher . . .*

Councilor—or Member of the Council— . . . *His memory be blessed . . . Peace."*

"What Council would that be?" asked Cromwell.

"The Jewish Sanhedrin, of course. That's the very term used in the Gospels."

Silence ruled the cavern.

"Awesome!" Cromwell finally exclaimed. "Just awesome!"

Jennings said nothing at all. He merely wiped tears from the corner of his eye.

SEVEN

Jonathan . . . Richard . . . I needn't tell you the implications here." Jennings had finally found his tongue while driving back to Ramallah in the Land Rover. "The sarcophagus may be empty. Or it may not be. If not, then this could be one of the first biblical personalities *ever* discovered. We have *inscriptions* relating to people in the Bible—like the Pontius Pilate stone at Caesarea—but we don't have their remains."

"And *such* a personality! The man who buried Jesus in Jerusalem!" Jon exclaimed. "This could shape up to be the find of the century, Austin!"

No one said anything, until Jon added, "But I suppose that's exactly the sort of speculation we should avoid at this point."

Jennings nodded. "We could be building ourselves up for a huge letdown."

Cromwell, who was driving, disagreed. "That sarcophagus alone—empty or full—will make history, believe me. Do we spill the news to our staff?"

"Oh no. Not yet," Jennings replied, instantly. "First we must open the sarcophagus. Don't forget to bring along two chain hoists and quadripods tomorrow. Several pry bars and flat irons too."

"*And* my video camera," said Cromwell. "All this is too *historic* to shoot only in stills."

At Ramallah, the other members of the staff wondered why they were so preoccupied, and several asked questions about what was going on over at the escarpment. But they fended off all inquiries.

The next morning they straddled the sarcophagus pit with two quadripods. Then they inserted pry bars into the seam under the lid and ever so slowly pried it apart from the ancient clay-mortar seal that had bound it to the sarcophagus. As Cromwell bathed the grotto in light from three more gas pressure lanterns he had brought along for his videos, Jennings and Jon inserted flat irons under both ends of the stone lid, attached chains to the tips of the irons, and joined these to small chain-hoists they had secured to the quadripods.

"Let's do this in unison, Jonathan," Jennings directed. "The world would never forgive us if we broke the lid! Now pull your lift chain in exact cadence with mine."

Jon smiled. For all Jennings's warnings not to inflate their hopes, he was already thinking in "world" terms, evidently. He carefully tugged away to parallel Jennings's efforts. "Good, Austin," he said, "we're keeping it level."

"All right, that's high enough." The lid was now suspended more than four feet over the sarcophagus, and at least two feet above the cavern floor. Both aimed flashlights down inside the stone coffin, but said nothing for endless moments.

"What in very *blazes* do you see?" Cromwell finally cried, racked with suspense.

"Put down your camera and come look."

Cromwell hurried to the edge of the pit and looked down. He saw some yellowed and partially decayed linen grave wrappings enshrouding a human skeleton, the vacant eye sockets of the skull not really a haunting sight. There was almost a smile of welcome in what appeared to be a fine set of teeth.

"It's as if he's saying, 'So, friends, you've *finally* found me!'" Cromwell commented.

"Ibrahim," Jennings finally called outside, "run and get Clive and Shannon for me. And Noel Nottingham."

When the three had arrived and crawled inside, Jennings said, solemnly, "Shannon, your entry for this morning's log will begin as follows:

At 10:45 AM, this date, the presumed remains of the first biblical personality ever discovered—on a demonstrable basis—were uncovered inside a cavern at the escarpment northwest of the Hellenistic-Roman excavations at Rama."

"Good Lord!" exclaimed Shannon. "Who?"

"Joseph of Arimathea."

At the hotel, two nights later, Jennings convened a meeting of all dig personnel. After announcing the discovery, he explained why the news was a bit tardy, and then had Dick Cromwell show slides of the cavern, the pit, and the stone coffin. When he had finished, Jennings promised to let all of them see the find in groups of four at a time. "And now," he continued, "our anthropologist, Professor Nottingham, will discuss his initial findings."

Noel Nottingham was a tall, gaunt, quintessential Cambridge don with omnipresent pipe and soiled field-khaki Bermudas. He looked something like David Niven, and tried to ape the devil-may-care insouciance of the British actor. He began with a *caveat*. "*Do*, understand, won't you all, that these observations are *extremely* preliminary, and subject to change after much additional study. First off, the remains are remarkably well preserved—most of the skeletal structure is articulated and intact—and the bones don't have that much calcareous accretion. This was an upper middle-aged male, approximately five foot, eight or nine inches in height. His bodily frame seems well proportioned—the shoulder width suggesting a person we'd style as strongly built rather than stocky. Ditto the hip area. His diet was good—all bones seem properly rounded and normal—and his teeth, which are intact, show no cavities. This was in an era before candy bars and junk food, of course!"

The audience tittered, as Nottingham intended they would. He resumed, "The remains show someone who was not used to hard physical labor, since no joints show the sort of wear we find in those of slaves and common laborers, such as were discovered in the shoreline excavations at Herculaneum."

"Of course not," Shannon whispered to Jon, who was sitting next to her, "Joseph of Arimathea was one of the fat cats."

"Well, the New Testament tells us only that he was a rich man," Jon whispered back, "quite apart from any bodily girth."

"I'm speaking American, Jon. Don't you recognize your own colloquialisms?" She gave him a playful jab in the ribs.

Nottingham continued. "No degenerative illnesses show up in the skeletal structure. Hands and feet are normal, though fingers and toes seem on the slender side. And finally, the facial features would suggest a slightly oblong rectangular visage, with high cheek bones, ample mouth, and less than prominent nasal septum. He also had dark hair. We hope to learn more shortly. Are there any questions?"

"Yes. How do you know he's a man and not a woman?" asked Eloise Bancroft from Bennington College, whose questionable performance at the dig thus far hinted that her future lay not in the mysteries of archaeology, but in those of heterosexuality.

"*Was* a man, Eloise," replied Nottingham, good-naturedly. "I do believe the past tense applies! The pelvic structure in women is wider and rounder than in men to permit the birth process. And the general bone structure is smaller too. But our skeleton has larger bones and a smaller pelvic area. Hence, a man. Yes?"

"You said the remains came from 'an upper middle-aged' man," Dick Cromwell led off. "Would you like to quantify that more specifically? And how do you determine age?"

"In answer to your first, I'd venture that the man was at least fifty years of age at death. And we determine that by the spurs or knobbing from calcium deposits at the joints, as well as the grinding and wear on the tooth enamel."

"How do you know he had dark hair?" Regina Bandicoot wondered.

"There's a shock of it still attached to his skull."

"Oh. What'll eventually happen to his bones, Noel?" she persisted.

"A good and worthy question, Regina. We surely *will* show due respect for the dead. Eventually the remains will be re-interred, but because we may have a 'celebrity' on our hands here, much scientific testing lies ahead."

"In any case," Jennings intruded, "we'll remove the remains to the Rockefeller Museum in Jerusalem as soon as possible, because they must quickly be covered with a PVA emulsion as a preservative—polyvinyl acetate. Otherwise they'll disintegrate in this dry air."

Jennings now asked Jon to explain to the students the larger significance of the find. "Some years ago that wouldn't have been necessary," he whispered. "But never underestimate the biblical illiteracy of the younger generation today!"

"Our evidence is still presumptive," Jon opened, "and we must *not* jump to conclusions. But our sarcophagus inscribed with the name 'Joseph of Arimathea, son of Asher, Councilor' may very well prove to be that of a so-named individual in the New Testament, who arranged the burial of Jesus of Nazareth after his crucifixion. He was a member of the Jewish Sanhedrin, but, along with a friend of his named Nicodemus—who also assisted at Jesus's burial—he had *not* voted to condemn Jesus. In fact, he offered his own rock-hewn tomb in Jerusalem for Jesus's burial. Now *if* we've uncovered the tomb and the remains of this same Joseph, he evidently returned to his hometown after his service in Jerusalem and must have been buried here. In that case, this will be one of the first biblical personalities ever to have been discovered archaeologically. The bones of others *may* have been uncovered before this—like those of Joseph Caiaphas—but no firm identification has been possible. Are there any questions?"

A buzzing of ohs and ahs resonated in the room at several points during Jon's statement. The hand of Scott Ferguson shot up, a Yalie in Near Eastern studies. "The evidence would seem *conclusive* that this *is* the one and the same Joseph of Arimathea. Why do you call it 'presumptive'?"

"For several reasons. In biblical times, sons often followed their fathers' professions, so this Joseph might have been the father or son or another-generation relative of the Joseph mentioned in the Gospels. Or no relative at all. Or he might have been a member of a village 'council' here at Rama rather than Jerusalem. And even though the bones inside the sarcophagus *appear* to be his, they could conceivably belong to another—even though that seems a *very* remote possibility. Still, I give you the case of Jesus of Nazareth, buried in someone else's tomb in Jerusalem."

"But all things considered," Ferguson persisted, "what do you see as the *probabilities* that these *are* the bones of the Joseph of Arimathea cited in the Gospels? On a scale of one to ten?"

Jon smiled and then huddled briefly with Jennings. Both nodded. "Seven or eight," Jon reported. "But in the interests of scientific archaeology, don't *ever* say I told you that!"

After the laughter, Jennings stood up and wore a very tense
expression. "You may not realize it," he warned, "but our dig is
now in profound *danger*. All we need for disaster to strike is any
one of you to fail to maintain *absolute* silence about this find. The
Hasidim would be on our necks with an unholy vengeance if they
learned! You saw how they demonstrated over *empty* tombs! And
that's not all. In view of the possibly 'sensational' identity of the
remains, we'd also be set upon by hordes of reporters out here,
and the work would suffer. So I must ask for *absolute* secrecy. I
want each of you to raise your hand in a personal pledge."

All hands shot up immediately, and the meeting ended. The
senior staff, however, stayed behind to continue the discussion on
confidentiality.

"What about your Arab workmen, Achmed?" asked Clive
Brampton.

"Ah!" Sa'ad commented, "they are no problem. They know
what brought 'the bearded plague'—as they call them—to the dig.
I have told the few who know to keep a wise silence, in the name
of Allah the All-Compassionate. They will do so."

"What about Gideon and the Antiquities Authority, Shannon?"
asked Cromwell.

"No problem. Gideon's out for scientific archaeology. And
even if he *does* learn that we hit bones here, he's hardly going to
send a wire to our friends, the S.O.B.'s!"

"The S.O.B.'s?" Jon inquired.

"The Super Orthodox Brethren."

"What else!" Jon chuckled, duly gulled. Then he added, "We
should also remember that these are *hardly* the first human remains
to be discovered in Israel. 'Grave robbers' we are not!"

Several days later, Jennings, Brampton, Shannon, and Jon were
sifting out materials inside the base of the sarcophagus, now that
the remains had been removed by Nottingham with meticulous
care. Four people on their knees, hovering over the open stone

coffin proved to be a clumsy quartet, since they were constantly jostling each other. "Enough!" Jennings announced. "Clive and I will go outside and process your spoil, Shannon and Jonathan. Pass the material to Ibrahim, and he'll hand it out to us."

Jon and Shannon carefully began removing the grave cloths and fragments of what proved to be matting from the bottom of the sarcophagus. Although they were passing out rotting wrappings and other debris, the men outside seemed delighted with each scrap of ancient textile.

Just before midmorning break, Shannon exclaimed, "Oh, oh . . . I think I have something!" Turning the gas lamp brighter, she grabbed a brush and gingerly whisked away the debris encasing the object.

"Shannon's found a lamp!" Jon called outside. "A ceramic oil lamp—eight or nine centimeters long. Looks Herodian to me."

"That would be typical," Jennings commented. "Tombs often contain lamps."

"Yes indeed, symbols to shed light for the journey to the next world, as it were," Brampton added. "The old Egyptian idea."

The moment Ibrahim brought the lamp to him, Jennings exclaimed, "It *is* Herodian! We've seen dozens like it, and it helps fix a first-century BC/first-century AD time frame. Come out and sketch it, Shannon."

Crawling outside, she took a ruler, pen, and pad, and drew this sketch:

"There's lampblack at the burn spout," she said. "Shows that this one was really used. Can't wait to show it to Naomi." Then she returned inside the cavern.

Just before lunch, she uncovered another funerary lamp on the opposite side of the sarcophagus, similar in size, but with some ornamentation in contrast to the first. Jennings pronounced it Herodian as well.

If he hadn't switched sides with Shannon, he *would have discovered the*

second lamp, Jon thought, in a moment of pettiness. Then he reflected on how small humanity's inner thoughts can be at a time when they ought to be expansive instead. The gong for lunch at the mess tent delivered him from further self-accusation.

Crawling outside, he saw Shannon busily sketching the second lamp. "That one *could* be a little earlier than the first," said Jennings. "Late Hellenistic—early Herodian. Let's see what Naomi says."

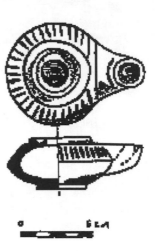

Over the lunch table, Naomi fondled the lamps with a ceramicist's special appreciation, brushing away the last specks of dust on them. "Both these oil lamps were formed from pinkish buff clay, as you can see," she told the staff table. "No glaze or slip was used prior to firing. And both were actually used at one time, as you'll note from the soot marks. The plain one's a bow-spouted Herodian lamp. Rather commonplace for the period from Herod the Great to, say, the Roman conquest."

"We're talking *circa* 40 BC to AD 70?" asked Cromwell.

"Yes, except I'd make that 40 BCE to 70 CE. I'm Jewish, you'll recall, and I deal in terms of 'Common Era'."

"Of course. Sorry!" Dick's face was red.

"Now, the ornamented lamp is the Delphiniform type, which is a little earlier. Quite a few have been discovered in late Hellenistic strata."

Jon had better luck in the afternoon. Just after lunch, he uncovered two narrow vaselike bottles or flasks, lying on their sides. Dusting them off, he showed the creamy buff vessels to Jennings and Brampton.

"Well, now, you're *finally* earning your keep around here, Jonathan," said Jennings. "What do you think they are, Clive?"

Brampton studied them and replied, "Perhaps oil flasks for the lamps?"

"Now it's your turn to sketch, Jonathan. Meanwhile I'll go get Naomi."

Jon sat down and reached for a pen. "Clive," he said, "I've never understood this 'drawing' bit in archaeology. I mean, with the precision of photography available, what good is this primitive routine of sketching artifacts?"

"It brings out the highlights and contrasts you'd never find on a photograph, Jon."

"Something like a caricature, then?"

"Well, let's say a caricature *without* the exaggerations. Get it?"

"I suppose," he groaned. "An artist I am *not*, but here goes . . ." He started to sketch. Five minutes into the first effort, he crumpled

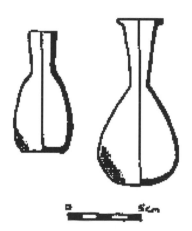

up the page in disgust and tried again. The next attempt was at least passable, he thought, and he finished the sketch just as Jennings arrived with Naomi.

She took one look at the vessels and said, "I would've expected those. They're unguentaria, mid-Herodian to the Roman conquest. We find many of those in tombs from, say, 20 BCE to 70 CE."

"I thought maybe they were oil flasks for the lamps," said Brampton.

"One of them *could* be—the larger one. But the other would have been used for balsam or other burial ointments."

"So," said Jon. "This is . . . rather typical pottery inside first-century tombs, Naomi?"

"How do you Americans put it: 'standard equipment'? Yes, this is very typical. I'd have been surprised to find a grave without out ceramics like these."

Just before closing, Jon was cleaning out the base of the sarcophagus where the foot bones had rested, when his trowel struck
onto something. Prying beneath it, he dislodged an oblong object
that promptly broke in two as he tried to extract it. He muttered
a quiet curse.

Shannon trained her flashlight on the item, and together they
lifted out the pieces. It was a rotting slab of some kind, several
shades lighter than the debris encrusting it. With excruciating
care, they brushed off as much dirt as they dared and then passed
the pieces out to Jennings.

Seconds passed. Then a full minute. They heard nothing from
outside. Finally Jon knelt down at the threshold and called,
"What do you make of it, Austin?"

"*Sweet Jupiter!*" he bellowed, abruptly. "Get out here, both of
you! It's an *inscription*, I think!"

Jennings was bending over the pieces of slab and dusting them
off with a broad camel's-hair brush. "We have parchment here,"
he said, "And it's bonded onto what seems to be wood that's rot-
ted. You can just make out faded lettering of some kind. . . ."

For a time, Jon could see nothing, since he was blinded after
the darkness of the cavern. When his eyes had adjusted, he scrutinized the parchment and said, "Incredible! I can make out a
delta here, so it's probably Greek."

"There's the gong. Quitting time," said Jennings. "We'll examine this after dinner."

The two pieces of slab lay on a worktable in the dig's small laboratory at the hotel. Jon used a compressed-air gun to coax more
encrustation off the parchment, the soft clup-clup-clupping of the
compressor replacing any conversation among those clustered
about the artifact.

Placed together at the crack line, the slab measured over two
feet in length by one in width. Lettering appeared on three lines,
some characters nearly faded.

Jon stared at the writing for some time, but then shook his
head. "I can't quite make it out. Can you, Austin?"

He also shook his head.

"You don't have an ultraviolet lamp here, do you?"

"Yes! *Jolly* good idea! Clive—"

Brampton hauled out a small ultraviolet apparatus, waited several minutes for the lamp to gain intensity, and then shined it on the parchment.

"Better! That's much better," said Jon. "We certainly *do* have Greek on the middle line. But . . . but *Aramaic* below it?" He leaned over and studied the lettering for some time. Then he looked up and asked, "And what about that top line? It's . . . it's . . . by George, it's *Latin!*"

Silence followed, as all eyes adjusted to the ultraviolet light. Most of the lettering was now recognizable.

"Oh . . . my . . . Lord," whispered Jon, for he deciphered it first.

"*I* still don't have it, Jonathan," said Jennings, although I do make out 'Nazareth' . . . 'king' . . . Oh! *Oh!* . . . Oh, oh, oh, dear boy! Saints preserve us! I have it now!" Jennings dropped his arms, and his mouth sagged open in wonderment. Then he staggered to the nearest chair and sat down, holding a hand to his forehead. Jon felt his own legs turning gelatinous and he slumped to the floor, sitting on a throw rug with legs spread apart.

"Is this going to be some professional secret?" Shannon groused. "Translation, please! My Aramaic's a bit rusty."

Her father said nothing. Jon finally muttered, "It's the *titulus*, Shannon, the *titulus.*"

"What's *that* supposed to mean?"

Jon explained in tones of awe. "It's the sign Pontius Pilate nailed to Jesus's cross on Good Friday, when—"

"'*And Pilate had an inscription written and put it on the cross,*'" Jennings interposed, quoting John's Gospel. "'*It read: JESUS OF NAZARETH, THE KING OF THE JEWS . . . And it was written in Hebrew, in Latin, and in Greek.*'"

"Now we *know* that the remains are those of the biblical Joseph of Arimathea, Austin, don't we?" asked Jon, triumphantly.

"Oh, yes *indeed!* Fabulous, Jonathan, just *fabulous!* This confirms it!"

"I . . . don't quite follow," Brampton admitted.

"Well, Clive," Jon explained, "Joseph of Arimathea must have preserved the *titulus* as a sort of sacred memento of his services in burying Jesus that evening in Jerusalem—even to the point of directing that it be buried with him in his own tomb here."

Now Brampton beamed enthusiastically, and said, "*Incredible!* This is one dig that'll go down in history—"

"Right up there with the Dead Sea Scrolls!" Shannon chirped.

"Notice that '*of the Jews*' is partially missing in the Latin top line, as well as the Aramaic bottom," Jon noted. "We ought to search the sarcophagus for the two missing corners."

"You haven't excavated it all, then?" Brampton wondered.

"No. We still have a little to do."

By now, the numbness in the group had faded, replaced by waves of elation. Jennings, however, still urged caution. While they had no doubts about the authenticity of their discoveries— something like this was beyond contrivance, after all—anyone *not* present at the dig would, almost viscerally, have to greet anything as phenomenal as this with massive skepticism. The more extraordinary the find, the greater the demand for its verification.

"Until all tests are completed," Jennings warned, "we simply *must* withhold the news—even from other members of our own staff, I regret to say. This is just too spectacular to announce, even in house, until we have validation. Can we *please* agree on that?"

Shannon, Clive, and Jon nodded emphatically.

"Oh! Someone else will have to share our momentous secret. Clive, go and fetch Dick Cromwell and his photo equipment. He'll have to be privy, of course, but he can keep a confidence."

In clearing the sarcophagus base the next morning, they found a missing corner of the *titulus* that completed the first or Latin line. Because it had been protected by a bunching of grave linens, the ink of that lettering was much darker than the rest of the sign. Several other fragments of the parchment were also sifted out.

Since most of the *titulus* was now recovered, Cromwell took a series of photographs against a neutral matte background, using both panchromatic and color film. Then he repeated the process using infrared and ultraviolet light and corresponding film.

Jon scanned the lines intensely under ultraviolet, recalling a similar effort at the Vatican. Had the parchment been a palimpsest—written on previously but erased for reuse—the earlier writing would have left visible traces under UV illumination. "I see nothing else," he said, finally. "Pontius Pilate, evidently, was no chintz. He used fresh parchment on Good Friday."

Late that night, Cromwell delivered a series of maximum-contrast prints that brought out the lettering more distinctly than the parchment itself:

"Excellent!" said Jennings. "We'll work with these right after breakfast tomorrow."

The five could barely sleep that night.

"Let's get on with the paleography, Jonathan," Jennings urged, the next morning. "What do you think?"

"Well, let's start with the top line. The Latin is *very* similar to lettering I've seen on the election posters at Pompeii, and since those signs got buried by hot ash in AD 79, a first-century origin for the Latin here would seem logical enough."

"So far, so good," said Shannon. "What about the Greek?"

"Greek lettering style didn't change that much between the Hellenistic and Roman periods, so it's a little difficult to pin it down to a century. But handwritten notices I've seen at Athens from the first century resemble this quite closely."

"We're in the ballpark!" Cromwell enthused. "But look at the bottom line. The Aramaic separates the words, like we do today. Didn't the Jews run them together at that time? The Greeks and Romans obviously did."

"No, they were strangely modern about that. They separated their words as early as the fifth century BC . . . Now, as to style, there's no question but that this is a somewhat crude first-century Aramaic in Herodian script." Jon stopped and tapped his nose in thought. Then he wrinkled his brow and said, "But we *do* have two problems here, friends. The first is minor: John's Gospel tells us the sign was in 'Hebrew, Latin, and Greek,' but our sign here has *Aramaic* rather than Hebrew. . . . Well, on second thought, that's nothing serious. Aramaic is sister to Hebrew, and we know it was the language spoken by the common people in Jesus's day. The sign was put up for their benefit, after all. But now the second problem is more serious—"

"Yes, the *order* of languages is different in John versus this sign," said Brampton. "This has Latin first."

"Oh, that's not significant, Clive," Jon replied. "Pilate would inevitably—officially—have put Latin on top, whereas John would give first place to his own tongue. In fact, I think that adds a touch of credibility. . . . No, my concern is the third line. Don't you find the Aramaic a little off-key, Austin?"

"You mean the lettering?"

"No, I mean a grammatical error: that should be *malkah* for 'king,' not *melek*, shouldn't it?"

Jennings scratched his head and said, "I do believe you're right."

"Oh, jeez. It's a *fake*, then?" Cromwell asked. "All that film down the tube?"

A long silence ensued. Suddenly Jon broke out laughing. "No, no, no. We all missed something, and it just occurred to me. That error in Aramaic helps *prove* its authenticity, I think. What, pray tell, were the circumstances behind that *titulus*? Pilate, a non-Jew, or, more probably, one of his non-Jewish aides, wrote the inscription. Now, a Gentile would write the errorless Latin and Greek that we find here, but likely not Aramaic too."

The room was quiet until Brampton broke the silence. "That certainly makes sense to me."

"Yes. Brilliant, Jonathan," Jennings concurred.

"No, anything but. We'd all have thought of it."

Jennings smiled and said, "Well, then, on to the scientific tests. I propose that we take a fragment of the parchment with no lettering—a bit of the wood rot backing too—and send them to the Weizmann Institute at Rehovot for radiocarbon testing. Why are you frowning, Clive?"

"It's just that I'd hate to see *any* part of this extraordinary discovery destroyed."

"I, too, Clive," Jon agreed. "If this were an ordinary find, we wouldn't even bother with carbon 14, since the evidence from the pottery and the writing styles all point to the Herodian period. But in view of what we have here, the world would demand radiocarbon testing. But how much will the Weizmann Institute need by way of samples, Austin?"

"Let me check. I have their schedule here somewhere." He opened one of his filing cabinets, extracted a manila folder after a brief search, and read the requirements. "Of the items we could supply 100 grams of human bone would be necessary, fifty grams of linen, two grams of wood, two grams of parchment or papyrus—"

"Well, even if it's only two grams, that would be a *very* sizeable fragment," Jon observed. "So why don't we do this: since they use the conventional C-14 tests at the Weizmann, let's send them only materials we have in quantity—the grave linens and wood-rot backing. But let's save the precious parchment for testing by the mass spectrometer method. That system requires a sample only *one-thousandth* as large. That's the method we used for testing the Shroud of Turin."

"Excellent, Jonathan," Jennings concurred. "Just splendid."

"But is the Weizmann reliable?" asked Jon, who would have preferred his own team, were they not thousands of miles away.

"Oh, they do fine work. The British School of Archaeology, the American School, the École Biblique all use them."

"I'll throw in the towel, then," Brampton conceded. "But let's make sure Dick has a 'take' on all the photos first."

"Obviously."

EIGHT

Two weeks later, Shannon and Jon drove to Rehovot to pick up the radiocarbon report. Rehovot lay to the west in the Plain of Sharon, about an hour-and-a-half drive from the dig. Jon was playfully probing Shannon's relationship with Gideon Ben-Yaakov as their Land Rover sped down the hills west of Jerusalem.

"Have you told Gideon what you and I pulled out of Joseph's tomb, Shannon?"

"Don't be silly! He doesn't even know there *is* a 'Joseph's tomb.' Did you tell the people at the Weizmann Institute?"

"*Touché!*" Jon laughed. "So how are things between you and Gideon? When do you plan to get married?"

"Tomorrow, if Gideon had his way."

"I can sympathize with that." The words were out before, on second thought, he would have held them in check.

Shannon looked at him curiously and asked, "Is that supposed to be a compliment?"

"Not 'supposed to be' . . . *is.*"

"Well . . . thanks, in that case. I thought you had eyes only for Aramaic and dusty inscriptions, and—"

"Delightful little Irish terrorists who scamper about digs in white shorts, hopelessly distracting all males within range."

"Oh. I never thought of that. It gets so hot out there. You disapprove?"

"Yes, Shannon. I'd really recommend a *chador.* Arabs have this marvelous way of keeping their women gowned, veiled, and quite undesirable."

She laughed. "Male chauvinist *goat!*"

"I thought it was a 'pig.'"

"We're in Israel, remember?"

Jon chuckled, and commented, inwardly, *You're some lucky fool, Ben-Yaakov!* He remembered the time Shannon was working next to him at the sarcophagus, and their hands and arms, even faces brushed against each other as they were extracting the material, and how each contact induced a tiny tingling in him that had nothing at all to do with the excitement of archaeology.

"Tell me more about your wife, Jon," she said, ending his reverie. "I was so sorry to learn about her . . . terrible accident in Switzerland."

They were just driving into the plain when Jon began a long answer to Shannon's query. It was a little difficult to manage— telling of a lost love to a woman for whom a strong attraction was building, despite the frustratingly bleak prospects of any reciprocation. He kept looking ahead and to the left as he drove, so she would not see the film in his eyes. Finally, he changed the subject abruptly and asked, "What do you think they're going to tell us at Rehovot, Shannon?"

"It's a test of *their* equipment, not our samples. We *know* they're authentic."

"Yes, the context *is* overpowering, especially the *random* nature of the find itself."

"You'll think me a dunce, Jon, but—one last time—tell me how they do a carbon 14 test."

"It's not a dumb question, because they're continually improving on the old Willard Libby method. He was the genius who discovered the technique in the 1950s. Now, when cosmic rays strike the earth's outer atmosphere, they hit nitrogen—the commonest gas in the air—and convert bits of it into carbon-14 atoms, a radioactive isotope of regular carbon that will disintegrate over time. Are you with me so far?"

"Of course."

"Okay, all living things are carbon-based. Plants take it in from the atmosphere via carbon dioxide and pass it on to animals. And so both absorb not just regular carbon but carbon 14 as well— *until they die*—at which time ingestion ceases. After that the carbon 14 in their systems slowly disintegrates back into nitrogen, according to the half-life of radiocarbon, which is about fifty-seven hundred years. . . . Follow me?"

"Meaning that half of the carbon 14 vanishes every fifty-seven hundred years?"

"Exactly. So Libby had this brilliant idea of simply measuring the amount of radiocarbon still present in any sample to determine when it died—*the less carbon 14, the older the sample.* And this, of course, applies to any part of the plant or animal—lumber from a tree, animal skins turned into leather or parchment, linen—like our sample—whatever. Libby got the Nobel Prize for that hunch, and he should have! He gave archaeology one dream of a timepiece—a clock that runs backward."

"But how did he know the normal amount of C-14 in something still alive?"

"To get a base level? Believe it or not, he started measuring it from methane gases provided by the sewage works in Baltimore—the bowels of the people there providing the first evidence of normal C-14 levels in living creatures."

"How kind of them—excretions as evidence!"

"How genteel, my dear! You could have used the *S* word! . . . Next, Libby demonstrated that the levels of C-14 were virtually identical across the globe, and back in time too. He tested objects of a known age—wood from early tombs in Egypt, for example—and the scheme worked! Not perfectly, of course. Some Egyptian artifacts dated a couple centuries 'too young,' but they adjusted their standards to allow for variations in cosmic ray bombardment that produced greater or lesser amounts of C-14. So it's a *superb* tool for—oh, oh, we're coming to a high-security zone."

"You bet! It's the Weizmann Institute that develops the nuclear warheads for Israeli missiles."

"I thought they did that down at Dimona in the Negev."

"That's where the uranium's processed."

"My, we're well informed!"

"It's an open secret. Soon everyone will have 'The Bomb,' Arabs included. Thank God Saddam Hussein didn't quite get the hang of it."

Their mission explained at the guardhouse, they were waved

through the gate to the Isotope Laboratories. Dr. Reuben Landau met them in his office, a kindly-faced, white-bearded patriarch who looked like Sigmund Freud.

"Ah, my friends, sit down, sit down," he invited. "Would you like some refreshment? Yes? Some tea?"

"No. But thank you, Dr. Landau."

"And how is my good friend, Professor Jennings?"

"He sends you his warm regards," said Jon. "Did you have any problems with our samples?"

"A little. We had hoped to use only half of the wood and linen you brought us, but it just wasn't enough. We needed most of the linen, and this small fragment is all we have left." He handed them a piece four centimeters square on a steel tray, which Jon put into a lead-lined pouch. "And we had to use all of the wood sample."

"No problem."

"Otherwise, we had quite normal readouts. The wood had traces of calcium carbonate that *could* have added ambient carbon, but we were able to clean the linen thoroughly. In any case, it seems your linen came approximately from the Second-Temple era—the wood a little earlier—both give or take the usual century."

Jon and Shannon looked at each other, eyes taut with excitement.

Landau continued, "Here's our full report. We date the linen at about 50 CE, and the wood at about 5 BCE, plus or minus the usual hundred years."

"Smashing!" Shannon whispered to Jon. "Right on target!" Then she said, "You have fine equipment here, Dr. Landau."

"Thank you, Miss Jennings. Ah . . . might I be so bold as to ask where the samples came from?"

Jon cleared his throat and replied, "It's just . . . material from Professor Jennings's dig at Rama, Dr. Laundau. We found this at a . . . at a separate site there, and wanted general confirmation of the time frame."

"I see, I see." Landau was peering curiously at Jon. "But in preparing the wood sample—it's olive wood, by the way—we noticed bits of what seemed to be parchment embedded in the wood. Did you find parchment too?"

Instantly Jon would have to decide between truth and falsehood, reality or cover-up. If he admitted to the parchment, the next question would have been, "Was there any writing on it?" He looked over to Shannon and found only an anxious stare. No, there was a third alternative.

"I'm sure Professor Jennings will be in touch with you shortly."

"Yes, certainly. And do give him my best wishes. I've enjoyed working with him on several occasions." Landau smiled as he bade Shannon farewell. "Your father is a great archaeologist, Miss Jennings. But you are very much his finest achievement!"

"Why, thank you, Dr. Landau. We're very grateful for your help."

They could hardly keep a lid on their mood as they left the premises. Once on the open highway, however, both let out a whoop of joy. "They're *authentic*, Shannon—the finds of the century!" said Jon, almost breathlessly.

"Fabulous! Just fabulous! I'm *so* happy for Papa. For all of us. Even you, Jon!" She gave him a playful jab in the ribs.

Jennings was waiting for them in the lobby of the hotel when they returned to Ramallah. "Well?" he asked, his eyebrows a pair of arches.

"You, Shannon, have the honor of reporting," said Jon, gallantly.

"Sorry, Papa. Landau dates both the wood and the linen to the twelfth century AD. All this seems to be a hoax by the Crusaders."

"*What?!*" he bellowed.

"Just spoofing!" she chuckled. "We're talking *AD 50* for the linen, and *5 BC* for the wood. Plus or minus a hundred."

"*Hooray!*" Jennings yelled.

"Looks like it's all as genuine as the Sea of Galilee, Austin. Congratulations!" said Jon, extending his right hand while delivering Landau's report with the left.

"Congratulations yourself!" he countered. "*You*, after all, discovered the cavern."

"But it's your dig, Austin."

"*Our* dig, Jonathan."

NINE

What to do?

They felt obligated to report the astounding discovery to the rest of the dig personnel, but they also knew that, once announced, word about so extraordinary a find could never be contained. They decided to finish the excavations at the tomb area first.

"We really ought to take every thimbleful of dust and debris out of that cavern," said Jennings. "Armies of archaeologists will want to comb this place one day, Jonathan, and it would be dreadfully embarrassing if we overlooked something, now, wouldn't it?"

"I think the only rubble left is in the pit. After that, it's solid rock. So we should go after that gravelly material. Same configuration? Shannon and I inside? You, Clive, and Ibrahim outside, sifting what we pass out?"

"Well, we've had jolly good luck with that configuration so far, wouldn't you say?"

They began troweling away all remaining debris in the pit around the sarcophagus. Several buckets of material were passed outside, but no further artifacts were found. Jon hardly minded. Again he was continually brushing against a woman who intrigued him as they spooned out the past—the light and fire of a kindling affection against the dark and cold of death. Love was supposed to flourish on Mediterranean cruise ships slicing through moonlit waves, not in a dank cavern digging out a *sarcophagus*, which, after all, meant "flesh-eater" in Greek.

But such a stunted love! Shannon seemed to have no feelings whatever for him, and he could thank not only Ben-Yaakov but

81

the general ambiance for that, to say nothing of their age difference. *Blast* such one-sided attractions!

"Are you both *blind* in there?" Jennings's stentorian tones con-
veyed some sense of urgency. "Come out here! Immediately!"

They crawled outside, Jon following Shannon, to find the three
men clustered about some object Jennings was holding in his
hand. "It's a bronze *quadrans,* I think," he said.

Jon took the coin, rubbed it clean, squinted at the inscription,
and said, "It's from Nero's time!"

Over lunch in the mess tent, they passed the coin around for all
staffers and students to enjoy. As it went from hand to hand, Jon
explained what they were seeing. "It's a bronze 'mite' minted by
one of the Roman governors here, either Felix or Festus. St. Paul
stood before both of them when he was in prison at Caesarea,
you'll recall."

At that moment, the coin was in Scott Ferguson's hand. He
looked up and said, "I don't see either of those names on it."

"Aha! But whose name *do* you see?" Jon probed, ever the professor. "Look carefully."

"Well, on one side, the Greek is '*LE KAISAROS.*' Well, the last
is 'OF CAESAR,' obviously, though I don't know what '*LE*' is."

"In a moment. Now the other side."

"'*NERONIS*' . . . 'OF NERO'."

"Exactly. Now the *L* is simply a warning that what follows is not
a letter, but a *number,* even though it's the Greek epsilon: *E.* If you
number the letters in the Greek alphabet, what number is epsilon?"

He counted: "*Alpha,* one; *beta,* two; *gamma,* three; *delta,* four;
epsilon, five. Okay, five."

"Now you've got it: '*The fifth year of Caesar Nero.*' And since

Nero became emperor in AD 54, we know that this coin was minted in 58 or 59."

"Awesome! But what about Felix or Festus?"

"In Nero's fifth year, either Felix or Festus was governor. The chronology there is still a little hazy."

When the coin had made its rounds, Jennings reminded the students that this proved only that Joseph's burial could not possibly have occurred *before* AD 58/59. Then he went on to anecdotes about how he had once tried to gull the great Père Roland de Vaux at Qumran by "discovering" a Byzantine coin in what was supposed to be a first-century BC stratum. The bearded French Dominican had merely shot him a cold Gallic smile and said, "It eez *impossible!* Remove zat 'spook,' *s'il vous plait.*"

That afternoon, the buckets contained nothing but a little remaining rubble. Jon and Shannon had now met each other at the western end of the sarcophagus, having troweled down to solid rock around the entire perimeter. Jon called outside, in dig argot: "The clearance of the cavern is complete!"

"Are you *sure,* Jonathan? Nothing else?"

"Have a heart, Papa!" Shannon called back. "Hasn't this cave given us enough?"

They heard chuckling. "Well, I suppose it has. Come out, then. It's nearly time to quit anyway."

Shannon crawled out of the sarcophagus pit and through the threshold. Jon gave his trowel a parting shove into the floor of the pit—a good-bye gesture—and climbed out as well.

It was his wretched Teutonic thoroughness that was responsible, Jon would later claim. He did a "double take," recalling that his last shove with the trowel had clattered a bit differently than when it merely hit bedrock. Then again, he was just imagining things, he decided, and continued crawling through the threshold. Then he stopped again. It was hopeless. He would have to go back.

Feeling somewhat ridiculous, and hoping the others had not noticed his halting performance, Jon climbed back down into the sarcophagus pit and shoved his trowel into the same spot a second time. This time there was a sharper, high-pitched chatter or squeal. He started troweling carefully around the area, which was in the floor just outside the head end of the sarcophagus. Soon, a small ceramic object came into view, lying on its side. After brushing off the upper side that faced him, he stared at a small pinkish juglet only slightly longer than his hand, and about three or four fingers wide. Had he been a newcomer to the dig, he would have extracted it immediately, but he recalled Jennings's chiding Shannon and himself for removing the ceramic items from the sarcophagus before they had been photographed *in situ*.

"Austin, you'd all better come inside here," he called out. "But first have Ibrahim get Cromwell and his camera."

Several minutes later, the five were hovering over the sarcophagus pit, which flickered with blue-white flashing from Cromwell's cameras. "That should do it, Dick," said Jon. "May I continue?"

"Just one more," he replied, the universal litany of photographers anytime, anywhere.

With enormous care, Jon gently removed the juglet from its matrix, and then proved his archaeological maturity by handing Jennings the artifact, ignoring it, and carefully spooning away further material from the cavity he had just discovered. Ten more minutes of excavation-in-miniature revealed nothing else. Outside the cavern, Jon winced at the two scars his trowel had scored along the side of the juglet, which had produced the squeal. "Sorry about that," he apologized. "But what do you make of it, Austin?"

"I don't know. It's obviously a juglet of some kind . . . perhaps a small flagon for perfumes or ointments."

"Look inside," Shannon suggested. "Take out that plug. Or lid."

For some moments Jennings examined the pluglike stopper that capped the juglet. "It's clay," he said, "unfired clay, probably as a sealant." Silence commanded the group. Finally Jennings said, "Obviously we'll open it. But not here." Then he put his arm across Jon's shoulders and said, "You always provide us with as much homework as we can handle, Jonathan. There's a good professor!"

Another letter from Vatican City awaited Jon when he returned from the dig. Sullivan was making progress on the agenda Jon had suggested, but the solution was nowhere in sight. "Strong ultraviolet on the *Sinaiticus* in London showed nothing more at the end of Mark," he wrote. "The Holy Father now gives full approval to your proposal for scientific tests. Feel free to assemble your panel at any time."

Jon filed the letter, amazed that what had seemed so "earth-shaking" in Rome some weeks ago now seemed much less pressing. Rama was the reason!

Just after dinner that night, the same fivesome gathered around the work table at the hotel. After washing and drying the bottom and sides of the artifact, Jennings put it under strong light and inspected it with a large magnifying glass, giving Shannon a running commentary to record in the campaign log:

This date, *Area 15, Registration Number 027*: one oblong vessel—a juglet or small flagon with handle—18 centimeters in height, 9.5 centimeters in diameter at its widest, tapering to 7 centimeters near its mouth, giving an elongated pyriform configuration. The mouth is occluded with unfired clay molded into the orifice, resulting in a rather tight seal. Color is pinkish beige, and there was no glaze or slip used prior to firing.

"I hope you're sketching this thing, Jonathan."
"*Must* I?"

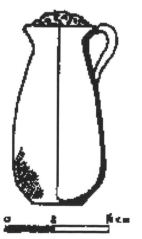

"You found it; you sketch it!"

Jon groaned and got out his pad. A graph grid underneath it helped him with the general dimensions, and soon he produced the drawing, passing it around for all to mock.

"Rather acceptable for now, Jonathan," said Jennings. "Give us time. We'll make an archaeologist out of you yet!" He then resumed his dictation:

The juglet base is flat, the fired clay of fairly uniform consistency, with a few flecks of white. The unfired clay seal is gray and desiccated, but undisturbed. There is no inscription, design, or art on the exterior. This item was found—where?

"Below the head end of the sarcophagus, at the western base of the pit," Jon answered.

"Use those words, Shannon. . . . There, that's enough log entry for now. It's time for your photography, Dick."

Cromwell photographed the juglet from every angle—particularly the mouth, since no one doubted for a moment that the plug of sealant would be removed. While his films were developing, the other four took turns examining the flagon or juglet—whatever it was—with gloves on, turning it every which way for clues as to its nature.

"It looks for all the world like an ancient martini pitcher," Jon suggested, "though I doubt we'll find ice cubes inside."

"Film's Okay," a voice from the darkroom called out.

Jennings now took a small scalpel and meticulously, almost surgically, cut into the edges of the clay seal. Brittle, dry, and crumbly, the ancient clay offered little resistance as he slowly pulled the plug out of the juglet's mouth and put it into a small box lined with cotton-batten. Then he held the open juglet under a high-intensity lamp and peered inside.

"Beyond belief!" he exclaimed. "I see a . . . a coil of some sort of material inside. This lamp won't do! Give me a penlight, Clive. On second thought, don't bother. Just lay out a base of cotton on the work table instead."

That done, Jennings turned the mouth downward and very gently tapped the base of the juglet to let the contents drop onto the cotton. The material inside started moving, but caught at the neck of the juglet. Clive offered him a pair of tweezers.

"I need a *toothpick!*" Jennings roared, as if he were a world-class brain surgeon and a nurse had just handed him a drill instead of a sponge. Shannon hurried out to the dining room and came back with a handful of toothpicks. Jennings took one, inserted it with agonizing care under the material, and gave it a tiny nudge. Suddenly, it slipped out intact onto the cotton base.

Jon stood transfixed. Shannon and Jennings seemed in suspended animation. It was left to Clive to find words for the group. "Great God on High!" he whispered. "It's papyrus! It's a small *scroll!*"

Silence again draped the chamber, broken only when Cromwell exclaimed, "*Fantastic!* Unroll it so I can photograph it!"

"Not on your life, Dick!" Jon warned. "We'll most likely have to humidify it first so it doesn't break up. Right, Austin?"

"Yes, yes, *yes!*" said Jennings, lifting his head off the table. "We can't do any more here. Tomorrow we'll take it to Nikos Papadimitriou at the Rockefeller Museum in Jerusalem. If anyone on earth can unroll this thing without destroying it, it would be Nikos!"

TEN

Nikolaos Papadimitriou was born into the Greek Orthodox community in Jerusalem and had spent most of his forty-five years not far from the gleaming golden-white limestone walls of the Palestine Archaeological Museum, usually called "The Rockefeller" in honor of its donor. As a teenager, he had apprenticed with the teams that unwrapped the Dead Sea Scrolls, and now, as director of the museum's laboratory, his was the court of first—and sometimes last—resort for dealing with fragile materials uncovered by various digs in Israel. Jennings had known him ever since his own days of work on the Dead Sea Scrolls, and they had pursued a close friendship ever since. If anyone could be trusted with a confidence, it was Nikos Papadimitriou.

When Jennings arrived, he closeted himself with Nikos for some earnest, quiet dialogue, handed him a shoe box filled with cotton surrounding the papyrus scroll, and then discussed the process of unrolling it. Nikos studied the coiled scroll for some minutes and said, "It's extremely brittle . . . very, very dry, Austin. Let me humidify it gradually. About a week should do. Come back, let's say, next Wednesday for the 'unscrolling.' Will that be convenient?"

"Same time? In the morning?"

"*Kalos.*"

"Fine, then. *Eph charisto, Nikos!*"

It was a restless seven days for "The Quintet," as Jon now styled those who were privy to the papyrus. The juglet had been sealed: someone, long ago, had wanted the papyrus preserved for some reason. Although they all *hoped* it would contain writing, Jennings cautioned them again that no writing whatever had appeared on the exterior of the scroll, nor in whatever of the core he could see via penlight.

On the drive to the Rockefeller Museum a week later, Jon reminded the other four that there could have been a reason for sealing a blank scroll. "Joseph of Arimathea might have had an Egyptian servant or aide who believed that a model of something was enough to secure its existence in the next life. King Tut's tomb had many such models—slaves, chariots, ships—to serve him in eternity. Knowing that Joseph was educated, maybe the blank scroll was to be some sort of 'memo pad' for the future life, so to speak."

"A little farfetched," Clive objected. "And you found the juglet *outside* the sarcophagus."

"Well, *just* outside, and at the head end. Look, Clive, obviously, we all hope there *is* writing on that papyrus. I'm only trying to prepare us in case we draw a blank."

"Hmmmm," Jennings finally commented. "Consider the case of Yigael Yadin at the Dead Sea caves. He found this marvelous tied roll of parchment from the time of Bar-Kokhba, but when it was unrolled, it was all blank! The scroll was simple 'stationery,' waiting to be used!

"But here we are at the Rockefeller. We'll use the *back* entrance to the laboratory because the Israel Antiquities Authority has the south wing here. Gideon had better not spot you, Shannon!"

The Land Rover climbed past the golden octagonal tower of the Rockefeller Museum, overlooking the Kidron Valley and the Mount of Olives, and squeaked to a halt in the rear parking lot. Nikos Papadimitriou met them at the door of his laboratory office. Jon liked the dapper Greek's firm handshake. Fairly tall, though overshadowed by the lanky Jennings, Nikos had salt-and-pepper hair and a moustache that accented a friendly face that could be trusted.

"I admire your scholarship, Professor Weber," he said. "And I look forward to reading your latest book."

"You'll find your own work cited in several key passages, Dr. Papadimitriou," said Jon. "Delighted to meet you!"

"Come, come, sit down, my friends. I've ordered tea and cakes for all, yes? Ah, my little Shannon, you grow more beautiful each time I see you. No wonder Gideon Ben-Yaakov is so moonstruck!"

"Why, thank you, Nikos." She smiled graciously. "How did our scroll fare?"

"The scroll . . . yes, of course. Please be kind to close the door. Ah, fine." Then he lowered his voice. "For the past week, the scroll has been inside this humidifier here, and I've slowly raised the humidity to 85 percent. That *should* be enough to restore, ah, how you say? . . . ah . . . flexibility to the papyrus so it won't crack, yes? Here, you can see it through the glass door."

The scroll had swollen to three times its original diameter in partially uncoiling itself because of the humidity. Nikos now opened the door, reached for large cotton-tipped tongs, and with steady hand extracted the scroll, placing it onto a sponge-rubber mat atop his worktable. All the while, Cromwell was taking photographs with gusto, switching his lenses, his cameras, and his stances. He included portraits of the entire group as well, sensing that either archaeological history was in the making, or photographs for the dig's scrapbook, to be captioned: "The Furtive Five, discovering Joseph of Arimathea's toilet paper."

With excruciating deliberation, Nikos now took rubber spatulas and ever so slowly started prizing the coil open. Several pieces of papyrus flaked off at the edges, but, happily, the central trunk remained intact. Not a sound was heard, other than the clicking of Cromwell's cameras. With microscopic movements, Nikos pried further. "Nothing so far," he said, in a soft voice.

The silence was sepulchral. Now he leaned over very close to the scroll to peer into its open end. "*O Thee mou!*" he erupted. "There's *writing!* I can see it *just* beginning to show!"

Cheers filled the room. "*Smashing!*" cried Clive. "Absolutely *smashing!*" Jennings tossed his orange cap into the air, while Jon grabbed Shannon around the waist and squeezed her hard as she squealed with delight. Nor did he miss the opportunity of planting a warm kiss on her cheek.

There was a rapping at the door, and it flew open. Gideon Ben-Yaakov looked first shocked and then pleased as he stepped into the laboratory. "What are we having here, my friends, a *party?* We hear you all over the museum! . . . Shannawn! Why didn't you *tell* me you were coming to Jerusalem!"

"I was just about to drop in on you, dear."

As Gideon walked over to embrace her, his back turned briefly, Jon grabbed the lid of a huge amphora awaiting inspection on Nikos's table and placed it squarely over the scroll.

"So what was the celebration about?" Gideon turned and asked.

No one said a word.

Therefore Jon had to. "Well, it's really not *that* much to cheer about," he drawled. "I . . . just got a call from my publisher, and he said that 200,000 copies of my new book have been sold."

"Well, well . . . that *is* something to cheer about! Congratulations, Jonathan! But why are you all here rather than digging at Rama?"

"Cromwell here is taking photos of laboratory procedures to show our students on the dig," fibbed Jennings. "Some of the museum pieces too."

"Well, don't miss this . . . what is it . . . this amphora lid, then," Gideon responded. "Where did they find it, Nikos?"

"Caesarea."

"Oh yes . . . Holum's dig." Then, to everyone's horror, he picked up the lid. "Why, it must weight six or seven kilos." He set it down again and said, "Well, I must be going, friends. Lunch, Shannawn?"

"Fine, Gideon. In about an hour?"

"Good. Just come down to my office."

Nikos followed him to the door, this time bolting it after him.

"*Blast!*" said Jon, as he raised the lid. "He caught the end of the scroll and knocked off another flake of papyrus. No real damage, though."

Gently Nikos resumed the uncoiling procedure, stopping from time to time to let the papyrus adjust to its dramatic new environment. Eight lines became visible. Then there were twelve.

Jon peered closely at the writing. "We have Aramaic square script here," he said, "a hand that wrote *very small* but careful lettering. Looks Herodian, pre- or post-, more or less our first century BC/AD horizon. Though these are just first impressions."

Nikos now reached for a strange-looking device that looked

like a giant *C* with felt-covered tabs along the sides. "This is a scroll-holder I designed for shorter documents like this one," he explained. With endless, almost loving care, he slowly insinuated the half-opened scroll onto the holder, and ever so gradually opened the remaining coil over the last quarter of the document. Now they could see the whole text without waiting for it to be stretched flat, which would require additional hours. Several cracks had developed, despite Nikos's care.

"Look!" said Jennings. "A tiny worm must have been sealed inside the juglet. It chewed a couple of worm highways into the scroll here and here." He pointed. "But that worm was *intelligent*, let me tell you: it dieted on the papyrus *between* the lines of ink!"

"Worms probably don't like the taste of ink," Shannon offered.

"Good heavens! The text seems almost intact!" said Jon, as he scanned the document. Then something brought him up short. "There—down there at the bottom. Don't you all see it?" He pointed.

"Looks like a different hand, doesn't it?" said Jennings.

"Different everything! Different hand, different ink, larger size, broader margins. A postscript of some kind? A codicil?"

"Well, what does the text *say*, gentlemen?" Shannon wondered. "You might *then* learn what that trailer is. Or am I being too obvious?"

"You know your Aramaic, Austin." Jon smiled. "Be our guest."

"Not *nearly* as well as you do. Now start translating this thing, Jonathan, and *finally* earn your keep on this dig. Be a good chap . . ."

"I'll have a go at it."

Jon took a magnifying glass and studied the text for several minutes in order to familiarize himself with the script. He nodded from time to time, mumbling and mouthing several of the consonants. Then he started chuckling, shaking his head in wonderment.

"What *is* it, Jon?" Shannon demanded. "The suspense is just intolerable!"

"You just won't *believe* it, my friends!" he exulted. "It seems to be a letter . . . a letter from 'Joseph, son of Asher' to 'Nicodemus, son of Simeon.' Here, listen to the opening line: '*Yosef Bar-Asher le-Naqdeymon Bar-Shimeon shalom!*'"

"True, Jon?" Jennings asked, then put on his reading glasses and looked for himself. "Oh, it is. It is indeed!" he whispered in awe. "How . . . how *glorious!* Please, God—Let it be *the* Nicodemus of the Gospels!"

"He was the other man involved in Jesus's burial," Brampton reminded Cromwell, who was not famed for his biblical knowledge.

"Read on," Jennings crooned. "Read on!"

"'*I hope . . . you are in health, friend . . . Not ever did I . . . or . . . I was never sorry . . . to leave Jerusalem when you . . . or . . . even though you . . . wanted me to stay.*'" Jon threw up his hands and said, "It's a little difficult to give a command performance like this. I'll do much better with a pen and pad of paper."

"We have to break for lunch anyway," said Jennings. "Will you join us, Nikos?"

"My pleasure."

They returned from lunch minus Shannon, who had been assigned the task of distracting Gideon Ben-Yaakov. Nikos unlocked the door of his laboratory and then gasped. The papyrus and its supporting apparatus were gone! In its place on the work table was the large amphora lid.

"Oh . . . Lord of Heaven and Earth!" Jennings cried. "This cannot be!" He turned to Cromwell and asked, "Did you get any photos of the text this morning?"

"Only a few lines . . . over Jon's shoulder."

Nikos darted from his office and presently returned with a younger associate, who sheepishly confessed that he had put the papyrus holder on another work table at the end of the laboratory in order to take scrapings of the amphora lid. Nikos quickly retrieved the papyrus, looking approximately as sheepish. "That's fine, Vasilios," he said. "You may go and continue your clay analysis later."

"No more chance!" said Jennings, swimming in relief. "Dick, take some photographs of the text immediately. You can do the formal ones later on when the papyrus is flat."

"Yes," Jon agreed, his heart finally resuming its normal cadence. "Photograph the very *devil* out of that text!"

"Piece of cake," said Cromwell. "That ink's darker than most of the *titu*—" He caught himself just in time, realizing that Papadimitriou was present and had no membership as yet in The Quintet. Loading high-speed pan film into one of his cameras with a macro lens, he photographed the papyrus from four different vertical angles, to compensate for the curvature of the scroll. "Okay," he finally said. "I have enough overlap. It's all yours, Jon."

Jon sat down at the table, scrutinized the Aramaic, and began translating onto a yellow pad of legal-sized paper. Cromwell tried to read Jon's writing, but Brampton stopped him, whispering, "Let's not distract him, Dick. It's hard enough to urinate while someone's watching, isn't it? Same goes for translation."

Jon put down his pen and laughed. Then he returned to the text, writing down phrase after phrase, line after line, though not without a good deal of backtracking and crossing out words. Meanwhile Brampton invited Cromwell out for a coffee, Nikos went into the museum, and only Jennings shared his vigil, pacing from one end of the laboratory to the other, doing his best to contain his excitement.

From time to time Jennings glanced at Jon, and noticed a gradual change in his mien. Jon had begun with a look of intense interest, but then a slight frown had developed, along with a wrinkled brow. Later his eyes constricted, and his breathing sounded somewhat labored. His writing became more intense, while the line-outs became veritable slashes from his pen. Then he dropped it entirely, staring boggle-eyed at the papyrus.

"What is it, Jon?" asked Jennings. "Anything wrong?"

Jon said nothing. He only stared blankly over the top of the papyrus at a case of books along the wall.

"What's the matter, Jon?" Jennings demanded. "Are you all right?"

"Fine," he responded at last. "Get Nikos and see if he has Koehler-Baumgartner's Aramaic-English dictionary."

He had left blanks in his translation when he encountered

words or phrases unfamiliar to him. Several were crucial verbs, on which the whole thrust of the document might depend, and he was grateful that Jennings had not demanded any translation thus far. He now returned, dictionary in hand.

Jon thumbed through it quickly, filling in some of the blanks in his translation. Then he returned to the text. Jennings quickened his stride as he walked from one end of the laboratory to the other, reminding himself of putative Simian cousins in the ape cages of the London Zoo—*a rather inane comparison,* he thought, but only such humoring would contain the volcanic suspense building inside him. He engaged every shred of self-restraint, for otherwise he would have dashed to the yellow pad and read off the translation for himself.

But nothing could stop him from reading Jon's mood, which grew alarming. All color had drained from the younger man's face, perspiration drenched his forehead, and his hands seemed to tremble as he flipped another page on his pad and continued writing, looking up words, crossing out, and writing again.

Finally Jennings could stand it no longer. "What in very *blazes* is wrong, Jon?" he exclaimed. "What does that document *say?* You look like Scrooge facing the Ghost of Christmas Future!"

"And you look like a bloody caged tiger! Can't you leave me *alone* for just a bit?"

"All right."

Instantly Jon shook his head with a wan, forlorn smile. He rubbed his eyes wearily. "Sorry, Austin," he said. "Do forgive me?"

"Of course, Jonathan. Of course." Jennings patted him on the shoulder and left the laboratory.

An hour later Jon emerged, the legal pad and dictionary clutched tightly at his side. He had regained his composure but not his color. "Nikos," he said, "could I borrow the dictionary for a short time?"

"No need to," Jennings interposed. "We have one at Ramallah."

Jon then turned to Cromwell. "Do you have enough photos, Dick?"

"About three times as many as we need."

"Can you give me several prints of your sharpest negatives this evening on high-contrast paper?"

"No problem."

"Fine. Why don't we go back to Ramallah, then?" Jon suggested. "Nikos, you *do* have a humidity-controlled safe here, don't you?"

"Of course. When the papyrus is ready, I plan to put it under glass and inside the safe. Is that acceptable?"

"Excellent," said Jennings.

"And thank you for your strategic help, friend," added Jon. "Soon I'll be in a better position to give you—all of you—the translation," he said with a strange detachment. "This document is too important for any errors, even in a *preliminary* version. You'll understand why soon." He faltered, and there was a catch in his voice. "Very soon."

As they walked out to the Land Rover, Jon beckoned Jennings to one side and said, "It's your dig, Austin, so you have the right to know what I have so far. I destroyed the first draft with all the cross-outs and recopied it. Here, if you can read my writing." He handed the pad to Jennings. "The blanks are words and phrases I still can't decipher."

Jennings walked over to the shade of a pine at the edge of the parking lot and sat down to read. Jon watched as his hands tensed slowly, his eyes glared, and he jerked the legal pad closer. A muscle twitched in his cheek as his lips tautened. His features locked on to each paragraph, which he seemed to read and then reread intensely. When he finished, his head slumped down to his chest, and he remained motionless for what seemed to the others like a small eon.

Finally he raised his head and called, "Jonathan."

Jon walked over.

"What . . . what time was it when the meaning of this letter first dawned on you?"

"About an hour and a half ago. Why do you ask?"

"Mark the time well. That was the moment our world began to change."

Under any other circumstances, Brampton and Cromwell would have demanded to know at least the main thrust of what Jon had deciphered. But both he and Jennings seemed so shaken that the drive back to Ramallah passed in total silence, broken only when they reached the hotel and Jon promised to read them his translation the next day.

Dick Cromwell delivered several razor-sharp prints to Jon's room an hour after dinner. The high-contrast paper made the document easier to read in photograph than the original text, and that night Jon worked till 2:30 AM. Several key phrases eluded him, and half a dozen all-important verbs.

Sleep proved impossible. At 4 AM, he startled the hotel operator by putting in an overseas call to Massachusetts, knowing that his colleague, Frank Moore Cross, Jr., would certainly still be up at 9 PM. Cambridge time. Professor Cross was the one man in America who knew more Aramaic than he did, Jon cheerfully conceded. The call went through in surprisingly quick time.

"Frank?" Jon called into the phone. "This is Jon Weber, in Israel."

"Hello, Jon! You don't have to shout. We have a good connection. What are you doing up so early over there?"

"Checking out an extraordinary document here, Frank. I'll explain later. Right now I need some help in Aramaic. We don't have Marcus Jastrow's Hebrew-Aramaic lexicon over here, so can you help me out on several vocables?"

"Of course."

Jon listed the words and phrases that were giving him problems, spelling out the Aramaic. Cross, that linguistic genius, was able to answer some of Jon's queries on the spot. He promised to phone him the rest after checking.

The next morning, The Quintet closeted themselves in Jennings's office. Jon, bags under his eyes, asked their pardon for not reading them the translation as promised, and told them about his call to Cross. "You see, we're dealing with a rural dialect here, it seems, whereas the postscript, which turns out to be Nicodemus's response, looks like standard Judean Aramaic."

"Can you at least tell us if this Nicodemus is the same one mentioned in the New Testament?" Brampton inquired.

Jon looked to Jennings, who nodded. Then he said, "It *is* the same Nicodemus."

A low whistle was Brampton's only response.

"Now, Professor Jennings will be staying at the hotel today to get Cross's call, while I go to Jerusalem to see Claude Montaigne at the École Biblique. I hope he can shed some light on this dialect."

"*When* will you let us in on this, Jon?" Shannon demanded, a distinct bite in her tone.

"Tonight, I promise. I really do. Just after supper, Okay?"

"Is he being fair, Papa?"

"Yes, dear. He really is."

"Shannon," Jon asked, "when you had lunch with Gideon yesterday, did he say anything about our scene in the laboratory?"

"No. He knows nothing."

"Fine. *Please* keep it that way for now, no matter how much you love him."

"Who said . . . oh, forget it. Okay."

Jon had a 3 PM appointment with Father Claude Montaigne at the École Biblique et Archéologique Française, just north of the walls of the Old City. The scholarly Dominican was doyen of the Aramaic linguists in the world, and the library and archives at the École were among the finest in the Near East.

Montaigne met him just inside the walls of the institution—*everything* was walled in Jerusalem, Jon noticed. The celebrated scholar was diminutive in size, though gigantic in reputation. Everything about the man was silvery—his hair, his close-cut beard, his habit, and even his metal-rimmed glasses.

"*Bonjour, Monsieur Weber,*" he said, extending his hand. "Monsieur Kevin Sullivan in Rome wrote me that you'd be calling and that I must extend *every* courtesy!"

"*Bonjour, mon Professeur . . . notre Professeur,* for you have taught us all." Jon cheerfully ignored the French conceit that mandated a *Monsieur* rather than titles in face-to-face dialogue, a probable carry-over from the French Revolution.

"But now you teach me with your *Vie de Jésu.* I find many fine insights in your book."

"*Merci, Père Montaigne.* But the footnotes in that book demonstrate my indebtedness to your scholarship."

"*De rien.* It is nothing."

"You are gloriously mistaken. But I come on a very urgent errand. I beg you to keep it confidential for the moment."

"But of course. What is it?"

So that Montaigne could work objectively, Jon did not show him photographs of the entire document. He rather presented him the problematical words or phrases within the context of separate sentences, which he had written out ahead of time.

Montaigne studied the material handed him for some time. "Aha!" he said, at last. "This is Aramaic from the hill country. We have an old lexicon in our archives that should help us." He left his office and returned several minutes later with an ancient tome in hand. Then he set to work. Remembering how he, too, had craved the luxury of someone *not* looking over his shoulder, Jon excused himself and explored the library of the École Biblique.

Montaigne summoned him an hour later. He had cracked at least half of the "untranslatables." Here, obviously, was another linguistic prodigy, and with such a scholar one must be honest.

"Père Montaigne," said Jon, "I will now give you photographic copies of the entire document. I beg of you two things. One, please be kind enough to give us your translation so that we can compare it with ours. And two, please let no one see this document, or learn of it, until we confer again. The text will explain this urgency."

"*Certainement,*" he replied with a quizzical expression.

The moment he took his leave, Jon noticed Montaigne's silver spectacles tilting down toward the photocopy.

Toward evening, when Jon returned to Ramallah, Jennings told him that Frank Moore Cross had called, suggesting translations for some of the words and phrases in question. "He hasn't gotten them all yet, but he'll get back to you."

"Fine," said Jon, as he read what Jennings had written out. Between Montaigne and Cross, most of the gaps in translation could be filled, and he could now type up a more accurate version of the document.

At supper, Shannon, Brampton, and Cromwell ate next to Jennings and himself. Jon saw their eyes daring him to renege on his promise to reveal the translation that night. After a final course of Jericho dates, Jon faced them directly and pleaded, "One more night? Please? I have to coordinate the new information we have from Cross and Montaigne. Just after breakfast tomorrow, I swear it? All right?"

Their forced assent was anything but enthusiastic.

"Don't take the bus in the morning," Jennings advised. "Stay here, and we'll drive out to the dig later in the Land Rover."

Jon sat at the desk in his room. As his fingers addressed the keyboard of his laptop, he quivered at the significance of what he was typing—words that would change the future. These were lines that would render every book on Christianity in the world obsolete, including his own best seller. And that effect was only superficial. This shift was seismic, elemental. Nothing could be the same after this became public knowledge.

Another howl from a jackal skewered the night air. Was it the same beast? Was this some mascot of Ramallah? Or of hell? But this time, the mournful cry was answered by a whole chorus of ululating yowls, moaning a canine lamentation at life. Or fate?

"It's a paradigm for the future," Jon muttered, intentionally using one of the most trendy theological buzzwords of the century.

ELEVEN

We'll have to change our nickname," said Jon, in the workroom after breakfast. "'The Quintet' is too bland. Something like 'The Fateful Five' might do—well, maybe not—but after I read this, you'll certainly see why. I know this sounds pompous and bombastic, but it's true nevertheless. This document could change Western civilization. Maybe parts of Eastern too. I need your pledge, under oath, that you'll not reveal a *syllable* of this to anyone for now. Do I have it?"

All nodded emphatically.

Jon, who was not looking for hands on Bibles, continued, "This translation still has several gaps, but we're now sure of the main flow of the text. Which is . . ." Jon took up his typescript and read:

Joseph, son of Asher, to Nicodemus, son of Shimeon, peace! I hope you are well, friend. I was not sorry to leave Jerusalem, even though you wanted me to stay. Arimathea, the home of my youth, serves me well also in old age. I seek only the peace of God before I stand in His presence. To find that peace, I write you. A painful stone is lodged in the sandal of my soul, and I must remove it. Do you remember the rabbi Yeshua [Jesus] whom we buried in my tomb a score and seven years ago during the—

"We're not sure of the next word, but it looks like a Hellenism in Aramaic—hegemonya—"

—during the [*hegemony*, governance] of Pontius Pilatus? I could not sleep after the Passover that night. I feared that the noble rabbi, a man of much suffering, would not have the rest that

103

should come to him after his pain. My servants heard rumors in the city that the priests had a plot regarding his body. I feared they might harm or mutilate it. Later I learned that they only wished to seal the tomb. O that I had known! Not many hours before cock crow, my servant Eleazar and I went to the sepulcher. We removed the body of Jesus and returned the stone to its place. We put the body onto a donkey cart, covered it with logs of olive wood, and returned to my house in Jerusalem. The evening after Shabbat [Sabbath] we drove the cart to Rama where we—

"We don't have the next word either, but we think it means 'buried again'—"

—where we reinterred the rabbi in the sarcophagus I had ordered for myself, but not yet taken to Jerusalem. Only later did I learn of the excitement over the empty tomb. Before my Lord, I do not know why the priests did not examine the tomb before they sealed and guarded it. It was empty on the first day of the week because it was empty already the day before. When I returned to Jerusalem, I found you and the other followers of the Nazarene in such great joy over what you thought his resurrection, that I could not drown by truth the very—

"We don't know the next word—"

—I could not drown by truth the very [blanks] that had overcome your sorrow. Forgive me, dear friend. My health is poor, my eyesight dim. Before I die, I must seek your pardon for hiding the truth these many days. When you read this, I may be dead. If so, I shall be buried not in the sarcophagus with my name, for Jesus is there, but in another tomb. May the Lord give you wisdom to use these words properly or to destroy them. Be in peace. Farewell, beloved friend.

The room was deathly silent. All eyes—some filmed—were staring at Jon vacantly, almost as if he personally had authored the document that would tear Easter from the world's calendars.

Almost defensively, he added, "And now comes Nicodemus's note at the bottom of the letter:

> I, Nicodemus, am here at Rama for Joseph's funeral on the eighth of Elul [September 10]. I cannot express the great disturbance of my mind and heart. But Joseph's reasonings for withholding the truth are also my reasons. I am burying this letter next to the tomb of Jesus. The truth is now in the hands of *El-Shaddai* [the Mighty God]. If He wills, the truth will come to light. If not, then it may be His will that The Way [Christianity] survive, for it is a teaching of hope. Amen.

Jon laid his typescript on the table.

Shannon dropped her head and wept. Clive sat as if he had been fettered to his chair, eyes glazed, his skin sallow and jaundiced. Jennings remained silent as a living corpse.

Dick Cromwell struggled for logic and coherence. "You . . . you mean, then, that the bones we found are *not* Joseph of Arimathea, but . . . but *Jesus?*"

Ever so slowly, Jon nodded. "At least, that's what this letter claims."

"Oh, my Lord! *Jesus?*"

They sat in a circle of shock for several minutes before anyone said another word. Jon watched in knowing sympathy as Shannon, Clive, and Dick recapitulated his own experience in responding to the wrenching revelation. Were *they believers who affirmed the bodily resurrection of Christ?* he wondered. He had certainly been raised to believe that. If so, this was the most corrosive information they could ever hear. But even if they had doubts or were outright skeptics, the Easter concept had been such a part of Western culture that nothing could be the same henceforth.

Jon now broke the silence. "Under any other circumstances, this would be one of the greatest archaeological discoveries ever— no, *the* greatest. But when you have two billion Christians believing that Jesus rose from the dead . . ."

He did not finish the sentence. A hush hovered over the room again for endless moments.

"I just thought of something . . . something rather inane," Cromwell admitted.

"Be our guest."

"Remember those buttons that used to show up on college campuses in spring? 'NO EASTER THIS YEAR: THEY FOUND THE BODY!' Well, we've gone and done just that!"

Again there was mortal silence.

And again, Jon broke it. "Now, of course, the process of authentication becomes *heroic!* If this gets out, the Christian world is going to *scream* for tests of every kind. Which is also why we *have* to keep this under wraps until all the tests have taken place."

Jennings finally came to life. "Oh, there will be *dozens* of tests before we're through! Dozens! But let's start with *internal* evidence, Jonathan. Read the whole translation again, and let's all of us search for any flaws."

When he had finished a slower, more deliberate reading the second time, Brampton inquired about the one chronological clue in the text. "They claimed to bury Jesus 'a score and seven years' earlier. That's twenty-seven years, right?"

"Right."

"Well, relate that to the coin we found and see if it all jibes."

"Good thought," Jon replied. "Scholarly consensus leans to the years AD 30 or 33 for Jesus's crucifixion, but I've always argued for 33. So 27 years after 33 would bring us to AD 60 as the time this letter was written. Our coin, you'll recall, dates to 58 or 59, so it all fits." He paused, touched the tips of his fingers together, and then added, with a smile, "But the earlier date for the crucifixion—AD 30—*doesn't* fit, so score one for 33!"

"*Beautiful,* Jon," commented Shannon, acid in her voice. "Go strut your chronological stuff—over the dead body of Christianity."

"*Sorry,* Shannon. I . . . just got carried away for a moment. I think we've all got to stay more objective about this and not leap to *any* conclusions, however compelling they may seem."

"Ah yes," Jennings agreed. "Tests, tests, and more tests! Only then the conclusions."

Claude Montaigne had called, and his appointment with Jon was set for the following afternoon. He greeted Jon in a state of high agitation, his Gallic forehead wrinkled with furrows. "*Voici . . .* my translation," he said, handing it over to Jon. "But I have *many* questions, *mon ami.*"

He now fired a volley of further queries about the dig and the discovery, and Jon provided a full description. When they moved on to writing analysis, Montaigne commented, "Yes, it looks like *premier siècle*—first century—but do let me look at the original, *s'il vous plait.*"

"Why, of course. Shall we go to the Rockefeller? Can you get away?"

"*Certainement.*"

A ten-minute walk brought them to the museum laboratory. Nikos Papadimitriou smiled when he saw Montaigne. "Ah! I'm glad that *you* are involved, Père Claude."

"*Kalimera,* Nikos!" said Montaigne, for whom Greek was an active sixth language.

Nikos quickly opened the safe at Jon's request and drew out the papyrus, now safely ensconced between plates of glass, and then left the room. Jon beamed a strong lamp over the text and handed Montaigne a magnifying glass. The black ink of the lettering showed up clearly, as did the brown-black of the Nicodemus response.

The French scholar studied the document for some time before he said anything. Then he and Jon broke into spirited dialogue over the problem words and phrases, and finally compared the two script styles with various lines of Aramaic from different centuries on a chart Montaigne had brought along.

"The writings on this document *do* look very much like our first-century sample, don't they?" Montaigne offered. "Have you sent a copy to Frank Moore Cross at Harvard?"

"We're sending him a fax as soon as Cromwell, one of our staffers, photographs the papyrus now that it's flat. He's coming in any time now."

"Good. Well, both script styles seem to be Herodian or the Roman period up to, perhaps, the Bar-Kokhba revolt."

"So we have a time frame of about 40 BC to AD 135, Père Montaigne?"

"*Oui.* Probably only one man on earth could narrow that frame . . . *and* give us better definitions at places where I have question marks in the translation."

"Who's that?"

"Alexandros, the former archimandrite of St. Catherine's monastery at Mount Sinai. He's devoted his life to Aramaic, even the dialects." Montaigne smiled wistfully and added, "I hate to admit that he knows more Aramaic than I do. But he does."

"I'd love to discuss every syllable of this text with him personally, if possible." Jon strummed his fingers on the table, then turned and said, "Israel and Egypt are at peace. Couldn't I drive to St. Catherine's from here?"

"*Oui.* There are two routes. One is the highway: no problem. But if you take the wadi route, which is shorter, then you must have . . . how do you say it. . . power on every wheel?"

"Four-wheel drive?"

Montaigne nodded, and said, "And you must also have provisions in your car. I would be glad to arrange an appointment for you. Alexandros has helped us before."

"I'd be *greatly* obliged to you, Père Montaigne."

"Ah, does Nikos know what this document is? Or claims to be?"

"No, he hasn't pressed us, probably out of professional courtesy. I told him I'd discuss it with him once we're sure of the translation."

Then Montaigne shook his head slowly and said softly, "So far, I've dealt with this only as a scholar, *mon ami.* I've not even *begun* to . . . to respond to this as a theologian. Or as a Christian."

"Nor have I, Père Montaigne. Nor have I!"

The moment he saw Jon drive off, Claude Montaigne stepped back inside the Rockefeller and returned to Papadimitriou's office. "Oh, Nikos," he said, nonchalantly. "I want to look at one more item on that papyrus."

"Help yourself, Père Montaigne. It's still on the laboratory table. We're waiting for the Rama photographer."

Alone inside the laboratory, the smallish Dominican performed the most risky act in his otherwise sheltered, scholarly life. Hands trembling, but with the tenderest care, he lifted the top plate of glass off the papyrus, set it aside, and then cut a rhombus-shaped fragment from the bottom of the papyrus, using one of the laboratory scissors. He inserted the fragment into a small envelope, which he then slid into his coat pocket, all the while glancing furtively through the lab's window divider at Papadimitriou, who had his back turned. Since the bottom edge of the papyrus was chipped and serrated anyway, no one would notice anything amiss. Montaigne replaced the glass, smiled at his success—small but potentially strategic—and left the Rockefeller.

When Jon returned to Ramallah, Jennings closeted him in his room and said, "While you were gone, Nottingham returned from Jerusalem with Dr. Itzhak Shomar's report on the . . . on the remains." Now that these had a catastrophic new identity, he could not bring himself to say "bones." "Shomar, you recall, is the Rockefeller's pathologist."

"Does Noel have any idea what this is all about?"

"No. He assumes those are the remains of Joseph of Arimathea."

"And Shomar?"

"Noel told him nothing."

"Good! Let's keep it that way as long as possible."

Jennings handed him Shomar's report, which was thirty-five pages in length. Before he opened it, he asked, "Does it address *the* problem, Austin?"

"It does."

"How?"

"Read for yourself, Jonathan."

The pathologist's report, however innocent and unknowing, now carried overwhelming import. *If* the papyrus were authentic, there was one piece from a different puzzle that did not at all fit. The bones suited Joseph of Arimathea handsomely—the name on the sarcophagus, after all—but *not* a Jesus who was a young man—33 to 36—when he was crucified. Nottingham had insisted on an age range of 50 to 60 for the skeletal remains, numbers that now assumed critical importance.

While Jennings went out to fetch a bottle of sherry, Jon perused the report. He was on page five when Jennings returned. "Nothing much different from Nottingham's preliminary so far," he commented.

"Read on."

"Here are some interesting points: 'The bones show slight calcium deprivation, though not of a serious nature.' Hmmmm. 'The teeth show no dental caries of any kind.'"

At page twelve, Jon suddenly sat up straight in his chair and took a long sip of wine. "Listen to this, Austin:

> The distal ends of the right and left radius show a grooving or abrasion of some kind, as does part of the metatarsal assembly. While this may be due to dietary deficiency, the similarity of this defect in all four extremities is strange.

"The wrist ends of both arms and the middle foot bones *grooved?*" Jon exclaimed. "As from *nails?* As in *crucifixion?*"

"What else?" Jennings groaned.

Jon continued reading. Several pages later, he stopped, looked up, and said, "Listen to this:

> There is also a lateral scoring on the upper side of the seventh left rib, which tapers from a width of 2.5 to 1.7 centimeters. The cause of this abrasion, whether naturally or artificially induced, is not determined as of this writing. The latter, however, must be suspected, since this phenomenon is not paralleled in my experience.

Jon closed his eyes and quoted from John's Gospel: "*'But one of the soldiers pierced his side with a spear, and at once blood and water came out.'* Shomar just gave a perfect description of the imprint of a spear's head!"

"Read on, Jonathan. You'll find more shovelfuls to heap on the grave of classic Christianity," said Jennings, a dour, woebegone expression clouding his features.

Some minutes later, Jon said, "No, that's about it. Well, wait, here's the final evaluation section." He read further to himself, then out loud:

In terms of the absolute age of these remains, methods of radiocarbon, fluorine, and other procedures for bone datings were not attempted, as such determinations must be decided upon by Professor Jennings. With his permission, however, a small portion of the left femur was subjected to amino-acid racemization. Assuming a temperature history inside the cavern at Rama parallel to other such caves in Israel at this latitude and altitude, the analysis suggests a bone age of 1,940 years BP [before the present] with an uncertainty factor of 15 percent. As to the age of the individual *at death*, however, a preliminary report suggesting an attained age range of 50 to 60 should be revised downward, since there is less dental and joint wear than was first suspected. Furthermore, the extraphytic accretions—i.e., spurs or knobbing from calcium deposits—on the spinal vertebrae, acetabular fossa, and other joints are not as pronounced as would be the norm for advanced age. A more appropriate range for age at death would be 35 to 45.

Wearily, Jon closed the report and set it on the table. He took another long sip of sherry, and Jennings refilled his glass. "Well, there it is," Jon sighed. "This missing piece fits after all. Or, let me put it another way: the last nail in the coffin of traditional Christianity is nicely in place, and the purely 'spiritual resurrection' of our liberal theologians nicely vindicated."

"But isn't 35 to 45 still a little too old for Jesus, Jonathan?"

"Tut, tut, Austin. I thought you read my book. The chapter on chronology puts Jesus at 32½ to 33 at the start of his ministry, and 36½ at his death."

"Oh, that's right."

Neither said anything more, both staring vacantly out at the last roseate glimmer of daylight fading on the hills. Jon was waiting for another jackal's howl, but the local canine soloist was not performing that evening.

Suddenly Jennings stood up and started pacing the room. "You know, Jonathan, this thing is getting absolutely out of hand. I wonder if we shouldn't simply destroy the papyrus, the juglet, and all the photographs and negatives to avoid maiming the faith of countless millions—perhaps civilization itself. Let the world think we discovered Joseph—isn't that a find enough? Christianity would remain intact, and we could always—"

"Are you serious?"

"I . . . well, I . . ." He paused, faltered, and then slammed his hand down on the table, rattling the wine bottle. "No, I suppose I'm *not* serious. After all, how could an archaeologist destroy *anything?* And yet I . . . I tremble now, Jonathan. I tremble—"

"So do I, Austin. And even if we wanted to destroy the latest items, we could hardly bring it off now. Shannon, Clive, Dick, Montaigne, and Cross all know . . . or will know. Nikos half knows—"

"Yes, scientific objectivity and dispassionate scholarship have to rule from here on." Jennings seemed to regain his composure. "We're getting too much personal involvement here—by the very nature of the find, of course. But we *must* keep open minds."

Jon nodded emphatically and said, "What we've discovered is either authentic or the most diabolically elaborate hoax ever contrived. We have to determine which. I know, I know, we feel in our very *bones* that this is all genuine—we were there, after all, and how could anyone, however warped, 'salt' *this* much? But verification is now the name of the game."

An Arab concierge knocked at the door and told Jon he had an international call from Rome on the hotel's telephone. Jon hurried downstairs, assuming it was Sullivan. It was. Jon apologized for not responding to his latest lines, and said, "Kevin, I can't explain now, but something *exponentially* more important than the Markan conclusion has just come up here, and I simply have to sidetrack your project for some weeks, maybe months, to come. Can you please put everything on hold? I'll tell you more as soon as I can."

Sullivan sounded surprised and mystified, but finally agreed. After Jon hung up, it suddenly occurred to him that the deleted line in Mark corresponded exactly with the papyrus. In both cases, Jesus's body had been taken. Two widely separated sources of evidence agreed perfectly.

Was this the start of a new era? *Were* they turning the corner on planet earth? For better? Or for worse?

TWELVE

Claude Montaigne's version of the papyrus so closely matched his own that the problem of translation was nearly surmounted. That of authentication was not. Jon debated the testing strategy with Jennings.

"The biggest mistake in the Shroud of Turin affair," said Jon, "was their spending years doing every possible test on it except the right one: carbon 14."

"True," Jennings agreed. "Think of the forests that were lost to paper pulp for the hundreds of worthless articles and books 'proving' the Shroud genuine, when in fact it turned out to be a medieval forgery, thanks—*finally*—to your efforts and radio-carbon."

"Well, not just mine," said Jon. "But let's *not* make the same mistake. What I propose is this: we'll have to test our papyrus and parchment with C-14 at *some* point, so I suggest we bite that bullet *now*. It would save us endless grief if they turned out to be forgeries."

"Fine, Jonathan, though we have precious little of the papyrus to spare."

"Granted. But we'll use the same tandem accelerator mass spectrometer method we used on the Shroud. TAMS requires samples only *one-thousandth* of the sizes we brought to the Weizmann. Now, remember that large papyrus fragment that broke off during the unscrolling at the Rockefeller? It's just large enough for TAMS, and we could also take one of the larger scraps of *un*lettered parchment from the *titulus*."

"Where would you take them? Arizona?"

"Yes, but first I'd stop off at the Smithsonian and have Sandy

115

McHugh give them a complete analysis. He's the scientific advisor to the ICO. He was a great help in the Shroud tests."

"Fine!" Jennings nodded. "Let's do it, then. That's really the best plan."

"Want to come with me?"

"Love to! But no, someone has to ride herd on the dig here."

Jon flew to Paris—the fragments inside two small lead-lined envelopes in his attaché case—and thence to Dulles Airport at Washington, D.C. He was inside the Smithsonian almost before jet lag could set in.

"Sure 'n it's good to see ye again, Jonnie, me boy," said Sandy McHugh, dressed in his laboratory whites and looking nothing like the leprechaun he sounded. He generally conversed with Jon either in proper English or the worst Irish brogue this side of Dublin. Today it was the latter. Ample girth, round face, and reddish-blond hair marked the man, while twinkling turquoise eyes reflected the personality.

"Hello, old top!" said Jon, giving him a cheerful cuff on the shoulder. "Been keeping busy?"

"An' I'll be thankin' ye fer that!" he nodded. "'Twas quite the riddle ye sent us with that erased-line business. So tell me now, did the Holy Faaather agree to our little testin' scheme?" McHugh knew only that a papal document was involved, not that it was the conclusion to Mark's Gospel.

"That he did, Sandy."

"And what might be these scraps of paaarchment and papyrus yer bringin' me now? Some proof that the Holy Shroud is genuine after all?"

"No," Jon laughed, "nothing like that. But they *are* from some *incredibly* important documents. When you handle them, just imagine that these flakes came from the Declaration of Independence itself. Or a letter from St. Patrick."

"I get the picture," said McHugh, switching to proper English. "No foul-ups."

Inside the laboratory, Jon opened the envelopes and gingerly extracted the pieces of parchment and papyrus. Sandy studied the fragments for some time under various lamps, filters, and scopes. "They certainly look medieval, if not ancient," he finally commented.

"I *do* hope that you can narrow that down somewhat!"

"Obviously," he grinned. "All right, then, here's what I propose. First we'll do the nondestructive analysis in the laboratories here—mainly microscopy and electronmicroscopy—with a photographic record throughout. That'll take the rest of the day. You spend the night at my place in Georgetown—yes, I insist!—and tomorrow we'll take your precious samples and catch a flight to Tucson. I've already phoned Duncan Fraser at the University of Arizona to drop everything and fine-tune his mighty TAMS apparatus for those two bits of paper of yours."

"Superb, Sandy! Arizona's still the best for our purposes? Not Oxford or Zurich?"

"Put it this way, Jon—it's the only place on earth with a machine like that *and also* a collection of bristlecone pine samples as testing controls. If God Himself handed me the first page of Matthew's original Gospel and said, '*Date it,*' that's where I'd take it!"

They landed at the sprawling Spanish hacienda that was Tucson International Airport and drove a rent-a-car to the University of Arizona, a vast collection of structures in red brick. While walking inside the Physics Building, Sandy commented, "This is holy ground for the world's archaeologists, Jon. These are the boys who recalibrated the radiocarbon clock via tree-ring datings from the bristlecone pine."

A midsized man with dark hair and genial smile approached them, hand outstretched. "Hello, Sandy!" he said. "Good to see you back in Tucson!"

"Greetings, Duncan! You know Jon Weber here from his letters the time we tested the Shroud."

"Indeed!"

"Delighted *finally* to meet you, Professor Fraser," said Jon.

"Sorry I was too tied up in Cambridge to get out here when you were working on the Shroud samples."

"Honored to have you aboard! Sandy said your fragments were extraordinarily important. But he didn't say why."

"That's because I don't *know* why!" Sandy interjected.

"*After* the tests I'll explain, gentlemen," said Jon. "A matter of objectivity, you understand."

"Quite right," said Fraser. "Well, gentlemen, let's go over to the accelerator laboratory."

He led them to an underground annex where the TAMS apparatus was housed in a vast, lofty chamber. Jon looked at the massive T-shaped accelerator and its conduits bending around the room and said, "This looks nothing like the glass beaker array I saw at the Weizmann Institute in Israel!"

"No," said Fraser. "Their conventional method counts the blips of carbon-14 decay, whereas our TAMS measures the C-14 directly. Here, let me explain it to you."

As Fraser hauled out a chart, Jon cautioned, "Better keep it elementary, friend! My physics is pure Newtonian!"

He handed the chart to Jon and said, "First we burn each of your samples into carbon-dioxide, which we then convert to graphite. Next we load that carbon onto a plug and insert it into the ion source—Number 1 on the sketch." He pointed his pencil to the left side of the chart.

"Then we bombard that plug with a beam of cesium ions, which transforms neutral carbon into *negative* carbon ions. Now these ions make a mad rush toward our transformer—Number 2—finding its two million volts *very* attractive—if you'll pardon the pun! However, *en route*, our slits and magnet—Number 3—separate our regular carbon 12 and 13. Are you with me so far?"

"I actually think so," said Jon. "Do continue."

"So now the isolated carbon 14 ions dash into the waiting arms of our stripper—Number 4—which shamelessly removes their electrons, turning them from negative to *positive* ions. Now, of course, they're *repelled* by that sordid affair and fly *away* from the transformer."

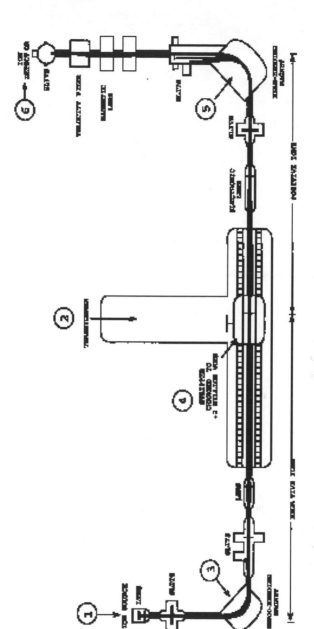

Tandem Accelerator Mass Spectrometer (TTAMS)

"See, Jon, that's the *tandem* part of the TAMS system," Sandy broke in, "the double acceleration."

"Now—at Number 5—we have more slits and magnets to deflect everything but the C-14 we want to measure. And finally, the ion detector—Number 6—counts the number of C-14 ions that survived this journey and feeds the data into our computer. And that's it! I've given you the . . . ah . . . popular version, of course, but basically, it's that simple."

Jon laughed. "I *do* think I caught it!" Then he grew serious. "But how do you know you're reading *all* the carbon 14? If you miss some, wouldn't your samples seem older?"

"This machine can spot *one* part of C-14 in *100 trillion* parts of regular carbon."

"Incredible!"

"Now let's have a look at your samples," said Fraser, offering them seats around a lab table. Jon removed the two lead-lined envelopes from his attaché case, and Fraser studied the fragments of parchment and papyrus.

"Please tell me we have enough material there," said Jon, anxiously.

"Oh, yes, more than enough. How old do you think they are?"

"Should I really say? Someday, when this is all written up—and it *will* be written up, mark you—I wouldn't want anyone to claim I suggested any dates to you."

"Of course," Fraser smiled. "But I'm only looking for a 'ballpark' sort of range—the nearest five thousand years will do."

Jon laughed in relief. "In that case, our range would be anything from very recent, say ten years ago—*if* they're forgeries—to as far back as, say, two thousand years or more if not."

"Duck soup!" said Fraser. "Here I thought you might be stretching our capacities by bringing in something *really* old!"

Fraser and his associates now began a meticulous preparation process on both samples, which commanded the rest of the day. Jon was held in thrall by the entire scientific spectacle, wondering what his life would have been like had he elected physics instead of Near Eastern studies.

"We have our graphite," said Fraser, at day's end. "It all went well. Very well, in fact. So come back tomorrow and we'll fire up our monster here."

Jon pitched and turned and flailed at his bedsheets that night, fighting for a sleep that never came. The *titulus* and papyrus fragments were *everything* now—*far* more significant than old ceramics, linens, or even bones, all of which were available to a really supple Near Eastern forger. It was better that neither McHugh nor Fraser knew that the course of history could bend as much as ions in an accelerator depending on the C-14 present—or absent—in those flakes. That would have stripped cool dispassion from any scientific procedure.

Poised at his control console the next morning, Duncan Fraser flipped his master switches and scanned an array of gauges and dials. Associates reported a checklist of readings, which reminded Jon of Mission Control in Houston:
   "Accelerator terminal at 2.0 million volts."
   "Cesium generator at 25,000 volts."
   "All magnet potentials at nominal."
   "Ion detector nominal."
   "Computer nominal."
A carefully orchestrated chorus of electronic humming filled the laboratory. For Jon, the suspense was almost beyond endurance.
   Fraser now switched on the cesium-ion bombardment of one of the plugs from the *titulus* parchment. Jon and Sandy hovered over his head at the computer console, and saw a grid appear on the screen, which was now overlaid with two green bars showing the relative amounts of carbon 14 and regular carbon.
   "The one to watch is the right-hand C-14 bar," said Fraser. "The lower it is relative to the left-hand normal carbon bar, the older your sample is."
   Jon looked intensely at the screen and saw a considerable difference developing in the two heights. No one said anything. His pulse was throbbing.
   "What age is it showing, roughly?" he finally asked.

Fraser quickly looked down at his master reference table and said, "About the 1960s."

"*Good Lord!*" Jon exclaimed. "It's a *forgery*, then, done some forty or fifty years ago!"

"No, no," Fraser laughed. "The 1960s *BP*, before the present. We're talking, oh, about the 30s or 40s AD."

Sandy, blissfully unaware, let out a whoop of joy. "It's bloody *authentic*, I'd say!"

Jon merely tasted his heart, which was galloping in a mad cadence. Now civilization might indeed shift.

After some minutes of testing and recording his data, Fraser left the console, went to a lead-lined locker at one end of the laboratory, and returned with another tiny graphite plug in hand which he inserted into a carousel of targets at the ion source. Then he turned to his guests and said, "Now I have a little surprise for you. For something as important as this seems to be, we'll parallel test some bristlecone pine specimens of known age to match our readouts here. If they agree, we'll have a guarantee of accuracy. The plug I just put in came from the core of a bristlecone pine known to be exactly two thousand years old from tree-ring analysis."

The accelerator again hummed to life, as three heads scrutinized the screen. Soon, the array of bars materialized, taking shapes nearly identical to those of the parchment sample.

"Aha!" said Fraser. "That certainly shows we have our machine tuned properly, doesn't it?"

"Right on," said Sandy.

"Shall we move on to the papyrus sample?" he asked.

"Yes, by all means," Sandy replied, since Jon seemed strangely subdued.

Fraser moved the carousel, returned to the computer screen, and resumed the testing procedure. Again the dark screen came to life with bars of brilliant green.

"This one's just a tad younger," he said. "See?" he pointed. "The C-14 bar's a shade higher."

"Where do you peg it, roughly?" Jon had finally located his voice.

"Around the 1930s BP, maybe a little more."

Again Jon cringed internally. The letter of Joseph of Arimathea would certainly have been written later than the *titulus,* and thus appear "a tad younger."

Fraser returned to his shielded cabinet, extracted another tiny plug, and explained, "This one's from a nineteen-hundred-year-old bristlecone."

The readouts from its test showed only a twenty-five-year deviation from that of the papyrus. "All in all, our little machine was on good behavior today," said Fraser, giving the console an affectionate pat. "Though we still cushion our test dates with an error range of plus or minus eighty years."

"Why's that?" asked Jon. "The readings seem so much closer."

"Varying cosmic ray bombardment across the centuries."

"Obviously. I forgot. My mind was on something else."

"Well, congratulations, Jon!" exclaimed Sandy. "Looks as if you have the real things there, whatever they are!"

"Aahhh . . . thanks, Sandy."

"You don't look very pleased."

"I'll . . . explain shortly."

"We'll send you both a detailed statistical report, of course," said Fraser. "You'll learn, for example, the exact number of C-14 ions we counted, that sort of thing."

"We can't thank you enough, Professor Fraser," said Jon. "Also for using some of your precious bristlecone samples. We're *deeply* in your debt! When I'm finally at liberty to reveal the nature of those fragments, I promise that you'll be the first to know. They *are* of incalculable importance."

"I certainly understand."

On the flight back to Washington, Jon felt the same roiling, corrosive, emotional acids that had overtaken him when translating the papyrus for the first time. If, or rather *when*, the news was announced, the impact across the world would be staggering, and his own future would be held hostage to Rama.

McHugh was showing admirable restraint in not badgering him for further information, and Jon told him so. "Great of you not to harass me for the facts, Sandy. I'll spill everything when we get back to Washington. Can we have dinner someplace with *lots* of privacy?"

"Sure. The wife and kids are up at Chesapeake Bay. I'll get us a back booth at Hogate's."

By the second Tanqueray martini, Jon had given the history of the dig. By the salad course, Sanford McHugh was wearing a huge grin at the news that Joseph of Arimathea's estate, tomb, and even remains had been discovered, along with the *titulus*. A staunch Roman Catholic, he found the tidings ever so congenial to his faith. It was during the entrée that Jon looked about to make sure he was not overheard and then read his translation of the papyrus.

The transformation in Sandy's appearance was so quick and alarming that Jon feared for his health. Globules of sweat erupted across his freckled brow and cheeks. His ruddy complexion had drained off to a pasty gray. The man was on the verge of collapse. Suddenly he got up from the table and hurried to the rest room, where he reached the toilet just in time to surrender his dinner.

"Hold on, Sandy," said Jon, as he helped him back to the table. "There's still a . . . a very *remote* possibility that a forger could have used the blank beginning or end of a genuinely ancient papyrus for writing material, and we'd get the same C-14 results. That's why we have to discuss other tests as well."

That seemed to revive Sandy somewhat. He fired a volley of questions at Jon concerning the tests at Rehovot, and asked for a detailed description of all artifacts that had been discovered inside the cavern. They spent the rest of the evening discussing the most appropriate tests for each.

When Sandy saw him off at Dulles the next day, Jon's closing comment hardly needed expression: "You see, now, why all this *had* to be kept utterly confidential?"

Sandy merely threw up his hands and bowed his head, almost in despair.

THIRTEEN

Again, Jennings's tall dome crowned with orange sun hat towered above the waiting crowd at Ben Gurion Airport. Again Jon told him he should have sent Clive Brampton or one of the students instead.

"Not on your life, Jonathan. I *had* to know the results, obviously! What did you find?"

"Tell you on the way back to Ramallah."

Jon's report on his experiences in Arizona and Washington took half the trip. At first, Jennings said very little in response, but then he groaned, shook his head, and warned, "Maybe we no longer have a dig, Jonathan, but a snarling, hissing fuse instead, which is about to set off a *catastrophic* explosion! You're sure the tests were managed properly?"

"Yes, I'm sure. In fact, the results were quite impressively *proven* by comparison with samples from a bristlecone pine that was growing in Nevada just about the time Herod the Great was finishing the Temple in Jerusalem."

Again Jennings shook his head. "Well, what now?" he asked.

Jon detailed some of the testing plans he and Sandy McHugh had projected for the other artifacts they had uncovered in the cavern.

At the hotel that night, he scrutinized papyrus prints for the dozenth time while Jennings paced the workroom, hands behind his back, trying to decide his next move. "If *only* we could somehow test the *writing* alone—the *ink*—to see if it's ancient or recent. But I suppose that's impossible, Jonathan?"

"Afraid so, for two reasons. One, no archaeologist would *ever* destroy any writing for such a test. And two, what if he did? He'd get only an infinitesimal amount of carbon from the ink—too small even for TAMS. No, I think we'll have to go back to writing *style* for an answer. And we still have that dialect problem with our 'untranslatables.'"

Jennings stopped, stretched out his arms, and said, "Well, then, we'd best make that pilgrimage down to Mount Sinai, don't you think?"

"I think so. Alexandros could well be our last resort. Why not call Montaigne and have him arrange an appointment with our archimandrite friend?"

When she heard that her father and Jon were planning a trip to Mount Sinai, Shannon begged to go along. Why miss seeing the place where Moses received the Ten Commandments?

"Fine, my dear. You can help us drive," said Jennings.

"*And* cook our meals if we get marooned in the desert," Jon added.

"Then you'd starve," she retorted smartly. "I go along as an equal or not at all."

"Only kidding, Shannon! Only kidding."

"So was I," she laughed. "I'm really not *that* hard to get along with, Jon."

They stocked their Land Rover with extra jerry cans of gasoline and water jugs, since the trip across the Sinai Desert to Saint Catherine's would not be easy. They also carried emergency food supplies and first-aid materials, as well as *two* spare tires, since the wadi shortcut to Mount Sinai was studded with flint rock that had a great appetite for rolling rubber. The most important part of the cargo, however, were the papyrus photographs. Cromwell had done a second set of the document under glass, as well as special enlargement photos of the remaining "untranslatables," along with the sentences in which they appeared.

Setting out well before sunrise, they reached the Negev in the still-cool of the morning, Jennings providing a running commentary on the topography all the way to Elat and the Gulf, where they had lunch. Since all three had valid Egyptian visas, the border crossing at Elat went smoothly enough, and they continued south along the coast until they turned westward onto the wadi road that led to Mount Sinai.

Here the trip turned into first-class adventure. Although it was getting unbearably hot, Jennings had fallen asleep, his lanky frame sprawled across the backseat. Jon was perspiring at the wheel in front with Shannon, using the four-wheel drive to all possible advantage in maneuvering the vehicle through a lunar landscape of hills in polychrome earth tones. While dodging boulders and vehicle-devouring chasms at the very shoulders of the wadi road, he resumed his favorite sport—probing Shannon's personal relationships, especially including Gideon Ben-Yaakov.

"Why are you always asking me about Gideon, Jon? Do you disapprove? Are you anti-Semitic or something?"

"No, of course I don't disapprove. And even if I did, what difference would it make? And no, I'm *not* anti-Semitic. I was only wondering if you'd checked everything out. Would your children, for example, be raised Christian or Jewish?"

"Gideon's a secular Jew, not a religious one. Since I'm a Gentile, the kids wouldn't automatically be Jewish—you have to have a Jewish mama for that. But they could become Jews—and Israeli citizens—later."

"Are those your plans?"

"I don't know, Jon. At first I wanted any child of mine to be baptized Christian in general, Church of England in particular. My mother was an Irish Catholic, of course, but I was raised Anglican by my father."

"You say, 'at first' you wanted your kids baptized. What now?"

"Well . . . so far as my faith is concerned, I . . . I'm reeling, Jon. *Reeling.* Now I don't know what to think . . . what to believe. When you get down to basics, the reason Christianity succeeded so incredibly is because it promises 'the resurrection of the body and the life everlasting'—those phrases at the end of The Creed. Now it seems that even Jesus, the Founder, didn't make it. Which would also cut out his divinity, of course—"

"Hold it, Shannon. Let's not draw *any* conclusions—theological or otherwise—until we're sure of what we have here."

"Yes, yes . . . I know. But, between the two of us, how in

bloody blazes could *anyone* have faked all this? We troweled it all clear, Jon. We were *there!*"

"I . . . we . . . don't have the answers yet, Shannon, *if* there are any. But back to you and Gideon—"

"You're a blinking broken record, Jon! I may marry the man. I may even convert to Judaism if Christianity is shot. Or I may not."

"May not convert? Or may not marry the man?"

"All of the above."

"Don't you love him?"

"Yes . . . but not all the time. I think love comes and goes. Maybe I'm not entirely sure what love even is."

"*I'm* sure," said Jon. Love, to him, now began and ended with the radiant woman sitting next to him. Love was Shannon. Shannon was love.

"*Why* are you so sure?" she asked, "and—"

Suddenly a huge cavity yawned open in the road that threatened to devour the front end of the Rover. Jon screeched his brakes, swerved to the left, and missed it by inches.

Jennings, jolted awake, cried, "Merciful Minerva, Jon! I know we have a problem on our hands, but let's not get suicidal!"

"He couldn't help it, Papa," said Shannon. "We shouldn't have used the wadi route. This road was designed in hell. So was this climate!"

After grinding, grueling hours that exhausted their water supply, they finally arrived at the broad, sloping plain in front of Mount Sinai.

"Here, presumably, the Israelites pitched their tents while Moses went up into the mountain," Jon explained. "And see that walled compound on the lower side of the mountain? That's the Monastery of Saint Catherine—our goal—a *fabulous* place! See those walls? They're a meter thick, and still the very same ones the Byzantine Emperor Justinian erected in the sixth century to guard the monks from desert marauders."

"Tell her about Tischendorf, Jonathan," came a voice from the backseat.

"Aha! I give you the tale of Constantin Tischendorf," said Jon, magisterially. "He was a German scholar in the last century who got fed up with critics claiming the Gospels were late writings and untrustworthy. He would have loved nothing more than to discover the original Gospel manuscripts. But, failing that, he correctly assumed that the earlier the manuscript, the better. And so he came here on camelback in 1844, suspecting that the holy men of the desert might have some ancient documents in their archives. Well, they certainly did, but—idiotically—they were using parchment pages of what proved to be the world's oldest Bible as *waste paper!* Tischendorf rescued what was left of those precious parchments and later borrowed a volume of them—the *Codex Sinaiticus*—in order to publish his critical edition.

"The Russian Czar gave the monks nine thousand rubles for it, you English bought it from the Russians, and today it's in the British Museum. Meanwhile, the monks here want it back, and quite obviously they're no longer in the lending library business!"

"What's the date on the *Sinaiticus?*" Shannon inquired.

"A little before AD 350. In 1975 they even discovered some of the missing pages of the *Sinaiticus* here. With any luck, we *may* get to see them."

"Quite a tale! You know, Jon, you'd do well as a tour guide," she quipped. "So you'll still have something to fall back on when our discoveries blow Christianity out of the water."

"Try to control yourself, Shannon," said Jennings.

"Don't be such a fuddy-duddy, Papa. You're far too serious! In another life, you were William Gladstone."

Jon stopped the Rover at the monastery gate, got out, and pulled a cord that rang a small bell. "Be glad we have a gate," he said. "When Tischendorf got here, there was no door. They lowered a bar imbedded in a rope for him to stand on, and then winched him up over the wall!"

An ancient porter with black skin and white beard appeared, clothed from neck to toe in a cream-colored *galabiya*. Opening the gate, he beckoned them inside and led the way across a stone courtyard. But they stopped following when they came to a well. Jon wound up a bucket of crystal cold water, and they drank it dry.

At the door of the monastery, a stocky, bearded figure received them, clad totally in black. He was the abbot, Archbishop Paulos Kalaramas, who greeted them with quaint formality. "Our abode is your abode, my friends, and our food and drink are yours as well. Our fare is humble, but you will, I think, find it wholesome."

"Thank you, Beloved-of-God," said Jennings, hoping the English translation of the Greek form of address to an abbot would suffice. "It's *very* kind of you to extend this hospitality."

"I regret, honored friends, that Brother Alexandros is not here to greet you personally. He was very tired and has returned to his quarters. You may find this strange, but his vast learning has made him—how do you call it—a little 'eccentric' . . . yes?"

"No matter," said Jennings. "We're grateful indeed that no less than the abbot himself extends us this welcome."

After a simple supper, garnished with a little palm wine, the abbot took them on a tour of the premises, identifying the various mosaics and icons inside the Chapel of the Burning Bush, as well as the library where Tischendorf discovered the *Sinaiticus*. Then he conducted them to separate monastic cells and bade them goodnight.

"Anybody know where I can get a cold beer?" Shannon whispered to Jon.

"Ah-ah-ah! It all begins with self-denial."

"Shut up, Jon!"

"And we must also cleanse our speech patterns in this holy place, Miss Jennings. There's a good little girl." He gave her a chaste good-night kiss on the check. She giggled and tickled his ribs.

"Ky-ri-e elei-son . . . Chris-te elei-son . . . Ky-ri-e elei-son." The chanting that implored the Lord and Christ to have mercy awakened them at dawn the next morning. The monks were already at matins, and the rich melodies of Greek Orthodox worship resonated throughout the compound. Jon found himself torn between admiration for the centuries-old liturgy and concern for what would happen to that liturgy—indeed, all liturgies—should the papyrus finally prove authentic.

After a simple breakfast of tea, dark bread, and honey, the Archimandrite Alexandros presented himself, a tall, gaunt ascetic, gowned like the others in black, from cylindrical edged hat to shoes. His mane of hair, like his full and flowing beard, was a silver-gray and black mix, and his eyebrows were two minor forests of the same.

"I bid you welcome in the holy name of our Lord," he said, bowing to his guests. His voice was such a deep and resonant bass, it might have been the Lord Himself speaking. "Père Montaigne said that my small talents might be of some use to you in appraising a papyrus you have discovered. Please to join me in my office."

Alexandros led them to a study cell lined with books from floor to ceiling on all four sides. After brief amenities, Jon asked him to view first the enlargements of the few remaining phrases that had resisted all efforts at translation. In the process, he asked him also to evaluate the time frame for the scripts in question, providing samples from both the letter and the Nicodemus postscript.

Alexandros studied the photographs for some time and then replied, "I am pleased to answer your second question first. These are the work of two different hands, but both hands wrote, I would judge, from the time of Herod until . . . I would say . . . until the Roman conquest."

"About AD 70?" Jennings inquired.

"Of course." He studied the photographs intensely. "Yes . . . without question. I would place them at that time. Your first samples seem to come from the hill country of Palestine . . . how you say . . . a countryside version of Aramaic?"

"Rural dialect?"

"Yes, rural dialect. Exactly."

Jon, Jennings, and Shannon exchanged meaningful glances.

"And this last sample, I think, came from Judea, probably the Jerusalem area."

"Are you able to translate these sentences, honored Archimandrite?" asked Jon, pointing to the "untranslatables."

"Why do you not show me the whole document?"

"We will very shortly."

"Well, then . . ." He studied the phrases that Jon had circled with red pen. "Your sentence reads, 'The rabbi Yeshua whom we

buried in my sepulcher a score and seven years ago during the
. . . ah . . . the government, the *administration* of Pontius Pilatus.'
The Aramaic is a corruption from the Greek *hegemonia.* Is that
clear? Yes?

"Well, then, we go on to your second problem: 'The next
morning we drove them—ah—we drove the wagon to Rama,
where we put . . . *put into the ground again* the rabbi . . . in the
sarcophagus I had—ah—built for myself.' Does that make sense
for you?"

"Yes, it surely does," said Jon. "And I must congratulate you
on your *great* command of Aramaic!"

"It is nothing," he protested. "Then, to your final problem. Let
me see. It reads: 'We were not able to kill by drowning the very'—
what is the word in English?—'the very corks, the very floatings'
. . . fishermen use them in their nets . . ."

"Buoys?" Shannon volunteered.

"Yes, 'the very buoys that had defeated your grief.'"

Jon looked at Jennings and said, "Well, that's it. We have it all
now." He also continued to marvel at Alexandros, a very much living fossil who could read primitive Aramaic on sight almost as if it
were the Op-Ed page of the *New York Times.* He made Montaigne
and himself look like amateurs. "Again, I must express my astonishment at your *superb* command of Aramaic, Brother Alexandros!"

"It is nothing. I learned old Aramaic at some villages in
Syria. But when may I see the whole document?"

"Now." Jon handed him Cromwell's most recent photographs
of the papyrus. "But please be prepared for a shock, Brother
Alexandros, a *very* great shock."

The monk looked at Jon strangely and started reading. Almost
maddeningly, his face registered no response but for a tightening
of the eyes as he reached critical sections of the text. Having read
the document, he now reread it, his lips silently mouthing a translation into his native Greek. When he had finally finished,
Alexandros looked up and asked, "Where did you find this?"

Jon recounted the history of the dig, the discovery of the cavern,
and all its contents. As he did so, the constriction in Alexandros's
eyes seemed to tighten. Then he studied the copy of the papyrus

text for another considerable time, during which not a sound was heard. At last he stood up and walked slowly back and forth across his study, lost in thought, and seemingly oblivious to their presence. Again he stopped abruptly and devoted another quarter hour to a close scrutiny of the papyrus copy and particularly the enlargements, using a magnifying glass.

Again he paced the chamber, chin in hand. Abruptly he stopped and said, "I will consider this further. Please to meet me after lunch?"

"Certainly."

After lunch, however, Alexandros asked for more time. "I must consult other old works in Aramaic to . . . to compare the writing. Please to meet me after supper."

As they left, Shannon leaned over and whispered to Jon, "His voice sounds like a laryngitic hippo gargling at the bottom of a cave."

"A boy soprano he is *not*," Jon agreed.

Jennings and Jon spent the afternoon examining the monastery library. First they would build confidence in their hosts, they decided, and on the morrow ask for permission to look, however briefly, at the newly discovered *Sinaiticus* parchments. Jon wondered if they might somehow have a bearing on the *Vaticanus* problem. Shannon, meanwhile, went out to climb the foothills of Mount Sinai.

Just before dinner, the abbot graciously conducted them to privileged sections of the monastery not shown to visitors at Saint Catherine's, such as the kitchen, disciplinary cells for recalcitrant monks, and the charnel house. The last, in the rear of the compound, sheltered the remains of hundreds of monks from earlier centuries, their bones stacked up in one area, and their skulls neatly pyramided in another, all awaiting the great day of resurrection.

Jon and Jennings shot immediate glances at each other, shouting what remained unsaid: "Are we just in the process of destroying the very hope for which this charnel house—indeed, this monastery—was built?"

On the way to the dining hall, Jon whispered, "All those smiling skulls, Austin . . . each of them seemed to have eyes in those hollow sockets . . . eyes that seemed to know what we're about . . . eyes that seemed to plead, '*Don't* take the Resurrection away from us!'"

"'Our *one and only hope!*' Yes, Jon, I heard them too. Good Lord! In that environment, Easter is no theoretical nicety!"

Alexandros asked them to come up to his study cell after supper. When they were all seated, he touched the tips of his long fingers together, stared at them with deep brown eyes that had an almost fearful fluorescence, and said, "Your papyrus is false. It is a . . . an invention . . . how you say? . . . a forgery. It is a forgery." He said nothing more.

Jon, who was stunned when the evidence had so strongly supported the authenticity of their finds, was nearly as stunned by Alexandros's statement.

"What leads you to that conclusion?" he asked.

Instantly, Alexandros clenched both his fists and pounded them down on his desk, shrieking, "Because our Lord *rose from the dead!* How could His *bones* be in any *grave? How,* I ask you?" His lips trembled, his hands quivered, his eyes filled with tears. Then he stood up and shouted, "*And so that papyrus is either a modern forgery, an ancient forgery, or an invention of the devil!*" He waved his arms as if he were preaching to a multitude of thousands rather than three people.

Shannon and the men were too shocked to respond. Jon studied the floor of the cell to avoid having to look at the manic monk. But at last Alexandros seemed to gain control of himself and said, "Please to excuse me for a moment."

He walked into an adjoining bedroom cell, where he bent over a basin of water and splashed sobriety and composure onto his face. Then he returned to them and said, "I beg your forgiveness, my friends. The papyrus . . . troubles me very deeply."

"It troubles us, too, Brother Alexandros," said Jennings.

"But again," Jon persisted, "how did you detect a forgery?"

"It is a matter of how the pen was held in the writing, for one thing. I can show you when I see the original. Where do you have it?"

"At the Rockefeller Museum laboratory."

"Yes, of course." Alexandros sat down slowly and stroked his long black beard. "Ah . . . would you please to present me a note of authorization so that I might look at the papyrus when I go again to Jerusalem?"

"Yes . . . we'd be glad to send you an authorization," said Jennings. "Agreed, Jonathan?"

"Agreed. Of course."

"Ah . . . my problem is this, honored friends. I plan to be in Jerusalem very shortly, and I would prefer, if possible, to have your written permission now. I will, of course, call you when I reach the museum."

Jon opened his attaché case, took out one of his letterheads, and handed it to Jennings, who wrote out the authorization, which Jon countersigned. Alexandros received it with thanks and then asked, "Who knows about the papyrus besides you three? Père Montaigne?"

"Yes. But we've tried to keep this as secret as humanly possible."

"Yes. You surely *must!*"

"And the photographs, the negatives. Where are they?"

"At our headquarters in Ramallah."

"Fine, fine. But now, my friends, I think you should retire early, because I would like to do you a favor, perhaps to . . . how you say? . . . make up for my poor behavior. Have you ever seen the sunrise from the top of Mount Sinai?"

"I've never climbed Sinai," said Jennings. "Nor has Shannon. Have you, Jon?"

"No."

"Well, then, I would like to guide you up the holy mountain. It is a . . . a magnificent spiritual experience. Would you like that?"

"Yes, indeed!" Shannon cried, as the men smiled their assent.

"But we must arise *very* early. Otherwise it will be too hot to make the climb."

"Fine."

"The porter will knock on your doors at two o'clock in the morning. We begin to climb a half hour later."

They started their trek in total starlight. The blazing oven of the daytime desert had cooled to an enchanted realm of fragrant breezes, spangled with the greatest profusion of stars they had ever seen and arched by a broad, snowy belt of Milky Way.

"Good heavens! This is majestic . . . awesome!" Shannon sighed.

"There's no pollution in the desert," her father explained. "No competing city lights."

"'*The heavens declare the glory of God,*'" Alexandros bellowed in front of them, "'*and the firmament shows his handiwork,*' just as the psalmist says!"

"That voice of his spooks me out," Shannon whispered to Jon. "He'd make a good Boris Godunov."

"More like Rasputin, I'd say."

The path of pink granite rock was strangely visible in the starlight and led ever upward. It began as a comfortable grade, but soon the nearly three-hour climb grew precipitous and demanding. Yet the towering silhouette of their guide stalked on, taciturn and relentless. Several times Jon had to beg him to halt so that Jennings could catch up and regain his breath. Alexandros stopped only grudgingly, but then quickly resumed the climb, almost as one possessed.

They were beginning to have second thoughts about this "favor" of Alexandros when dawn finally exploded over the mountain peaks, precipices, and valleys about them, unveiling a panorama of breathtaking splendor. Twenty minutes later they finally reached a tiny chapel at the summit, just as a ruddy golden yolk of sun orbed onto the eastern horizon.

"Behold the hand of God," said Alexandros, sweeping his arm in all directions. "Moses may have used this path up the mountain to receive the Ten Commandments. Or he could have used a steeper one to the south. Let me show you. Come here to the other side of the chapel."

Alexandros guided them to the edge of the summit precipice and pointed downward. As they craned their necks warily over the edge to peer at a drop-off hundreds of feet down the southern face of Mount Sinai, he moved behind them and suddenly rammed into Jennings and Jon with both arms, pitching them headlong over the edge of the cliff.

Shannon screamed, and he lunged for her. She dodged him desperately and ran down the mountain path they had just used. Recovering instantly, Alexandros pulled up his confining robe with one hand and pivoted across the rocks with the other, scampering over ledges to cut across several switchbacks on the path to intercept her.

Pulling out of a hairpin turn, Shannon saw the lofty hulk blocking her way. Shrieking, she ran back up the path. She was almost to the summit again when a powerful hand locked onto her right shoulder and pulled her to a halt.

Crying for help but with no one to hear, she turned to fight him off. But it was no contest whatever. He sneered at her desperate pummeling and grabbed her around the waist, dragging her toward the precipice. She screamed, struggled, and kicked, trying to break his hold, but he merely locked on to her left wrist with a grip of iron and hauled her over the ridge of stone before the edge of the cliff. Suddenly she planted both feet on the rib of rock for leverage and drove her right fist into his genitals with all her might.

Alexandros groaned heavily and released his grip as he shielded his anguished scrotum with both hands and hunched over in agony. Shannon picked up a large rock and smashed it onto his skull again and again until he collapsed in a great heap of black linen. Then she ran to the precipice.

Her father had somersaulted over the edge and begun a slide to the death on the nearly vertical slope when his outspread legs caught a spur of rock jutting out from the precipice and he jerked to a halt. But Jon had tumbled past him, his back and buttocks scraping the cliff and his arms flailing in a desperate effort to find something—anything—to hang on to. But there was nothing.

The speed of his slide increased. His brain boiled with thought. *So this is how life will end? Just like Andrea's—on a mountainside?* Another part of his mind screamed, *Stop the slide or you'll die!*

At least I'll die trying, he vowed. Looking down, he saw his one and only chance—a narrow vertical gully of sand and gravel nestling in a hollow on the mountain face. But it was just to the right of the path of his fall. He started kicking and heeling in with his left foot, which finally veered him to the right. The next instant he felt sand and dug in both heels and elbows with all his might. They scraped and burned fiercely, but they slowed his fall.

Still he didn't stop, and the agonizing slide continued again. He was losing heart when at last his feet hit a small ledge and he stopped abruptly, doubling his legs and flaying the skin off his kneecaps.

"Thank you, Lord," said Jon, his first prayer in months, he realized ruefully, as he checked his shaking, bruised, and bleeding limbs to make sure they were still attached. "And thank you, Harvard Mountain Climbing Club." There he had learned that desperate maneuver back in his college years.

"*Jon! Are you all right?*" Shannon screamed from the summit.

"Yes," he called up to the tiny figure in white at the crest. "What about the monk?"

"I've either knocked him out or killed him!"

"*Great,* Shannon! What about your father?"

"He caught himself on a rock up here. He seems okay!"

"Well, I'll probably survive," Jennings called down to Jon. "But my bum may never be the same. And I don't know how in ruddy blazes I'm going to get out of here!"

"Shannon!" Jon called. "You've got to run down to the monastery as fast as you can. If that bearded maniac is still alive, he may come to. Tell the abbot to send help . . . men with lots of rope. *Hurry!*"

"Okay! Hang on, both of you! I'll be back as soon as I can!"

Then the waiting began. It would be several hours before help could arrive, Jon realized. Survival was no problem, but what about the murderous monk? *Mistake!* He should have asked Shannon if he were still breathing. What if the reptile recovered and started dropping boulders on them?

"Austin, can you hear me?" he yelled.

"Yes—"

"If that madman's alive and comes to, he may try to stone us. Do you have any way to protect yourself?"

"Well, not really. It's awfully precarious here."

"Okay, stay put and hug the cliff! I'll think of something. But why in the very *devil* did he do this to us?"

"God only knows! The papyrus, probably."

"You have an extraordinary daughter, Austin! Do you know that?"

"I've no idea how she ever did it!"

Jon studied his situation. He looked up toward the summit. He was too far down the precipice for anything but the longest rope to reach him. Would the monks even bring enough? Then he looked down and scanned the terrain below him. It all looked hopeless, a sheer and dizzying drop-off with murderous outcroppings of rock, broken only by . . . Incredible! Why hadn't he noticed it before? A narrow pathway threaded its way diagonally down the face of the mountain. Probably it was Moses's southern route the crackbrain wanted to "show" them.

How to get to it? He searched the face of the cliff for a route. *Aha!* There, perhaps. Take I-75 south to Atlanta, then head east on I-20 to Columbia, then south again to the Promised Land. *Weird humor was the ally of sanity,* he told himself, while also thanking God that he had never suffered from acrophobia, or he would have died ten deaths ere then. I-75 was a long crack running down the rock face, into which he could jam some oblong stones lying on the ledge where he was standing. These would serve as pitons, and he could use a flat rock near his feet as hammer. The traversing parkway eastward—I-20—was another small ledge, and the final route southward to Moses's pathway, another gravel gully.

Slowly, he inched his way downward, and somehow the weird journey held together until the final bar of gravel, which proved too shallow to have much holding power. He started to slide again, even though he was facing the mountain this time and digging in his toes while his hands clutched two flat stones that were madly combing the gravel as brakes. But the pathway itself saved him after a painful landing.

Salvation! Now he could get down the mountain safely. But

no, he'd have to *climb* instead, to protect Jennings. That black-draped devil masquerading as a man of God might revive and smash Jennings's skull. The southern ascent of Sinai was much steeper, he saw, but it was also quicker for someone in condition, and Jon was in condition, thanks to his weeks at the dig. Despite his lacerated arms and legs, he made the climb in a frenzied fifty minutes.

Drenched in sweat, heart pounding, and lungs screaming for air, he finally gained the summit. He searched desperately for Alexandros, but the monk was nowhere to be seen. Then he hurried to the edge of the precipice. To his immense relief, Jennings was still there, riding the rock spur as if it were a docile donkey.

"Are you okay, Austin?" he called.

"Yes, thank the good Lord! But how did you *ever* get back up here?"

"Where's Ivan the Terrible?"

"No idea!"

Again Jon scanned the whole summit area, but saw nothing. Then he heard some anguished croaking from inside the little granite stone chapel at the crest of Sinai. Dashing inside, he found Alexandros on his knees at an oratory, shaking his head to and fro in tortured worship, tears streaming down his face and matting his beard. He looked at Jon only momentarily and then returned to his Lord with the words "*Pater, heymarton eis ton ouranon kai enopion sou.*" Jon recognized them as the words of the Prodigal Son in Luke's Gospel: "Father, I have sinned against heaven and before You, and I am no longer worthy to be called Your son."

While climbing back up Sinai, Jon had vowed vengeance on the wretch who had tried to murder them, but the broken figure before him made for a poor target.

"*Why*, Alexandros?" Jon cried. "*Why* did you try to kill us?"

"I pray to God that your colleague is also safe?"

"He is, but why did—"

"I was acting as a tool of Satan, yes? With the three of you dead in a terrible 'accident,' I had planned to go to the museum in Jerusalem with your authorization to examine the papyrus, and then tear it to shreds. That document can destroy the Church. I *had* to save the faith . . . save our Lord . . . and His resurrection."

"But you claimed it was a forgery. You said you could prove it a fake if you saw the original."

Alexandros buried his face in his arms and sobbed. "I lied. I found nothing . . . nothing wrong with it." Then he looked up at Jon and cried, "But it *must* be false! It *must!* Our Lord lives! He *lives!*"

"But there were photographs of the original . . . and negatives. How could you hope—"

"After destroying the papyrus, I would have placed the tray back in the vault—as if the papyrus were intact—and then gone on to Rama and tried to destroy the photos as well. Even if I did not find them, they could no longer be . . . how you say . . . supported . . . verified."

Jon thought it unnecessary to tell him about Brampton and Cromwell and how sadly impossible was his whole weird scenario. Instead he asked, "But *murder* three people? In cold blood?"

"Yes. Three martyrs, if you please, to save the faith of millions. To my mind, the mathematics were . . . acceptable. But it was a horrible, *horrible* sin, for which I must—"

Shannon suddenly burst inside, followed by the abbot. "Jon! *Thank God!* Are you all right?"

"Yes, but let's get to your dad."

Abbot Kalaramas and the dozen younger monks he had brought along hurried to the edge of the precipice and dangled a shoulder harness down to Jennings. With some difficulty, he slipped into it, and they slowly pulled him to safety. Jennings hugged his daughter, and Jon too, before his shaky legs gave out and he had to sit down. One of the monks poured glasses of very cold orange juice for them from an insulated canister. Another tended to Jon's wounds.

The abbot now unloaded a barrage of angry Greek on Alexandros, who provided tearful replies in the same tongue, the other monks standing in something of a judicatory circle around him, a gathering look of horror on their faces.

Finally, the abbot stepped over to them and issued the most

sadly abject apology Jon had ever heard. Then he asked, "Do you wish to press charges with the police in Abu Zenima?"

Jon looked to Jennings for a reply, but Jennings shook his head. "No. No, that won't be necessary. Your brother needs help, much help, and I'm sure that can best be provided here."

"His brilliance, I fear, is driving him mad," the abbot explained. "As archimandrite, he used to be head of this monastery, but I had to replace him. And what is this terrible document he speaks of, one that could destroy the cause of Christ?"

"The . . . ah . . . brother was overreacting," Jon replied. "Much, much work lies ahead before this could be a threat of any kind. Meanwhile, it would be best for all of us to keep this matter confidential. At least for now."

"I understand. It is gracious of you to be so forgiving after . . . after the terrible thing that has happened. This is the way of Christ indeed!"

By now it was becoming unbearably hot, and they all hurried down the mountainside in silence. Just after lunch, when they were leaving, an anguished Alexandros sought out Jon to plead for forgiveness.

"Pray for me," the monk said, in a trembling voice. "But pray for the faith also!"

They were driving back through the arid wilderness, all three too stunned by their brush with death to say very much. Shannon wondered if they shouldn't have pressed charges. "That weirdo would've *killed* us! He should've been put away for life!"

"The last thing we'd need would be to get the police involved," said Jon. "Alexandros would use the papyrus as his defense, and the world would know. I think the brothers will keep a lid on him. Besides, we may yet need his fevered brain for the papyrus."

Jennings, in the back seat, suddenly reached for his Hebrew Bible and translated from Exodus 19, the giving of the Ten Commandments. "Listen," he said, "to how Moses warned his people about Sinai: '*Be careful not to go up the mountain or touch the foot of it. Whoever touches the mountain shall be put to death!*'"

"I guess that prohibition must still apply," Shannon commented. "Look what happened to us. Or almost happened."

"That *infernal* papyrus!" Jon muttered. "It's taking control of our lives. Some are even ready to *kill* for it!" He kept shifting about in his seat, trying to reduce the pain from his injuries. "But now, Shannon," he added, "tell us, at long last: How in the *world* did you ever stop the mad monk?"

FOURTEEN

Claude Montaigne had a morning appointment with them at the Rockefeller a week after their Sinai trip. He and Jon, armed with Alexandros's final definitions, would edit an authorized translation of the papyrus text. They found him poring over the papyrus under a strong light.

"Find anything amiss, Père Montaigne?" asked Jon.

"No. But I am still convinced that . . . that this thing is *not* genuine."

"Are you speaking as a scholar? Or as a man of faith?"

"I try not to separate the two."

"That was unfair. Sorry! But now let's try out the remaining definitions from Alexandros. He surely is a genius, albeit a disturbed one."

"Disturbed? What do you mean?"

"It's a long story. Quite a story! But let's finalize the translation first. Then I'll tell you."

For the next hour they worked on the wording, Shannon taking dictation and Jennings providing the most apt English synonyms, like the living *Oxford English Dictionary* he clearly was. The authorized version was not much different from Jon's original translation, but now all idioms had been properly rendered.

Afterward, they all went to lunch at the Seven Arches Hotel on the Mount of Olives, overlooking Jerusalem. Sipping Carmel red table wine along with the salad, Montaigne asked about their Sinai experiences, and Jon proceeded to relate the full, incredible tale.

Strangely, though, Montaigne did not seem unduly shocked by Alexandros's murderous conduct. "I fear we shall see more of such violence if the world learns about the papyrus," he warned.

"You are witnessing only the tiniest tip of a monstrous iceberg, *mes amis*. Have you *really* thought about all the . . . the ramifications of your discovery? Non-Christians will be unaffected, of course. And among Christians, many liberal theologians, critics, and sophisticates will have little trouble, even if everything proves authentic. But this group, for all its influence, numbers less than 1 or 2 percent of world Christendom. The great majority of believers confess that Jesus materially—*physically*—rose from the dead, and your discovery will lead to a *devastating* crisis of faith throughout the Christian world."

"We're fully aware of that, Père Montaigne," Jon assured him. "It's been a burden on our minds ever since we first deciphered the document."

"I'm sure it has. But I also foresee mass despair, collapse of religious and perhaps political authority, suicides—"

"Isn't that a little premature, Father Montaigne?" Jennings remonstrated. "We still have *many* other tests to perform."

"Yes, yes, I know. But this fraud seems to be so *diabolically* clever that the other tests may not reveal the hoax either, and then—"

"Please don't use terms like *fraud* or *hoax* until—"

"But of course, but of course. However, I am sure they apply. Or will apply! Nothing is more certain to me! And so, to avoid giving horrible offense to the whole Christian world, I . . . I must respectfully implore you to *destroy* the papyrus, all of the photographs, the negatives, and the *titulus,* and then rebury the remains in the sarcophagus where they were found. Seal up the cavern and finish the other sectors of your dig instead."

Jennings, Jon, and Shannon exchanged glances of amazement. Montaigne pressed the case. "Or failing that, at least destroy the papyrus. If you *must* have a 'great discovery,' let the world think Joseph of Arimathea has, in fact, been found."

Jon was angry. "I bitterly resent your suggestion that we '*must* have a great discovery' at our dig. We merely—"

"Forgive me, *mes amis!* That was . . . that was unworthy of me." Montaigne dropped his eyes. "It's just a *terrible* thing to see our faith under such attack. I ask you again, will you consider destroying the papyrus? The *titulus* too, I think, because it could lead to speculation as to the remains you discovered?"

Shannon looked at her father, then at Jon. Jon looked at Jennings, who finally responded, "It *is* a thought, Jonathan. It *is* a thought. We'd spare the world a lot of agony—"

Jon could scarcely believe his ears. Was this a scientific archaeologist caving in? "All this talk is *premature!*" He sliced his syllables, emphasizing *premature* so loudly that several dining room guests turned to stare. "We won't make any such decisions until all the tests are completed!"

"Spoken as a true scholar, my friend," said Montaigne. "But we have an extraordinary, an unparalleled situation here, for which we must take extraordinary measures. Please, I *implore* you to consider destroying the papyrus!"

Jon merely shook his head.

Montaigne paused as the waiter brought the main course. Then he resumed, "Well, then, I am prepared . . ." he faltered, "I am prepared, on behalf of the agency I represent, to offer you the sum of five million dollars if you will give me the papyrus. I have revealed nothing to this agency, other than to state that a certain document could falsely subvert the Christian faith, if not destroy it."

Jon's jaw sagged. He shook his head as if to dispel a bad dream. "You cannot be serious, Père Montaigne. Please tell me you jest—"

"I do *not* jest. I am absolutely serious."

"I find this in extremely bad taste. What agency do you represent, the Jesuits? No," he corrected himself, "that's not their style today."

"The Society of Jesus is not involved. But please take me very seriously—you *will* receive *five million dollars.*"

Jennings's eyes widened, while Shannon stared incredulously at Montaigne. Again Jon gave the response for the group, no longer bothering to check with Jennings. "No. Not for five million or whatever sum you try to bribe us with!"

"I resent the term *bribe*. This is merely a gift of appreciation from the agency in question to prevent the faithful from suffering horribly because of a fraud!"

"What agency? I ask you again."

"I'm . . . not at liberty to say."

"And we're not at liberty to 'sell'!" Jon shot back.

"I raise the offer to *ten* million dollars. Ten million! Imagine how that would underwrite your archaeological campaigns for many years to come."

"I can't *believe* a scholar of your international reputation resorting to huckstering! I simply can't believe this conversation is taking place!"

"Nor can I, *mon ami!* But, as I said before, we have a unique problem here in the world's history, for which we must devise unique solutions."

"Are you certain you can't tell us the agency involved?" Jennings asked. "What if we swore to keep the information confidential? Otherwise, your offer has no credibility."

Montaigne pondered the point for some time. Then he looked up and said, "*Will* you give me your word to keep it confidential?"

"We will," Jennings responded.

"It's some very wealthy members of the Opus Dei—the Spanish branch—who are acting on their own."

"Well," Jon replied, "now you have credibility!" The organization of extremely conservative Catholics was known the world over for dedicated—some thought fanatic—efforts in behalf of the faith. "Nevertheless, I'm opposed to *any* sellout," Jon affirmed. "Categorically."

Silence was mandated as a waiter cleared the table of the main course. The bizarre conversation resumed over coffee.

Montaigne now pressed his palms together, almost in a mode of prayer, and said, firmly, "You must leave, my friends, as must I. But I shall now make the only further offer I will *ever* make in this regard. Henceforth I shall never raise the issue again. Indeed, I shall have to deny that this conversation ever took place, and will cheerfully do so if I'm ever accused of it. I am authorized to offer you *fifteen* million dollars, to divide as you see fit, for possession of the papyrus, the *titulus,* as well as *all* relevant photographs and negatives.

"Before you respond, I would remind you again of how such an endowment could support not only your future campaigns,

Professor Jennings, but also your Institute of Christian Origins, Dr. Weber."

Jennings's eyes widened further. "You said *fifteen* million dollars?" he exclaimed. "Do you mean *nine or ten million pounds sterling?*"

"*Absolument!* Not a *sou* more, not a *sou* less!"

Jennings's hands trembled a bit as he slurped his coffee and looked a little anxiously at Shannon and Jon.

My Lord, is he weakening? Jon thought to himself.

Several times Shannon had bit her tongue to keep from intruding into the grotesque dialogue, but she could restrain herself no longer. "I find this all surrealistic," she said. "So what if we *would* sell you those items for fifteen million? What would prevent our telling the world about the papyrus anyway? Or hiding a negative or two to prove our story?"

Montaigne smiled, for he had thought of such a possibility in advance. "I certainly rely on your sense of honor in that regard, *ma chère mademoiselle*. But, more than that, I know that you would *never* tell anyone about this transaction, let alone the world."

"Why not?"

"Because your reputations as archaeologists and scholars would be destroyed. In our profession, one never sells, hides, or disposes of anything, particularly something as important as this."

"Yes, he's right, of course," Jennings admitted. "So, then, my colleagues, do we sell out at fifteen million and enjoy the rest of our lives? Or keep the papyrus and bring pandemonium on the world, while wishing fanaticism, hatred, and bodily harm—up to and including assassination—on ourselves? And if you think that's farfetched, I give you the Salman Rushdie affair and what Muslims did after his *Satanic Verses* was published."

Jon clenched his fist and said, "You put that beautifully, Austin. It sounds to me like a directed verdict to sell!"

"Oh, not really, dear boy. It's just that I'm getting a bit unnerved by it all. Hanging over that abyss at Mount Sinai was hardly sipping a glass of gin-and-Schweppes at Wimbledon! No, let's be democratic about all this. There are three of us, so no tie is possible. How do you vote, Shannon?"

"No, Austin, it's your dig," Jon interposed. "You decide."

"No, I insist. Your desires, Shannon?"

Shannon looked at her father, then at Jon, and replied, slowly, "I . . . I could never live with myself after selling out. I don't care what they offer. I vote no."

Jon smiled, reached over, and squeezed her hand.

"And I vote no too," Jennings quickly responded, "so it looks like hard luck if you wanted to sell the papyrus, Jon." He had a twinkle in his eye, as Jon broke out laughing in relief.

"I think it is only fair to warn you," Montaigne sulked, "that under no circumstances do I want my name connected with this project in any way. I want no mention of my participation in the translation, or in consultation, or in—"

"Thanks for your help thus far, Dr. Montaigne," Jon seethed. "We'll respect your wishes to the letter. And now take your fifteen million dollars and stuff them up . . . no, on second thought, why not use them over there," he pointed down toward the Hinnom Valley. "Use them to buy another potter's field, next to Judas's!"

Jon sent Montaigne a note of apology the next day for having overstepped his role as dispassionate scholar. Montaigne's conduct had been no better, of course, but the French Dominican had, after all, provided strategic help in translation. Montaigne was equally gracious in reply and now registered his mortification that he had ever gone along with the Opus Dei offer. "But that papyrus seems to be turning all of us inside out," he wrote.

Jon had to agree. It was time for a vacation to soothe everyone's nerves. It was now the end of August, and the students at the dig were returning to their universities. Jon had planned to drive up to Galilee with Jennings and Shannon, but Jennings backed out at the last minute. "I want to scout out a possible new dig site near Qumran, and I need Clive along before he has to return to England," Jennings explained. "But don't change your plans on my account."

"You still want to go, Shannon?" asked Jon.

She thought for a moment, then replied, "Why not? Sounds like fun."

And so it proved to be. Galilee was easily the most picturesque section of Israel, the least spoiled by time and the urban sprawl that characterized Judea. Jon and Shannon drove along the Mediterranean coastal road, through the Megiddo Pass, around Mount Tabor, and they finally reached their first night's destination at Tiberias on the Sea of Galilee.

They had reservations at the Plaza in Tiberias, right on the seashore. After checking into adjacent rooms, they dined by candlelight in the restaurant overlooking the Sea of Galilee, *a magnificently romantic setting for any but Shannon and himself,* thought Jon—an improbable couple trying to flee their consuming secret. Here was easily the most famous body of water in the world—the very lake where Jesus presumably walked on the water, stilled the tempest, and produced the miraculous haul of fish. Near it he delivered the Sermon on the Mount and fed the five thousand. But all of it, *all of it,* would be grotesquely undermined if their papyrus proved genuine.

"Shannon," said Jon, looking out over the lake, "do we really have the . . . the right to destroy people's faith? This responsibility thing is creeping up on me."

"Me too. For a while it was fun-and-games trying to sleuth out the truth. Maybe it still is. But if word ever gets out, say good-bye to all peace, tranquility, and sanity."

"And all orderly scholarship. Yes, any premature revelation *would* be the worst-case scenario."

"Jon, did you ever wonder if maybe Montaigne was right after all? I mean, not because of the money, but his motivation—not wanting to hurt people?"

Jon gritted his teeth. "Yes, I've thought about that. More than I care to admit."

Suddenly she chuckled. "Wouldn't it be ironic if we all decided to save Christianity and destroy the papyrus anyway, *after* letting fifteen million dollars slip through our hands?"

"At least we could live with ourselves . . . I hope," Jon laughed. "We didn't do it for cash, we did it for principle."

At the moment he found himself entranced once again by the changing moods playing across the face of the ever-so-beautiful woman looking at him across the candlelight. She toyed with a strand of her lustrous hair that spilled generously onto her shoulders. Whenever she spoke, the coral pink of her lips danced invitingly before a backdrop of perfect teeth, parting for smiles that effortlessly took him captive. The laughing sparkle in her eyes set fire to his soul. He fiddled with the stem on his wine glass, trying valiantly to return to the mainstream of their conversation.

"Who knows?" he said. "Maybe something will still turn up in the other tests—"

"Do you *really* think anything will? Tell me the truth."

The arrival of their entrée mercifully cancelled his need to reply. "Let's talk about something happier, Shannon," he said. "You, for instance. Let's have your life story!"

"Oh, fine. Just like that! Well, 'I was born at a very early age,' as they say." She went on to speak of the death of her mother, and of her first memories in Oxford.

"Tell me about her, Shannon . . . your mother."

"I know very little about her. I was only a baby when she died. But she was very beautiful. You can see that from her photographs. She died quickly of some rare form of pneumonia, and this really broke Papa up for a *long* while. She was Catholic and he was Protestant, green Irish versus orange, but that didn't seem to bother them, since they were very much in love."

"Do you resemble your mother?"

"Papa says I do."

Her mother, then, must have been something spectacular, thought Jon. "Tell me more about you and your father. Did your mother's death bring you two closer together, or—"

"Well, I was too young to know at first. My earliest memories are of good Miss Heatherstone, our nanny. She tried to mother both of us, I think. She'd have to tell Papa what to put on when he went out, since he was *so* absentminded. Once we went down to the Thames for a picnic. After we'd finished, Papa actually started to drive away without putting the blanket and leftover food in the trunk! But yes, he doted on me, I think. He tried in his own way to make up for Mother's absence. The only time I really felt like an orphan was when he sent me away to girls' school. *That* was the pits!"

"Oh, yes," Jon chuckled. "Your boys' boarding schools are even worse, I hear."

"I hated the rules, the picky, picky regulations, the uniforms . . . you wouldn't believe the hats! Several of the girls even taunted me for not having a mother. Kids can be *so* cruel."

"Did your father talk much about your mother?"

"Only when I'd ask. Then his eyes would seem to film over, he'd bite his lip, and his voice would catch. He can get quite emotional, you know."

Jon nodded, then asked, "What about the teenage Shannon?"

"Oh, somehow I survived those awkward years. Dear Miss Heatherstone died on my eighteenth birthday, and we had a string of housekeepers after that. But by then I was an Oxford student—as if I had any choice!—and became Papa's assistant at digs and such. The older I got, the better our relationship."

That I can understand, thought Jon, as he picked away at the last remnants of St. Peter's fish on his plate, almost intentionally averting his gaze from his partner at the table. Shannon-by-candlelight ignited his very being. He loved her. He wanted to scream to everyone in the restaurant that he adored her. The frustration was nearly unbearable.

What now? Should he simply declare his love to her, wait for her to register shock—or worse, amusement—and then apologize for mentioning it, and so play the role of unrequited fool for the rest of their vacation? No, he couldn't take that chance. It was time to cool off.

"Ah, you don't want dessert, do you?" he asked.

"No. How'd you guess?"

"Because that would crowd too much into your tummy for our moonlight swim. C'mon, let's change. Then I'll race you to the beach. Last one in's a bearded monster of a monk!"

"You're on!" she chuckled.

Shannon won. There she stood with her ankles in the Sea of Galilee, sporting a bikini that glowed white in the moonlight. "Ha, ha, you lost, Rasputin!" she taunted. "Why're you looking around everywhere?"

"Just checking for the Israeli police. They'd arrest you for that miniswimsuit you're wearing."

"You nut!" She shoved out her foot and sent a wave splashing over him, then giggled and ran into the water. Jon plunged in after her, but she swam a rapid crawl far out into the lake. Jon followed suit, but failed to catch her.

Well, that figures, he told himself. *The most desirable woman in the world in one of the most magnificent settings imaginable, and I can't do a thing about it.*

A nearly full moon had floated up over the Golan Heights rimming the eastern shore of the lake, shooting a satin-sheened path of platinum toward Tiberias. The water, almost bath warm from the August sun, was barely ruffled by scented southern breezes blowing off the Jordan Valley. How he loved that radiant creature swimming out there somewhere! She would never know how much.

Suddenly, his feet were snatched off the sand bar where he'd been standing, and he fell backward into the water. The head of a dripping Irish sprite surfaced to claim responsibility.

He sputtered and laughed and threw his arms around her for a friendly hug. "I didn't know you were such a mermaid, Shannon. You seem to excel at everything, including beating up bearded monks."

She laughed, then noticed a long, vacant stare in his eyes. "Hey, what's the problem? Why're you so serious?"

"Oh, I was only thinking what an *incredibly* lucky fellow Gideon is."

"Gideon, Gideon, Gideon! Always Gideon! What about *us*?"

"Us?"

"Yes, *us!* Do I have to draw you a picture, Jonathan Weber? Won't you please, just once, take me in your arms and hold me a little? Would that be so *very* difficult?"

He let out a gasp of joy and clasped her tighter than she had ever been held. Then he rained down kisses on her wet cheeks, her ear lobes, her neck, her chin, and finally reached her mouth with the longest, most passionate kiss he had ever given anyone. She sighed with happiness. He quivered with the unexpected thrill of it all. "Shannon, Shannon, Shannon," was all he could whisper as his arms tightened again around her lithe body. "I loved you from the moment I first saw you at the dig, I think. And it's gotten worse since then, *much* worse!"

"I love you too, Jon! More intensely than I thought possible." She put her head on his chest in a haze of exhilaration. "But why did you take so long to express yourself?"

"I don't know. I just didn't think this could be possible—the Israel Antiquities Authority, the age difference, and all. Besides which, appearances to the contrary, I'm a *very* shy guy."

"Mmmmm," she purred, as she now kissed him rapturously. "It makes no difference. I'm only glad we were finally honest with each other."

Again he clasped her to himself, almost worried that somehow she might slip out of his life, that the dream might shimmer away like some mirage. "Darling Shannon! Incredible Shannon! You've been the one secret source of joy for me all these weeks, even though I thought you were absolutely out of reach. I really had no idea you shared my feelings."

"I thought I'd dropped a hint or two . . ."

"I guess I was too afraid of rejection to even notice. What a blinking coward I turned out to be!"

"You didn't seem very cowardly up on Mount Sinai."

"*You* were the one who was larger than life that day, darling. I'd had you on a pedestal before, but after your heroic performance there you hit the stratosphere. Beyond belief! Tell me once again how you took care of that crazed cleric."

Shannon laughed. "Want me to show you?"

"Oh, oh . . . better not! But where'd you learn how to do all that?"

"I have a weakness for Ian Fleming. It's what one of the James Bond heroines would have done."

Jon chuckled, and they walked onto the beach. The gentle southern breeze caressed away any chills as they ambled arm in arm for several hours, celebrating the exquisite new joy in their lives. First they shared delightful revelations of how they had *really* felt about each other at various points in their acquaintance. Clearly, Jon had fallen in love first. She had been detained by the Gideon complication. But before long, she confessed, Jon had quickly dislodged the Israeli, and she had only been waiting for him to show some initiative. On the other hand, she couldn't be too forward about her feelings for fear he was still hopelessly attached to the memory of Andrea. He admitted to her that he would never love Andrea the less, but there could hardly be any complication on that score.

"Why must we mask ourselves so?" Jon wondered aloud. "Why do people cover their feelings instead of expressing them? Look what it cost me: two months of love with you, and that's an *irreparable* loss."

She stopped, gently twined her arms around his neck, and murmured, "We can try to make up for lost time, my darling." Then she kissed him so vibrantly that all thoughts of time and space vanished from their horizons.

It was well past midnight when they returned to the hotel. Jon wanted desperately to spend the night with her, but there was a good chance she might resent the suggestion, to say nothing about the issue of morality. He would do nothing, absolutely nothing, to ruin the dream. He paused in front of her room, caressed her bare shoulders, and said, "Good night, my darling. You've made me the happiest man on earth at this moment. I know that's a *very* hackneyed expression, but I really can't find other words for it."

"I feel exactly the same way, Jon. Thank you for . . . for coming into my life." She gave him a long, tender kiss, stepped inside her room, and closed the door.

Courage, Jon, he told himself. *You have the rest of your life to spend with that marvelous woman, if—pray God—she'll marry me!*

He undressed and went to bed. Since the air conditioning was halfhearted at best, he lay naked on top of the sheets, luxuriating in the memories of the most sublime evening of his life. Sleep was impossible, as his whole being now focused on that grandest creation of God called Shannon Jennings. "Thank You, Lord! Thank You!" he said. It was the most honest prayer he had ever uttered.

What had started as a brief holiday, a little awkward because one of the vacationers was missing, had now turned suddenly romantic. Their lives would never, could never, be the same. Breakfast was much more than food. It was a daylight confirmation of their overwhelming attachment. Their planned itinerary stayed the same, but nothing else did. All awkwardness, all restraints had been buried at Tiberias. Now they felt free to be absolutely genuine with one another.

Like school children on their first picnic, they fairly sailed along the roadway around the western shore of the Sea of Galilee, past Capernaum, and up to Caesarea Philippi, where the apostle Peter first confessed Jesus to be the Son of God. Jon and Shannon cavorted about the caves and grottos there like young billy goats—teasing, racing, cajoling, touching, embracing, kissing. Here were the headwaters of the Jordan—clear, cold water gurgling out from a spring in the mountainside, a perfect spot for them to defeat the heat by plunging under the waterfalls there.

They climbed the Golan Heights, peered into Syria, and camped out at Ein Gev on the eastern shore of the lake. They found new joys in each other, unexplored thoughts, delicious sensations, invigorating emotions. Should they telephone Jennings and tell him of their great happiness? Time enough for that later on, they decided.

"Jon, take me for a boat ride on the Sea of Galilee," she said, after they had returned to Tiberias. "I've never done that, believe it or not, and I've heard about this lake ever since Sunday school."

"Done!" he promised.

They rented a sailboat in the harbor and headed out toward the middle of the lake. "Now if Someone comes along, walking on the water, *do whatever He says*," Jon advised.

"Just don't get us caught in a tempest. Your Friend may not appear on schedule."

No tempest, but a great calm overtook them near the center of the lake. Not even a zephyr ruffled their sails. They were dead in the water.

"I really think we ought to use this time to better advantage than just sitting here," said Jon. "Don't you agree, my love?"

Again they were in each other's arms, tumbling down into the shallow inner pit of the sailboat, caressing and kissing with a passion that astonished them. *Life can never be better than this,* they thought.

Suddenly they heard it before seeing it. A boat was bearing down on them, crammed with tourists singing, quite lustily, *"Blest be the tie that binds our hearts with Christian love."*

Jon jerked his head up over the gunwales and saw the ship, festooned with a huge banner: "ANOTHER BOATLOAD OF BAPTISTS IN ISRAEL." The pilgrims craned their necks at the couple from the starboard rail.

In panic, Jon tried to stand up to warn the ship, but his swim trunks caught on the jib line, pulling them down. The pilgrims could draw only one conclusion.

"Brothers and sisters," the tour leader boomed over the public address system, "avert your eyes from such carnal misdeeds! 'Flee youthful lusts!' the Bible says. Instead let's all sing hymn number 374, 'O Love That Will Not Let Me Go'!"

Jon—his swim trunks back in place—joined Shannon in a howl of laughter, and even the scandalized boatload chuckled at their leader's gaucherie.

"Are you Okay?" the captain of the ship called down as his ship pulled alongside the sailboat. "I thought you might be in trouble."

"No, no! We're fine!" Jon called back. Mercifully, the ship sailed on toward Capernaum.

"Oh, that'll look *great* in your dossier," Shannon guffawed. "'WEBER MOONS PILGRIMS IN GALILEE'!"

Jon chortled and said, "That Bible-quoting leader of theirs— I can quote some Scripture too." He bent to kiss her. "Like . . .

How beautiful you are, my love, how very beautiful!
Your love is better than wine; your perfume more fragrant than
  any spice.
The taste of honey is on your lips, my darling. What a magnificent
  girl you are!

The curve of your thighs is like the work of an artist.

Your navel is a rounded bowl that never lacks mixed wine.

Your breasts are like two fawns, twins of a gazelle.

You are graceful as a palm tree, and your breasts are clusters of dates.

I will climb the palm tree and pick its fruit!

Your kisses are like the best wine that goes down smoothly, gliding over lips and teeth.

How lovely you are, how exquisite, how complete the delights of your love!

"That's *so* beautiful, Jon. It's from the *Song of Songs,* isn't it?"

He nodded and said, "Or as it's sometimes called, the *Song of Solomon.*"

"Let's read it together sometime."

"How about for daily devotions?"

He looked a final time at the form lying so magnificently in the pit of their sailboat, smiled with infinite satisfaction, and murmured, "Up, little princess. We have to catch this wind and sail home."

They had one last dinner at the hotel that had changed their lives, and then packed for the drive back to Ramallah.

"Where do you think they should hang the bronze plaque?" asked Shannon, as they drove away.

"What plaque?"

"The one that reads: 'HERE THE GREAT LOVE BETWEEN JONATHAN WEBER AND SHANNON JENNINGS FIRST BLOSSOMED.' On the beach or in the hotel?"

"On the front lawn. In neon!"

She nibbled at his right ear lobe and then brushed his cheek with her lips. It was conduct like this that made them forget the car radio. Had they been listening instead to Kol Israel, the BBC, or any other station, they would not have been so shocked when they returned to Ramallah.

When they did arrive around midnight, they found their hotel surrounded by what appeared to be half the Israel Defense Force. Floodlights beamed against the entrance, officers with walkie-talkies patrolled the perimeter, and a pushing, shouting mob besieged the site, prevented from entering by the Israeli military.

"What in the very *devil* is going on here?" Jon asked the guard who blocked their access.

"Who wants to know?" he countered.

"This is Shannon Jennings. Her father's the director of the Rama excavation, and I'm Professor Weber. We live inside here." He pointed.

"Oh! We've been looking for you everywhere! Please follow me."

He cleared a path for their car. They drove in, got out, and walked inside to find a white-faced, perspiring Jennings stalking to and fro. "Thank God you're finally here, Jon . . . Shannon," he nearly croaked. "Somehow, word got out! Now the world knows!"

Jon gritted his teeth and clenched his fists. He looked over to Shannon and hissed, "*Worst-case scenario!*"

FIFTEEN

W hat in ruddy *blazes* happened, Austin?" Jon burst out, not even trying to disguise his fury. "Sort it out for me!"

"An idiotic lapse in security. Gideon here was showing his cousin around the dig and—well, you tell him, Gideon."

Ben-Yaakov looked crestfallen, chastened. "Well, it was a comedy of . . . no, a *tragedy* of errors," he confessed. "My cousin Schmuel Sanderson is a stringer for the Associated Press in Jerusalem. As you know, it's been a very 'low-news' August, so Schmuel was doing a potboiler on the various digs in Israel, and since yours is one of the best, it was only natural that I took him to Rama. After showing him the dig, I brought him here to see the workroom and the laboratory. Professor Jennings and Clive Brampton were gone at the time, and the other dig personnel saw nothing wrong with our little tour of your facilities. Inside the photo lab, I saw a print of your papyrus. I thought I'd show off my Aramaic in front of Cousin Schmuel, so I started reading off the first three or four lines. When I saw that this might be something . . . rather sensitive, I stopped translating immediately, and we left the hotel.

"Schmuel, of course, has this incredible nose for news. As we were leaving, he claimed he'd left something behind and went back inside the hotel. What the schlemiel did was to take photos of the print. Then he brought his photographs to Hebrew University for translation. They didn't get it all, but they did translate enough for Schmuel to realize he had the biggest story of his life on his hands. He never contacted me first. He simply broke the story. I'm . . . *very* sorry, my friends. So very sorry!"

"And just what in Hades was Dick Cromwell doing, letting prints like that lie around?" Jon demanded. "And where *is* Dick?"

161

"Dick had to fly to the U.S. His mother's ill," said Clive. "Austin and I were down at the Dead Sea caves when it happened. Maybe we're paying the price for not having had a resident here who knew the whole story."

"All right, first things first. How much does the world know?"

They showed him banner headlines from various international newspapers on sale in Jerusalem. The story was inchoate, but the main sensational facts were not lost on any of them.

"They don't know that the papyrus and the bones are at the Rockefeller," Jennings explained. "They think they're here. That's why we're under siege."

"We should be grateful for small favors, I suppose," Jon retorted. "Who's in charge of the army out there, Gideon?"

"Colonel Chaim Nahshon."

"Can he keep a confidence?"

"He's one of our best."

"Why not have him transfer a strong detachment of his troops to beef up security at the Rockefeller? They should stay out of sight, if possible, but be ready to appear on a moment's notice."

"Fine! Back in a moment." He walked outside.

The ghastly noise of an electronic megaphone now blared at them from the crowd gathered around the gate: "HELLO, PROFESSOR JENNINGS AND PROFESSOR WEBER! RODNEY CORNWALL OF REUTERS HERE. WE HAVE A NEWS POOL NOW, SO YOU'LL HAVE TO TELL YOUR STORY ONLY ONCE. MAY I PLEASE HAVE AN INTERVIEW?"

Jon quickly discussed strategy with Jennings, who nodded. Then he stepped to the window and yelled, "Come in, Cornwall!"

Gideon Ben-Yaakov had returned in the meantime.

"Where in Jerusalem would we have room enough for a news conference?" Jennings asked him.

"I'd say the convention room of the Diplomat Hotel."

"Would they let us?"

"Of course. Free advertising!"

"Would you call them for us?"

"Certainly."

Rodney Cornwall stepped inside, a mustachioed little Englishman who had been on top of many of the world's headlines over the past decade. "Frightfully nice of you to grant me this interview." He smiled his words.

"We're not granting you an interview, Mr. Cornwall. We're merely asking you to relay a message to that mob outside."

"Oh?" His eyebrows arched. "What message?"

Gideon, at the phone, gave them the thumbs-up sign, and asked, "Day after tomorrow? In the afternoon?"

"Fine." Then Jon turned to Cornwall and said, "Please tell everyone out there two things. One, none of the artifacts or remains discovered at the cavern site are on the premises here, so please tell everyone to leave."

"And where are they, then, Professor Weber?"

"No comment, Mr. Cornwall. The second message is this—we'll hold a general news conference, to which all the media are invited, at the convention center of the Diplomat Hotel in Jerusalem the day after tomorrow at 3 PM."

"That's it? That's all you can tell me?"

"That's it, Mr. Cornwall. Good night."

Cornwall turned and left. Soon his voice was heard again on the bullhorn, addressing the crowd.

"What do you know!" said Jennings. "For once the press got something right!"

"It actually seems to be working!" said Shannon. "The mob's starting to leave."

For the next hour, they plotted strategy. Jon, they insisted, should be the spokesman. But he was seething that their discoveries were now public. "This is a *horrible* complication for us! That bloody, snooping stringer—I'd like to take that creep and twist his . . . At the news conference, why don't we simply tell the media to bug off until we're finished?"

"It won't work, Jon," said Brampton. "Not with *this* story."

"I guess you're right. They'd hound us to death." Jon walked over to a window and looked out again at the Judean hills. In his present mood, he would have loved to *orchestrate* a whole pack of jackals, baying at the moon. Then he turned and said, "I suggest we tell the story simply and honestly, so we're not accused of a cover-up later on. But I'll stress—*over*emphasize—that everything is preliminary, there are *no* conclusions, *much* more testing is necessary, et cetera. Well, what do you think? Bless that strategy or shoot it down."

Jennings sighed. "It's really all we can do."

As Gideon turned to leave, he put his arms around Shannon and asked, "May I see you tomorrow night, my little *shiksa?*"

Jon overheard, and suddenly forgot all about the current chaos.

"Ah . . . Gideon," Shannon responded, "I . . . have something to tell you. Shall we . . . ah . . . take a little walk?"

Jon smiled exuberantly, then returned to the crisis at hand.

The convention center at the Diplomat Hotel was jammed to capacity. All five hundred seats were taken, and the world's press corps spilled over to the walls. The podium was festooned with a forest of microphones, television lights beamed in on the dais, and tripods supporting a network-headquarters' worth of television cameras rimmed the hall. Reporters of every skin color were standing or sitting in whatever space they could find, notepads at the ready. A special section, reserved for church leaders, was occupied by the Latin Patriarch of Jerusalem, the Greek Orthodox, Coptic, Armenian, Abyssinian, and other ethnic patriarchs, as well as emissaries from the pope, the archbishop of Canterbury, the Lutheran World Federation, and the World Council of Churches.

On his way to the dais, Jon saw a familiar face in the crowd. He stopped and walked over to give Kevin Sullivan a clap on the shoulder. "And what brings *you* here from Rome, old buddy?" he asked wickedly.

"Our mutual friend in the Vatican sent me to represent him, Jon. You'd best tell us what you've been up to!"

"I will indeed, Kevin. Let's hoist one later, okay?"

"Only one? See you afterward!"

The cacophony in the room stilled to a hush as Brampton, Jennings, and Shannon joined him at the green table behind the dais. At 3:10 PM, Jon stepped up to the battery of microphones and said, "Honored clergy, emissaries, and ladies and gentlemen of the news media, permit me to read a prepared statement, after which I'll entertain questions. But first let me introduce my colleagues here:

Dr. Clive Brampton, associate director of the excavations at Rama; Professor Austin Balfour Jennings, the distinguished director; Shannon Jennings, his daughter, who is the recorder; and I'm Jonathan Weber, their associate.

"We must first assure you that this news conference was forced upon us by the unauthorized and entirely premature publication of our discoveries at Rama. This was absolutely unwarranted, and it was accomplished by unethical means. According to all canons of archaeological science, we wanted to test our findings extensively before making any of them public. Several tests have taken place, but by no means all of them. Accordingly, I can't emphasize strongly enough that all our findings to date are extremely preliminary, and that no conclusions whatsoever have been made about the significance, or, indeed, the basic authenticity of our discoveries. We expect you to be absolutely clear on that point, and I hope your questions afterward will reflect that clarity."

Jon went on to give a brief history of the dig and its discoveries, as well as the tests they had applied to date. He made no mention of the attempted murder at Sinai or the role of Claude Montaigne.

Finally he stated, "Because a quite inadequate, at places garbled, version of the purported letter of Joseph of Arimathea has been published, we will now supply you with copies of the authorized translation, as well as photographs of the *titulus*, juglet, and papyrus. I'm sure the world's scholarly community will be interested in helping us gauge the final authenticity—or lack of same—in these items. We're now open for questions."

More than fifty hands shot up. Jon recognized them as best he could.

"Hans Steinle, *Frankfurter Allgemeine*. Why don't we have a photograph of the bones you discovered? And where are the . . . ah . . . the remains at present?"

"We have no present plans to provide photographs of the human remains. Aside from the matter of taste, further evaluation will first be necessary. You should also be satisfied with the photographs provided. Many archaeologists take months or even years to publish their photographs. We did so only because of the potential significance of these finds. . . . Yes?"

"Blandford Morgan, *Manchester Guardian.* You didn't tell us where the papyrus and other items are at present."

"No, and that was intentional. . . . Yes?"

"Louis Rambeaux, *Paris Match.* The radiocarbon tests you've applied thus far *prove* the validity of your finds, I would think. Why don't you simply accept them as genuine?"

"Too much is at stake here for any simplistic conclusions in that regard."

"But if there had been no parchment or papyrus to identify these remains so . . . so sensationally, wouldn't you by now have been convinced that your discoveries are authentic?"

"Probably. But we'd still do more tests and far more study. On second thought, I'm going to ask you to strike that word *probably,* for it could be misinterpreted. Make it *possibly.*"

"Arthur Blake, *New York Times.* What other tests do you plan?"

"Perhaps Professor Jennings would be kind enough to clarify that."

Jennings moved to the battery of microphones and said, "We plan thermoluminescence for the ceramics, additional radio-carbon samplings, metallurgical studies of the coin, pollen analysis of the parchment, papyrus, and linen. Perhaps collagen fiber analysis too. And, of course, general spectroscopic studies of all the artifacts, as well as neutron activation analysis to gauge their origin. There may well be other tests, as this series progresses."

"Helen Cronin, *Melbourne Daily News.* Suppose the tests all support the authenticity of your finds, and you and the other scholars declare them genuine. Would that spell the end of Christianity as a viable religion?"

A buzzing of whispers augmented into general commotion in the crowded hall. Jon motioned for quiet, and replied, "I don't like responding to such a question for several reasons. One, we just don't have time for speculation involving matters of such urgent concern. Two, this is more a theological question than one relating to scientific archaeology. Purely as a *personal* reaction, I'd certainly hope that neither this nor any other archaeological discovery would ever undermine the Christian faith. . . . Yes?"

"Dan Rather, *CBS Evening News.* Now clearly, Professor

Weber, these finds are either genuine or they are not. If not, how could the papyrus ever have been forged? How could it date back so accurately if it's a hoax? How could you set up first-century bones in a first-century grave?"

"It's called 'salting a dig,' Mr. Rather. The perpetrator plants the artifacts or buries them for 'discovery' later on. Perhaps Dr. Clive Brampton here can give us a brief rundown on some of the more celebrated archaeological hoaxes in the past."

Clive stepped to the microphones and listed some of the great fakes, ranging from the familiar Piltdown Skull in England to the Runic Stone in Minnesota. He went on to celebrated art frauds, like the supposedly ancient Scythian gold tiara of Saitapharnes which fooled the French—it was all crafted in the nineteenth century AD—or the Hacilar double-headed pot from Turkey that duped English experts at Oxford. Its origin was not the claimed fiftieth century BC, but the twentieth AD! Brampton concluded with famous written forgeries, ranging from the "Donation of Constantine" to the "Hitler Diaries."

Rather stood up again. "But that still doesn't explain how the papyrus tests out as an ancient document in your carbon-14 readings. *If,* that is, it were a fraud."

Jon returned to the microphones and said, "The perpetrator could have used the blank beginning or end of an ancient scroll for fabricating his message."

"But how could he write such perfect Aramaic? In so convincing a script?"

"I . . . don't really know. . . . Yes?"

"Howard Go Whu, *Hong Kong Telegraph.* Don't you professors wonder how *all* these things could have been fabricated? The complexity, dear sirs, seems enormous. And who would attempt something like that? And why?"

"I'll admit, if this does prove to be a hoax, it will also be the most elaborate fraud in all of history."

"But again," Go Whu persisted, "it *may* not be a hoax at all. And the more I hear of your discoveries, the more genuine they seem to me. And I believe this feeling is also shared by many of us gathered here."

"No comment, because you are opining, not asking." Again there was a loud commotion.

Jon fielded questions for another hour before he made his closing statements. "I must again ask you to curb any speculation about the Rama discoveries, since definitive conclusions simply do not exist at this point. I would urge all the media to show restraint in your reporting and avoid any sensationalizing for reasons that are obvious enough. Otherwise, you'll be doing a profound disservice to the cause of truth.

"And now, finally, I should like to introduce several other members of our archaeological staff at Rama: Naomi Sharon, our ceramicist; Achmed Sa'ad, who is in charge of our labor force; and Professor Noel Nottingham, our anthropologist. None of them knew of the *titulus* or the papyrus until this past week, when they learned along with the rest of you. They had every reason to feel affronted that we kept these items from them, but they've been gracious enough to forgive us in view of the unparalleled circumstances."

A round of applause brought smiles to the entire Rama crew.

"We'll keep you informed of our progress with the subsequent tests. Meanwhile, thank you, ladies and gentlemen, and good day."

Jon and Kevin Sullivan sat at a secluded table in the bar of the Jerusalem Hilton, caressing frosty bottles of Heineken. There were some attempts at levity and a few smiles, but both were weighing the effects of Rama on the world.

"This, obviously, was what sidetracked our problem with Mark in the *Vaticanus,* right?" asked Sullivan.

"You've got it, friend!"

"At the time, I wondered what could possibly have been more important than *that* potential bombshell, but you certainly came up with it! In spades!"

"It's really frightening how that deleted line seems to blend in with Rama, isn't it?"

"Exactly what I thought too."

"I promise that as soon as this nightmare is over, Kevin, I'll pull out all the stops for St. Mark."

"Fine. By the way, you did a masterful job at the press conference."

"Not at all. The whole business is idiotically premature. I'd like to smash the silly face of that stringer AP has in Jerusalem for breaking the story!"

"Well, it's out, for better or worse. Probably worse. And now you'd better prepare for the tidal wave."

"What do you mean, Kev?"

"I mean, 'you ain't seen nuthin' yet,' as the saying goes. Up to now, the world has had only fluff and froth, unsubstantiated rumors, sensational stuff. You find it all the time in *National Enquirer* and the other tabloids. You know the headlines: 'Woman Bites Herself in Half,' 'I Slept with a Hooker from Outer Space,' and 'Team Finds Body of Jesus.' Get it? But now the world has *authoritative* information that substantiates what seemed impossible at first. Now's when it *really* hits the fan!"

Jon wrinkled his brow. "You're probably dead right. Did I spill too much out there?"

"At first I thought you did. But on second thought, maybe your 'honest and open' approach is the best after all. Nobody can accuse you of holding back."

"You see, the problem was this—they already had a poor translation of the papyrus circulating, so we had to correct that. The rest they'd have found out inevitably."

"True enough. But you'd best batten down your hatches, pal, because a real storm is brewing. Mark my words."

"What do you think'll happen?"

"Anything. Remember, religion and fanaticism are next-door neighbors in too many brains in this world. Touch people's faith and they go looney. You can expect anything from feces sent you in the mail—I mean real ones—to assassination attempts. How many are now dead because of Rushdie's book? And that was *fiction!* The Fundies will call you and Jennings the 'Judases of the Twenty-First Century,' and that'll be the kindest of their phrases."

"Well, I'm more concerned about the effect on the rest of the Church. If our stuff proves authentic, how would you gauge the impact?"

"*Devastating.* Absolutely *devastating!* Sure, it won't bother some of our liberals, but it'll savage the faith of 98 percent of our membership. Christianity is tough enough to believe in a secular age. This could well-nigh do it in."

Jon nodded, sadly. Then he asked, "By the way, how did the pope react?"

"He turned absolutely ashen when I brought him the first reports. Then he wanted to issue an immediate statement that the discoveries 'must be an impious fraud,' but I begged him to hold off until I saw you."

"Let him go ahead with his statement, I'd say. It'd be a nice counterpoint to what'll doubtless be some sensationalizing reports from that crowd today. But now you *do* have me worried, Kevin. Yeah, I'd best batten down those hatches!"

"Please stay in close touch, Jon. Here's my private number at the Vatican. Favor an old friend and keep the Holy Father and me as closely posted as you can, will you?"

"Of course. I promise."

Jon had no sooner stepped out of the Peugeot at Ramallah that night than two arms twined themselves about his neck and he was pulled down for a delicious kiss. After that, Shannon asked, "So how did it feel to be the center of the world's attention, my darling?"

"All I felt was this ache to be alone with you."

"Oh sure, sure, Jon! That's why you handled all those questions so brilliantly."

"No way! And even if the old noggin stayed in gear, my heart was with you the whole time. By the way, I never had the chance to ask. How did your talk go with Gideon?"

"Maybe I should've been easier on him or broken the news gradually. He's taking it *very* badly. He seemed shocked out of his mind."

"Can't say I blame him. If I lost you, I'd fall apart too." He paused, and then added. "I can't believe it. My eyes are actually getting filmy just *thinking* about that! What have you done to me?"

"I love you, Jon. I love you *so* much!"

"*Ani ma-aritz otach,*" he replied, holding her snugly in his arms.

"What does that mean?"

"It's Hebrew for 'I adore you'."

SIXTEEN

The tidal wave struck more ferociously than anyone had forecast. Over the next days, the world shook. Not a newspaper on earth failed to give the story front-page headlines, including *Izvestia* and the *Peking People's Daily.* In the United States, the story dominated all network newscasts, with full-hour ABC, CBS, NBC, PBS, and CNN specials after the evening news and again in the morning, when much of the Jerusalem news conference was replayed on television. *Newsweek, Time,* and *U.S. News & World Report* brought out special editions featuring photographs of the dig, background stories on the principal excavators, interviews with parents and relatives, and a galaxy of quotations from leading church officials, theologians, and politicians. The same media saturation blanketed Latin America, Europe, and Australia, with Africa and Asia providing only a shade less coverage. Rama covered the earth.

The New York Stock Exchange suffered its worst one-day loss in the history of the Dow-Jones Industrial Average, while the London Stock Exchange delayed opening by more than half a day. The Tokyo Exchange was flooded by waves of sympathy selling, the bond market was devastated, and only gold and precious metals attempted a rally. The public mood curdled into surliness, boiling up into weird demonstrations and riots, particularly in the Bible belt. Worried cabinets convened in many of the Western capitals, as queens, kings, prime ministers, and presidents puzzled over a proper response to the crisis. Rama shook the earth.

Then Newton's Third Law took effect: "To every action there is an equal and opposite reaction." Now the shock waves were reflected back to Israel in general, the dig personnel in particular. Jon felt the first jolt through an overseas call from Hannibal, Missouri.

173

"Jon? This is your father." His tone was hollow, weak, disoriented. "What have you done, son? What ever have you done?"

"Please don't overreact, Dad. I know this is a ghastly shock, but it's all too premature to—"

"Overreact, Jonathan? Do you know what day this is?"

"September 10. Why?"

"Well, it's Sunday noon here in Hannibal. I just came home from church. I don't know how I got through the service. When I was leading the congregation in the Apostle's Creed and we came to 'On the third day, He rose again from the dead,' one of our elders, Martin Fischman, yelled out, '*Maybe not!*' Then he ran out of the church weeping. I could barely preach—my throat kept closing up."

Jon's stomach knotted as he groped for words. Then he asked, "How did the rest of the congregation react? What kind of attendance did you have?"

"You'd have thought it was Christmas. Or Easter. It was absolutely packed because people want to know. They're looking to us for answers. . . . Oh, their response? Stunned beyond belief. You'd have thought I was conducting a funeral."

"Dad, you've got to tell the people *not* to jump to conclusions. It's much too early to—"

"What else can they do? Your tests are all positive. The radio, TV, magazines, newspapers all make it seem like a lead-pipe cinch that those are Jesus's bones you've found."

"Well, they shouldn't. I warned them *not* to!"

"I guess the worst part of it is"—his voice began to crack—"is that I've spent my whole life serving our Lord, and here *my own son* destroys the Christian faith!"

"That's not fair, Dad. I tried my darndest to keep this secret, but—"

His father broke out sobbing. "Here, talk to your mother."

The conversation with his mother was even more excruciating, and a chilling perspiration moistened his body as he hung up. "Kevin was right," he muttered. "It's a tidal wave. Nothing less."

Ben Gurion Airport was jammed with news and media people from all over the world. Their hotel at Ramallah was under siege again by a fresh wave of reporters, hoping to get additional statements from the staff. The Rama dig site was so thronged with press people and photographers that the military had to erect an electric barbed-wire perimeter. The congestion in Jerusalem was suffocating, with religious leaders, luminaries, and writers converging on the city from all points of the globe, desperately seeking interviews with Jennings, Jon, or any of the dig crew who would give them the time of day.

The fanatic element streamed into Jerusalem like iron filings to a magnet. As he left the Rockefeller one afternoon, Jon was hit by a stone that left a two-inch bruise on his left temple. Huge rallies of Fundamentalists, fed by chartered aircraft from America's South, publicly denounced Jennings and Jon as antichrists, almost exactly as Kevin had predicted.

All hotels were sold out when the World Charismatic Congress, scheduled coincidentally for October, now had five times the expected registration. Their closing rally on the slopes of the Mount of Olives saw thirty-five thousand of them dressed in white and waving their arms in prayer. The air was filled with a torrent of glossolalia. One of their leaders interpreted the tongues with a great bullhorn: "THE ABOMINATION OF DESOLATION HAS NOW BEEN REVEALED NEAR GOD'S HOLY TEMPLE MOUNT! ANTICHRIST HAS MADE HIS APPEARANCE! IMPIOUS DEVILS ARE TRYING TO SNATCH OUR JESUS AWAY FROM US, BUT THEY SHALL NOT SUCCEED!"

"*Amen!*" the multitude responded, "and *amen!*"

Prophecy fanatics across the world were busier than ever relating Ezekiel, Daniel, and the book of Revelation to the recent events. Hal Lindsey seemed a stodgy conservative compared to the claims they now made. Jesus would return, not in a matter of years or months, but in *weeks*. People were selling their businesses, cashing in their stocks and bonds, donning white robes, and—the most complicating factor of all—coming to Jerusalem for "the last days."

The tidal wave was splashing.

"The situation is nearly out of control," said Israeli Premier Mordecai Zevulon, a dapper chub of a man with wavy gray hair.

He was addressing not only Jennings and Jon, who were invited as guests, but the whole Israeli cabinet. "Our facilities are taxed to the breaking point. The crowds are impossible, and even our Hasidim are demanding to know where 'The Body' is so they can give it a decent burial! I've never seen *anything* like this, and here we thought those Scud missiles in the Persian Gulf War were the worst thing we'd have to face! Now, we have a crisis center set up at the King David Hotel, and we've called up some of our reservists so your police can be relieved, Teddy."

Teddy Kollek, the resilient, crisis-inured mayor of Jerusalem, smiled and nodded. The genial magistrate seemed to have been in charge of the Holy City ever since Creation, and had been summoned out of retirement.

"But our priority concern," Premier Zevulon continued, "is that this crisis be *resolved*. And *soon!* And so, Professor Jennings and Professor Weber, when can you complete your tests?"

"We probably would've been finished with many of them by now if the media hadn't gotten involved," said Jennings. "Professor Weber will soon be returning to America for their completion."

Avram Heshbon, the interior minister, offered a suggestion. "Because of the *gravity* of these discoveries, gentlemen, I wonder if it wouldn't be better to have our Antiquities Authority take over control of the Rama excavation and its finds. I'd never suggest this under normal circumstances, but, as we're sadly aware, the circumstances are *not* normal! They are in fact chaotic!"

"You're suggesting *what?*" Jennings thundered.

"Please understand, Professor Jennings, that this is no reflection on your fine work at Rama," Heshbon continue. "It's just that we now have extraordinary problems because of an excavation in our sovereign territory, so I think it's the government's responsibility to step in."

"Hear, hear!" several voices echoed. Zevulon seemed to be nodding slowly.

Though as shocked as Jennings, Jon momentarily analyzed it as a quick fix for the gargantuan problems that had surfaced. But no. Didn't they realize what a disaster that would create?

One did. Moshe Breitenstein, minister of tourism, raised his pencil and was recognized by the prime minister. "Gentlemen, I find this an *appalling* suggestion for several reasons," he said. "One, it would be lunacy for Jews to control this dig, which seems to be so embarrassing to Christians. If the discoveries *do* prove to be authentic, we'd still be accused of 'a master Jewish conspiracy' to undermine Christianity. Anti-Semitism would rear its vicious head, as it always does in times of crisis. All Jews beyond Israel would be in danger. Or, the opposite scenario—if we demonstrated that the finds were fraudulent, we'd be accused of a cover-up, with one monotheistic religion helping another. In either case, a no-win situation."

A general nodding of heads around the cabinet table heartened Jennings and Jon, for the logic was unimpeachable. Breitenstein paused briefly, then resumed: "The second objection is a simple question of expertise. Who would be more qualified to ferret out the truth in this business: those who dug from the start, or those who come in at the end? And if this affair is botched, or if Christianity really suffers, let me add an economic footnote to this discussion. Do you know how much income religious pilgrimage brings to the state of Israel? More than a billion dollars annually! Tourism ranks just after diamonds as our largest industry. If the pilgrims stop coming, our economy will be in even *worse* shape, if that's possible! And the balance-of-payments deficit will take on heroic proportions."

Silence blanketed the cabinet room, until Avram Heshbon said, "I withdraw my suggestion."

"Good, I agree," said the prime minister.

"May I have the floor, Mr. Prime Minister?" asked Jon.

"Certainly, Professor Weber."

"Professor Jennings and I have had some lengthy discussions on the most appropriate *modus operandi* here. Our plan is simple but, we hope, effective. First, we want to expedite the testing, and we'll announce the results as soon as the analysis is firm, unlike some archaeologists who take *years* to publish their results. We all remember the forty-year delay in the case of the Dead Sea Scrolls!

"Now, the week after next, I'll be driving down to El Arish and Cairo, so that I can fly Egyptair to the States and avoid the swarm of reporters waiting for us at Ben Gurion. I would ask your government's help in alerting your frontier post on the border to

wave us through. I'd also ask you to contact your Egyptian counterparts so that they permit similar courtesies at El Arish and Cairo
Airport."

"Yes . . . excellent," the prime minister observed. "We should
be able to arrange that."

"Then, when a *very* comprehensive series of tests has been
completed," Jon resumed, "our staff will publish the results, and
invite scrutiny by the world's scholarly community. We'll be providing a 'manual,' as it were, for specialists across the world to
ponder over the next months . . . or years. Let an international
consensus draw the final conclusions."

Zevulon nodded. "Good," he said. "And you have our sympathy, Professor Weber. If only you and Professor Jennings had been
left alone!"

"How very true, Mr. Prime Minister! Our task is now complicated. *Severely* complicated."

Several calls to Sandy McHugh resulted in a general "shopping list"
of what his panel at the Smithsonian required for the test series:

A. A complete file of all photographs ever taken at the villa
   and the cavern at Rama.
B. The two "Joseph" jar handles.
C. Another piece of the *titulus* parchment, including a
   quarter-inch incursion into one of the darker letters, and
   any of the wood rot backing.
D. More of the grave linens and matting.
E The two clay oil lamps.
F. The two flasks, now differentiated as F-1 (the
   unguentarium) and F-2 (the oil flask).
G. The juglet in which the papyrus was found.
H. The clay plug of the juglet.
I. Packets of material debris from inside the sarcophagus, its
   pit, the floor of the cavern, and the earth just outside the
   threshold.

Despite the length of the list, it was no massive cargo that Jon would smuggle into the United States, with the approval of all governments concerned. It all fit inside two fat attaché cases that were stuffed with cotton and foam rubber and lined with lead foil. Those valises would not leave his side until he was safely inside the Smithsonian in Washington.

Clive Brampton sat at the wheel, driving Jon to Cairo. The border between Israel and Egypt at El Arish, once the scene of fierce tank battles in the Sinai Desert, was now a tranquil tourists' crossover. The Israeli border guards waved them through, and the Egyptian frontier police detained them only momentarily. Above all, they eluded the world's press. No flashguns. No television minicams.

They filled the hot desert kilometers with chitchat about Jennings, Brampton providing a wealth of additional detail on the celebrated archaeologist. Now they reached the Suez Canal tunnel and then took the desert road to Cairo Airport, where they stayed overnight at the Sheraton.

The next morning, Clive saw Jon off. "You'd best wear those sunglasses Shannon bought you, Jon," said Clive, as he was about to drive off. "You're an international celebrity now, you know."

"Oh, beyond all doubt," Jon chuckled. "But you're part of the same constellation, Clive!"

"The desert hyenas are unimpressed."

"Give my love to Shannon. You knew her before I did—as an adult, that is. How could you fail to fall in love with her yourself?"

"Who says I didn't? But she was 'the boss's daughter,' so I fled for safety into the arms of Naomi. Still, well, I've never told you this, Jon, but I'm really glad you've replaced Ben-Yaakov in her life."

"Thanks for the vote of confidence, Clive. Take care on the return trip."

"I will. But put those shades on."

"Okay. . . . there. Do I look like Paul Newman?"

"More like Omar Sharif. He goes with this territory. Cheerio!"

While waiting for Egyptair's flight 201 to New York, Jon bought a copy of *The Cairo Telegraph*, Egypt's English-language daily.

He looked at the front-page feature and winced. "ISLAM NOW
THE WORLD'S LEADING RELIGION?" the header ran, just
over a photograph of Cairo's chief mullah, Muhammed Abu-
Bakkar, who was quoted as saying:

> Islam's views of the prophet Jesus are now a proven fact.
> Muhammed taught that Jesus of Nazareth was not a divinity who
> rose from the dead, but only a prophet like our fathers Abraham
> and Moses. It was the Christian heresy that sought to make him
> something more, bestowing on him the honors that belong to
> Allah alone. And now the very dust of the earth has proven the
> prophet correct! The recent discoveries in Israel will surely sound
> the death knell for Christianity as the world's largest religious sys-
> tem, opening the way for Islam to assume that role. With 2 billion
> adherents, Christianity had twice the following of Islam's 1 billion.
> But no longer, thanks to archaeologists Jennings and Weber and
> their discoveries several months ago.

Jon shivered, even in the boiling heat, as he climbed the ramp
onto the Egyptair 747. Now he had a new role: killer-of-
Christianity. Why had life lost its symmetry?

Having logged hundreds of thousands of flight miles, Jon had
long since abandoned any fear of flying. For the first time in years,
however, he wondered what would happen if the 747 packed it in
somewhere over the Mediterranean or Atlantic. Or terrorists continued their noble sport of "My bombs can slaughter more people
than yours can." His concern was less for himself and more for his
attaché cases and their curious contents: an assortment of objects
that were already changing the world's culture.

What if the stuff finally *did* prove genuine? What difference
would it make in his own life, Jon wondered, as the jet climbed
out over the Mediterranean. If Christianity became mortally
wounded, what about basic theism? Would it fall too? *Was* there
a God, after all? Or not? Planes did furnish a welcome oasis of
time, a good chance to think. Rather than thumb through a travel
magazine full of mummified pharaohs, Jon gazed out at the endless blue blanket of sea, nicely pockmarked by tufts of ivory

clouds. It was time to sort through his real beliefs . . . or doubts.

Why not begin as Descartes did? Doubt *everything*—not just God, but any so-called "reality"—space, time, material, his own existence, for that matter. *Not too convincing*, thought Jon. He was, after all, doubting and thinking. And so, like the French philosopher, he too had to agree: *Cogito, ergo sum* (I think, therefore I exist). And if he existed, as truly as the 747 he was flying in and all people aboard, then it could well follow from the argument of cause and design that there must be a supremely intelligent, powerful, and rational Being, since neither the jet nor its human cargo could be self-created or self-existent. In short, God exists. *Sum, ergo deus est* (I am, therefore God exists). Descartes had also affirmed that, and Aristotle long before him with his arguments for a First Cause. Creation intuits a Creator.

Or does it? Descartes had *not* said, *Malum est, ergo deus non est* (Evil exists, therefore God—at least a good, all-powerful God—does not exist). Once again, Jon was on the tenterhooks of the ultimate arguments pro and con Deity. Put simplistically, creation proves God; evil disproves.

He admitted that there were plenty of reasons to doubt God's existence: Andrea's death, evil and disaster in any form, the cruelties and periodic insanities of history, no contact with God through any of the five senses. *Those cheap evangelists on the tube or in the tent who claim regular conversations with God (in which He replied audibly) had to be hypocrites, liars, or blooming idiots*, thought Jon. *Yet why did their hearers, who heard no such voices, ever believe them? Or contribute to their support?*

But he was digressing. He had always finished the volleys of arguments pro and con God's existence with the same conclusion. *Until I can find another answer as to where I came from, I'll side with Deity.* Pascal's wager had never been disproven, namely: By all means, believe, because if you win (God exists), you win everything; if you lose (God doesn't exist), you lose nothing.

And, granting God's existence, Jon found Christianity equally credible; no other religious faith on earth had such strong historical and archaeological credentials. Unless, that is, archaeology and faith were about to part company.

The *Cleopatra,* flagship of Egyptair, dropped through scudding clouds over eastern Long Island, glided onto runway 31 Left at JFK, and taxied to its gate at the international terminal. While the jet turbines wound down their deepening dirge at being deprived of fuel and ignition, the voice of the chief steward filled all eighty speakers in the plane's PA system. "Attention, please: Will Mr. Ernst Becker please identify himself?"

"*Rats!*" Jon muttered. Ernst was his father's middle name, Becker his mother's maiden name, and it was his alias for tickets, for the "special" passport the American embassy had issued him, and for clear passage through customs by all governments concerned. He raised his hand. The steward walked over and said, "Please take all your belongings and follow me, Mr. Becker."

Jon grabbed his attaché cases and the garment bag he had stowed in a forward compartment and followed the steward to the exit. There, filling the doorway, stood a brute of a fellow with whitish, crew-cut hair and ruddy skin.

"Mr. Becker," said the hulk, "I'm George Tollefson, with the Central Intelligence Agency." He flashed his credentials. "Did you check any luggage?"

"No. I have everything here—"

"Fine. Then please put on those sunglasses and come with me. Here, let me carry your bag."

Convinced that he would fail miserably in the world of international espionage and intrigue, Jon sheepishly put on the glasses and let the CIA carry his garment bag. When they reached a secluded corridor, Tollefson stopped and confided, "The president would like to see you as soon as possible, Professor Weber. We have Air Force Two warmed up and waiting just outside this terminal."

"But . . . but I was simply going to take the shuttle to Wash—"

"Yes, yes, we know that. But we took the liberty of canceling your reservations in view of the developing crisis."

"Our discoveries in Israel?"

"More than that. The president will inform you, I'm sure. Now, we'll fly to Andrews Air Force Base, and one of the marine helicopters will shuttle us to the White House from there."

Jon studied the bluish carpet in the arrival lounge, scratched his head, and said, "Let's go."

There was a strange feeling of *déjà vu* about it all: the sleek 707 that had been Air Force One, carrying presidents and their parties in convenience-laden luxury; the dark-green chopper whirling down onto the White House lawn like a giant maple leaf; and the majestic façade of the White House itself. But such scenes had always come via the television evening news. Now, strangely, he himself was within the frames of those familiar backdrops.

By now it was almost midnight, Cairo time, but only late afternoon in Washington. He no longer looked like a savage, thanks to the shaving facilities in the president's former private restroom in the plane. He had even dared place his buns on the presidential padded toilet, recalling that this was his first cheek-to-cheek contact with any of America's chief executives. But now would come the more socially acceptable encounter. The door of the helicopter opened.

"What, no red carpet? No marine band?" Jon asked Tollefson, who only looked at him strangely. Then again, the CIA never was known for its sense of humor.

They were escorted westward to the Oval Office in the executive wing of the White House, where the dour Tollefson finally took his leave. Ushered inside by the president's secretary, Jon was greeted by The Man himself.

President Sherwood Bronson was a Republican from Michigan who had a bodily frame similar to JFK's, projected piety-in-the-presidency as did Jimmy Carter, and was a media master like Reagan or Bush in expounding the New Conservation that still held the nation in thrall. His rugged good looks reminded some of the man in the Marlboro ads, but without cigarettes and assorted livestock. Having ridden to power on his promise to balance the federal budget, "Woody" Bronson astonished the pundits by only moderately failing to achieve that utopian goal.

"Nice of you to drop in on us, Professor Weber," said the president, extending his hand.

Nice of you to have such a great sense of humor, thought Jon. What he said was, "Honored to meet you, Mr. President."

"I'm sure you recognize our secretary of state, Mr. MacPherson, and our secretary of defense, Mr. Hammar."

"Indeed. Glad to meet you, gentlemen."

"Please sit down, everyone," the president beckoned. "And please forgive us for this detour in your travel plans, Professor Weber, but we have something of a crisis on our hands. Scott, perhaps you'll be good enough to brief Dr. Weber?"

"Certainly, Mr. President," said MacPherson. "Shortly after your first press conference in Jerusalem, Dr. Weber, *Pravda* published a front-page editorial that—"

"*Pravda?!* Didn't they shut down years ago?"

"Of course. This is the first issue of what they call *Novaia Pravda . . . New Pravda.* Here, maybe you'd best read it first before we go any further." He handed Jon a photocopy of the original, along with English translation:

MARXISM IS VINDCATED AT LAST!

Communists across the world can now celebrate the truth of Karl Marx's statement that "Religion is the opiate of the masses." The discovery of the very bones of Jesus of Nazareth, announced in Jerusalem two weeks ago, proves that Christianity—the misguided faith of the majority in the decadent, counterrevolutionary, capitalist West—has no basis in fact. (The Christians have a myth that Jesus came back to life again after he died, and believers expect the same for themselves.)

Whereas the Christian church tries to hide the ills of the working classes with nebulous promises of how much better things will be in the "heaven" after death, Marxism has the honesty to inform workers that there is no "heaven," and that they must rather band together to improve their lot in this life, since it is the only life. We have made our advances through truth and collective effort, not through empty myths and promises, as has capitalist Christianity.

But now the world knows the truth. Socialism has been correct about religion all along. We now have a marvelous opportunity, comrades, to seize the present advantage and win the world back to the truth of Marxism-Leninism. "Workers of the world, unite! You have nothing to lose but your chains!" Even as these are the

last words in the *Communist Manifesto,* so we would now cry,
"People of the world, unite! You have nothing to lose but your
outmoded superstitions!"

"Incredible!" said Jon, when he had finished reading. "This
sounds like something straight out of the Cold War . . . certainly
not *glasnost, perestroika,* and the new Russia. Is anybody buying
this rot?"

MacPherson smiled wanly and replied, "A cabal of diehard
communists in Moscow is trying to orchestrate this into a campaign to regain control of Russia, then the former Soviet
republics, and then the world. The Russian ambassador to the
UN seems to be coming down on *their* side! He delivered a major
address in the General Assembly a couple of days after this
appeared. The neutrals, the Afro-Asians, and the Third-World
bloc were very impressed. They disagree with the atheistic part of
this campaign, of course, but they have no great love for
Christianity because they favor their own native religions instead.
And now we have a new wind of anti-Westernism blowing across
the globe."

"But this isn't the new Russia!" Jon objected. "It's just *not*
Rozomov's style!"

"You're right, and it's not *his* doing. He's still on a long state
visit to North Korea, but he may well get booted out of power
when he gets back. *If* he gets back. This all broke while he was
gone. It's the work of disgruntled diehards in the KGB, the military, and Stalinist apparatchiks in the Kremlin who are much better organized this time than they were during their fizzled coup
against Gorbachev some years ago. They've never forgiven Gorby
for losing eastern Europe, and now they're madly trying to use
Rama to breathe new life into the corpse of communism."

"Those ding-bing hardliners will exploit any and every weakness they can manage to find in the West," the president added.
"The old-guard red ratfinks did it to us every time they could
years ago. And now those bleeding Neanderthals seem to be taking on new life."

Jon noted that Bronson seemed to have attended the Richard

Nixon School of Rhetoric. Then Jon asked, "What's the mood here in the States?"

"We have nothing less than a *morale* crisis here," said President Bronson. "Church attendance is plummeting, worship services are getting disrupted—people cursing the clergy for misleading them—and every atheist or freethinker on the block is screaming, 'We told you so!' at the top of his effing lungs. Not a day passes that we don't get a horror story. Like last Sunday: the cardinal archbishop of New York is celebrating the Mass at St. Patrick's Cathedral, and one of his parishioners throws the wafer back in his face as she cries, 'Enough of this sham!' and stalks out."

Harold S. Hammar, the secretary of defense, joined in. "We all have our personal horror stories, Dr. Weber. My uncle was a missionary in Mozambique. He'd worked there twenty years for *three* converts. A week ago, my aunt found him hanging from a banyan tree in the jungle. His suicide note read: 'All for Jesus, the Great Deceiver. All for nothing! Forgive me, Sarah'!"

Jon clenched his teeth and shook his head. "This is all *premature . . . ridiculously* premature!"

"Yes, but meanwhile, the Church—and maybe the country— seem to be going to the warm place in a handbasket," said the president. "And that's not all. Harold, tell him the rest."

Hammar cleared his throat. "The old guard in Moscow seems to be doing more than just cackling over our crisis. One of their idealogues quoted Sun Tzu of ancient China, who said something like: 'Fighting on the battlefield is stupid. The highest art of warfare is not to fight at all, but to subvert your enemy's culture. Then, when he is demoralized, destabilized, confused, you may strike.' We think they'll use this crisis to try to pull a Sun Tzu on the West—America in particular—*if* they win out in Russia."

Jon shook his head. Never had he anticipated a *political* fallout from Rama. Then he said, "Well, gentlemen, I . . . much appreciate this update. But how am *I* involved in all this? What can I do?"

It was the president who responded. "To make a long story short, Dr. Weber, we'd like to know how long it'll take for you archaeologists and scholars to come to some conclusions on this thing. America and the Western world are in suspense and pain.

Personally, I'm a practicing Methodist, and I feel like the very heart's being ripped out of my faith. Now, *if* your discoveries do test out authentic, then we'll just have to try and rebuild one way or another. Maybe the liberal theologians will have some ideas. Haven't they been telling us for years that it'd make no difference to the faith if Jesus's bones *were* discovered? Or, better yet, if your finds prove to be a hellish hoax, we ought to know that as soon as humanly possible so that we can go back to the business of being a great nation. At the moment, there's panic and malaise in the air. So *when*, I ask, will you know?"

Jon took a deep breath and said, "Well, gentlemen, I owe you an update too." He then gave them a synopsis of all tests projected, and when they hoped to have the final results. He also put his two attaché cases on the president's desk and opened their lids to identify some of the ceramic pieces, explaining the tests for each.

The president and the two secretaries stared at them without saying a word.

"So this is the bric-a-brac that's tearing our world apart!" the president finally muttered. "I'd love to smash those knickknacks beyond recognition. All right, Dr. Weber, tell me this: Is there *any* way our government can assist you in the tests? Or otherwise?"

Jon thought for a moment, but then shook his head. "No. Beyond greasing the rails with customs for my return flight to Israel, the government should give us a wide berth. Otherwise, the world would suspect political intrusion."

"All right," said the president. "But you *will* get those tests under way as soon as possible, won't you?"

"Certainly."

As they were all leaving the Oval Office, the president caught Jon's arm and asked him to stay for a moment. Shutting the door behind him, Bronson said, "I just *have* to get a better handle on the probabilities here so I can try to guide the ship of state through some heavy weather. If necessary. At this point in your investigation, and on a scale of one to ten for authenticity—ten being absolutely genuine—how do you rate your discoveries as of now?"

Jon wrinkled his brow, opened his arms, and said, "I really wish I could answer that question, but—"

"Come on, man! This is for my ears only. You'll never be quoted."

"But—"

"Is it a nine or ten?"

"No."

"An eight?"

"Well . . . no."

"A seven?"

"Well . . . no comment."

"I see you've learned to speak government language!" Bronson chuckled. Then he grew serious and said, "I hope you'll work as hard as you can to . . . ah . . . demonstrate a fraud or hoax here, Dr. Weber. The stakes are enormous, I'm sure you realize. You'd be doing your country a favor—an enormous service—if you could end this nightmare by blowing the whistle on these discoveries of yours. Would to God you'd never opened the ground over there!"

"Yes. I've often thought the same thing."

Now the president took his arm and almost whispered. "Dr. Weber, may I call you Jonathan?"

"Certainly. But make it 'Jon'."

"Fine, Jon. Now, wouldn't it be possible for you to . . . couldn't you see your way clear to . . . *find* something wrong with those artifacts of yours?" He pointed to the two attaché cases. "That really would cut the Gordian knot. The world, certainly the Christian world, really *wants* to believe in their resurrected Lord—"

"What are you saying? Are you suggesting that I . . . *falsify* the evidence?"

"Now, Jon, I . . . didn't say that. But if you chose to assign, let's say, maximum weight to any possible flaw in your evidence, the Western world and certainly the whole Christian church on earth would be in your debt."

"I've been searching for any flaws, I can assure you, Mr. President. But I intend to remain deadly honest in dealing with the evidence. The stakes are too high, too incredibly high."

"I know . . . I know." The president wrung his hands and now started pacing the Oval Office. Then he stopped, looked at Jon, and said, "And yet it's been said that no one approaches any project,

anything . . . with total neutrality, without *some* bias. I only hope
your modicum of bias inclines in the proper direction."

"It does, Mr. President. And let me prove that. If this were *any*
other excavation, *any* other discovery, we wouldn't have bothered
with all these additional tests."

"Why not?"

"Because the circumstantial . . . the surrounding evidence is
overpowering. The ceramic typology, the paleography, the
anthropology, and the radiocarbon tests are also overpowering.
We'd probably have rated all this *a solid ten* some time ago!"

"My God!"

"Exactly."

President Sherwood Bronson hung his head over drooping
shoulders as he looked down at his desk for some moments. Then
he pulled out a card and wrote on it. "Here, Jon. This is my private phone number. It bypasses the White House switchboard.
Call me the moment you have your test results. Will you do that
for me?"

"Yes, certainly."

"One of the limousines will take you wherever you wish. Send
us any expenses. Ah . . . I'd ask you to dinner, but we're due at
the French Embassy this evening. Another time?"

"Another time. Thank you, Mr. President."

SEVENTEEN

The White House limousine delivered Jon to the address he had specified in Georgetown. Sandy McHugh wouldn't hear of his staying at a hotel, though Jon did have one proviso: that evening, when he would be fighting jet lag, they would simply enjoy themselves, sipping the margaritas for which Sandy was famous. Maybe for one night only they could forget Rama and its tyranny over their lives. Sandy cheerfully indulged the scheme—his wife and children were visiting her parents in Philadelphia—and that evening he recited so many ribald limericks that Jon, already punchy from jet lag, was reduced to tears of laughter.

But it was all business the next morning. McHugh had assembled a panel of twenty of the nation's foremost scientists at the Smithsonian, and he introduced each of them and their specialties. Jon now unloaded his attaché cases onto the large, mahogany conference table, explained each item, and passed the photographs around for all to study. Next he gave a color slide presentation of the Rama dig that focused on the cavern area and its artifacts, after which he detailed the carbon 14 tests that had already taken place in Israel and Arizona. Then he fielded technical questions from the scholarly specialists.

After a break for lunch, they reached a consensus on testing procedures. "As to the specific samples," Sandy announced to the group, "we've agreed on the following schedules. Let me read the list again so that we all concur:

> For the *two jar handles* inscribed "to Joseph": magnification survey of the inscribed seals to determine if they were fashioned by ancient or modern tools, followed by optical emission and X-ray

fluorescence spectrometry, neutron activation analysis, and thermo-luminescence, to determine the age from kiln firing.

The *two oil lamps, unguentarium, oil flask, juglet,* and *clay plug:* ditto the above, omitting the inscription survey.

The *"titulus" parchment:* pollen analysis, texture analysis via electron microscopy, pigment/ink analysis of a small portion of one of the letters.

And thanks for allowing us *that,* Jon!"

"I had a choice?" he chuckled. "I regret it, but it has to be done. Otherwise, critics would point to it as the big chink in our testing procedure."

"Absolutely. We've also agreed to do a PIXE on the ink."

"What's that?" Jon wondered.

"Particle Induced X-ray Emission Analysis. That procedure's particularly useful for very small samples. We've used it to test for metal oxides in the ink of the Gutenberg Bible, for example."

"Superb! Can it tell the age?"

"Unfortunately, no. Most of these tests, except for thermo-luminescence, are merely analyses, but they've spotted as many forgeries as C-14 by finding traces of elements *not* used at the time claimed—Yale's notorious Vinland map, for example. So, if we find any iron oxides in the ink or pigment, we'll suspect forgery, since pure carbon inks were the norm then."

"Well, you *could* find some copper too," Jon replied. "In the Dead Sea Scrolls, the earlier ones used pure carbon-based inks, but the later ones show some copper."

"We'll bear that in mind," Sandy commented, then resumed reading the schedule:

The *wooden backing* of the *"titulus":* ditto procedures for the parchment.

The *grave linen* and *matting materials:* ditto, with special emphasis on pollen analysis.

The *bronze coin:* optical emission and atomic absorption spectrometry, and neutron activation analysis for metallurgical assay and comparison with similar bronze coins of known authenticity.

The *four debris packets:* separation of materials, quantitative and qualitative analysis of ingredients, further testing as deemed necessary.

"Does that about cover it?"

All nodded.

"Some of these tests will be done elsewhere, of course," Sandy concluded. "After we're through with the pottery, for example, we'll take it to the Museum Applied Center for Archaeology at the University of Pennsylvania, since they have the finest thermoluminescence laboratory in the country."

The late fall symposium of the Institute of Christian Origins convened in Cambridge, Massachusetts, as usual, but this time the one and only theme on its agenda was Rama. Jon provided a comprehensive report on the dig, including video footage Cromwell had fortuitously shot. Dick himself was also in attendance, en route back to Israel, and he assured Jon that he had *not* left the papyrus prints lying exposed in his darkroom.

"Are you *sure*, Dick?" asked Jon.

"Absolutely! And I *did* lock the darkroom before flying to the States."

Jon frowned, drummed his fingers on the dais, and then asked, "Who else has a key to the darkroom?"

"Oh, gosh! I guess most of the senior staff members there do."

"*I* don't."

"Well, you're a Johnny-come-lately!"

They tittered briefly and moved on to the second part of the conclave, which was a report back to Jon on how the nation and the world were reacting to Rama. All symposium members wanted to speak at once, it seemed, and Jon listened to them one by one, each offering a colorful or lurid or tragic piece of a panorama entitled "Crisis."

"So, the spectrum looks something like this," said Jon, when they had finished. He stood up and wrote from right to left on a blackboard, Hebrew style:

LIBERAL LEFT	MODERATE LEFT	CENTRIST	CONSERVATIVE RIGHT	ULTRAORTHODOX RIGHT
Full acceptance with no concern	Some acceptance with much concern	(Mainline churches) Very troubled response with much shock	(Evangelicals) Terrified rejection, but anxiety that Rama could prove authentic	(Fundamentalists) Horrified rejection and open hostility

"Give me some further examples of the extreme left," Jon asked.

Heinz von Schwendener, the renowned New Testament scholar from Yale, replied, "Well, you recall those theologians who've been claiming that the discovery of Jesus's bones wouldn't surprise them?"

"Yes."

"Well, they're now issuing genteelly worded 'I-told-you-so' statements in seven languages. And, of course, way-out sorts like Harry Nelson Hunt are claiming that your discovery really favors the *conservatives,* Jon."

"How in the world?"

"Because it proves that there *was* a historical human being named Jesus after all! Hunt had his doubts."

"Predictable. All right, colleagues, you've reported on the theology out there. Give me a little more on the grass roots. Anecdotal stuff."

Jon almost wished he hadn't asked. A potpourri, prepared in hell, seemed to boil over in tales told by symposium members: a country parson so choked up in his pulpit that he collapsed and died halfway through his sermon. Trappist monks who had taken a vow of silence now screaming their disillusionment. Fall registration at seminaries and divinity schools down a catastrophic 85 percent as trend pundits promised they would close altogether, along with monasteries and convents. Futurologists predicting the conversion of empty churches into restaurants or beer halls. Suicides, mental and moral breakdowns, vastly increased crime, and the reduction of world Christianity to cult status.

"Enough!" Jon threw up his hands. "For my money, the most tragic thing I've heard this afternoon is how the dying had the hope of the Resurrection torn away from them when they needed

it most. But we've got to move on. The third part of this symposium has the elegantly phrased theme, 'Where Do We Go from
Here?' We're open to suggestions."

What followed was the liveliest debate in the annals of the
ICO. The conference room rattled with suggestions, counter-
suggestions, and passionate exchange. Late in the afternoon, however, a consensus developed. The Smithsonian test series would be
of critical importance, obviously, but they also worked out a master contingency plan pending the results. Jon endorsed it enthusiastically, but all members swore to keep the plan confidential.

To brighten the mood, just before closing the session, Jon asked,
"What's the most *inane* reaction any of you have come across to
date? I mean, something really off-the-wall."

Katrina Vandersteen, professor of Semitic paleography at Johns
Hopkins, raised her pencil. "I give you the case of one Maharishi
Yogananda, a guru at a commune near Monterey, California. He
claims that your dig has now proven the truth of *Hinduism*, Jon!"

"*How*, for goshsakes?!"

"Well, it's true, isn't it?" she teased with a twinkle in her eye.
"What's the chant you hear from those bald sorts in peach robes
wandering our airports? '*Hare Krishna, Hare Krishna . . . Hare
Rama, Hare Rama.*' Well, the Maharishi claims that the very name
of your dig, which has just 'buried Christianity,' exalts Rama, who
is Lord over all!"

The symposium rocked with laughter, and they got up to leave.
Suddenly the door flew open and a small, slender man with thin-
ning white hair stormed into the conference room, slamming the
door behind him. He stalked over to Jon and glared at him.

"Well, hello, Mr. Nickel," said Jon. "We're delighted to see you!"

Joshua Scruggs Nickel was clearly in furious fettle. He opened his
mouth and roared, "*Why* wasn't I notified of this meeting today?"

"I'd intended to give you a résumé during our appointment
tomorrow morning, Mr. Nickel, as in our previous meetings. I didn't
think you wanted to sit through all the technical discussions."

"You assumed wrong! Especially when our faith is at stake!"

"Well, you know you're always more than welcome at—"

"Hear me, all of you!" Nickel cut him off. "I provided the

seed money for this Institute, and the seeds were pretty big, as I recall: an endowment of *five million dollars!* The purpose of the ICO—at least as *I* saw it—was to explore ever more deeply the story of how our Lord and His holy apostles founded the Church and sent it out to conquer the world in His name. You were supposed to provide fresh data about Christ's life and ministry. And for a while you succeeded. I was quite satisfied with your book, Jonathan."

He now took another step toward Jon and, emphasizing his words with one long finger, said, "But now you've overturned everything you've achieved! Instead of the *proofs* for the *truth* of Christianity you were supposed to supply, you've plunged a terrible dagger into the very *heart* of our faith! When I first learned of your horrible discoveries I was going to send you a wire, Jonathan, but I couldn't find the words. I *still* can't find the words . . . other than to say that this is a . . . a treacherous way to reward my investment in you . . . in you all. In place of truth, you're supplying deceit and *fraud!*"

The little man quaked with fury, his gray eyes filmed with tears, and his wrinkled skin took on an apoplectic red. Jon tried to calm him. "Please, Mr. Nickel, take a seat and let's—"

"Let me quote from Psalm 1, which *I*, at any rate, still regard as the Word of God. 'Blessed is the man who *sits not in the seat of scoffers.*' No, I shan't sit down, Jonathan. And now let me tell you my plans for the ICO. I'm cutting off the annual subsidy of $250,000 I've been providing you, effective immediately, and I will seek legal counsel about retrieving my original endowment!"

A vein throbbed visibly in the middle of his forehead, and Jon feared the man might suffer a stroke. "*Please*, Mr. Nickel," he pleaded, "can't we discuss this over dinner tonight?"

"No, my mind's made up. In fact, only one thing could change it."

"What's that?"

"If you go on record as admitting that you must have been *duped*, Jonathan. And I'd also want the ICO to denounce the Rama 'finds' as a devilish fraud, which you all intend to expose by further research."

"But that's just the point, Mr. Nickel," Jon protested. "We've just laid out the most comprehensive plans to continue research on possible fraud."

"Yet, in the meantime, you're poisoning the world with evidence that seems to *affirm* this fraud. As the discoverer, one word from you that this must all be a fake would help to calm the world and save the Church."

"I can't do that, Mr. Nickel. That would go against the principles of sound scholarship. And honesty."

Nickel glared at Jon several moments more, then at the entire symposium. "Very well, ladies and gentlemen," he now sliced out his syllables. "My support for the ICO is at an end!" He whipped about and left the room.

The symposium sat stunned for some moments until von Schwendener said, "I move that from here on we all donate our time. And that we also help raise alternate funding for the ICO."

"Hear! Hear!" many sounded. The rest applauded.

The motion passed unanimously.

The remaining days of November and early December were not his own, Jon soon discovered. While trying to coordinate the work of the ICO—now fiscally threatened—and consult with Sandy McHugh on the progress of the test series, he had all he could do to dictate answers to the huge stacks of mail that had accumulated during his absence. But he and his word-processing prodigy of a secretary, Marylou Kaiser, worked up twenty different letters in the computer's memory that covered almost 90 percent of the correspondence, including cancellations of a host of speaking engagements that had been on Jon's docket before Rama exploded.

Yet the hardest task, by far, was fending off the broadcast media and the press. Reporters had dogged him constantly, ever since some enterprising cub drove into the rolling countryside west of Cambridge and did a stakeout at his home in Weston. If it wasn't the media, it was the maniacs. Police had to put regular patrols in his neighborhood after some madman smashed a spear through his window, claiming he was the prophet Elijah sent to skewer the Antichrist.

No, he had a harder task yet—surviving without Shannon. She had sent a booklet of love poems she had composed for him and illustrated with sketches of their favorite haunts in Galilee. Jon, ordinarily a prosy sort, thought the verses unspeakably beautiful, and wondered what it was about poetry that made it *the* medium of communication for love. One incandescent chapter, entitled "Our Love Is . . . ," was followed by burning descriptives on pages that followed, the first being "Eternal." Its definition, "I will love you until the ends of earth and time," brought tears to his eyes and only enlarged the hollow ache that gripped him from the brushing of teeth in the morning to the shedding of shoes at night. He missed her more than he thought possible. *A packed schedule should have dulled the emptiness,* he thought, *but it had not.* Unintentionally he had been conducting his own test of attachment to the girl, and those results were in. It was true love, and more. Yet the English language had no word for it.

He told her as much in torrid overseas calls, pleading for her to fly to Boston so they could spend the Christmas holidays together. He had to stay in the States because the test series was almost concluded. While sharing his need, she felt she could hardly leave her father, who seemed exhausted in the aftermath of all the excitement. "I love you more than I can ever express, my darling," she added. "*Do* spend Christmas with your folks in Missouri. But then *hurry* back!"

Jon's jet landed at Lambert Field in St. Louis on Christmas morning, and he booked a rental for the ninety-mile drive north to Hannibal. It was 9:30 AM, and if he sped up Highway 61, he'd make it just in time for his father's 11 AM service at St. John Lutheran Church. His visit would be a surprise—possibly an unwelcome one. Rama's tentacles reached everywhere.

Blowing snow mixed with sleet delayed him, and when he arrived at the very church where he'd been baptized and confirmed, he slipped into one of the back pews as surreptitiously as possible, since the congregation was already singing the final verse of the pre-sermon hymn. Jon recalled that, when he was a boy, Christmas and Easter were the record-attendance days, and he was startled to find the church half empty. Perhaps the sleet had something to do with that. Or perhaps a certain excavation in Israel.

Was the figure in the wheat-colored alb who mounted the pulpit really his father? It was two years since he had seen him last, but the Reverend Erhard Weber seemed to have aged at least ten. The salt-and-pepper hair was now all salt. The full rectangular face was now trapezoidal due to sunken cheeks, and a pallor clouded his features. Mercifully, though, his voice was the same, and he began his sermon in firm tones, though with a sad pun:

It seems more of a *wary* than a merry Christmas. The world is asking the Church if it intends to celebrate this year. Two thousand years ago, wise men came from the East to worship the baby Jesus. But now we have "wise men" from the West denying the very heart of the Christian faith! Doubts, not angels, hover over Bethlehem, as modern-day Herods would seek again to kill the infant Christ—

Jon squirmed uncomfortably, wondering how his father would greet him after the service—as Jonathan, Herod, or Judas? He always did have a way with words.

Now the Reverend Weber continued:

The text I've chosen may not sound very Christmasy, but I hope you'll find it appropriate all the same—Matthew 24:23–24, where Jesus tells His disciples, *"If any one says to you, 'Lo, here is the Christ!' or 'There he is!' do not believe it. For false Christs and false prophets will arise."* I truly believe that this prophecy is being fulfilled at the present moment, my fellow believers. They're telling us that what's left of Jesus Christ is somewhere in Israel, but, as our Lord told us, *do not believe it!*

Once again, Jon shifted uneasily in the back pew, and quickly donned his shaded glasses so no one would recognize the "false prophet" in their midst. But suddenly the man in the pulpit brightened, even smiled, as he said:

No, my Trudi and I plan to celebrate Christmas! We'll sing with the angels, worship with the shepherds, adore with the Magi! No matter what my own son or any other archaeologist *thinks* he may have discovered in Israel, they'll *never be able to take Christ out of Christmas!*

The rest of the sermon was less polemical and more seasonal, but Jon still felt he should not embarrass his father by waiting in line at the church door to greet him after the service. He slipped out of St. John when his father stepped down from the pulpit.

The sleet had stopped, and the sky was brightening. But with awful reciprocity, Jon's own mood was darkening. He took a walk down to the Mississippi waterfront he had loved and haunted as a boy. Sauntering onto a rickety old dock, he leaned against a mooring post, and stared at the icy gray waters tumbling and foaming their way to New Orleans before they froze. So this is what he, Jennings, and the team were doing to church life at the grass roots . . . and likely across the world. Good Lord, maybe they should have gotten a bulldozer and heaped tons of dirt on that corner of the dig rather than causing an international crisis. His own father all but disowning him in public. It had come to that.

He looked at the hill-topped island in the middle of the Mississippi he had explored so often as a lad, the land of Tom Sawyer, Huckleberry Finn, and Mark Twain. *How Sam Clemens would have cackled over the present crisis,* Jon mused. Aside from Twain's rollicking humor and razor wit, there was also that bitter, antireligious side to Hannibal's most famous son, as witness his *Letters from the Earth.*

And maybe Mark Twain was right, Jon finally had to admit to himself. And not only Twain, but all of liberal theology, which had been denying a physical resurrection of Jesus ever since David Strauss and Ernst Renan did so in nineteenth-century Germany and France. Yes, maybe all the higher critics, particularly Rudolf Bultmann, were right all along. The Resurrection never happened, but it was the *faith and belief* that it did that was important. And all his conservative, Lutheran Church—Missouri Synod Sunday school and Bible classes, and all the endless sermons . . . wrong!

Yet if this were truth, and if truth were liberating, why did he feel such gloom? And why was he so restlessly anticipating Sandy McHugh's promised phone call on Monday? And where would he take that call, now that he no longer intended to visit his parents?

Jon ambled off the wharf, wrapped his scarf more tightly to block a frigid blast from the north, and headed briskly back to his rent-a-car. He had driven only six miles back toward St. Louis on Highway 61 when he told the steering wheel, "This is some *stupid* way to celebrate Christmas!"

Braking onto the shoulder, he engineered a U-turn across the median, nearly slid off the other shoulder, spun his wheels just in time, and headed back to Hannibal. "Let's see if Mother will serve Sunday chicken and cherry pie to a heretic."

His opening line was predictable: "Hello, Dad. Your prodigal son has returned." The Reverend Erhard Weber was stunned only momentarily, and then threw his arms around Jon. His mother openly wept for joy as she hugged him. "O Jonathan, my Jonathan, you've *finally* returned."

"Sorry I haven't stayed in better touch, Mom. You know the situation—"

"Of course, of course!" She was instantly crestfallen. But soon the slender, graying woman with patrician features and twinkling blue eyes revived and served up Sunday dinner in the grand old style Jon had missed for years.

He spent much of the afternoon with his father, listening to how America was responding to Rama. "Oh, Jon, you can't believe what's happening to our beloved church. And the other churches, for that matter! Pastors are leaving the ministry, congregations are leaving their pastors, seminaries are closing down. And the agnostics and the atheists are howling their 'See? We were right' line. Four A—the American Association for the Advancement of Atheism—has revived . . . well, not only revived, but its membership is exploding. Oh, and, of course, every liberal theologian in the country is crowing, even in the Bible Belt."

"What's been the Jewish response?" Jon wondered.

"Restraint. Admirable restraint. I think, though, that some

Jewish leaders may feel that a great opportunity is opening for them. They're ready to declare that atheism is *not* a proper response to this crisis, and that Judaism may well be."

"Understandable! You can't blame them for that, though it's still too premature." There was that adjective again. Jon was beginning to hate it.

"Rabbi Judah Weiss at Hebrew Union in Cincinnati made a telling comment. He said, 'Christianity became vulnerable the moment it claimed that God took on flesh in the person of Jesus. Judaism has never exposed itself that way. Only God is God. No one else.'"

Jon nodded. "By the way, how's the 'electronic church' dealing with this?"

"The TV evangelists? They're basket cases! You'd think they'd have learned from the Jim Bakker affair, or the Jimmy Swaggart scandals, but no, one's worse than the next."

"You mean they're in a panic? Flaking out? Giving up the faith?"

His father smiled. "No, not giving up the faith, but yes, 'flaking out,' as you put it. They're more hysterical than ever with all their sensationalism and showmanship. Oh, they'll 'save' the faith for sure, and right over Jesus's dead body." He suddenly winced and whispered, "I can't believe I said that."

"What's Melvin Morris Merton saying?"

"You mean 'Millennial Mel'? 'Three M's for the Master'? He's the worst of the lot. End-of-the-world pronouncements . . . 'Touch your TV set so we can hold hands in prayer!' . . . 'Send for my prayer cloths!' . . . '*Heal! Heal!*' . . . 'Sell what you have and send me some of the proceeds for this great crisis!' Why, you're the best thing that ever happened to that scoundrel, Jon! Although," he chuckled, "he's quite sure you're either the Antichrist or his First Lieutenant. Not a show of his goes by that he doesn't rebuke the evil spirits inside you and Professor Jennings. In fact, he wants to perform an exorcism on you in Israel. Atop the Mount of Olives, no less!"

"Oh? *He's* the con artist who needs the exorcism, and I'd *pound* the devil out of that bilious geek if he ever laid a finger on me!"

"I feel the same way about any leech who tries to profit from the crisis, Jon, and many of them are. Maybe you don't see it so much in New England, but ever since cable hit the rest of the country, we're bombarded with *sleazy* Christianity on some of the channels not only every day, but some of them are on twenty-four hours a day with their *terrible* perversions of the gospel. Down South you even have to fight with the remote on the TV to find good old secular programs. 'Cause everything in between will be some Elmer Gantry haranguing his viewers to send in cash for Christ, often with some painted queen at his side, whooping it up with equally moronic studio audiences fawning on their every word. And talk about taking the holy name of Christ in vain! These birds are masters at it. 'Give generously, my brothers and sisters! *Sacrifice* for the Savior, and *JEEEZZUSS* will bless you!'"

Jon was delighted to find his father in such rare form. Obviously, neither Rama nor age had dimmed his mental powers. "But how're the TV pirates handling our dig?" Jon asked.

"Tell you in a moment. I'm not finished with that ilk. And what passes for *music* on those shows! Some overripe soprano will warble away about how Jesus has cured her hot flashes, or a chorus of exploited kids from their college—they *all* have colleges now, you know, status symbols. Anyway, the kids will sing their hearts out in order to touch yours . . . or put the touch on your wallet! And the come-ons—'Let me send you my latest booklet, *Jesus Told Me When the World Will End!*'

"Whatever happened to the cross? To responsible preaching? To Bach or Handel for that matter? As a Christian minister, I'm embarrassed before the whole world if *this* is the faith!"

"Calm down, Erhard!" Jon's mother called from the kitchen. "Your sermon should have ended in church!"

He smiled and called back, "I know, I know, Trudi. But now to your question, Jonathan. Yes, the worst of these television 'apostles' *are* exploiting the crisis. And, come to think of it, Mel Morton isn't the worst. For my money, the worst is a bearded freak from Alabama who dresses in some outfit from *Star Wars* and whips his audiences into frenzies with a gargling sort of drawl. Lately he's been opening each of his programs with painted portraits of you and Professor Jennings. '*Heeyah* are the whelps of Antichrist!' he bellows. '*Ah do rebuke, ah do condemn you in the name of the Faahhthuh*'—he then lets fly with a dart into each of your portraits—'*and of the Suuhn*'—another pair of darts— '*and of the Holy Speerut!*' And the studio audience goes wild. Yes, he's the absolute pits, but Mel Morton has far and away the biggest following, which is why they *had* to have him as one of the panelists on the special this evening."

"What special?"

"The CBS special. 'Christianity in Crisis,' they're calling it. CBS cancelled *60 Minutes* tonight—they hardly ever do that—for a two-hour special. The first half is supposed to be a documentary on your dig, and the second will be a panel of—"

"Oh, the one Marty Marty's going to chair? Yes, I remember now. They wanted me on the panel, but I couldn't clear it. That's tonight?"

"Yup. They're tying it into Christmas, of course. CBS has given it a tremendous promotion. Probably half the country will be watching."

After the matriarch of the manse had served his favorite Sunday supper, Jon sat down with his parents in the living room to watch the show. Dan Rather hosted the documentary segment, which featured background footage from the Rama dig and Jon's first press conference in Jerusalem.

"My, you look handsome, son," his mother purred. "But who's that *very* lovely girl sitting just behind you?"

"That's Shannon Jennings, Professor Jennings's daughter." Just the sight of her on the tube made Jon take a deep breath. "I intend to marry her."

"*What?!*" she cried. "Did you hear that, Erhard?"

"Shhhhh! Yes, I did. *Great* news, son! But look, they're interviewing world leaders now."

The United States president, the Canadian and British prime ministers, and other Western chiefs of state all warned that no one should draw hasty conclusions from not-yet-completed investigations. "I'll drink to that!" said Jon, as his father brought in a couple of cold beers from the refrigerator.

World religious leaders were then interviewed, the pope affirming: "Not for a moment *did* I think, *do* I think, or *will* I think that the bones discovered in Israel are those of Jesus!" The Archbishop of Canterbury, the Berlin bishop who was head of the Lutheran World Federation, and the president of the World Alliance of Reformed Churches expressed similar sentiments, though without use of the future tense.

Response from the non-Western world, however, was somewhat different. The Russian president was much more diplomatic than the original—and now much-quoted—*New Pravda* editorial. Looking into the CBS camera permitted inside the Kremlin, Arkady Rozomov sat at his desk and said, through an interpreter:

> I should like to greet my American friends during your Christmas festival. We also sympathize with you on the problems that have developed by the discovery of what may be Jesus's remains in Israel. While it is not our place to comment on this, we would urge that you be open to new spiritual directions, if necessary. Let Nature and Science, Logic and Goodwill be the props for our future, not what may be mistaken opinions of the past. And now join us in a worldwide celebration of Father Frost and the beautiful New Year he has in store for us. And so I say to all of you, not "Merry Christmas," but "*S Novom Godom!*"—"Happy New Year!"

"Thank God Rozomov won the power struggle inside the Kremlin!" said Jon, raising his beer can in salute to the screen. His mother, however, was dabbing her eyes with a handkerchief. Jon did not ask why. He wondered for how many other millions in the world the new symbol for Christmas was not the shepherds or the Magi, the manger or star—but the question mark. And what would Sandy McHugh say in the morning?

No commercials had interrupted the program until the first hour had passed. Then IBM provided a very tasteful one, although it was lost on that half of America taking a bathroom break.

And now the camera zoomed in on the smallish, balding genius who was Dr. Martin E. Marty. Deemed the most influential figure in American Christianity after Billy Graham, Marty digested and interpreted more articles and books on the current state of the Church than anyone on the planet. Some claimed that God himself subscribed to Marty's *Context* newsletter in order to stay fully informed, although Marty always denied this—a little wistfully, some thought. He now opened, in his piping tenor voice:

> Good evening, ladies and gentlemen. We've assembled here a panel of commentators on the recent archaeology in Israel, and I'm only sorry that Professor Jonathan Weber couldn't be here also. To my extreme left, but at the extreme right on your screens, in accord with his theology, is the Reverend Dr. Melvin M. Merton, who represents the most conservative segment of today's Christianity. Next to me is the man for whom any introduction is redundant, Dr. Billy Graham. To my right, your left, is the Roman Catholic archbishop of New York, the Most Reverend Patrick Cardinal O'Neill. And finally Dr. Thomas Aquinas Avery, professor of Systematic Theology at Union Theological Seminary in New York.

"Oh, great!" said Jon's father, ruefully. "They have 'Doubting Thomas' Avery on the program. He'll be sure to celebrate what you've found, Jon. Or claim to have found."

Marty continued:

> Gentlemen, the excavations at Rama in Israel have been the central story in all the media for the past months. Tonight, we'd ask you to comment on the possible *implications* of this discovery, rather than on questions of its authenticity, which is still being decided. The implications, of course, rest entirely on the authenticity, and if Rama proves to be a fraud, we've all been exploited. But our question this evening is this: "What would be the impact on the Christian faith *if* the discoveries should prove to be authentic?" First, Dr. Merton.

Easily the most studied showman on the panel, Melvin M. Merton—a black-haired, deep-jowled, ham-fisted, pulpit-pounder—gave a bravura performance, attacking the Israeli finds, and the finders, with caustic wit. Jonathon Weber was another Charles Dawson, who had foisted a new version of the "Piltdown man" hoax upon a gullible world. "The Spirit of Antichrist has returned," Merton announced, grandly. He continued:

The book of Revelation tells us that Antichrist shall sit in the very Temple of God. We've always understood that to mean a new Temple in Jerusalem. But, after much study of the Bible, and after a special revelation from *Jesus* Himself several weeks ago—which is too holy to describe to mortal ears—I'm now sure that "Antichrist sitting in the Temple" means "the ultimate attack on Christ in the very heart of the Church." These archaeologists, then, applauded by our agnostic church leaders, are directly fulfilling the book of Revelation, and this means that the end times are upon us. Oh, thank You, Jesus, thank You!

Merton raised his arms and nearly shouted in conclusion:

You've shown us that You'll be coming *soon,* O Lord! And now please condemn the perpetrators of this fraud to the inner corridors of hell! Amen! And *Amen!*

"Dad, do you know where I can get an asbestos jogging outfit?" asked Jon. "Poor Marty Marty. How can he possibly handle this yo-yo without losing his cool? I'll give you a hundred-to-one odds he tried to argue CBS out of having him on the panel."

Marty, showing admirable restraint, turned to Cardinal O'Neill for the Roman Catholic riposte.

Patrick Cardinal O'Neill, a silver-haired sage whose broad shoulders and stocky frame visually dominated the panel even though he was not, that evening, draped in the red-purple of the cardinalate, began deliberately:

While the Catholic church agrees with Dr. Merton that the bones discovered in Israel are *not* those of Jesus, it agrees with him on almost nothing else.

"*Great!* Give it to him, O'Neill!" Jon's father shouted into the screen of their Zenith. They all chuckled as O'Neill proceeded to

dismantle Merton's rabid millennialism and self-serving claims to
a private revelation:

> Can we really believe in a Christ who talks only to Melvin
> Merton? And so far as his timetable for Jesus's return is con-
> cerned, prophecy fanatics have played that game for ages, and
> their "batting average" to date is zero. But now let *me* make a
> prediction: as we move through the first century of this new mil-
> lennium, these sorts will be coming out in frenzied swarms with
> frantic forecasts. Remember what former Secretary of the
> Interior James Watt told a congressional committee? America
> needn't worry about her resources beyond the year 2000, since
> the great millennium would either wipe out or transform the
> existing world? Well, that's the kind of irresponsibility spawned
> by your unholy emphasis on end times, Dr. Merton, and dozens
> of prophecy preachers like you!

He glared at Merton for some moments, and then gave views
on Rama that were similar to what the pope had affirmed.

Moderator Marty, who had had a difficult time controlling a
catbird smile during O'Neill's presentation, now introduced the
third panelist:

> Professor Thomas Aquinas Avery, of Union Theological Seminary
> in New York, studied under Rudolf Bultmann, and he has publicly
> stated that the Rama discoveries, which he considers genuine,
> are, in his words, "congenial to Christianity and even expected."
> Professor Avery.

An older Boston Brahmin with accent to match, Avery had a
full thatch of snow-white hair carefully framing an aristocratic set
of features. A glad sparkle in his olive-green eyes, he began:

> Even though there are hundreds of different church bodies, there
> are only *two* basic theologies—with some variations, of course.
> One is the conservative, if not fundamentalist, view that insists on
> a literal interpretation of the Bible as "God's inspired" or even

"errorless Word." The other is the more scholarly and logical view that has honestly dealt with the obvious errors in the Bible, tried to identify the very human—not divine—sources on which the biblical writers drew, how they edited those sources for their theological purposes, and which also dismisses the so-called "miracles" in Scripture as simple mythology. And this includes such claims as Jesus's raising someone from the dead, or that He was Himself raised from the dead. Consequently the discovery of Jesus's bones in Israel surprises us not a bit. Quite on the contrary, some of us even predicted that they might indeed be found one day, and that this would have no effect whatever on Christianity—properly understood.

"Oh, *of course not,* Doubting Thomas!" the Reverend Erhard Weber shouted at the TV screen. "It just contradicts the very core of the faith, that's all!"

"Quiet, dear!" cautioned Mrs. Weber. "I want to hear him defend that point, if he can."

Avery continued:

Many of my colleagues and I are also somewhat chagrined that the Rama archaeologists have been so reticent about the authenticity of their finds. Had anyone else's bones been discovered with that sort of documentation, they would have been declared genuine *long* before this!

"Not so fast, Avery!" Now it was Jon's turn to address the screen. But Avery paid him no heed, as he resumed:

Many of you may wonder how I can say that an *informed and mature* Christianity will not be affected by these discoveries. What's important about the first Easter is *not* the resuscitation of a lifeless corpse—that was impossible then just as it's impossible now, even for experts like Dr. Mel Merton! What *is* important is the *faith and belief* that we can overcome evil and fear of death triumphantly, just as Jesus did. He sets us the great example. By nobly facing death, He truly "conquered" it. Jesus shows us how,

even as He points the way to a renewed life for all of us, if only we
follow His example.

"Pure Bultmann," Jon's father commented. "I hope Billy Graham
nails him to the wall."

Graham's face had reddened somewhat during Avery's presentation, and when Marty gave him the floor, the lanky, likeable
evangelist chose words that quickly picked up tempo and intensity:

I only wish Professor Avery would try out his message on someone
who is dying. "This is the end, friend," he'd have to say. "Stiff
upper lip! Try to take it on the chin like Jesus did. There's no hope,
no afterlife—nothing. Prepare for dissolution!" Compare that to
the faith that has always pulsed through Christianity: that Jesus
truly rose from the dead—physically, historically, factually, materially. *This* is the sort of Easter proclaimed by all the earliest witnesses, and by the whole Christian church until some theologians
thought differently in the last century—and this.

"Go, Billy, go!" said Pastor Weber. "Give them St. Paul!" And
Graham seemed to hear, for he continued:

The earliest writing in the New Testament came from the pen of
St. Paul, and for him the matter was simply categorical. "If Christ
was not raised, your faith is *in vain!*" he said. "If we have only
hope in Christ, we are of all people most to be pitied!" Now I can
certainly understand someone like Professor Avery doubting the
Resurrection—that's his prerogative. I only object to any claim
that this is historic Christianity. It is *not!* The Jesus you describe,
Dr. Avery, is only a teacher in a line of noble teachers, like Socrates,
Aristotle, and the rest. And your so-called "Christianity" is merely an
ethical system, not a religion.

"Good, Billy!" said Mrs. Weber, now joining her husband in
one-way conversations with picture tubes. "Billy Graham, at
least, has managed to preach the faith all these years without

the additional trash foisted on us by so many of the other TV evangelists."

Moderator Marty resumed:

Thank you, gentlemen, for your position statements. We now open the panel to discussion. Professor Avery.

What followed was one of the most memorable hours in the history of television—a debate that would become classic in time, since rarely were the various schools of Christian thought expressed so clearly or pointedly. Avery defended liberal theology with great skill, claiming that many mainline clergy agreed with him, but were silent in order to hold on to their positions. He continued:

According to one survey, about half the Methodist ministers in America don't believe in a physical resurrection. Nor do a third of the Presbyterian and Episcopal clergy. You see, Jesus surely rose again, but He did so *in the minds and hearts* of His followers. And His life and death have had such a radical effect on the world since then that His cause certainly *has* been resurrected. And that, I think, is what Easter's all about.

The debate grew progressively heated, opinions more sharply barbed. Mercifully, Merton was largely ignored in the exchanges, much to his evident disappointment. Cardinal O'Neill questioned whether the theology of the left had pervaded *that* great a segment of American Christendom.

Avery responded quickly:

A professor at Berkeley claimed that of the nine Catholic and Protestant schools in the Graduate Theological Union there, he didn't know of *any* in which a significant part of the faculty accepted a physical resurrection. You see, a vast chasm has yawned open between what theologians and scholars believe, on the one hand, and what church leaders, priests, and pastors teach their flocks on the other. Had they been more honest with their people, they *wouldn't* be suffering such agony now!

Open applause from the studio audience greeted that remark, and equally vocal hissing. Referee Marty did his best to maintain order and keep the debate on track. Now he called for final summations. Avery reinforced his warning that the Christian world had better get ready to accept what "honest scholarship" had been telling it for years:

> Some wit put it very well: "When a long-held idea is falsified, for the scientist, it's a triumph; for the politician, an embarrassment; but for the theologian, a disaster." Well, clergy with intelligence are skirting the disaster by realizing the truth of our position. It's now *high* time for them to help educate the laity. Jesus still has much to teach us. We *don't* have to abandon His example now that His remains have been found. Indeed, the very bones prove Jesus more historical than ever!

In Hannibal, Jon squirmed again at the presuppositions now paraded as fact, though he also could not resist trying to project a Christianity without a bodily risen Christ. What *would* Sandy have to report?

It was now five minutes to cutoff, and Billy Graham was given the honor of the last summation, as befitted the nation's most famous religious figure. His face tanned from a recent crusade in the South and his penetrating blues eyes afire with conviction, he said:

> Although I don't claim the gift of prophecy like Dr. Merton here, I do predict that Rama will prove to be the most elaborate hoax ever concocted. As to Professor Avery's attempts to teach a Christianity without a true Resurrection, a leading Jewish scholar, Dr. Geza Vermes, put it best. Those who believe Bultmann's (and Avery's) theology, he claims, "have their feet off the ground of history and their heads in the clouds of faith." St. Paul had nothing so nebulous in mind when he stated: "For I am persuaded that neither death nor life, nor angels, nor principalities, nor powers, nor

things present, nor things to come, nor height, nor depth, nor anything else"—including fake discoveries, he would add—"shall be
able to separate us from the love of God that is in Christ Jesus, our
Lord"—our risen Lord, who truly triumphed over death on that
first Easter, and whose victory over the grave is also our promise
of life everlasting!

While his father burst into applause and his mother was wiping her eyes, Jon took the liberty of answering the phone, which
had started ringing just after Martin Marty's closing comments.

"Pastor Weber's residence," he said.

"Jonathan?"

"Yes—"

"This is Sandy. We have the results. Can we talk?"

EIGHTEEN

For weeks, Jon had been impatient to get the test results from Sandy, but now that he was about to receive them, he almost would have preferred one last evening of not knowing. Perhaps another beer with his father and Bach's *Christmas Oratorio* on the stereo would have served as pleasant counterpoint to Rama.

"Jon, are you there? Can we talk?" the receiver repeated.

"Sure. Shoot, Sandy. I thought you were going to call tomorrow."

"I didn't know how long you'd be there in the morning. Did you see the TV special?"

"Yeah. We just turned it off."

There was silence on the eastern end of the line.

"Sandy? Are you still there?"

"Ah . . . yeah. I just don't know how to handle it, Jon. So *incredibly much* is riding on this. I mean, who am I—who are we—to act as the hinges of fate in—"

"Can the 'tools of destiny' bit and give me the results, Sandy." Jon tried to sound businesslike, although his pulse was racing, probably in even tempo with Sandy's.

"You're sure we can talk? No wire taps?"

"Not likely! They generally use smoke-signals out here in the boonies."

"Okay. Well, you'll get all this in pages and pages of detail—377 to be exact—but I'll just give you the upshot now."

"Fine."

"All right, then, the two 'Joseph' jar handles show an *unevenness* in the seal impressions consistent with ancient tools rather than modern ones. Thermoluminescence dates the one with Aramaic as fired *circa* AD 15, plus or minus 150 years. The other, with Greek, left the kiln about twenty years later. Same error range."

Both fell easily within the authenticity horizon. Sandy resumed, "We can tell you the kind of clay used in the jars, the temperature at which it was fired, and lots of additional data, but that's all in the report."

"Yes, skip that for now. Just give me the highlights."

"Okay, we'll move on to the *titulus* parchment. We used PIXE on the ink and didn't find any metal oxides. Then we checked it chemically and found that it's the same sort of pure carbon ink with gum arabic binder used widely in the first century."

"What about the parchment itself?"

"The pollen analysis was interesting. We isolated pollen from it and also from the grave cloths and then called in a botanist who specializes in the Near East. She found it all quite consistent with the floral sequence of that area."

"How nice!" Jon felt like responding, sensing again the irony that authenticity is invariably *gladdening* in archaeology, but for this, the only exception in the annals of that science.

"The burial linens also contain traces of aloes," Sandy continued.

"That was Nicodemus's contribution, according to the fourth Gospel."

There was a prolonged silence, until Sandy resumed. "The two oil lamps—thermoluminescence dates the 'Herodian' lamp to *circa* AD 40, plus or minus, and the decorated lamp to about 25 BC. That was an oldie. One of Joseph's heirlooms?"

"Probably. They stopped making that kind at the end of the BC era, so your testing seems validated."

"Now, on to the two flasks. Both tested closely with the Herodian lamp—not more than twenty to thirty years difference. Ditto the juglet."

"The juglet too, eh? What about the clay plug?"

"We couldn't do much with that plug, since it wasn't fired. But it's a different story with the Nero coin. No question that it's genuine. We have another at the Smithsonian, and the copper:tin:silver ratio in the bronze is virtually the same in both."

"What about the debris samplings in the packets?"

"The particulate wasn't as valuable as we'd hoped. But we didn't find any spooks, although I, for one, was looking for a transistor or microchip, let me tell you!"

Jon chuckled, but then another long silence muffled both ends of the line. Finally Jon said, "Well . . . thanks, Sandy. I'll be flying there tomorrow noon. Call you when I get in." After he hung up, Jon reported none of the conversation to his parents. *Why spoil their Christmas?*

Jack Anderson, Woodward and Bernstein, Evans and Novak, Andrew Tully, George Will, and James Kilpatrick were stars in the skies of journalism, but Radford Morrison of *The Washington Post,* at least by his own claim, was "all of the above," the whole constellation. His column was read across the world by statesmen and scholars, politicians and pundits. Morrison had the uncanny knack of uncovering "the big story" before anyone else through his own brand of investigative reporting. "Unnamed sources" were his *only* sources, detractors claimed, but his material had a .940 batting average for accuracy. Even his letterhead boasted the slogan, *"Ask not the source . . . but it's true, of course!"*

Convinced that Rama and its consequences would be the story of the century, Morrison had shuttled between Washington and Tel Aviv for weeks now, gathering material for what would be *"the* authoritative book" on the dig. Half of his staff had been recruited from electronics laboratories and detective agencies, the other half from the CIA and cousin organizations. Some of the best exposés had come through the monitoring efforts of Willard Fenske, who read microchips like road maps, and he was the one Morrison picked for special services that Christmas.

The Rama staff had never cooperated with Morrison. They wanted no one from the press underfoot at the dig while everything was still in flux. But somehow Morrison learned that the Smithsonian findings would be relayed to Jon around Christmastime. Salivating at the possibility of learning them at the same time, Morrison put a tail on Jon both in Weston and Cambridge the week before Christmas, expecting that he would fly to Washington to get the results. Morrison's travel agent kept putting

Jon's name into the computer to see which flight it might be, and the screen surprised them with details of a St. Louis destination. So it was that Willard Fenske watched Jon get off his jet at Lambert Field, shaded glasses almost identifying rather than concealing him. So, too, Fenske had rented a car just after Jon and tailed him to church in Hannibal.

Unlike Jon, however, he had not stayed for the service. *Obviously, sonny boy is going to have Christmas dinner back home, so we'd best make the necessary arrangements,* he told himself. A quick check of the public phone directory steered him to the parsonage, where he parked in an alley behind the house—though not before he had fastened a large "SBC Communications" decal on both doors of the cream-white rental. Changing quickly into a phone repairman's uniform, he rang the back doorbell. *Good, no answer.* Glancing about to make sure no one saw, he moved to the living room windows and slapped a small, self-adhering bug onto the corner of one of the lower panes, doing the same to the kitchen. Now both window panes would act as microphone resonators that would broadcast into one of the cassette recorders he had with him.

Then he climbed the telephone pole looming over the rear of the parsonage. *Rats!* The back door was opening and a woman was throwing some crumbs to the birds. Suddenly she looked up at him and said, "My, my, do you people have to work on Christmas Day?"

"Yes, ma'am," said Fenske. "No rest for the weary. Something's wrong along the line here. Had any trouble with your phone?"

"I don't think so."

"Be finished shortly. Aren't you supposed to be in church?" he trifled.

"Oh, I just got back from early service. Let me know if you'd like a cup of coffee or anything."

"I will. Thank you, ma'am."

Fenske moved swiftly to the junction box and spliced in a three-wire lead to his own porta-phone. Then he climbed down the pole and dialed the Erhard Weber residence. His genial profferer of coffee answered. He assured her he was only testing, and all was well. She was ever so grateful.

Fenske drove the car to another street and then walked back into the alley. He drew his wire lead into a clump of bushes at the base of the pole, where he was hidden from view. It became an afternoon and evening of state-of-the-art eavesdropping. He turned on one of his tape recorders when Jon arrived—the two bugs delivering an almost broadcast-quality signal into his monitor headphones. The other recorder was switched on only when the telephone was in use. More than anything else, he was grateful that the Webers' taste in pets, if they had any, did not run to Dobermans or German Shepherds.

There must be a better way to make a living, Fenske groused, as he sat shivering despite thermal underwear and sheepskin jacket and pants. *What a way to spend Christmas!*

Morrison, though, would relish the juicy tidbits the younger Weber dropped about the Rama dig during dinner. But hearing them munch away was too much for his own growling stomach. Switching his equipment to automatic, Fenske drove into town for a hot dinner and several even hotter toddies. Then he returned to his lonely post and put on his headphones. Supper at the manse was just concluding with animated jabber about the forthcoming television special.

"Oh, oh. Their reaction to that could be pay dirt," he muttered to himself. Less than an hour later, his hunch proved correct, as he lovingly recorded every syllable of reaction from the three Webers. But he grew positively elated when the phone finally came to life with McHugh's call, and he checked the modulation meter with a penlight to make sure he was recording every sacred syllable. Well briefed on Rama, Fenske smiled into the darkness as he listened to the results. He was not a religious man himself.

When Jon hung up, Fenske turned off his equipment. He even managed to sneak back to the windows and remove the bugs. Then he returned to his car and Lambert Field in St. Louis where he phoned Morrison.

"Fabulous! Just fabulous!" Morrison exulted. "You get a very special bonus *this* Christmas, Willard, my boy. But only if you get your tail back to Washington by breakfast so I can hear those tapes!"

Jon spent Monday afternoon and evening at Sandy's place, digesting the bulky official report. At 10 PM he called the private number the president had given him, bypassing the White House switchboard. It rang and rang. Evidently the president was out.

At 11 PM—6 AM Israeli time—he put in a call to Jennings in Ramallah. They had worked out a code for communication in advance. "Can you hear me clearly, Austin?" Jon opened.

"Yes. Yes indeed."

"All right, then, I have the results."

"You do? Fire away."

"Well, *all* items tested within the nominal range, except for H and I, which were indeterminate."

Jon heard nothing on the other end. "Are you there, Austin? Did you get that?"

"Yes, Jonathan. All but H and I . . . nominal, you say?" He sounded a little vacant. Then again, it *was* early morning in Israel.

"That's right, Austin. How's Shannon?"

"She misses you terribly, dear boy. I do believe she's in love. Shall I wake her?"

"Well . . . no. Just assure the fair lady of my endless devotion when she arises. In any case, the report weighs in at 377 pages, and I'll bring it along when I fly back there day after tomorrow, via the . . . ah . . . planned approach. I suppose we'll have to unveil Phase III when I get back."

"Indeed. I see no other way."

"Take care, Austin."

He then translated for Sandy's benefit. The "planned approach" involved his flying KLM to Vienna; Alia to Amman, Jordan; and into Israel via the Allenby Bridge, all to avoid the press that had been camping outside Ben Gurion Airport. But it took him a quarter hour to explain Phase III.

Sandy approved it enthusiastically. "'Tis really the only way, Jonnie, me boy." It was the first rotten brogue he had heard from

Sandy in weeks, and it gladdened him as a kind of throwback to a less complicated and happier past.

His last call in the wee-hours-Stateside-but-early-morning-Rome time went to Kevin Sullivan, as he had promised. After learning the main results of the Smithsonian test series, Kevin sounded shaken, almost despairing. Jon tried to firm him up. "Steady, sport! This isn't over yet. We have lots more digging to do. Please assure the Holy Father of that."

"*Great*, Jon," he replied, sardonically. "You sound like a deck steward on the *Titanic*, pouring tea into cups at a thirty-five-degree angle! Great balls of fire, man, do you think the libs have been right the whole time? Any physical resurrection was just mythology?"

"*Premature* is the key word, Kevin."

"Haven't you at least *thought* of that possibility?"

"Yes, of course I have! And let me prove that. It just *may* be time for us to do a heavier exegetical study of John 20:26. Keep the faith, Kev!"

"Carry on, Jon."

He knew that Kevin would be opening his New Testament to read about that post Easter evening when the resurrected Jesus appeared to his disciples right through the walls of a closed room. You don't need bones for that sort of mobility.

Jon never made his flights on KLM or Alia. Nor did his alias, Ernst Becker. Early the next morning, Sandy's phone started ringing incessantly. After answering it, Sandy stalked to the front door to pick up the morning edition of *The Washington Post*. Bleary-eyed, he stared at himself on the front page, his photograph next to Jon's, under a banner headline, "ARTIFACTS DATE TO JESUS'S TIME," and subheader, "Smithsonian Tests Add Further Credence to Belief That Jesus's Bones Have Been Discovered." The story opened:

> According to "absolutely unimpeachable evidence" uncovered by Radford Morrison and Associates, Professor Jonathan E. Weber of Harvard University, who made the original discoveries in Israel, arranged for a secret series of tests of the artifacts found near

bones purporting to be those of Jesus. The tests were conducted at the Smithsonian Institution and other selected laboratories under the supervision of Dr. Sanford McHugh. All laboratory analyses of datable artifacts, particularly thermoluminescence, point to origins from c. 25 BC at the earliest, to c. AD 60 at the latest, plus or minus minor error margins—dates which accord very well with information from the now-famous "Joseph papyrus."

Sandy knocked on Jon's door. "Time to get up, bucko," he said. "And don't ask about the morning's news. We're it!" He thrust the *Post* under Jon's widening eyes, adding, "Welcome to hell!"

Again the phone rang. Sandy was of a mind to leave it off the hook, but for some reason he answered it. Then he passed it on to Jon. "It's the White House."

"This is Sherwood Bronson, Professor Weber," said the president, a touch of pique in his voice. "I thought we had an agreement that you'd give me your results *before* going public."

"We certainly did, and I respected that, Mr. President. I learned the complete results only yesterday, and I *did* try to call you last night. But no one answered."

"You did? Oh, that's right. My wife and I were at the Kennedy Center."

"I'd planned to give you a full briefing today, if possible, but Mr. Radford Morrison had other plans, as you know."

"How in *blue blazes* did he find out about the tests and the results?"

"We've no idea. A mole at the Smithsonian? A wiretap? Who knows?"

"Didn't they find *anything* suspicious or wrong in the tests?"

"Afraid not. At least not yet."

There was a long silence, finally broken by the president. "Well, what now? Are you simply going to stand there, with your arms hanging down, and let the faith of a hundred eighty million Americans go down the tube?"

How very quaint and provincial, thought Jon. *What about the faith of ten times that many outside the U.S.?*

"Well, that was unfair of me," said the president. "We're all on edge. I thought of convening a blue-ribbon panel of psychiatrists and psychologists and charging them with the task of finding a way to help our citizens through this crisis. Do you think that'd be a good idea?"

"With all due respect, not really, Mr. President. I think I have a better one. I'll be announcing it at a press conference the day after tomorrow. I hope you and the nation will find it helpful."

"Oh? Good . . . good. But in the meantime, is there any way I can help you?"

"Yes, there certainly is. To implement our plan, I'll need a secluded office somewhere—no bugs—and three or four *clear* phone lines—no wiretaps. Could you arrange that? The long-distance tab could get formidable, but we'd reimburse—"

"*Done!*" the president replied. "And don't worry about the bill—this is in the national interest. You can use an office in Blair House as soon as you like, and we'll have extra phone lines in there about forty-five minutes from now."

"Thank you, Mr. President!"

Jon's first call at Blair House was to Harvard, where he asked his secretary, Marylou Kaiser, and ICO general secretary, Charles Ferris, to drop everything, hop the next shuttle to Washington, and plan to stay overnight.

His next call went to Jennings. Jon spilled his pent-up fury into the phone: "Austin, do you remember that sly-and-skulking snake of a journalist from the U.S. named Morrison? The one who wanted to do a book on our dig?"

"Yes, I seem to recall him. But he looked more like a weasel than a snake, didn't he? A weasel with jaundice?"

"Whatever! Yes, that's the one! Well, the bilious little pup found out our results somehow, and published them in this morning's *Washington Post*. The other media are now saturated with the story. You'll read about it in the next *Jerusalem Post*. So things are in an uproar over here, and I'm calling you for permission to unveil Phase III now, rather than waiting till I get back to Israel."

"Oh yes, by all means! But do you have agreements from all concerned?"

"We're working on those now."

"Go for it, lad! There, that proves I can speak American too, not?"

"Cheerio, Austin!" said Jon. "I'm ringing off." Two could play that game.

Marylou Kaiser and Chuck Ferris walked in just four hours later. "What took you so long?" asked Jon, a little smile tugging up the corners of his mouth. Then all three set to work at telephones, calling a long list of names on various continents.

That afternoon and all the next day, the calls went out across the nation and across the world. To reach the object party was like a Byzantine intrigue in some cases, a quick success in others. Kevin Sullivan, for example, was on the line in just two minutes, and he called back an hour later with word that the pope, though horrified at news of the test results, most heartily approved Phase III and implored God's blessing upon it.

The inevitable press conference, on December 29, was held in the grand ballroom of the Shoreham Hotel, where presidential inauguration galas regularly took place. The vast hall was filled with media people from across the world, as well as academic, religious, and political luminaries who had abandoned their holiday plans to come to Washington for the occasion. For that reason, Jon's opening statement was apologetic. "I deeply regret, ladies and gentlemen, that your year-end festivities, when you should be with your families, have been interrupted by this press conference. Certainly Professor Austin Balfour Jennings, director of the Rama excavation, and I would never have been so thoughtless. But when a certain columnist, without any authorization, published results of the Smithsonian test series, we had no choice, particularly in view of the at-times hysterical response here and abroad.

"Nor shall the columnist be nameless. However he came by the information, Radford Morrison has violated either the law or basic ethics, or both. His implications that our test series was 'secret' and would probably have remained so but for his 'investigative reporting' are absolutely *false!* We fully intended to announce the findings, and shall do so now.

"An epitome of the test results is being distributed to you at this moment. If you fail to receive a copy, please raise your hand and one of the pages will accommodate you. I'll entertain your questions shortly. First, I'd like to introduce the other person on the dais here—Dr. Sanford McHugh, of the Smithsonian Institution.

"Now, I must strongly emphasize that, although our various samples registered an age of origin approximately in the first century AD/CE, we have *not* abandoned our research into the authenticity of the cavern-area discoveries at Rama. A greatly augmented program of excavation there has been decided upon that will eventually expose the entire first-century town. This is the start of what we call 'Phase III' at this dig. *Phase I*—so named in retrospect, of course—were the campaigns conducted by Sir Lloyd Kensington and Austin Balfour Jennings. *Phase II* was the discovery of the cavern tomb and its artifacts, tested as of this point. *Phase III* is what we plan from now on. And I'll have more to say about that in my closing statement.

"After reading the epitome, I'd urge all of you to postpone any conclusions until *after* the final phase of this enterprise. We've been dismayed by many of the responses to Rama and horrified by others. Rumors have been added to assumed 'facts,' resulting in conclusions that are poorly conceived and sensationalistically expressed. Truth suffers. If two unethical members of the press— one in Israel, the other here—had acted responsibly instead, the masses would have been spared much agony. Lives have been lost, as you certainly know. And so, ladies and gentlemen of the media, I appeal to your integrity and sense of responsibility. I'm now open for questions."

"Jeffery Sheler, *U.S. News & World Report.* I'd like to explore your personal reactions to this latest test series, Professor Weber. Were you shocked that all the items tested to the first century? Or not so surprised?"

"Not so surprised."

"Why is that?"

"Since the radiocarbon tests in Arizona dated back to that time frame, it would have been extraordinary not to find *all* materials from the same locus similarly datable. . . . Yes?"

"Tadaki Arioshi, *Tokyo Shinbun*. "But why, then, does this not *prove* all your finds to be genuine?"

"First-century artifacts, let me explain again, could have been 'salted,' that is, planted there as a fraud. In that case, the perpetrator would hardly have been foolish enough *not* to use first-century materials throughout. That's why I wasn't too surprised by the results. . . . Yes?"

"Everett Sinclair, *Toronto Globe and Mail*. Could you explain to us what *thermoluminescence* means?"

"Let's have Dr. McHugh answer that one. Sandy?"

Sanford McHugh tilted the microphone a bit and responded, "Back in 1664, Robert Boyle discovered that a diamond would emit a faint glow in a darkened room when he warmed it with his hands. That was the earliest demonstration of thermoluminescence. Now, natural clay has traces of radioactive impurities, such as uranium and thorium, which emit radiation that gets trapped inside the clay. But when the clay is formed into pottery and then fired, the heating process releases all this stored radiation in the form of visible light, hence 'thermoluminescence,' leaving *zero* radiation energy left in the pottery.

"In time, though, the radiation builds up again at a constant rate, and when the pottery is heated a *second* time in the laboratory, the amount of luminescent glow can be measured to determine the age of the pottery since its original firing."

"I, ah, *think* I caught that," Sinclair responded. "But how accurate is this method, Dr. McHugh?"

"Plus or minus 10 percent, certainly, and probably plus or minus 5. . . . Yes?"

"Tom Brokaw, *NBC Nightly News*. It would seem, Dr. McHugh, that *if* a forger were able to 'borrow' all the props from first-century sources—ceramics, parchment, papyrus—the one thing he could *not* borrow was the *writing*—the ink, if you please—"

"Yes. That's true enough."

"Well, then, what did your tests reveal about the ink?"

"Three different inks came to light: one in the so-called 'Joseph papyrus,' a second in the 'Nicodemus postscript,' and the third on the *titulus*. Only the last could provide the sort of quantity we required for analysis, and even that was too slight for radiocarbon testing. Instead, our most successful analysis came via PIXE— Particle Induced X-ray Emission Analysis—which showed it to be a pure carbon ink, made from lampblack or soot. A liquid adhesive was added to stabilize the carbon: gum arabic. The other two inks appear to be the same, the 'Nicodemus postscript' just a shade brownish-black."

"Was that formula typical for ink in the first century?" Brokaw inquired. "And what about the color or tonal range, including brown?"

Sandy looked to Jon, who returned to the microphone and said, "Yes, it's a common formula for that era, and all three color tones fall within the spectrum we find in the Dead Sea Scrolls."

The questioning went on for an hour and a half. Jon knew it was time to close when the questions waxed theological, and Doris Dinwiddie's was the last he fielded. An aging but widely read columnist for the Hearst chain with several presidential scalps dangling from the considerable circumference of her belt, she was predictably provocative: "Professor Weber, don't you think it's high time that all of you stop your heroic efforts on behalf of a dying Christianity? No one on God's green earth could have faked all this. I mean, you have the smoking gun— you have the *very bones* of Jesus Christ! So why don't you give them—and the Christian faith—as dignified and decent a burial as you can?"

A raucous commotion and some hissing boiled up in the ballroom. "Your assumptions are premature, Miss Dinwiddie," Jon replied, evenly. "Quite apart from that sector of Christianity which believes only in a spiritual resurrection and therefore remains unaffected, the majority belief in a physical resurrection is *not* suddenly invalidated at this point. I'd think twice before sounding any death knell for the one religious system on earth whose origins, like those of its parent Judaism, involved real people in historical contexts, rather than being rooted in the misty fables of mythology."

The acerbic newswoman shot back immediately: "I wonder if your obvious bias in favor of Christianity shouldn't disqualify you from a leadership role in this enterprise?"

Slapping a lid on his inner seething, Jon responded, almost gently, "In view of our discoveries, Miss Dinwiddie, how do you think the world would have reacted had I been biased *against* Christianity?"

The moment of silence was followed by prolonged applause. Now it was time for his closing statement. Jon nodded to the pages and said, "We'll now distribute a brief outline of what we've termed *Phase III*. Besides completing the Rama excavations, we intend to establish an international congress of scholars who will review all of the methodology and findings at Rama from the first Kensington days until the present, as well as any discoveries from this point on. Membership in this congress is being decided through nomination from our ICO, the International Academy of Archaeology, the Society of Biblical Literature, and the American Academy of Religion, as well as their British counterparts. The leadership of the world's primary Christian church bodies will have representation, ranging from the pope and the Eastern Orthodox patriarch to all other church bodies with at least five million members. Observers from Judaism, Islam, and other world religions will also be welcome.

"Page five in your handout sketches the division of labor in various sectors and panels."

Jon then commented on each of the following:

I. SCIENTIFIC SECTOR

PANELS	CHARGES
ARCHAEOLOGY	Review and advise on all past, present, and future excavations at the Rama site.
ANALYSIS	Review and advise on all past, present, and future testing of the Rama artifacts and remains, as well as any yet to be discovered.

| LINGUISTICS/ PALEOGRAPHY | Analyze all Hebrew, Aramaic, Greek, and Latin inscriptions discovered as to script, vocabulary, syntax, and grammar. |

II. INVESTIGATIVE SECTOR

| INVESTIGATION | Probe the history and ownership of the Rama site, as well as the personal backgrounds of the principal excavation staff. Review forgery techniques attempted in the history of art and archaeology. |

III. THEOLOGICAL SECTOR

| OLD TESTAMENT | Research burial customs, eschatology, and all relevant religious/cultural data. |

| INTER-TESTAMENT | Same |

| NEW TESTAMENT | Same, all three panels to explore a revised theology of the Resurrection if Rama is finally deemed authentic. |

"After months of review and deliberation," Jon continued, "the final conclusions will be published in a monographic series, and doubtless be widely translated. Now it's very late and time to close. I thank you for your patience, ladies and gentlemen."

Just as Jon and Sandy were leaving the emptying ballroom, a slender figure with white hair approached them. "I . . . I acted too hastily in Cambridge," Joshua Scruggs Nickel confessed. "I was upset then, Jonathan. I know you're trying to . . . to do the right thing in all this."

"Well, thank you, Mr. Nickel. That means very much to me."

"But won't you have tremendous expenses now with your international congress?"

"Yes, indeed!"

"How do you propose to underwrite it all?"

"Our telephoning in the last two days brought pledges of cooperation and financial support from many church bodies and scholarly societies."

"Well, you can count me in again too. At double my previous subsidy."

NINETEEN

Shannon Jennings was about the only joy Jon savored over the next cluttered months back in Israel. Their love, carefully pruned by separation, was blooming again luxuriously, at least during the rare moments when they could escape the now-crowded dig, questions from the press, and meetings with the scholars' congress in Jerusalem. The patrolled, electric fence held back the curious at Rama, but hired helicopters fanned overhead several times each week, generating television footage via zoom lenses. Inside the fence, Jennings was now commander-in-chief of his largest archaeological army to date, his staff tripled in size with experienced excavators supplied by the Phase III effort. Jon helped Jennings coordinate it all, dictating memos to himself on a micro-cassette recorder, as he darted from one sector to the next. Rama was rapidly giving up her secrets.

None of the secrets, however, proved "sensational." All new artifacts dated unspectacularly to the eras where they belonged, and most of first-century Rama would soon be exposed. Jennings, however, greeted each new find like a doting parent, reverently dusting it off as a fresh trophy for his bulging collection.

Specialists from the Archaeology Panel were given *carte blanche* to explore the entire dig. They fully endorsed the methodology and record-keeping, and selected very few artifacts for further testing. Samples nearly always were returned with identifications close to what Jennings or Naomi Sharon had proposed. "Well, this whole dig is a magnificent window into the first century," commented Dr. Walter Rast, one of the panelists who had dug for years in Jordan. "But what else would you expect of Austin Balfour Jennings?"

The focus of the world's interest, of course, was the cavern tomb area, where Clive Brampton and Jon were in charge. Inside the grotto, their spoonful-by-spoonful, well-nigh thimbleful-by-thimbleful scouring of the interior yielded nothing more than additional dust, bat guano, and cave debris.

"Well, may that cursed cavern rest in peace!" Brampton sighed. "Lord knows it's given the world enough to chew on!"

Archaeology panelists studied every inch of stone on the sarcophagus, and then did a survey of all known first-century sarcophagi in Israel. Joseph's was similar in proportions though larger than the mean and yet smaller than the largest. "Clearly inside the ballpark," Jon noted, shaking his head.

Paleography panelists took wax impressions of the sarcophagus inscription, and then studied plaster-cast reproductions of it for hours on end. Next they launched a broad survey of all first-century tomb inscriptions in Israel to determine lettering size and style, length of line, and the average cutting angle and depth of the cut. Computerization of the results showed a bewildering variety. "Obviously, each local stonecutter did his own thing," commented Dick Cromwell, who had photographed so many tombs recently that he was starting to feel like a ghoul.

Clive and Jon now scoured the open cavern tomb higher up the escarpment. "This, probably, is where Joseph finally had himself buried 'in another tomb,'" said Brampton, "probably along with his family—*if* that blinking papyrus is genuine. And I, for one, think it is. I tell you true, Jon. All this looks nothing like any put-up job to me. How about you?"

"I've got to agree, Clive, though that's not for publication. The evidence is simply overwhelming. But I doubt we'll find much in this cavern. Grave robbers must have cleaned it out centuries ago."

But he was wrong. They did uncover shards from several cooking pots in one of the loculi and fragments from a funerary lamp. Naomi placed both in mid-first-century, and thermoluminescence would shortly bear her out. Most of the time, in fact, her ceramic typology proved even more accurate than thermoluminescence in pinpointing dates.

"She's a magnificent woman, Clive," Jon told him one day as they watched her washing pottery, faded denim cutoffs and a rather skimpy halter barely concealing her beautiful contours. "She's not only a gorgeous woman, but one of the finest ceramicists in Israel. You're a lucky fellow, you know."

"I *know!* Thanks, Jon. I'm really mad about the woman. And I intend to marry her."

"As you should! What an archaeological team you'll make!"

Noel Nottingham was a changed man. The breezy, tweedy, witty Cambridge anthropologist had felt embarrassed by his miscalculation of the age-at-death of the bones discovered, and fully agreed with Dr. Itzhak Shomar that they were at least a decade younger. "Those joint spurs looked so large to me," he later confessed, "but of course I was looking at them through a huge magnifying glass!" He had laughed at his own "stupidity" at the time, blissfully unaware of the possible alternate identity of the remains he had so carefully examined.

The day he finally learned, along with the rest of the world, he suffered a severe psychological trauma. White and sweaty, he poured himself too many gins, and then spent the rest of the night washing his hands, drying them, and then washing them again, drying, mumbling, washing again until dawn. Over the next few days, Nottingham came to better terms with reality, but still had taken several Valiums to make it through the first press conference in Jerusalem.

The compulsive handwashing remained a problem for weeks, however. He found it hard to pass a wash basin without indulging, and took to wearing gloves to hide the angry red wrinkles on his hands. Jennings had to issue Nottingham an ultimatum: get professional help or leave the dig.

Noel was minded to do the latter, but finally consulted a psychiatrist in Jerusalem who quickly exposed the problem. Noel had been a good Anglican in his youth, but later lost his faith, though not a ponderous guilt for having done so. Now, he assumed, Jesus had come back into his life in a bizarre way, and his hands had in some way violated Him. Those hands had to be purged, scrubbed, purified. But recognition and catharsis eventually cured what Jon called Noel's "Pontius Pilate Syndrome."

While every aspect of Phase III was being conducted under the most scrupulous ethical standards, one major deception was intentional. Ever since the Jerusalem press conference, the ultraorthodox Hasidim had been staging periodic demonstrations at Rama, demanding that the human remains be reinterred. They shouted, chanted, engaged in token stonings, and tried to block traffic in and out of the site. While foreign television crews rejoiced at some "action"—any action—to spice up their arid vigil, the Hasidim nettled the Rama staff.

Naomi Sharon returned from one of their confrontations with very bad news. "They're trying to establish your mother's name, Austin," she said. "But don't *ever* tell them!"

"Why not?"

"As a last resort, they're now planning the old medieval 'Rod of Light' ceremony to curse you."

"Sticks and stones may break my bones, but words will never—"

"No, listen. First they read from an eight-hundred-year-old text based on the Cabala. Then they burn black candles while someone sounds a ram's horn, and they invoke your mother's name to curse you. After that you face a horrible fate, or so their rabbis claim. I asked him what it was, and he said, 'There are many ways of dying, some less pleasant than others.'"

"I tremble, Naomi," said Jennings, playfully. "But let's have done with all this and give them their ruddy funeral!"

One night, they secretly exhumed one of the skeletons discovered and reinterred at the Rama cemetery back in the Kensington days, brought it back to the artifact shed, and placed it into a wooden coffin. The next morning, Jennings beckoned the chief Hasid inside the dig, showed him the remains, and agreed with him that it was time to rebury the dead *if* the Hasidim would keep the ceremony confidential. The next day, the Hasidim gathered again in their best clothes to hold a formal reburial rite along with the dig staff. Their rabbi had at first demanded that the remains go back into the cavern tomb, but finally compromised on one that Jennings had specially dug for the occasion. And so it was that the bones did, in fact, return to their original grave. End of demonstrations.

Editorials in the London press had complained about the "Americanization" of Rama, which, after all, had a British director and associate director, to say nothing of financing. While this was no problem for Jennings, the staff agreed that much of the analysis and testing be sent to British laboratories henceforth— Oxford University for radiocarbon and Cambridge for thermoluminescence. English scholars were also included on the various panels because of their international renown, quite apart from any Fleet Street pressures. But Shannon's idea was a masterstroke. With her insatiable appetite for English spy novels, she asked, "Why, for pity's sake, don't we simply turn the whole Investigative Panel over to them?"

Jennings pondered, smiled, and said, "Brilliant, child. Positively brilliant. Is that all right with you, Jon?"

"Superb! A U.N. roundtable is *not* what we need for *that* particular panel!"

The British had responded with Reginald Glastonbury of Scotland Yard to chair the Investigative Panel, and Tom Paddington of MI-5—the British CIA—as vice-chairman. Glastonbury had a Robert Morley sort of corpulence and hairlined pate to match. He was particularly delighted to be called up, since, because of his name, he was a "Glastonbury Legend" buff, according to which Joseph of Arimathea eventually sailed to England with the Holy Grail and built a chapel at Glastonbury before he died and was buried in a crypt there. Jennings twitted Glastonbury that he would likely prefer that the remains *be* Jesus's rather than Joseph's so that his precious legend could remain intact!

Tom Paddington, on the other hand, looked enough like a younger Sean Connery that the students referred to him as James Bond, while Glastonbury became "Sherlock the Fat." Both men and their aides were given free run of the dig, as well as all the facilities at the Ramallah hotel.

The Investigative Panel had been charged with probing the personalities involved at Rama, locating any blind spots, detecting any flaws, and sniffing out any hoaxes. Panelists had just done a grand tour of the British Museum in London, the Louvre in Paris, the Uffizi in Florence, and the Prado in Madrid, where they had interviewed the respective officials on celebrated art frauds and techniques of forgery. Armed with this information, Henri Berthoud skillfully worked up various scenarios as to how everything *might* have been concocted. Berthoud, a youthful expert on loan from the Deuxième Bureau in Paris, had a meticulously combed thatch of dark hair with well-trimmed beard, and eyes by Roentgen that seemed to look *through* rather than *at* anything. Every scenario that Berthoud played before the group showed a rather warped genius.

"You'd make a superb faker yourself, Henri," said Paddington. "Are you sure *you* didn't concoct all this?" But panel members always brought up some flaw in Berthoud's elaborate schemes which doomed that particular scenario. Several months passed, and they had found nothing that even hinted at fraud.

Glastonbury called the group together for its final meeting in spring. Making a triangle of his fingers and thumbs, he said, "Enough of this search of the effects. We have to go back to the cause—*if* such exists—and discover motives—*if* such exist. The hypothetical perpetrator must know archaeology and Aramaic absolutely, and he must truly hate Christianity for some reason. I think we can all agree on that, not?"

They nodded.

"That really would be the only explanation," said Paddington. "You see, forgery is almost always done for money, like the Hitler diaries. This would have to have been done for ideology alone . . . again, *if* this is a hoax."

"Well," said Glastonbury, "it's time for us to go our separate ways for now. Tom and I have agreed that he should stay here in Israel and do a title search on who owned the Rama property years back, while I go to Britain and the U.S. to do a run-down on everyone connected with the archaeology staff here. We'll meet again in late July. Agreed?"

Before leaving Israel, Glastonbury reported their plans to Jennings and Jon, who readily endorsed them. "I've nothing to hide in *my* record," said Jennings, a twinkle in his eye. "Do you, Jon?"

"Be my guest, Reginald," Jon smiled. "Off the record, it looks less and less likely that we're dealing with fraud here. But if we are, I hope you find the perpetrator and hang him by the gonads. Situations like this turn the brains of experts into jelly and demolish reputations overnight. Back in the twenties, Carl Sandburg thought the Lincoln letters in the *Atlantic Monthly* were genuine, and they weren't. Mussolini's son Vittorio declared that diaries supposedly written by his father were authentic, and they weren't!"

Glastonbury nodded and said, "Our own Hugh Trevor-Roper at first thought the Hitler diaries were authentic, and, of course, they were *not!*"

"But the opposite is even worse," said Jennings. "The renowned Solomon Zeitlin declared that the Dead Sea Scrolls were medieval forgeries! So did my colleague G. R. Driver of Oxford! And they—God knows—were *not!*"

"We'll do our best to bag the blighter if he's out there, gentlemen," said Glastonbury. "Cheerio!"

Month after month saw an ever steeper decline in church attendance across the world, though an actual *gain* in some of the rigorist groups. Jon had predicted that phenomenon. "At times of crisis," he told the staff, "people gravitate toward authoritarian leaders in state or church."

"But what rattles me are the lunatics out there," said Jennings. "They're outdoing one another in trying to prove to the world that you and I are apostles from hell, Jon—spawns of Satan, walking antichrists who bear the sign of the beast! They're even trying to find number values of 666 in R-A-M-A."

Jon nodded. "Unfortunately, many of that crowd are coming to Jerusalem this Easter."

"Why?" Shannon wondered. "Other than the usual Holy Week pilgrimage?"

"Because Easter Sunday is now being trumpeted as *the very day* of Christ's return!"

Although Melvin Merton was not the first to suggest this, he quickly agreed with the logic. Since God had created the world around 4000 BC to his reckoning, and the great date of AD 2000 had just passed, that would make six millennia for the age of the earth. The seventh would doubtless be the great Sabbath millennium, the thousand years predicted in the book of Revelation when Jesus would return. Now that Antichrist had appeared, could Jesus be far behind? And what better day for His return than Easter! And what better place than Jerusalem! Merton called a press conference and issued this statement: "It would not surprise me a bit if Jesus descended to the Mount of Olives in Jerusalem just about dawn this coming Easter Sunday."

The response astonished even Merton. A horde of his followers and those of other prophecy fanatics booked every available seat on the standard overseas airlines, and then chartered 747s when these were filled. As Holy Week approached, the pilgrims started arriving in groups of tens, hundreds, thousands. Once again, hundreds of troops from the Israel Defense Force had to supplement the overwhelmed Jerusalem police.

On Palm Sunday, Jon and Shannon stopped by St. Stephen's Gate in the eastern wall of Jerusalem to look in on the pilgrims processing into the Old City. The narrow street was forested with waving palm branches. Some of the groups bore signs, like *"HE* IS COMING NEXT SUNDAY!" or "THAT'S *NOT* JESUS AT RAMA!"

"Good Lord, Jon, what a circus!" Shannon commented.

"That was *some* Pandora's box we opened at Rama."

"You mean *you* opened! Don't blame the rest of us."

"Aha! Comes the crisis, and we all blame someone else?"

She beamed and gave him a warm kiss.

"*That's* better!" he murmured.

"Hah! Look at that dropout and his sign!"

Marching directly behind a nicely groomed college student who was carrying a sign: "*OUR* JESUS LIVES! SORRY ABOUT YOURS," was perhaps the earth's last representative of the beat generation. Heavily bearded in soiled T-shirt and jeans, he carried a sign that had only a large question mark painted on it. He had barely crossed inside the gate when he was attacked by enraged pilgrims who tore into his sign and pummeled him until he slumped down onto the street. Police quickly intervened and dragged the hapless fellow—dazed and bleeding—to the sidewalk.

Not a minute later, who should come strutting by at the head of his massive following but Dr. Melvin Morris Merton himself, singing hymns at the top of his Texan lungs. He looked for a moment at Jon, looked away, and then looked back, this time noticing Shannon at his side—two faces he knew well enough from news photos across the world. Jon now paid for his dislike of sunglasses.

Merton stopped, held up his hands for quiet, and said, "Professor Weber, I presume? And Miss Shannon Jennings?"

"Let's get out of here, Jon!" Shannon whispered. But it was too late.

"*There*, my friends," Merton pointed, "are the authors of the world's agony, the deceivers who claim to have discovered Jesus! *He* is the Antichrist named Weber, and *she* is the daughter of the other devil named Jennings!"

An angry growl bloomed up from his followers, and several rushed toward Jon and Shannon.

"*No, no, no!*" Merton remonstrated. "Don't hurt them. They're only fulfilling prophecy—Antichrist shall be revealed at the Temple of God!"

But it was no use. All the months of despair among some of Merton's followers had only thinly been compensated for by his exuberant prophecies, while others, who never doubted, now wanted to do battle for their Lord by attacking the enemy. A score of them broke ranks, stormed into the crowd, and made a lunge for Jon and Shannon, dragging her, shrieking, into the street, while others grabbed Jon's arms and legs and hoisted him after her. Now they had something better than signs for their procession, and they carried their two struggling trophies triumphantly through St. Stephen's Gate. A soprano in the front ranks started singing the "Hallelujah Chorus" from Handel's *Messiah,* and hundreds of voices joined her.

"Jon! *Do something!*" Shannon screamed.

Jon kicked and thrashed violently. "Let *go* of me, you fanatic fools!" he shouted. "I'm no Antichrist! *You* seem to be!"

Suddenly they were surrounded by a company of khaki-clad Israeli troops, each clutching a snub-nosed Uzi machine gun.

"*Put them down,* I tell you!" Merton cried, red-faced at losing control of his followers, who grudgingly released their captives.

Surrounding Jon and Shannon in a cordon, the troops marched them away to a waiting van and loaded them inside. There they found the battered dropout. He squinted at them, massaged his aching scalp, and said, "Like wow, man! That was pretty *heavy* out there, wasn't it?"

"Yeah, man," Jon replied. "It was strictly a bad scene."

"Where do you wish to go, Professor Weber?" asked the driver.

"Our car's over at the Rockefeller. Thanks!"

On Good Friday, so many pilgrims tried to crowd into the Church of the Holy Sepulcher that people fainted. Claustrophobes grew hysterical. Rescue teams had difficulty threading through the jammed lanes and alleyways of the living labyrinth that was the Holy City. But the Arab souvenir shops were making a killing, hence the joke: "What is the favorite Muslim hymn? Answer: 'What a Friend We Have in Jesus'!"

Easter, though, would be more manageable, since the pilgrim masses planned to celebrate it at dawn on the slopes outside the eastern wall of Jerusalem. This would give them a perfect vantage point from which to see the returning Lord when He *descended* onto the Mount of Olives to the east, the very summit from which He had *ascended* after His resurrection. Probably half the multitude had some doubts that Jesus would put in an appearance, but the rest had donned white robes to greet the returning Lord. Their eyes blazed with joy as they sang their hymns in a candlelight procession out to the eastern slopes of the Old City, each looking expectantly toward the dawn.

Jon and Shannon saw it all from their own vantage point. As a brief holiday, they had returned to Jerusalem for the Easter weekend, and, through the courtesy of the manager, had gotten a suite atop the Seven Arches on the Mount of Olives. Just before dawn on Easter Sunday, Jon had awakened her with the words, "Let's get outside as soon as possible, darling. We may never see anything like this again!"

While munching on rolls and drinking coffee from a thermos, they stood on the esplanade in front of the Seven Arches and looked westward at the incredible scene. The far side of the sprawling Kidron Valley was obliterated by people. Some hundred thousand on the hillside were singing ten different hymns concurrently, in as many languages. At the southern edge, a huge charismatic assembly was speaking in tongues, the sounds from many thousands of mouths blending into a thunderous general din.

As dawn broke, Jon and Shannon could read the long, serpentine banners that had been unfurled, some thirty-people long: "WELCOME BACK, LORD!" "GRÜSS GOTT, HERR JESU CHRIST!" "AVE, JESU!" "BONJOUR, SEIGNEUR!" and a dozen other languages. Some, assuming that Jesus would prefer His own native tongue, had carefully lettered "MARANA THA" in Aramaic square script. This ancient prayer, probably the Church's earliest, meant "Our Lord, come!"

A tiny figure below knew how to unify the crowd. Dr. Melvin Merton climbed onto a dais, took his place before a battery of microphones, and boomed out: "GOOD MORNING! HALLELU-JAH!" pausing as each phrase was translated into French, German, Spanish, Italian, Greek, and Polish. Then Merton dropped a word of Latin: "*VIVIT!* He lives! He is risen!"

That seemed to require no translation, as more than 100,000 voices easily resorted to the unifying Latin and chanted, in rhythmic unison: "*VI-VIT! VI-VIT! VI-VIT!*" for five long minutes. Then the Resurrection Gospels were read in the various languages.

Merton's Easter address, with pauses for translation, was scheduled to end just as the sun started peeping over the brow of the Mount of Olives—the time when many thought the Son Himself would also be appearing. And so Merton concluded, "He is risen! He is risen indeed! *And He shall return! Even so, come, Lord Jesus! Marana tha!*"

The multitude of pilgrims went wild: "*MARANA-THA! MARANA-THA! MARANA-THA!*" they started screaming, in a near-frenzied, hypnotic unison. The effect was so contagious, so overwhelming that even the doubters strained their eyes toward the summit for the possible luminescent glow of a Jesus returning at long last, as He had promised.

The chanting continued with thunderous intensity, terrifying all birds and other fauna on the Mount of Olives. The very atmosphere became so mesmeric that even Jon and Shannon caught themselves looking toward the crest of the Mount, Jon wondering for a moment if God *were* that much "The Wholly Other" as to render Merton and his followers right after all, and "normal" Christians wrong. But only nature's sun brightened the summit.

"Let's go, my love," said Jon.

While walking back to the hotel, Shannon commented, "I wish I could have followed Merton on the dais."

"Oh? What would you have told the crowd?"

"I'd simply have quoted Jesus on the subject of His own return: '*Of that day and of that hour knows no one.*'"

Jon smiled and said, "A student once asked Martin Luther what he'd do if he learned that Jesus was going to return the next day. The student expected that the good doctor would spend the night in repentance, maybe in one of those white robes. But Luther merely replied, 'I'd plant an apple tree.'"

"What in the *world* did he mean by that?"

"Well, the tree happened to be on his next day's schedule, and Christians shouldn't be leading the sort of lives that would compel a 'white-robed' scenario."

She laughed.

Jesus of Nazareth did not physically return that Easter Sunday morning.

TWENTY

Blizzards of letters from all over the world descended on the Rama staff and the scholars' panels. Some urged an immediate end to Phase III as a waste of time "in view of the obvious authenticity of your finds." Others offered advice on test procedures. Still others pounced upon some "flaw in the evidence that everyone seems to have overlooked." Jon soon had a bulging file of these, exposing such "errors" as:

- Both Aramaic and Greek would not have been inscribed on Joseph's sarcophagus. [Wrong: there are many such inscriptions from that era.]

- The *titulus* was simply a painted sign—no parchment was involved. [Nothing in the Gospels precluded a sign achieved with parchment. The "surprise" rather added a note of credibility.]

- John's Gospel tells of linen grave wrappings left inside the Jerusalem tomb. If Joseph had removed the body, he would not have left these behind. [If, as seems likely, they were soiled from Jesus's many wounds, he probably would have. He may also have left only the outer wrappings.]

- The onetime reference in the papyrus mandated Jesus's crucifixion later than AD 30. [In fact, the date was most probably 33.]

- Joseph would not have waited a Sabbath day before reburying the body, as claimed in the papyrus, in view of decomposition. [The remains had been packed with spices. A journey on the Sabbath would have attracted attention.]

243

And on down to the simplest flaw of all, born of faith:

• Jesus rose from the dead: How could those be His bones?

Another tumescent file contained letters of complaint. Elders of the Two-Seed-in-the-Spirit Predestinarian Baptists in the South wondered why no representative from their church body—hundreds strong!—had been invited to Jerusalem. Afro-Asian theologians felt scanted. Several lawsuits were filed against Jennings, Jon, and the Rama staff for having undermined the faith of someone who subsequently committed suicide. Inevitably, some of the letters were particularly virulent, others outright scatological, and the cheery note with membership applications sent by the Freedom *from* Religion Foundation hardly compensated for them.

But what disturbed Jon most was a long, confidential letter from Kevin Sullivan. The pope had sent him back to the States on a damage-survey mission, and his report was devastating. All Church statistics were plummeting, from attendance to contributions. Sunday school and confirmation classes were emptying, while parochial schools were closing. Sullivan wrote:

> I never realized how *vulnerable* is Christian public worship. The disruptions are increasing. Out in California, Robert Schuller was starting one of his sermons in the Crystal Cathedral, still wearing a confident smile and assuring the faithful that "*Possibility Thinking*" still exists, when a booming bass voice cut into his PA system and thundered, "*The 'possibility' is that Christianity is a fraud and you are a fake!*" It went all over the nation on TV. . . The same Sunday, while the organist at Riverside Church in New York was playing a Bach prelude, someone took an ax to the bellows of the great Aeolian-Skinner organ, causing a ghastly, deflating sound of dying music in the sanctuary.

Jon put down the letter and muttered, "The Lost Chord? Or a death knell?"

Was it just a coincidence that the glorious news broke at the summer solstice? The world would mark that moment! On the morning of June 20, Jon and Jennings were sitting in the auditorium of
the Hebrew University in Jerusalem, attending a plenary session
of the Theology Panels, when a page walked down the aisle and
handed them a letter. It bore an archbishop's coat-of-arms and
was signed by the Latin patriarch of Jerusalem.

> *My dear Professor Jennings and Professor Weber:*
> *With great joy, I am pleased to announce that a most definite proof*
> *of fraud in the cavern artifacts at Rama has been discovered by*
> *Father Claude Montaigne. He will deliver a public explanation of his*
> *findings tomorrow afternoon in the aula of the Latin patriarchate at*
> *2.00 PM. You and all your worthy colleagues in this investigation are*
> *welcome to attend.*
>
> *Sincerely yours in Christ,*
>
> *Umberto Cervantes*
> *Archepiscopos Ierusalemi*

Jennings turned pale and stared at Jon, who was also shaken,
for he uttered the most stupid question of his life, "What should
we do, Austin?"

"Make the announcement, of course!"

Jon stepped to the microphone, interrupted the proceedings,
and read the letter.

A vast hush blanketed the auditorium. Then bedlam.

The next afternoon, the aula or audience hall of the Latin patriarchate, seat of the Roman Catholic Archbishop of Jerusalem, was
thronged with scholars and media personnel. Lights and television
cameras lined the perimeter, and every chair in the structure, near
the Jaffa Gate, had been occupied since one o'clock, with hundreds
still begging for admission. Jennings, Brampton, Shannon, and Jon

would never have gained access had the patriarch not reserved seats for them in the front row.

Promptly at 2 PM, Claude Montaigne stepped into the aula. The diminutive Dominican was introduced by the Archbishop, and he opened with a prepared statement. His hands shook just a bit as he held his manuscript on the dais lectern, and read:

> With the greatest gladness, I announce to you that the Rama papyrus is a forgery. It was impiously concocted by someone who had a great command of Aramaic, but who wished to inflict a mortal wound on the holy Christian church. May God in His mercy forgive that individual for what he has done . . . for I cannot.

Montaigne stopped momentarily, giving way to his emotions. Then he regained control of himself and read on:

> After months of studying this document, I became aware of tiny lapses in syntax and grammar that would not have been made by someone as educated as Joseph of Arimathea must have been. I also found problems in the length of the document, its too felicitous "preservation," and the unlikely atmospheric conditions in the Rama cavern that somehow managed to be arid enough to "preserve" both the *titulus* so-called and the papyrus too.
>
> In sum, this is a masterful forgery, but a forgery nevertheless. My only prayer is that the entire world learn the truth about this deception as soon as possible, so that much needless agony can be ended. The hideous reports of despair among believers, mental breakdowns, suicides, abandonment of religious vocations, and the malaise of morale, particularly in Western countries, must stop immediately. I ask you, ladies and gentlemen of the press, to assist in this noble effort.

"I shall now try to answer your questions."

Several of the press corps had already dashed out to use their cell phones as Jon leaned over to Jennings and whispered, "That's *it?*"

But Jennings had his hand up. The little silver-haired sage recognized him, and Jon realized that this was the first time, in fact, that Montaigne had looked directly at them—unlike the television crews, who had been training zoom lenses on them to gauge their reaction to each syllable of Montaigne's presentation.

"Ah, Père Montaigne," Jennings's voice crackled. He cleared his throat and tried again, "Père Montaigne, what are some of the 'tiny lapses in syntax and grammar' you speak of in the document? We've had a congress of the greatest Semiticists in the world examining the papyrus, and nothing's been found amiss."

"*D'accord,* Professor Jennings. I did not see the flaws either, at first. On much further study, I did. . . . Yes—"

"Ah, before you take another question, Père Montaigne," Jennings interrupted, "would you please give us an example or two of those 'flaws'?"

Montaigne grew quite agitated, and his hands started trembling once again. "Surely they are much too technical for discussion here. Perhaps afterward we may discuss them. . . . Yes?"

A barrage of questions followed about how other aspects of Rama could have been fraudulently managed, and Montaigne replied with scenarios that were quite similar to Berthoud's.

Montaigne was on the point of closing when Jennings raised his hand. "Please, Père Montaigne, give us something to chew on. Professor Weber and I would like even *one* example of an inconsistency or flaw in the papyrus."

The pointed silver beard under the Dominican's chin started trembling, and his eyes were filling with tears. "Very well, then, I shall tell you. In fact, I shall do even more. Not only have I discovered the forgery, but . . . *the forger himself!* I shall name the forger!"

The aula hushed to a sepulchral silence. Montaigne glanced about in agitation and held both hands on the lectern to control their quivering. "The perpetrator—may God forgive him—the wretch who caused such misery in the Church and the world . . . is . . . *I myself!*"

Not a sound was heard. Then pandemonium broke out. The Latin patriarch held his head in his hands. Jon stared speechlessly at Shannon and Jennings. He groped for words and finally found them: "Incredible, Austin! That *would* explain why the Aramaic's so perfect in the papyrus, wouldn't it? Montaigne's the only one who could have brought it off!"

"Beyond belief!" Jennings sighed, shaking his head.

A forest of hands begged for recognition. Schmuel Sanderson of AP managed to get the floor with what, of course, was the universal question, "Why did you do it, Dr. Montaigne? What were your motives?"

"Quite simply this—I lost my faith years ago. I believed that the world would make much greater intellectual progress without the fetters of religion. You recall what the medieval church did to Galileo? In subtler ways, it has slowed the progress of science and knowledge ever since. Faith has blinded many people into believing the world is only a few thousand years old rather than billions. The truth of evolution is discarded. In America, I understand, Fundamentalist pressure has led to some textbooks' denying that dinosaurs ever existed, when their great bones clutter our museums, not? . . . Yes?"

"Renee St. Michel, *Figaro*. But *why*, Père Montaigne, did you then change your mind and reveal all this?"

"I had planned the whole scheme purely from an intellectual point of view. I didn't realize the . . . the terrible suffering it would cause. The response, especially within the Church, was much, much worse than I had dreamed. I could no longer bear it."

Jon's hand shot up. "Père Montaigne, I shall not break your confidence by reporting any details of a conversation we had in the dining room of the Seven Arches Hotel some months ago, but I should like *you* to recall it and—"

"You mean when I tried to purchase the papyrus for fifteen million dollars? I don't mind if you make that public. You want to know, of course, why I would have offered to purchase the papyrus with the intention of destroying it. Is that your question?"

"Yes, indeed."

"At that time, I still wanted to dupe the world. That was purely a psychological trick, a 'ploy' the English call it, I think, to make you believe the papyrus authentic. I *knew* you would never sell it."

Jon felt like a fish into whose mouth the fisherman had not only lodged the hook, but given it a firm, embedding tug. The canny little apostate had really brought it off, making fools of himself and the whole scholarly world.

Jennings waved his hand. "I hate sounding like a broken record, *Monsieur* Montaigne—and I shall call you that henceforth, since you have disgraced the priesthood—but we have many scholars in attendance here. I really must request that you tell us where the papyrus is flawed. If you forged it, why didn't you announce that immediately today, rather than faulting the Aramaic?"

"I . . . I was only trying to spare myself embarrassment. But, very well then . . . let me *prove* the forgery. When I wrote the papyrus, years ago, I intentionally cut a small fragment from its bottom edge—a sort of key to prove the forgery should I ever change my mind about it. I have that fragment inside this gold case." He held it up for all to see. "I suggest we proceed to the Rockefeller Museum and match it against the papyrus, yes?"

A long cavalcade of scholars, priests, monks, patriarchs, bishops, and reporters—looking like a Good Friday procession in reverse— filed out of the Latin patriarchate and turned eastward to the Rockefeller. Jon and Shannon hurried on ahead to prepare Nikos Papadimitriou for the onslaught. When everyone who could manage pushed inside the main hall at the Rockefeller, and with guards on all sides of a work table, Jon had Nikos bring in the papyrus. Then he beckoned to Montaigne, who opened the little gold case and extracted his small fragment with padded tweezers. "Aren't you going to lift the glass plate on top of the papyrus?" he asked.

"Yes, but first let's see if we have a general fit," said Jon. "Lay it into position on top of the glass, if you please."

"Very well," Montaigne placed the fragment directly over a rhomboid-shaped declivity along the bottom edge.

Jon and Jennings peered closely at the fragment. It seemed to fit indeed.

"Please step back," Jon told Montaigne. "*I'll* remove the glass and place the fragment." Carefully, he lifted the glass plate and slowly nudged the fragment into position. He and Jennings then examined it with a magnifying glass from various angles, and under a strong light.

Jon turned to the assembled throng and said, "The fragment is a flake of papyrus—of the same color and texture as the document here. It also fits perfectly. I presume, then, that Dr. Montaigne has told the truth in his confession, and that the 'Joseph Papyrus' is indeed a forgery."

A deafening roar swept the hall. The clergy started weeping for joy, embracing one another ecstatically. Someone started singing the great Common Doxology, and all joined in:

> Praise God from whom all blessings flow.
> Praise Him all creatures here below.
> Praise Him above, ye heavenly hosts.
> Praise Father, Son, and Holy Ghost!

The press corps stampeded out of the Rockefeller and television crews into their waiting vans. The world would not long be denied the earthshaking news.

Head bowed in shame and tears coursing down his cheeks, Claude Montaigne turned to the Rama staff and said, "I shall not even *try* to ask your forgiveness at this time, *mes amis*, though I do seek it. I only hope you will in time . . . *try* to understand what I attempted, however great my failure."

They said nothing. Montaigne continued, "May I . . . have my papyrus back, along with the fragment?"

"You may have neither," Jennings replied, evenly. "Good day, *Monsieur* Montaigne."

The chastened cleric bowed and left in the custody of his Dominican superiors.

Just as they were about to leave the Rockefeller, Jon had some disturbing second thoughts. "I wonder if I wasn't a little quick with my statement, Austin," he said. "We didn't examine that fragment very scientifically, did we?"

"Not really."

Jon furrowed his brow and reflected on the whipsaw developments that improbable afternoon. Then he turned and said, "If I were you, Nikos, I'd examine all the edges of that fragment under a microscope. The papyrus cavity too. See if it looks the same as the rest of the bottom edge of the papyrus."

"I had planned to do that in any case," said Nikos, smiling. "I'll phone you the results . . . probably this evening."

"What do you have in mind, Jon?" inquired Jennings.

"Only a thought. Nikos probably won't find anything amiss, but we've been splitting each hair five ways in this affair, now, haven't we?"

"True enough!"

The moment they returned to Ramallah, Jon had Dick Cromwell pass out photographs of the papyrus. Jon studied the sharp, high-contrast print of the flattened papyrus that scholars across the world had been using. The rhomboid cavity was plainly present at the mid-right side of the bottom edge.

"Funny, I never noticed it before," said Shannon. "But now it looks larger than life."

"Well, the whole bottom edge is chipped and irregular," said Jennings. "There was no reason for us to notice it."

"Seems to back up Montaigne's story, though, doesn't it?" said Cromwell.

"Dick, I've asked you this a dozen times, I know," said Jon, "and you've given me a dozen replies—all consistent. But, one last time, how in very *blazes* could that AP stringer have found a photograph like that lying open in your lab?"

"Omigosh! I've *told* you, Jon. I left *nothing* lying around the lab! And before I left for the States, I locked the lab tighter than a drum!"

"Do you suppose Montaigne had anything to do with it? Has he ever been inside the lab?"

"I doubt it," Jennings replied. "He did all his work at the École or the Rockefeller."

The phone rang, and Jon answered. "Yes . . . Nikos. What do you have?" Jon listened intently for some time. Then he said, "Fine work, Nikos. Fine work! Thanks extremely!" and hung up.

"Well?" Shannon demanded.

"Nikos says that all the edges on the interface between the fragment and the papyrus show *fresh cutting*. It's clean and compressed compared to the rest of the edging, which is irregular and fibrous."

"But wouldn't you expect that from Montaigne's original surgery?" asked Shannon.

"No. Montaigne claimed he did this years ago. In that time, Nikos says, the edges would have puffed back out more, especially after humidification."

"Well, *when*, then, could Montaigne have made his cut?" Brampton wondered. "The fragment was missing from the papyrus when we first discovered it, evidently—"

No one responded. Jennings beat a tattoo on the table with his fingers. "But *was* it, now?" he finally asked. "*Do* we know that it was really missing at discovery?"

"Hold it!" Jon shouted. "This 'authorized' print is not the earliest photo. Not by a long shot! Dick, where are those *very first* photos you took of the papyrus while it was still partially curled? You know, when you shot it from four different angles?"

"Well, those were a little fuzzy compared to these, so I threw them out."

"You had *bloody* well better be kidding!" Jon seethed.

"Of *course* I am," Cromwell laughed, while heading for the photo lab. He returned with the appropriate file. Jon quickly paged through the three photographs of the upper papyrus until he came to the print of the lowest quadrant.

"Great *balls* of fire!" he exclaimed. "Look, all of you," he pointed. "There. *No indentation!* The fragment hadn't been cut off yet!"

"Then *when* did Montaigne ever have access to the papyrus in order to do his dirty work?" Shannon wondered.

"We were always with him," said Jennings, shaking his head. "God only knows."

"And we do, too, I think," said Jon, brightening. "Remember that appointment we had with Montaigne at the Rockefeller after we got back from Sinai?"

"Oh! Yes, of course! The bounder was looking at the papyrus all by himself, wasn't he!" said Jennings.

"Won't work, fellas," said Cromwell. "I'd taken the 'authorized photos' long before that, and they show the fragment missing."

"*Darn!* That's right, Dick," Jon agreed.

Jennings, meanwhile, was dialing Nikos, but there was no answer either at the laboratory or at his home. "Stuff and bother!" huffed Jennings. "He probably left with his family for the weekend."

After a frustrating Saturday and Sunday trying to hold the media at bay, they finally reached Papadimitriou by phone on Monday morning. "We have an important question for you, Nikos," said Jennings. "Think back to the time we first brought the papyrus in to you and the days thereafter, all right? Fine. Now, was there ever a time when Montaigne was *alone* with the papyrus during that period?" Jennings covered the phone and whispered, "He's thinking."

"What's that? . . . You say it was the very first time we showed it to him? . . . He did *what?* . . . He came *back* into the laboratory after Jon left? . . . Well, thank you, Nikos. That solves it nicely."

The confrontation took place in the private living quarters of the Latin patriarch of Jerusalem. Present were the Rama Five, as well as the directors of the Albright Institute, the British School of Archaeology, and the École Biblique as witnesses. Besides the Latin patriarch and his secretary, the abbot of the Dominican Order in Israel and Père Claude Montaigne were also present. Out of courtesy to the Latin patriarchate, the press and public had not been notified. Kevin Sullivan, who had phoned from Rome the moment he heard the news "of proven forgery" on Radio Italiana, was expected to arrive imminently from Ben Gurion Airport, as personal representative of the pope. Jon had had the sad duty of calling Sullivan to report that any "proven forgery" was hardly that.

Umberto Cervantes, the patriarchal host, was a tall man with a full and generous face, elegantly crowned with a snowy mane and limpid emerald eyes. A good, honest man and a successful administrator, the Latin patriarch was unaware of the reason for the Jennings group's visit, other than, perhaps, to probe further into the motives of the now-disgraced Dominican.

Since it was midafternoon, the patriarch ordered tea for the group and bade Jennings open the discussion. Jennings began, but stopped when tea was poured. Lemon wedges and sugar cubes had hardly been distributed than Jennings resumed and Cervantes sat upright at the baleful tidings that Montaigne had lied about the fragment. At that moment, Kevin Sullivan burst inside, and, after briefest hellos, was updated on the discussion to that point. Jon then distributed Cromwell's original papyrus photograph, revealing no recess, along with subsequent views showing the cut.

Claude Montaigne said nothing. Sitting rigidly in his chair, he merely studied the patriarch's oriental rug. Cervantes demanded that he respond. He did not.

"I ask you again, Père Claude, answer these charges! As your ecclesiastical superior, I *require* that you answer them."

Seconds of silence passed. Finally, Montaigne grasped the handles of his chair and looked at the group for the first time. "*Oui,*" he whispered. Then, more audibly, "I cut off the fragment inside the Rockefeller laboratory, and not years earlier."

"Did you also lie when you claimed to have forged the papyrus?" the patriarch pressed.

"The papyrus is certainly a forgery," he responded. "The false nuances in grammar and syntax, the—"

"What *are* those 'false nuances'?" Jon interposed. "As I recall, you've never given us a proper answer to that question."

Montaigne began a long, technical soliloquy on tiny points of grammar that seemed less and less convincing—even to himself—for at last he threw up his hands and said, "All right, I'll stop. Ah . . . what was the question, Your Excellency?"

"Did you also lie when you claimed to have forged the papyrus?"

"Well . . . yes. *I* did not forge it. But I have no doubt that—"

"*Why?*" Jon boomed. "Why would you, one of the greatest Semiticists—you, who have given such *treasures* to the world of scholarship—why would you have committed professional *suicide* by doing what you did? You are *through* in the company of scholars, Montaigne! No one will look at your writing again! *How* could you do this?"

Montaigne was silent for several moments. Then he smiled wanly and said, "My greatest falsehood was to say that I had lost my faith. Before my God and in your presence, I tell you that *I have not!* And if Jesus could give His life for me, the very *least* I could do was to surrender my scholarship to the Savior. Oh, *happy* sacrifice!"

Now it was the others who were silent. All seemed strangely touched. Shannon had tears in her eyes, while it was Jon's turn to study the oriental carpet.

Montaigne continued, "Church bells are ringing again throughout the world, *mes amis!* Jesus has returned, as it were! People have faith and hope and love once again! First reports tell of churches crowded, cathedrals filled. Almost a million gathered in front of St. Peter's yesterday, as the Holy Father chanted a *Te Deum* that the forgery has been exposed. Will you now—*can* you—tear this renewed faith out of their very lives? *Can you?*"

No one replied. Again he took the initiative: "I was . . . how you say? . . . I was 'buying time,' *mes amis*. Someday Rama will be exposed as a fraud invented in hell itself. I have not been able to discover that, as yet. Nor have you. But in the meantime, how many hundreds, thousands, will have died without the comfort of the Resurrection? *How many,* I ask you?"

Again there was no response.

"All I ask, my colleagues, is that we let the world have its Christianity back, for it *is* indeed 'a teaching of hope'—the only thing that malicious forger ever said properly."

The silence, again, was deafening, until the host said, simply, "Why don't we have a brief . . . a brief interlude . . . or, rather, recess, my friends. I'll order more tea. Perhaps we can come back together in, shall we say, a half hour?"

The Rama Five walked onto a balcony overlooking Jerusalem, where Kevin Sullivan joined them. They stared eastward across the domes and cupolas, bell towers and minarets of the Old City toward the deepening gold of the setting sun against the Mount of Olives.

"*Was* it that way in Rome yesterday, Kevin?" asked Jon, quietly.

"Yes. I tried to get to the pope in time with your *caveat,* but I didn't make it. The Italian faithful were beside themselves with joy."

"Well, do you suppose we *should* let it go for now?" Jennings offered. "Continue our work secretly? Out of the glare of publicity?"

"Certainly would be easier that way!" Brampton agreed.

"What are *you* thinking, Jon?" asked Shannon.

"I . . . don't know. It would be our first false step in this whole unlikely affair." While gazing across the Old City, Harvard's motto came suddenly, incongruously, to mind: VERITAS, truth. *Let the Yalies cling to their LUX ET VERITAS,* Jon mused, *their "Light and Truth." Truth is enough. Light, without truth, is no light at all.* No "malicious forger" had been detected thus far. Likely, he didn't exist. Or, conceivably, he did. But meanwhile, nothing—however ancient, grand, magnificent, or sustaining—must ever, *ever* stand in the way of Truth. Truth in the past, in the present, for the future.

Jon turned to the others and said, "However you decide, I, for one, will *not* go along with Montaigne's scheme."

As they went back inside, Jon felt an arm across his shoulder. "Nor will I, friend," said Kevin, "much as it hurts." The others concurred. Emphatically.

"We've come to a unanimous conclusion, Your Excellency," said Jon, as they reconvened. "Truth is paramount. Admitting a false forgery now, however convenient, would make it more difficult to detect a true forgery later on, if such is the case. Truth, in any event, *must* prevail, whatever the cost. Our colleagues, the distinguished directors of the archaeology institutes here in Jerusalem, will have it no other way. The papal representative will have it no other way, and—"

"Nor will I," said the Dominican abbot.

"Nor I," said the Latin patriarch. "Brother Montaigne, while we can sympathize with your intentions, we *cannot* condone the means you employed to gain them. We must herewith strip you of your priestly functions for the time being and commend you to the spiritual care of your Dominican superiors. Under no circumstances are you to preach or teach or publish until further notice.

All of us will pray for you, I'm sure." Then he turned and asked, "And now, my dear professors, do you wish to draw up a public statement for the press? Or shall I?"

"We'll be happy to leave that in your hands, Your Excellency," said Jennings.

It seemed a particularly cruel trick to play on the world. Buoyant relief and exhilaration one day, a return to the pit of despair the next. Frustration, anger, bitter resentment boiled up at various corners of the globe. Some took the easy, the cheap, the obvious path, like Melvin Merton and his coterie, who were praising Claude Montaigne as "one very blessed Judas who repented" at the beginning of the week, and cursing him as "the excrement of the Evil One" at the end. "See?" said Merton. "You can't trust *any* of these would-be scholars, these so-called archaeologists. They're all in league with the devil!"

Just before he returned to Rome, Kevin Sullivan had lunch with Jon atop the Jerusalem Hilton.

"So, when will it all end, friend?" inquired Sullivan. "The Church has been trying to function with a razor across its throat for almost a year now."

"The panels should be winding up their work by late summer. Unless something new comes up, that should be it. Have you been working on John 20:26? Our New Testament Panel has."

"Yes, we have. You're saying Rama's all authentic, then? No put-up job?"

"I'm only saying that the Church had jolly well better be ready for something like that."

"Okay, that John passage says the resurrected Jesus appeared to His disciples *through shut doors*—He materialized through the walls. Fine, that certainly sounds like a *spiritual*—not a physical—posture for the Resurrection. But don't forget how that scene continues. Jesus invites 'Doubting' Thomas to touch the marks on His hands and side."

"John doesn't say Thomas did so, though I agree he might have."

"Quibble, quibble, quibble! But what about the parallel account in Luke?"

"I know." Jon held up his hands. "Jesus tells them, 'Touch me, for a spirit doesn't have *flesh* and *bones* as you see that I have.'"

"And after that, He *ate* a piece of broiled fish."

"Fine, Kevin. There we have the other pole in the Easter account, a very *physical* Resurrection. And yet where were the bones during that transit through the wall? Maybe that's what St. Paul had in mind with his magnificent illustration in 1 Corinthians 15: just as a seed planted in the earth is transformed into something much greater—a living plant—so, he says, 'it is with the resurrection of the dead. What is sown as a *physical* body is raised as a *spiritual* body.'"

"Agreed. But we've always understood that as true, glorified bodies, like Christ's. In that same chapter, Paul says we'll not be disembodied spirits but spiritual *bodies*. Any 'bones' are transformed. They're *not* left behind."

"I know, I know, Kev. It's the way we both were taught. Hah! I'll never forget how I reacted to an Easter article in the *St. Louis Globe Democrat* back in '79. Four area clergy were asked how they'd react to news that some archaeological team had discovered the bones of Jesus 'with scientific certainty'—"

"Sounds familiar, doesn't it?" Kevin commented.

"And how! Anyway, a Lutheran seminary president gave an orthodox answer, but he begged the question by saying it couldn't happen. A Methodist professor said he'd have to do a lot of rethinking. But an Episcopal rector said that finding Christ's remains 'would not affect me in the slightest.' I recall being totally *disgusted* at that response. The one I easily agreed with was a Catholic New Testament professor at St. Louis University who said that he 'would totally despair.' Now, *that* was honest! So you see where my heart is, Kevin. Or was."

"And now you're saying we'd better do that Methodist's 'rethinking'?"

"I'm saying we'd better be ready for *anything*. Surely you have Catholic theologians who agree with that Episcopal rector."

"We certainly do, even in Rome. Some of our ultraliberals have been smiling for months. Maybe you're not aware of it here in the sacred boondocks, Jon, but right now there's a *fierce* battle brewing inside the Vatican. It used to be polarization, but now it's almost war. The liberals are pleading with the Holy Father to accept a spiritual-only Resurrection even before you announce your final results here, because some of them figure the odds *for* authenticity at a hundred to one. The moderate middle and the conservatives, of course, know all about this pressure from the left, and Pedro Cardinal Gonzales has warned the pope to resist it."

"Warned?! And how *is* God's Watchdog-for-the-Faith? Still sniffing out heresy in every echelon of the Church?"

Kevin smiled and said, "Well, Gonzales and his Holy Office have the support of Augustin Buchbinder, Vatican Secretary of State, and his large following in the Curia. They want no tampering whatever with the Easter event."

"No one does. But what if there's no alternative?"

"I don't know." He drained the final suds from his second beer, and Jon did the same.

"When you have all the panel reports, Jon, could you let us know the results *before* you go public with them? Per usual?"

"I'll do better than that. I'll fly to Rome and go over them with you and the pope personally."

TWENTY-ONE

The Israeli government was hard pressed. The sacred catastrophe at Rama charged the land with a volatility that spread even to Palestinians in the West Bank. The *intifada* seemed to revive: Arab boys hurling stones, curfews reimposed, a bus bombed outside Bethlehem, kibbutzniks in reprisal raids—the same sad script of violence seemed to be plagiarized from the recent past.

Whether or not Rama was responsible, Gideon Ben-Yaakov continued to be the government's chief liaison with the Rama staff. To say his relationship with Jon showed signs of strain was to understate, and the reason—obviously—was Shannon. For his part, Jon tried to stay out of Gideon's way as much as possible, letting Austin Jennings handle most of their contacts. Early in July, though, he did run in to him at the Shrine of the Book in Jerusalem, where he had taken the Paleography Panel to examine the *titulus* more closely. All cavern artifacts were now being stored there. The greetings Gideon exchanged with Jon were quite professional, if a little frosty.

When Jon returned to Ramallah that night, Clive Brampton met him with happy news. "Guess what, Jon? Naomi said yes! We're going to be married in October!"

"Fabulous, Clive! I'm *so* happy for both of you!"

"I'm only afraid that with our backgrounds, we'll breed pots instead of kids!"

"No trouble dating them if you do!" Jon laughed.

After supper, he told Shannon the happy news and added, "I really *like* their plans, my love. What say we make it a foursome?"

She gave him an incandescent smile, but said nothing.

"No, on second thought, I don't want to share our joy with *anyone* else on that magic day."

"I wouldn't either," she agreed.

"When *will* it be, then? You know, you've never given me a clear 'yes,' Shannon!"

She pulled his head down to plant a long, tender, tingling kiss. "That's intentional, my darling. I want to keep you waiting, wondering, a little off-guard—the prince must fight for the affections of his lady fair, who is *never* to be taken for granted."

"Exquisite psychology, my dear. But terribly frustrating."

"Smashing! Let's keep it that way."

"Eventually, though, how does the concept of 'Shannon Weber' strike you?"

"Oh, I had the answer to that months ago."

"Which is . . ."

"If you can't figure *that* out, I may have to reconsider!"

He clasped her tightly, holding her locked inside his soul for some moments. At times, he reflected, hugging can be better than kissing, or even what can follow. "*When*, Shannon?" he finally asked, once again.

"When the crisis is over—one way or the other. You'll be hopelessly distracted until then, and I want you all to myself."

"All right, my darling. That *does* make some sense."

"Besides, now I don't even know what sort of wedding I want. Traditional Christian? Or just a civil ceremony?"

"Losing your faith?"

"I . . . could be. How about you, Jon?"

"Each passing day, it gets harder and harder to believe."

The "foursome" happened after all, though not in nuptial form. The two staff couples who were very much in love found rare happiness that pressured summer by escaping on weekends to the Mediterranean, since Clive had infected them all with a new hobby—marine archaeology. Piling scuba gear into the Land Rover, they made for Caesarea, where they dove down through crystal green waters and explored the huge jetties built by Herod the Great to enclose his magnificent harbor. On their latest scuba excursion, they also swam in the Mediterranean until sunset, and then lit a campfire to picnic along the beach.

"I think I'll transfer here after we've finished at Rama," said Clive.

Naomi tittered and said, "Some people think archaeology is only a matter of gluing cracked pots together. They should see us now!"

"I *knew* you couldn't get away for even half a day without thinking of your sacred ceramics," Clive joshed.

She playfully lunged for him and then chased him up the beach.

"She *is* a very beautiful woman," said Shannon. "I wish I had her legs. How come you didn't fall in love with her instead, Jon?"

"Who says I didn't? She'd make *some* consolation prize if you turn me down!"

She made a small fist and cuffed his shoulder.

"Well, Shannon, it's only—let's see if I get it right—it's only that 'I want to keep you wondering, a little off-guard . . . *never* to be taken for granted' . . ."

"Monster!" She pinched his arm. "That's Okay. Gideon will have me back."

He laughed, embraced the lissome figure across the length of her body, and lavished her smooth, tanned skin with kisses. Suddenly the place and the circumstances recalled a poignant parallel. Andrea! His dear—forgotten?—Andrea. Some of the next kisses were in her memory. Shannon would never know. He only hoped that, somehow, she'd understand and forgive him if she had known.

In late July, the Investigative Panel met inside the boardroom of the British School of Archaeology on the slopes of Mount Scopus in north Jerusalem. Since Jennings and Brampton were off scouting new sites, Jon represented the Rama staff. Henri Berthoud was at his creative best, unveiling a fresh scenario of fraud for the panel, but his latest effort failed to account for first-century human remains at the Rama cavern—*if* they were not authentic. He turned to Jon and asked, "Aren't ancient bones something of a rarity in Israel?"

"Not really," he replied. "At Qumran, for example, de Vaux found a cemetery just east of the structures there. They excavated about forty of the graves, and found something like thirty males."

"Oh?" Glastonbury asked, his eyebrows arching. "Where are the bones now?"

"All reburied, of course."

"Do we *know* that?"

"Certainly. That's standard operating procedure." Jon paused for a moment, then added, "And our bones couldn't have come from there. None of the Qumran skeletons had any 'Christlike' abrasions on their bones."

Glastonbury held up his plump hands. "Paddington, what did you find in your history of the site?"

The James Bondian figure stirred in his seat and replied, "Well, we now know the ownership of the site as far back as 1810. Only two Arab families, connected by marriage, have owned the property through their descendants since then, and Kensington was able to buy it from the last generation in the turmoil following the 1948 Israeli War of Independence. Here's a copy of the title from the Register of Deeds in Jerusalem." He passed out several photocopies.

"Then," Paddington continued, "I made a list of all staff personnel in the Kensington and Jennings campaign annuals, including Arab labor chiefs, and interviewed as many as remained in Israel or Jordan. The rest I sent on to you, Reginald. I trust you chased them down?"

"Yes, most of them. But continue."

"Well, I have several hundred pages of transcript from the interviews." He opened a fat file. "Shall I read them?"

"Good Lord, no!" Glastonbury chortled. "Just tell us where you found the flaw, the secret strange exception, the clue. Then we can happily solve this mystery—*if* it is a mystery—and all go home."

Paddington looked up wearily and said, "I didn't find any. It all bears out pretty well what's in the annuals, allowing for slight differences due, most likely, to the fallibility of human memory . . . And what did *you* find, Reginald?"

"Oh, a *little* more. I focused on the principal archaeologists—all British—with one strange exception—that American fellow—what was his name? Weavil? Weaver? Oh, yes, Weber . . . Jonathan Weber!"

As the panel duly snickered, Jon said, "Shall I excuse myself?"

"No, stay, stay! Because *you* did it, you see." Silence blanketed the boardroom. Glastonbury's eyes bored in on Jon, as he continued. "One international best seller wasn't enough for you. You also had to set up a second one, which will expose to the world how you brought it all off!" Glastonbury was not smiling.

Several panel members looked shocked. Jon actually started to squirm.

A vast grin broke across Glastonbury's face and his jowls shook with laughter. "I *jest*, you fools! We've come to a miserable pass indeed if we lose our sense of humor! No, Jonathan, my flight to the 'colonies' to check your credentials was quite useless indeed. They're not only frightfully impressive, but clean as the proverbial hound's tooth . . . which I've always thought a rather dismal expression, not? Imagine using that phrase in the case of the Baskervilles! But I digress—"

"You do indeed, Reginald," said Paddington. "Sign of dotage. Have you considered putting out to pasture?"

The chairman chuckled. "Yes, this *is* the case that could well force my retirement! But seriously, Scotland Yard now has a complete file on Lord Kensington, Professor Jennings, Clive Brampton, Noel Nottingham, and several other English archaeologists and scholars associated with the Rama dig in various seasons. Did we find *motives*, you'd like to know. Well, perhaps, but only *very* shallow ones. Kensington, if you can keep this confidential, was no Puritan moralist, let me tell you. With a wife and children back in Bristol, he had a contessa in Rome and some courtesan in Cairo to keep him occupied, and he was known to complain about the moral strictures of the established Church. But was *that* enough to have him engineer a hoax of this magnitude? One doubts.

"Now, Austin Balfour Jennings came from an Anglican parsonage in Ulster. Parents English on both sides, but they loved Northern

Ireland and moved there. Jennings deeply admired his father, who was killed in a traffic accident just before retiring. He then studied for the ministry at Oxford, but got sidetracked into Semitics and archaeology, where he performed so brilliantly that they invited him onto the faculty. Between stints in the classroom, he dug with Roland de Vaux at Qumran and then with Kensington at Rama. Just before Kensington died in '67, Jennings met a Catholic girl from Drogheda—that's on the Irish east coast. They married and had Shannon, who was born in 1974. While still a baby, her mother died, leaving Jennings despondent for the next year or so."

"What did she die of?" asked Jon. He knew Shannon's version, and was only checking out Scotland Yard's.

"Pneumonia. After that, Jennings conducted digs at Bethel and Shiloh before returning to Rama. Those are the high points. Of course, we have much more detail in the files."

"Any of the details give Jennings a motive?" Paddington probed. "Father died . . . wife died. Maybe he was mad at God. You said he was despondent."

Jon was getting perturbed, and said, "Pretty flimsy motives for fraud on *this* huge a scale! Jennings just isn't the charlatan type. A true hoaxer would have disguised his grief. Jennings has talked freely about it."

Glastonbury went on to open the Brampton and Nottingham files. Both were secularists, but hardly militant sorts, who wanted to kill Christianity. Next, he reached for the files of those scholars who had worked with Kensington or Jennings in Israel. Motives here were weak or nonexistent, but one name was well-known in archaeological circles—Gladwin Dunstable, of the University of London Institute of Archaeology. Jon knew him as "the British Sandy McHugh."

After presenting his *vita,* Glastonbury continued, "Dunstable dug with Jennings at Shiloh in '72. Now, of course, he runs the great analysis labs in London. What a memory that man has! When I interviewed him, he all but gave me details on what Jennings had for breakfast each morning! He's the one who introduced Jennings to radiocarbon dating. So when Dunstable left for the season and planned to see Italy on the way back to England, Jennings suggested he send him something from Pompeii so that he could test the new Weizmann lab at Rehovot to see how close they came to AD 79."

"Clever idea," commented Paddington. "What did he send?"

"Haven't the foggiest. In any case, that's our last name, my colleagues. Do any of you find anything amiss? Do you see any motives? Any flaws? Clues? Whatever?"

No one raised his pencil. Or hand. Or eyebrow.

"Well, then, homework for you all!" said the chairman. "We're copying every page in each of your files, and you will *all* read the fine work being done by your colleagues. Then we'll compare notes and have a final session in September. Meanwhile, ferret out anything else you can. *Anything.*"

As they stood up to leave, Glastonbury put an arm across Jon's shoulders and said, "You continue digging in your way. We'll continue digging in ours."

For Jon, it was simply *fun* talking with Naomi Sharon across the lunch table at the dig. He hoped everyone understood that, especially Shannon and Clive. Naomi's breathtaking appearance was almost a disadvantage, since people usually assumed the woman couldn't possibly have a brilliant mind with such an exterior, as though brains and beauty were mutually exclusive. The Rama staff knew better, of course, and Jon often consulted Naomi for the Jewish viewpoint on some aspect of the crisis, since she read widely beyond her specialty in ceramics.

One noon toward the end of summer, they were sitting apart from the group in the mess tent when Jon posed a startling question. "Put the case, Naomi, first, that our finds prove absolutely authentic; second, that the liberal interpretation of a purely spiritual resurrection for Jesus becomes the norm for Christianity as a result; but put the case, third, that instead of being accepted, there is instead a vast rejection and a tune-out of the Christian faith in general. Now, if all this happens, chart the religious future of our planet."

Naomi nearly choked on the pear she had been munching. "Well, Jon," she recovered, "that sounds like a one-question doctoral exam even the great Hillel would have been hard pressed to answer!"

"Try Nostradamus. He could see into the future." Jon winked.

"I hate to say this, Jon, but there may be more truth to that third possibility than you realize. Most people on earth, including believers, are very material, very tangible sorts. They have trouble with abstractions, and think only in the concrete. A spiritual-only hereafter may appeal to the Platonists—a tiny group—while leaving the masses untouched. Do you know what's boosted your Christianity into the world's highest religious orbit?"

"The Resurrection?"

"Exactly. Its teachings about 'the resurrection of the dead and the life everlasting.' No eschatology touches yours. What, after all, does any dying person want but the assurance that death is not the end, but rather the beginning of something better? And not 'better' in the abstract. Take away the Resurrection, and you lose probably 80 to 90 percent of your membership."

Jon nodded. "I always had my doubts that the common believer would ever accept the 'mature faith' being urged by our Christian left. So, now we're beyond hypothesis three. The church loses three-quarters of its members. Who, if anyone, picks them up?"

"Well," she peered into her water glass as if it were a crystal ball, "I see Islam making giant strides—not by picking up your ex-Christians, but by winning the undecided Third World, since it will no longer have the powerful competition of Christianity." She said nothing more.

"That's too bad, Naomi. I wish it could've been Judaism instead. Along with Christianity, it's the only other faith with rock-solid historical credentials."

"Judaism *could* benefit," she replied, slowly. "But only if it got its act together and learned a few lessons from the Christians about mission and evangelism. We have a resurrection, too, you know."

"As well as your very own country, no less!"

At that moment, Shannon walked over and said, playfully, "I've been watching you two. You're not trying to steal my man, now, are you, Naomi?"

"Of course!" she laughed. "Aren't all the girls?"

That night, Shannon was a little less playful when she asked,

"What were you discussing so *intently* with Naomi this afternoon, Jon?"

When he told her, she seemed dissatisfied. "Sure, sure, Jon!" she said. "You and this . . . gorgeous sabra were discussing the 'spiritual future' of humanity!"

"But we *were*, Shannon! It was all purely platonic."

"Exactly—play for you, tonic for her!"

He chuckled, but she continued to frown.

Words were exchanged. Dialogue grew heated. Voices were raised. Accusations flew. Emotions replaced logic. Her Irish temper flared. His Germanic temperament kindled. In a great huff, they stalked off to their rooms that night, slamming the doors behind them. It was a new, unwelcome milestone in their relationship—their first fight. Both spent a bad, restless night.

Something about the beauty and sobriety of daylight seems to bring resolution to life's problems. Jon and Shannon were back in each other's arms just after breakfast, confessing that they'd behaved at the maturity levels of high-school sophomores.

Rama was not so easily resolved. It was now late September, when Jon should have returned to Harvard, but the university granted him extended leave. All Phase III panels had completed their tasks except for Archaeology and Investigation, the former because all of Rama had not yet been uncovered, the latter because Glastonbury refused to throw in the towel. The international scholars' congress, however, meeting in plenary session in Jerusalem, felt the task was virtually completed, since the last digging to be done at Rama was nowhere near the cavern area, and Glastonbury had nothing fresh to offer. He was only a meticulous old bloodhound who, in fine Scotland Yard tradition, never closed a file on any case so long as the culprit had not been found. The probability that there was no culprit in this case had never really registered with Glastonbury. Paddington said as much at their final meeting, wishing him a happy retirement.

The Phase III findings were summarized in a fat, 585-page manual that represented only the *epitome* of the total research. The whole body would publish out to a dozen volumes. Rama was now the most meticulously researched archaeological site in history.

Jennings and Jon returned to Ramallah after the final session of the scholars' congress in Jerusalem, the ponderous typescripts of the epitome in hand. Shannon asked what they contained. "I'll tell you after supper, dear," said her father.

After supper, however, Jennings said he was too tired. "Why don't you ask Jonathan instead?"

Jon suggested they take a long walk. "I'll tell you along the way, my love." Then he added, "But we can't stay out too late, since you'll be driving me to Ben Gurion in the morning."

"Oh . . . your flight to Rome?"

"Right. I have to see Kevin Sullivan. And the pope. An old promise."

Dark glasses and banded Panama straw hat got Jon successfully through both Ben Gurion and Leonardo da Vinci airports. Sullivan whisked him away on the Via Ostiensis to Rome.

"Thanks for not demanding an 'epitome of the epitome,' Kevin," said Jon.

"Time enough for that later."

"What's the word on current Vatican politics?"

"Just as I told you before, only more so. A liberal consensus is growing that the Holy Father *must* accept the 'new theology' or see the ship of the Church founder and sink."

"And the Holy Office sorts?"

"Well, the ultras on the right are starting to make threats I never thought these ears would hear."

"Such as . . ."

"Such as . . . I really shouldn't be telling you this. In *absolute* confidence, Jon?"

"What else?"

"Well, Gonzales and Buchbinder have been holding secret meetings with their cronies in the Curia. I understand they're monitoring as much as they can of the pope's discussions with visiting theologians. And, of course, they fine-tooth comb each of his public statements."

"So, it's come to that? Do you suppose they've bugged his apartments? Or office?"

"I don't know . . . I hope not. In any case, the word's out in the Curia that if Benedict goes over to the 'new theology,' they'll try to have him declared *non compos mentis,* or whisk him away to Castel Gandolfo for a *long* rest. Incommunicado of course."

"Incredible! Could they get away with that?"

"Who knows? I think there'd be a horrendous outcry from the rest of the Church. There's also talk of forced abdication as a possible alternative."

"Any precedent for that?"

"Well, in the eleventh century, Pope Benedict IX took cash to step down in favor of a reforming successor. Then there's Celestine V, who resigned to become a hermit in the thirteenth. And, of course, Gregory XII abdicated in 1415 to end the Great Schism."

"But never a *forced* abdication, per se?"

"Of course, there's an even more *grotesque* rumor too. That's the one the devil sends our way each century or so—that someone might stop Benedict through physical harm *inside* the Vatican."

"Shades of the conspiracy theorists and John Paul I's month-long reign!"

Sullivan stopped in front of his apartment. "Let's freshen up inside," he said. "We're due in the papal apartments at 4 PM, which gives us a good hour."

"Welcome, *caro professore!*" said Benedict XVI, his arms spread wide to embrace Jon.

"I'm delighted to see you again, *Santissimo Padre!*"

"It's been almost a year and a half since we first met, and, ah . . . *much* has happened in the meantime, has it not?"

"To say the very least!"

"I thank you for having kept us closely informed of your progress, *amico mio.* Father Sullivan here has been very helpful in relaying your reports."

They smiled, and again let Benedict have the initiative in conversation.

"I also appreciate how carefully you've dealt with the evidence at Rama, good Professor. You've always stressed the conditional nature of the discoveries, and you've been sensitive as to how this would affect the faithful. But now, of course, we're eager to learn about your scholars' congress."

"Their conclusions are summarized in this rather ponderous volume. I know you'll read it at your leisure."

"I will indeed. Perhaps, though, you could report some of the, ah, important findings for me."

"Of course. First let me—"

"Better yet," the pope interrupted, "since it's so beautiful a day for early October, why don't we take a walk through our gardens, and you can tell me along the way. Yes?"

"That would be delightful," Jon replied, glancing knowingly at Kevin as the pope led the way. Sullivan caught the wordless comment perfectly and shrugged his shoulders.

And maybe they *were the paranoid, bug-seeking sorts,* Jon mused, while enjoying a pleasant stroll under the pine and cypress canopy of the Vatican Gardens behind St. Peter's basilica. At a small clearing near the center, illumined by the ruddy golden rays of a dropping sun, Benedict bade them sit down on a pair of rustic benches. He looked at Jon and said, "And now, I am anxious to hear your report, dear friend."

This would be the most difficult speech of his life, Jon knew, but his only option was to reveal the truth accurately rather than diplomatically. Slowly, specifically—and not unemotionally—he presented the final conclusions.

"The Archaeology Panelists praised the methodology of our dig, and found *all* of our discoveries to be authentic. The ceramic typology, they said, was a model of accuracy. The Anthropology/ Pathology specialists found no evidence of modern intrusion in the skeletal remains. The Analysis Panel endorsed all the radiocarbon and Smithsonian tests, and even narrowed the age-range in some of them. The Linguistics/Paleography specialists found nothing anomalous in the papyrus, parchment, or stone inscriptions, and thought the one grammatical error on the *titulus* quite natural, under the circumstances."

Jon paused to let the bitter tidings digest. This could only come as a cruel succession of shocks for his hearers. But the pope said softly, "Go on, my friend. Go on."

"The Investigative Panel, thus far, has found no indication of fraud, forgery, or foul play, despite many hypothetical scenarios they've discussed. Nor have they found any credible motivation for such deception among staff personnel, or anyone else."

Again, he paused. But when there was no response, he continued. "In the Theological Sector, the Old and New Testament Panels found no irregularities in the burial procedure at Rama, or implied in the papyrus. While ossuaries were in wider use than sarcophagi as of AD 60, the latter were still in fashion, especially among the wealthy.

"Accordingly," Jon now summarized, "the international scholars' congress finds itself compelled to conclude that the discoveries in the Rama cavern area appear to be fully authentic."

The sun had dipped lower, and a chilly breeze started whistling in the pines. The white papal cassock fluttered just a bit. Benedict XVI looked at the brown pine needles strewn about his sandals and said nothing. Finally, it was Kevin who spoke, very softly. "They conclude, then, that the . . . sacred bones of . . ." his voice caught, in great emotion, ". . . of . . . of Jesus . . . *have* been discovered?"

Jon nodded slowly. Then he added, "The books remain open, of course, for any further evidence that could turn up in the future." It seemed a hopeless consolation.

"And you, Jonathan?" the pope suddenly inquired, using his given name for the first time. "Do *you* think those are the bones of Jesus too?"

Jon said nothing, as eternal seconds ticked away. He almost felt as if he were standing before God Himself on Judgment Day, compelled to give the answer on which his eternal salvation depended. But no, this was no divine tribunal. This was merely the high priest for one billion believers. Or better yet, this was merely one Christian asking the opinion of another.

"Answer me, Jonathan," the pope asked again. This time Jon saw large tears welling up in his vivid brown eyes.

"*Santissimo Padre*," Jon began, his own voice now heavily

choked with emotion. "My heart says *no* to your question. But my head, in view of . . . of the *overwhelming* evidence, has . . . has no alternative but to say . . . yes."

Emitting a great groan, Benedict fell to his knees on the carpet of pine needles, put his elbows on the bench, and bowed his head. For long moments he said nothing. Finally his lips parted, and he whispered:

> *Angelo di Dio,*
> *che sei il mio custode,*
> *illumina e custodisci,*
> *reggi e governa me*
> *che ti fui affidato*
> *dalla Pieta celeste.*
> *Amen.*

He continued praying silently for the next quarter hour.

Jon and Kevin walked off a bit, to give the pope his privacy with God. "That's the common Italian *children's* prayer," Kevin whispered, tears in his eyes, "the first prayer Benedict ever learned. It must have been in Piacenza, when Mama Albergo taught it to her little Ricardo. American Catholic kids learn the English version as their very first prayer. I know I did."

> Angel of God, my Guardian dear
> To Whom His love commits me here,
> Ever this day be at my side
> To light, to guard, to rule, and guide.
> Amen.

Kevin's voice cracked at the "Amen," and he leaned against a tree, covered his face, and wept.

Jon peered through the pines at the great dome of St. Peter's basilica, shimmering gold in the twilight, and whispered, "Amen, indeed!"

TWENTY-TWO

At Ben Gurion, Jon spied them before they did him, thanks to the dark-glasses-cum-Panama-hat routine. This time it was two gorgeous women as the welcoming committee, but both Shannon and Naomi looked distraught. Naomi caught sight of him, rushed into his arms, and buried her head in his chest, sobbing.

"Clive is *dead*, Jon!" Shannon cried, eyes pink with tears.

"*Great God*, no! *No!* What happened?"

"He drowned, swimming at Caesarea."

"*No!* When?"

"Night before last."

Jon collapsed onto a bench, shaking his head and clenching his teeth as if to overrule the event by sheer willpower. Finally he groaned and said, "I'll get my luggage. Tell me on the way— *everything.*"

This time the kilometers to Ramallah were pure anguish. As Naomi sobbed quietly in the back seat, Shannon supplied the catastrophic details. "Naomi and I were in Jerusalem, shopping for her . . . for her," she burst out crying, "for her *bridal* gown! Papa was in Tel Aviv at the publishers. So Clive must have gotten bored, and driven to Caesarea with his scuba gear. After diving, he must have taken a final swim—like we always do—since the gear was repacked in the Rover. He never came back. They found the Rover on the beach, and his . . . his body washed up on shore a couple miles north, by the Roman aqueduct!"

"*Impossible!*" Jon objected. "It just *can't* be! Clive was a good swimmer."

"Yes," Naomi cried from the back seat, "but he also loved to

275

swim *way* out. Remember the time you yelled at him, 'Hey, Clive, if you're heading for Spain, you forgot your passport!'"

He smiled briefly, grimly, then returned to his grief and asked, "When did you say this happened?"

"We don't know for sure," said Shannon. "Probably the afternoon or evening before last. They didn't find him until yesterday morning."

"Any . . . any sign of foul play?"

"No. Nothing. Just a foolish, idiotic drowning that has no rhyme nor reason," Shannon cried. "Looks like God was sleeping again."

"He *does* take naps, you know," Jon replied, recalling a certain Swiss avalanche and not caring, at the moment, whether his comment bordered on blasphemy or not. Suddenly, another too-poignant parallel occurred to him. "So," he said bitterly, "we lose *another* great archaeologist to the Mediterranean!"

"Yes!" Naomi cried. "Paul Lapp! I thought of that later on. We use his *Ceramic Chronology* to type the pottery we find at Rama."

"What about Paul Lapp?" asked Shannon.

"He was scouting out a new site on Cyprus some years ago, and took a swim off Kyrenia Beach," Jon replied. "He got caught in the undertow and was carried out to sea. Like Clive's, a *terrible* loss to archaeology!"

When they reached Ramallah, they found a disconsolate Jennings, staring at the floor of his office, almost motionless. Wearily he raised his head as they walked in, and he said softly, "He had *such* a brilliant future, Jonathan. *Such* a brilliant future."

Jon slumped down next to him. "Why, Austin? Why?"

He shook his head. "They've asked that question ever since Job, I suppose. We'll likely be asking it till the end of time." He groaned and held his head in his hands.

"At times I wonder if a curse isn't hanging over this dig," said Shannon. "Rama seems to have brought the world nothing but agony. And now Clive's been snatched away too."

Jennings uttered a sad grunt and said, "Everyone must show Naomi all the love and support we can manage . . ." He choked on his words and then moaned again, "He would have had *such* a brilliant future."

The funeral was held at St. George's Cathedral in Jerusalem, with representatives of the international archaeology community in the congregation. The dean of St. George's conducted the Anglican service, and Jon delivered the eulogy. At the cemetery, the dean read from the *Book of Common Prayer* as he stood by the open grave:

> In sure and certain hope of the resurrection to eternal life through our Lord Jesus Christ, we commend to Almighty God our brother Clive Farnsworth Brampton; and we commit his body to the ground; earth to earth, ashes to ashes, dust to dust.

This was Jon's first funeral since Rama, and he found the words taking on a vastly modified dimension. Syllables of supposedly solid comfort in the dean's prayer now seemed hollow hopes:

> O, God, who by the glorious resurrection of your Son, Jesus Christ, destroyed death, and brought life and immortality to light: grant that your servant Clive, being raised with Him, may know the strength of His presence, and rejoice in His eternal glory.

As the mourners slowly left the grave site, Austin Balfour Jennings, tears running down his great bronze cheeks, threw a gilded trowel into the pit where they would shortly lower Clive's casket.

On a warm October Saturday, Shannon and Jon drove Naomi up to the Sea of Galilee for a day-long outing, the place that had ignited and fueled the fires of love for two of the trio. Naomi sensed as much. As they drove to Migdal on the west shore of the lake, she said, "Why don't you two enjoy the beach here? I'd . . . rather climb those hills and be by myself for a couple of hours. Meet you here about five?"

"Fine, Naomi."

Once she was out of sight, Jon and Shannon put on swimsuits, then scampered into the body of water they called "Our Lake." After a brisk swim—Shannon screamed at him *not* to head out so far, for poignant reasons—they lay on the beach, taking in the afternoon sun. Neither said anything for long minutes. Suddenly Jon sat up and gazed across the sea to the Golan Heights.

"What is it, Jon?" she asked.

"Oh . . . for some reason, that old Danish Lutheran hymn occurred to me:

> Built on the Rock, the Church shall stand,
> Even when steeples are falling;
> Crumbled have spires in every land,
> Bells still are chiming and calling.

"What's that supposed to mean?"

"Well, the Rock is Christ, but it's the falling steeples and crumbling spires that make the hymn look prophetic. Rama *will* wreak that sort of havoc when our conclusions are announced to the public in November. Those great cathedrals that took centuries to build—the Notre Dames, the Westminster Abbeys—Rama pulls out all their keystones and blasts away their foundations to boot!"

He stood up and skipped a flat stone across the waters of the lake, counting the number of times it skimmed the surface. Then he turned and said, "Let's move from architecture to music, Shannon. The most magnificent passages I've ever heard come in Bach's *Mass in B Minor*, where The Creed has just buried Jesus on Good Friday with the most somber tones possible; but then follows the glorious "Et Resurrexit," where full chorus and orchestra blast out sublimely joyful flourishes of triumph, trumpets blazing away to salute Jesus's Resurrection. You can't hear that marvelous music without getting tears in your eyes and tingling right down to your toes! But now I doubt I'll ever be moved like that again."

Sitting back down, he glanced at the exquisite features and stunning figure of the woman next to him and quickly corrected himself. "I'll never be so moved again *musicologically*." Then he brushed her hair aside and swept her cheek with gentle kisses. "But you, my darling, move me in every way imaginable!" he whispered, as his fingers tried to set out on an exploratory survey.

Shannon brushed away his hand while looking nervously about, grateful that they had the shore to themselves. "*Men!*" she yipped, as she stood up, grabbed a plastic container from their picnic basket, filled it with lake water, and splashed it across Jon's prostrate form. "There!" she cried. "*That* should put out your fire!"

Jon laughed and gathered her into his wet arms for a chaste hug.

"Men turn on so *instantly,*" she giggled. "It takes women a little longer."

"I have *endless* patience, sweetheart! But now that you've 'thrown cold water' on our romance, let's take a walk along the beach."

While strolling northward, arm in arm, Shannon said, "I think it's high time for 'accommodation' so far as Rama's concerned, Jon. The Church is going to have to put some elastic into its teachings on the Resurrection. Then maybe those steeples won't crumble after all."

Jon nodded. "Maybe. St. Paul does use the term *spiritual* in describing the resurrection body—to differentiate it from the kinds we have now which get sick, go to the john, et cetera, so I'd never have trouble with a 'spiritual resurrection' in *that* sense—a new dimension of reality."

"Well, why not simply go with that interpretation?"

"Fine. But the 'new theology' doesn't stop there. It goes on to claim that only a disembodied spirit or even 'idea' of Jesus drove the Church on. The physical resurrection, *à la* the New Testament, simply never happened: it was merely wish-fulfillment on the part of the disciples, maybe Peter's great idea for vocational rehabilitation. Can't you just see him gathering the disciples together after Good Friday and saying, "Well, fellas, we really blew it in following Jesus. But if you follow my plan, someday they'll name churches after us—"

"No," Shannon laughed. "I can't buy that scenario."

"See, if that *had* been the case, then the disciples were geniuses, rather than the dolts they seem in the Gospels. But I'll tell you when their scheme would have crashed—in Rome. In the arena. Just before he was hoisted up to a cross, Peter would have said, "Okay, friends. This was a great romp while it lasted, but a person could get hurt in this caper. I'll turn state's evidence!'"

"True. Someone said it well. *Myths don't make martyrs.*"

"Something about the papyrus has always bothered me," said Jon. "Okay, we have Jesus lying dead up in Rama. Meanwhile, they find the Jerusalem tomb empty. *Why,* in heaven's name, would they have thought anything other than grave theft? That should have been the end of Christianity. Now, 'Nature abhors a vacuum,' and so do I. You *don't* build on a vacuum, an empty tomb, a ghost, or a spirit. You build on *something.*"

"Don't critics say the 'something' was wish-fulfillment and—"

"Yes, and hallucination, visions of the departed loved one. Hey, if Mary Magdalene were the only one involved—" he stopped short and said, "*Incredible!* I just realized we were sitting on her beach here!"

"What? Oh, that's right. Migdal *is* the ancient Magdala."

"Anyway, if only Mary had been involved, I might have suspected hallucinations."

"Putting women down, Jon?"

"This has nothing to do with *gender,* Shannon. I'm talking *numbers:* one person."

"Oh."

"But beyond this one, we have hardheaded, skeptical sorts like Thomas or Saul of Tarsus, not to mention those five hundred up here in Galilee who saw Jesus after Easter. These people experienced a . . . an *extraordinary* personality transformation. How come they didn't turn tail when the authorities tried to clamp down on them in Jerusalem after executing their leader? That had been par for *their* course up to that point! But now they'll take on priests, governors, or the emperor himself! Why? They must have seen some enormously convincing *reality* in a resurrected Jesus. A ghost or a vision or a burgled tomb would *never* have been enough."

Shannon gazed out at the deepening azure of the lake in the late afternoon. "Well, solve the riddle, then, Jon," she said. "Rama looks absolutely *authentic* to me."

"I know . . . I know . . . I know." He stood up and scraped the sand off his legs.

"Here comes Naomi," Shannon said.

"Shannon, I have *one last* crack at it. Tonight I'm rereading the final draft of the epitome, since it has to go to the publishers day after tomorrow. If I find *anything* out of place—any hint, any inconsistency—I'll scream bloody murder!"

He found none. Late the next day, he asked, "Austin, do you remember when Gladwin Dunstable of the London Institute dug with you at Shiloh?"

"Yes."

"Glastonbury interviewed him, and he said that you once asked him to send you some radiocarbon-datable materials from Pompeii so you could test them at Rehovot to see how close they'd come to AD 79."

"Ah yes, the new lab there was 'on probation,' so far as I was concerned. That was, let's see, back in '72, I believe."

"What did Dunstable send you?"

"Oh . . . some carbonized material buried by Vesuvius. A small piece of wooden tool handle, I think."

"How well did the lab do?"

"The Weizmann did a rather worthy job, I seem to recall, pegging the material at, oh, about AD 50 to 60, plus or minus. Why do you ask?"

"I just finished Glastonbury's section in the epitome, and that jogged my memory. I looked it up in his log, but the information wasn't there."

"Oh, probably too trivial."

"By the way, I have to deliver the manuscript to the publishers in Tel Aviv tomorrow anyway, so why don't I simply drive you to the airport, rather than Dick Cromwell?"

"A worthy scheme, Jonathan! I hate to have to go back to Oxford just now, but we have the annual meeting of the Rama Foundation, and I have to face a pack of rabid conservatives on the board. You thought *you* had trouble with J. S. Nickel!"

"When do you get back?"

"In about ten days. I have some business to tidy up too. *Do* hold the fort while I'm gone, won't you?"

Later on, Jon would not be able to explain exactly why he decided to make the call, but he did. It was on the drive back from Tel Aviv that various options started boiling up in his brain. Stopping at the Albright Institute in Jerusalem, he put in a call to Dr. Reuben Landau at Rehovot and found him in. He asked if the Weizmann Institute had any records of radiocarbon testing back in the seventies. They did. Jon asked Landau if he might be kind enough to give him further detail on a sample that Austin Balfour Jennings had sent there, probably in 1972, which they dated to around 50–60 CE. Landau promised to check and call back.

Twenty minutes later, the phone rang and Landau reported. "We reference our tests both by years and also by clients, Professor Weber. And yes, this was the first time Professor Jennings used our facilities. It was on September 10, 1972, and the results were indeed about 50 CE, plus or minus the usual century."

"Fine," said Jon. "But what, specifically, *was* the sample? What did you test?"

"Let me see a moment here."

Jon heard the creak of an opening file drawer, and Landau flipping through his records. Finally he came on the line again. "Oh, yes, here it is. It was three grams of granulated carbon."

"That's it? Nothing else?"

"No."

A long pause ensued.

"Professor Weber? Are you there?"

"Ah . . . yes, Dr. Landau. I must have misunderstood something. But I'd appreciate your keeping my inquiry confidential."

"Certainly, certainly. Let me know if I can be of any further assistance."

"Thanks. I surely will. Good-bye."

After hanging up, Jon soon felt like a first-class fool. Jennings's sample had crumbled in transit. Or they *had* to granulate the tool handle for testing in any case. Any suspicions of

Jennings had to be galloping paranoia. If he didn't control it, next he'd be snapping at people who wished him a good morning: "What did you mean by *that?!*"

Jon left the Albright and was halfway to the street when the same Germanic gene that had caused him to discover the cavern juglet now compelled him to return inside. *Thoroughness is a terrible taskmaster,* thought Jon. It had convulsed the world with Rama. *Why* was he responding to it?

Consulting an international scholars' directory in the reference room, he found Gladwin Dunstable's number at the London Institute of Archaeology and put in a call. The overseas operator said the line was busy, but she'd try again and call back.

Jon had barely finished reading the front page of the Paris-edition *Herald Tribune* when the phone rang, and the operator said, "I have Dr. Dunstable on the line, Professor Weber."

Very little identification and small talk preceded Jon's inquiry: "Reginald Glastonbury of Scotland Yard told us he interviewed you, Dr. Dunstable, regarding your past contacts with Austin Balfour Jennings, and I understand you could do a Boswell to his Johnson."

"Oh, I doubt that," he chuckled. "But Jennings *is* quite colorful, you know."

"Indeed! But what interests me is one of your side recollections. Jennings asked you to send him some radiocarbon-datable material from Pompeii to test the new equipment at the Weizmann Institute in Rehovot—"

"Yes. That was on my way home from the Shiloh dig. Late summer of '72, I believe."

"What did you send him?"

"You know, that was sort of curious. He suggested that I scrape the soot off one of the bake ovens in a newly excavated sector of the Pompeii ruins—he didn't care which—and send it to him in a lead-foil envelope. And he wanted quite a quantity, as I recall, because C-14 testing required larger samples in those days. Strange I should remember that, but I found a bake shop—I think it was along the Via di Nola—and then brushed away for the best part of an hour to get enough of the blinking stuff. Why do you ask?"

"Ah, I'll explain in a moment. How much of the soot did you send him?"

"Oh, about thirty or forty grams, I think."

"But what about the larger sample—part of a wooden tool handle, wasn't it?"

"I . . . don't understand."

"I mean, what *else* did you send him besides that packet of soot?"

"Well, nothing, dear fellow. That was all."

"Are you sure?"

"Yes, indeed. The authorities at Pompeii would *never* have let me send anything else out of the country. It was all I could do to get them to agree to the soot."

"Yes. Of course."

"But what's the problem? Why do you ask?"

"Oh, nothing really," he fibbed. "We're publishing a summation of the Rama congress, and we have dozens of small details like this to nail down. This will just be anecdotal material to illustrate Jennings's thorough approach."

"Oh. Fine."

"Thanks for your help, Dr. Dunstable."

"Anytime, Professor Weber. Good-bye."

Jon walked outside the Albright Institute and paced its evergreen-shaded lawn fronting on Salah-El-Din Street, fighting to control his rampaging thoughts. Wringing his hands, he stared back at the green shutters and buff limestone that was the Albright, shook his head, and paced some more. "No, there's no other way," he told himself. "Time to call Glastonbury."

Linda, the Albright receptionist, a winsome brunette with deep brown eyes and endless patience, dialed the number Jon gave her and handed him the phone. What she heard next was clearly gibberish from another planet.

"You say you were trying to call *me*, Reginald? Why?"

For several minutes, Jon said nothing, although Linda could not help noticing his eyes getting wider and wider.

"Oh *no!*" he finally exclaimed. "That could be why . . . Good Lord, no! . . . No, what I have to say can wait till I see you . . .

Yes, no question but that I'll have to fly in. Let's see . . . today's Monday. I'll try to make it there by Wednesday, Thursday at the latest. I'll call you from Heathrow, if not sooner.

"But wait, Reginald: in the meantime, you *must* get to Gladwin Dunstable, swear him to secrecy, and explain how this seems to be shaping up. Then have one of your agents fly with him to Naples. There he'll be met by Kevin Sullivan from Rome. Here's Kevin's number: 39-6-772-4181 . . . Got it? See, you'll have to call Kevin first and have him clear permission with the Pompeii authorities. Then he must head for Naples to meet Dunstable's plane. Tell Dunstable he should brush off more soot from the *same* bake oven he used in 1972 at Pompeii, if at all possible. No! I *haven't* gone mad. I'll explain it all later! Tell Dunstable to try to replicate *everything,* using a similar brush with the same pressure. Then tell him we need *another* packet of that soot back in London as soon as possible. Got that? . . . Fine. All right then, repeat the whole arrangement so I know you've got it down pat."

A lengthy pause ended when Jon said, "Right! Not bad, Reginald. You can always fall back on secretarial work when you retire! See you soon!"

Handing the phone back to Linda, he said, "There, that all made sense, didn't it?"

"Oh . . . certainly, Dr. Weber! And where's your next dig? Mars?"

"Close! Thanks, Linda. And don't forget to send me the bill."

He left the Albright and looked at his watch. There should be time enough, but, Lord in heaven, how would he ever bring it off? He must go to the Shrine of the Book and perhaps commit a scholarly atrocity that would make Montaigne's little snipping job look like a kindergarten caper! What could happen? He ran over the various scenarios:

1. The ideal: the *titulus* is released to his care, and he flies to London with scrapings of its ink.

2. Shrine authorities refuse any release, but when he gets access to the *titulus,* he somehow manages to scrape ink from it without their notice and flies to London with it.

3. The authorities discover the "atrocity" and arrest him. He explains his macabre conduct, and they let him fly to London.

4. Ditto above, except that the authorities are *not* persuaded, and they throw him in jail.

I can handle all but the last, he mused. Again, he paced the front yard of the Albright, pounding one fist into the other, thinking rapidly. No, there was also scenario number

5. The authorities are not persuaded, but *he somehow escapes* and flies to London.

But he would be hunted, in that case. All borders would be sealed, and it would be open season on Jonathan Weber. *Though it was really quite simple,* he thought, with grim humor. He must merely escape across the borders of the most closely guarded country on earth per kilometer—Israel—after an all-points bulletin had been issued for him. Nice work if you can get it!

But stop *this madness!* he told himself. Instead, come clean—convince the Shrine authorities. Ask for permission.

Then again, what he would ask was unparalleled in the history of archaeology. They would *never* agree. Never. Nor, probably, would they ever believe his reason for making the outrageous request. Jon shook his head grimly. Montaigne sacrificed his whole professional reputation. Perhaps he would have to do the same.

Again, he faced the façade of the Albright Institute, wondering if its neatly cut blocks of limestone somehow held a solution. And *they did!* The Albright's sister institution, he recalled, was the American Center of Oriental Research in Amman, Jordan—ACOR—where Professor Walter Rast was editing his journal of the past summer's campaign along the eastern shore of the Dead Sea. Jon had dug with Rast earlier in his career.

"Hope he's still there," said Jon, as he headed back inside the Albright. "He's *got* to be still there!"

Again he approached Linda and said, "I know, it's been ages

since I saw you last, but this time let's make it a local call. Do you have a direct line to the ACOR in Amman?"

"Sorry, Dr. Weber, it's still international. But I'll put you through."

A short time later she handed him the phone, still smiling. Fortunately.

"Hello, is Professor Walter Rast still in Amman? . . . He is? Fine! May I speak to him? . . . Oh, he's out to lunch? I'll call back. Thank you."

"Be back soon," Jon promised. Then he went to the El Al office in West Jerusalem and purchased a ticket to London, stopping at a pharmacy next door for a package of five one-sided razor blades. Now he returned to the Albright and got through to Rast.

"Hello, sport! Jon Weber here . . . Great seeing you again at our final conclave! . . . Okay, Walt, I'm in something of a bind. First off, would you please check Wednesday morning flights out of Amman to London and buy a ticket in the name of Ernst Becker. You remember him, don't you? I told you over a brew after our last plenary here . . . Good, you've got it. Now the next part gets a little tricky, but it *could* be a solution to Rama. Remember how you and I were looking across the Dead Sea the evening after I arrived at your dig many moons ago? And what I said about that narrow tongue of land almost touching Israel? . . . You do? Good!"

Jon looked around and spoke in lower tones. "Ah, Becker *may* have to take a swim at the beach near Masada late tomorrow night. He'll . . . ah . . . be swimming eastward past the salt fields to Cape Costigan. And he wouldn't at all mind if the likes of you were there with a little flashlight around midnight to welcome him into Jordan . . . No, no. I haven't suffered a breakdown over Rama . . .Yes, I know it's dangerous, *very* dangerous . . . I am *too* playing with a full deck! And let me prove that. This is only a tertiary plan, which I doubt I'll—he'll have to use. It's just a fall-back in case of emergency. Now, can you be at the ACOR about, say, 5:15 PM tomorrow? . . . Okay, the call should come through telling you go or no-go at that time. I'll explain everything later on."

Again Jon looked around to see if he were being overheard, but Linda—mercifully—had left her desk. Then he resumed, "I know,

I know, Walt—possible mines, border patrols over there. You'll have an escort if we have to go that route. Our State Department will contact Jordan's . . . Sure, from the White House, no less . . . Yes, Becker will be in scuba gear, swimming past the canal and across to the base of the cape. Though again, I hope I won't have to bother you with all this . . . Right. Call is at 5:15 tomorrow afternoon . . . *Thanks,* Walt! You're a prince!"

Jon handed the phone back to Linda, who had returned in the meantime. Assuming a godforsaken smile, he said, "I . . . ah . . . know you'd *really* be disappointed if I didn't make . . . one last call. This one's to . . . ah . . . the White House in Washington, D.C." He handed her the card with the president's private number and smiled. *Where's a camera when you really need one?*

He checked his watch as he left the Albright: 2:30 PM. There was still time for a dry run to Masada. He drove out of Jerusalem and down the Jericho Road to the Dead Sea, where he checked his watch again, and then turned south along the shore road, past Qumran and En Gedi to the magnificent rock that Herod had fortified at the southwestern corner of the Dead Sea—Masada, the Gibraltar of Israel. The entire trip from Jerusalem had taken an hour and a half. Luckily he caught the last cable-car run for the day, taking the swift, spectacular ride from the base to Masada's summit.

Although he had brought binoculars along, he hardly needed them because of the coin-operated high-power telescope so conveniently provided for tourists atop Masada. Dropping coin after coin into the instrument, he scanned the entire border area between Israel and Jordan at the southern end of the Dead Sea. Because of dropping water levels, the tongue that Jordan thrust into Israel's face was now an almost solid land bridge between the two countries, broken only by a canal. The earth there, however, was soggy with pits of quick mud and crisscrossed with barbed wire—an unlikely route.

Next he scanned the beachfront at Masada and found the seaside spa he remembered from earlier trips. Tilting the telescope upward, he spotted his target near the base of Cape Costigan in Jordan. It looked to be no more than six or seven miles away.

He walked the twisting "Snake Path" back down to the base of Masada. Then he drove to the seaside spa and engaged in small talk with a lifeguard on duty there. "What's the sea bottom like in this area?" he inquired. "Anyone do any scuba diving around here?"

"Crazy salt formations," the guard replied. "They do a *little* diving, but you have to hang on extra weights or you won't sink."

"Right. Water's 25 percent salt, isn't it?"

"Yeah," he laughed. "I've seen 'em come here with regular equipment and bounce around like corks when they try to dive."

"How come you sound like an American?"

"I grew up in the Bronx. Became an Israeli five years ago."

"Small world!" Jon laughed. "Is there any . . . ah . . . danger to swimmers because this is so close to the frontier?"

"You mean mines? That kind of thing?"

"Right."

"Nah, I don't think so. Maybe down south there at the canal. But if you do dive here, don't swim out too far. I don't know what the Jordanians may have."

Jon made a mental note to take along the submersible metal-detector they had used to find coins while scuba-diving at Caesarea. "Ever have any trouble along the border here, with Jordan so close?"

"Not much. We have a live-and-let-live attitude with the Arabs down here."

"Thanks, friend. Take care."

It was doable, Jon decided on the trip back to Jerusalem. It was also surrealistic, the most maniacal scheme he had ever concocted. What if he *were* losing touch with reality, as Rast had gently implied? Was Rama curdling his brain?

That night he told Shannon the first lie in their relationship. He hated doing that. But the only alternative was her lying instead about his whereabouts over the next few days, if she were questioned, and he wanted to spare her that. He told her he had to go to the publishers in Tel Aviv for the next several days to do additional work on the epitome manuscript.

Dick Cromwell, however, got only the straight truth from Jon.

It was uttered in hushed tones over a bottle of sherry late that night in Dick's room at Ramallah. Jon watched, sadly, as Dick's face fell slowly apart. It took him a full hour to come to terms with the poisonous tidings.

"We still don't have an ounce of proof, Dick. I could very well be making the most horrible mistake of my life," Jon sighed. "It's an imbecilic risk, but I *have* to take it. Too incredibly much is riding on this, as you well know."

Slowly Cromwell shook his head. "I still can't believe this, Jon. But I . . . I guess I have to go along with it. Okay, tomorrow I'll shop for extra scuba weights at Divers Unlimited in Jerusalem and call in a reservation for myself at the Masada Youth Hostel."

"Get a couple of waterproof pouches, while you're at it."

"Okay. When do I drive you to the Shrine of the Book?"

"My appointment with the director is at 3:30 PM. We should leave Ramallah no later than 2:30."

Cromwell shook his head. "Are you *sure* you want to do this, Jon?"

"I have to. But reason *should* prevail. I calculate the odds at only one in ten that I'll have to get wet on my way to London. I'm just covering *all* the bases."

That night, Jon slept in fits and starts, fighting the sheets and thrashing about the bed. For all his surface assurance, a seismic uncertainty tingled in his very bones. "Father, if possible, let *this* cup pass from *me!*" he murmured, discovering a new sympathy for the scene in Gethsemane. Every discussion of testing at Rama had closed with the refrain: "If *only* we could test the *writing*— the *ink* itself." PIXE and chemical analysis had not been enough. He *must* get a larger sample, now that there was a possible standard of comparison. *Blast* their decision to let the Israelis have custody of the Rama artifacts! If they had still been at Rama, tomorrow's danger would have been bypassed.

"Nevertheless, not my will, but Yours be done." How rarely he had prayed in recent years, he reflected wistfully, except in a crisis like this.

TWENTY-THREE

I still think I should go in with you, Jon," said Cromwell as they drove up to the Shrine of the Book at the Israel Museum in West Jerusalem. "No reason you should take the heat alone."

"No, there's *every* reason for you to stay right here. Park over to the left there, next to Kaplan Street, and be ready to head out immediately, especially if I'm running. If I don't come out in an hour, or if the police arrive, then take off without me. In that case, call Glastonbury in London and tell him he'll have to come here instead—maybe I can smuggle the sample to him through prison bars—and call Rast too—5:15 PM—to tell him it's all off. Got that?"

"Right. Do you have the envelope with the false sample?"

"Yes."

"The empty plastic vial?"

"Yes."

"Razor blades?"

"Yes."

"You've got the infrared camera, I see. Okay, buddy, good luck!"

"I'll need more than that, Dick. You'd better pray!"

Jon stepped out of the Peugeot and headed inside the Shrine of the Book, his heart throbbing a pulse he could feel down to his fingertips. A walk down the ramp brought him to the office of the director, Dov Sonnenfeld. He looked at his watch: 3:33 PM.

The secretary glanced up at him and went in to report his arrival. Did she notice anything amiss? Already he was starting to feel like a criminal.

"Hello, Professor Weber," said Sonnenfeld. "Good of you to visit us!" The genial director, in his early forties, was a little taller

than Jon, had auburn hair, and ruddy, freckled skin. He had also
been a soccer star in his youth, and Jon cordially hoped he
wouldn't have to outrun *him*.

"Delighted to see you, Dr. Sonnenfeld. I've . . . ah . . . come in
regard to the *titulus* parchment from Rama."

"Oho! Before you say another word, please follow me."

Sonnenfeld guided him out into the museum, past display windows on either side that were illuminated in yellow light—"The
Bar-Kokhba letters," he explained proudly—and into the central
rotunda, where a facsimile of the Isaiah parchment was displayed,
greatest of the Dead Sea Scrolls. At the far end of the chamber
was a display window covered with dark cloth. Sonnenfeld
turned on the inside illumination and parted the cloth. "Well,
what do you think?" he asked, beaming.

Jon's heart nearly failed him. There, under the purple glow of
ultraviolet light, hung the *titulus,* all of its fragments placed in their
original position on a sheet of transparent muslin backing, and
enclosed between two plates of glass. A catastrophe, Jon thought.
Sonnenfeld would hardly release the parchment after they had prepared so elaborate a display, and the alarm wires threaded along the
perimeter of the locked glass doors of the display case would prevent
intrusion of any kind. He would *not* be able to get at the *titulus*.

"Well, it's . . . a remarkable display, Dr. Sonnenfeld," he finally
managed. "But I thought you'd wait until late November, when
the epitome of the scholars' congress will be released."

"Of course we'll wait. That's why we have a curtain in front of
it." He drew it closed again, and turned off the lights. "And, just
like the Isaiah scroll over there," he pointed, "this is *not* the original, but a *facsimile.* Couldn't you really tell?"

Swimming in relief, Jon shook with laughter. "A *fabulous* piece
of work, Dr. Sonnenfeld! Your artists caught it perfectly—the
diagonal crack, even the darker ink in the upper right corner.
Congratulations!"

"Oh, thank you, thank you! We thought we'd use the ultraviolet to add a note of realism. But let's go back to my office."

Once they had returned, Sonnenfeld asked, "Now, how may
we help you?"

Jon took a long breath and began, "We're a little embarrassed, Dr. Sonnenfeld. In our photography of the *titulus,* we took the usual analysis photos, but somehow we overlooked infrared. Just yesterday, when I delivered the epitome manuscript to our publishers, we noticed the omission. We have to do the photography as soon a possible, and we were wondering if you'd be kind enough to return the *titulus* to us for a day or two so we could accomplish that."

"Certainly, certainly. I see no problem whatever. Excuse me a moment and I'll fetch it."

Thank the good Lord! This was all going to come off infinitely easier than he had projected. The sense of relief was exquisite.

Minutes later, Sonnenfeld returned, but without the large padded case in which the *titulus* had been delivered to the Shrine. "I discussed this with the Director of the Israel Museum next door—they have final authority here—and he insisted that we first get permission from the Israel Antiquities Authority. Do you mind if I call them?"

"Certainly not." Exit relief, enter concern. But perhaps the director was out.

"Oh, yes, good afternoon, Gideon," said Sonnenfeld on the phone.

Exit concern, enter anxiety.

Sonnenfeld stated Jon's request properly and convincingly, and then waited for Gideon's response. It would, of course, be negative, Jon decided, bracing himself for the worst.

Sonnenfeld covered the mouthpiece and confided, "He says he wouldn't mind, but he has to get the approval of the Israel Ministry of Education. He's calling now."

Well, score one for fair-mindedness in Gideon, thought Jon, and shame on himself.

Four minutes passed. Sonnenfeld then came back to life on the phone. "Yes . . . yes . . . I see. All right, thanks very much, Gideon."

He hung up and said, "The Education Minister is out today, and they can't grant approval without him. Ben-Yaakov, therefore, can't either. He suggests you simply bring your camera equipment here and take the photos."

"No problem," said Jon. He opened his briefcase and took out the camera. "I thought that might be the case, so I brought along some infrared film."

"Oh? Splendid!"

"You do have infrared lamps in your lab here, don't you?"

"Of course. I'll bring several to the workroom in the archives. That's where we keep the *genuine* parchment."

The segments of the *titulus,* nestled between sheets of muslin, were removed from a large, humidity-controlled vault and set on a worktable. Sonnenfeld removed the covering sheet and helped Jon arrange the lamps to beam down on the parchment. Jon had eyes primarily for the darker letters in the upper right corner: the "DAEORVM" part of the Latin for "of the Jews." Those were the letters for which he was prepared to sacrifice his professional reputation.

If, that is, Sonnenfeld would ever leave the room. Like a solicitous mother hen, the director was fondly admiring the *titulus* once again, adjusting the lights, and hovering over his shoulders. But Jon steeled his nerves and waited him out, checking his watch to make sure he would not exceed the hour he had promised Cromwell. Photograph followed photograph after photograph, until Sonnenfeld finally dropped the delicious words, "Well, I'll go back to my office for a while. Call me when you're finished."

Almost tasting his heart, Jon quickly opened his briefcase and took out the razor blades and two plastic vials, one filled with crushed graphite—a fake decoy he would substitute if he were caught—and the other sterilized and empty, eagerly waiting to be filled. Bending down, he looked around one last time, then seized a razor blade and started scraping away the "DAEORVM" lettering, letting the blackish material build up below each letter. The stuff was coming off, thank God, not in the quantities he'd hoped, but perhaps it would be enough.

D was now obliterated, only a grayish stain remaining. *A* followed suit. *E,* for some reason, was balky, surrendering only half its substance to the scraping. Never mind. He went on to *O,* which succumbed readily enough, as did *R* and *V.*

There were footsteps in the hall. Jon froze, hovering over the *titulus* so no one would see. The footsteps continued past the door. He could have sung a *Te Deum*. *One more letter and I'll have brought it off,* he told himself. And what a magnificent letter: one *M* is worth three *I*'s when it comes to delivering tiny quantities of possibly forged carbon. By now his hand was getting skilled at the chore and in just eight flourishing strokes he had managed to denude most of *M*.

Now, and without touching the dark, granular spoil, he made slight trenches in the parchment and let the scrapings slide into the empty vial. He screwed the cap on tightly. Done! He secreted it in a pouch around his neck. Done! It remained only to put the muslin sheet back over the parchment and tenderly restore it to the vault. He had watched which drawer was used. With any luck, Sonnenfeld would not check it, and he would be in London tomorrow noon.

He glanced at the *titulus* a final time. "DAEORVM" had only half an *E* left. The rest was merely a gray, shadowy outline of the original lettering. It was either success—or the most miserable miscalculation in the annals of archaeology. For if Rama should finally prove authentic, he had just mutilated one of the greatest documents to survive from antiquity.

But why wasn't that *E* more cooperative? Perhaps another nudge would do it. He picked up the razor and scraped once again. The moment he did so, the door swung open and Sonnenfeld walked in, smiling and saying, "I just happened to think, Professor Weber, that you'd have a better—What are you doing there?" He bent over the parchment, his face tightening in shock. "What . . . what happened to the last part of that Latin line? . . . You . . . you used a *razor* on it? . . . You *scraped* it? *Elohim Shebashamiam!!* I don't *believe* this!!"

"Let me try to explain, Dr. Sonnenfeld—"

But the director ran out of the room, screaming in Hebrew, "*Guards! Guards!* Come in here!"

"Really, Dr. Sonnenfeld, there's no need to—"

"Grab that man and *don't* let him leave the room!" Sonnenfeld pointed. "I must call the Antiquities Authority!"

"Let me speak to Ben-Yaakov after you've talked to him!" Jon called to the departing Sonnenfeld.

The shaken director returned some minutes later and told the guards, "Bring him to my office." Their hands clasped tightly on both his upper arms, the museum police walked Jon to Sonnenfeld's office. The director grabbed the phone and said, "We have him here now . . . What's that? . . . Oh! Yes, of course." He put the phone down and said, "Let's have the ink powder you scraped off." Slowly Jon handed him the fake vial. *If they test* that, *it would date to AD 1990s!* he thought wryly as he struggled to keep from drowning in a sea of chagrin and humiliation.

"Here, he wishes to speak with you." Sonnenfeld handed him the phone.

"Yes, Gideon," said Jon, ponderously. "I know what I've done is unprecedented, but it *can be explained* . . . Yes . . . yes, of *course* I'll give you the explanation. But this is so incredibly sensitive that it must be for your ears only. May I *please* ask the others here to step out of the room? . . . Fine, I'll give you Dr. Sonnenfeld again." He handed him the phone.

The director listened, nodded, and handed the phone back to Jon. He then motioned to the museum police, and they all left the office. Jon now unveiled to Gideon the ominous information he had received from Dunstable and Glastonbury, as well as his plans to compare the *titulus* scrapings with soot from Pompeii.

"No," he concluded, "the evidence isn't *proof,* as yet, and maybe it isn't even circumstantial, but we've uncovered a strong *motive* for the first time. This was our one and only clue, Gideon, and I simply *had* to seize on it."

"I think you're making a mountain out of a speck, Jonathan," he replied. "Jennings had nothing more than a memory lapse, I'm sure. This is like saying that . . . that Dame Kathleen Kenyon was a prostitute!"

"But the motive, Gideon. I *have* to fly to London and learn more about it from Glastonbury and Paddington. We've also got to compare the *titulus* scrapings. It's like four or five hissing fuses. They *could* lead to a common, explosive conclusion."

"More like a dud . . . a fizzle! I'm afraid you need a psychiatrist,

Jonathan. I hate to say this, but I think you've gone over the edge. I know Rama's been a terrible strain, but—"

"Just give me the next two or three days, Gideon. After that you can do whatever you want with me. Lock me up and throw away the key, if you like. After I get back from London, I'll go directly to your office and tell you what happened. If I'm wrong, you can put me in handcuffs!"

"First of all, London is *out*, Jonathan. You don't *dare* leave the country. The Education minister . . . the *Prime Minister* . . . would have my scalp for letting you go after the atrocity you just pulled. And by the way, you should know that there's *absolutely nothing personal* about my decision here, though you may think so."

"I don't think that, Gideon," said Jon, although he did, the image of Shannon again commanding his mind's eye. "You're a bigger man than that."

"I'd have to decide this way if you were my own *brother*, Jonathan. Let Glastonbury fly in here with his little packet of soot, and you can test both samples at Rehovot."

"The Weizmann is excellent, Gideon, but it doesn't have the equipment to test something as small as what I scraped from the *titulus!*"

"I'm sure it does, Jonathan."

"It does *not*. We'll have to use a tandem accelerator on this."

"My patience is running out, Jonathan. I *should* be calling the police and having you arrested for malicious destruction of a national treasure—something really beyond any forgiveness—yet I'm—"

"Gideon, I'm *pleading* with you: just give me forty-eight hours out of the country and—"

"*Shut up!*" Gideon roared. "I'm giving you two options. One, you have twenty-four hours to set up the tests with Landau in Rehovot. Or two, I'll see you at the police station."

"All right, Gideon, all right. But please . . . *please* keep this absolutely confidential for now. And tell Sonnenfeld and his guard to keep it confidential too."

"Will you pledge to use Rehovot?"

"I . . . I'll pledge, Gideon," Jon sighed. Inwardly he continued,

*Sure, I pledge to bring a grain or two of the scrapings there . . .
someday.*

"All right, then, Jonathan. But don't even *think* of leaving
Israel. I'm alerting Ben Gurion, Ashdod, Haifa, the Allenby
Bridge, all our ports and frontier crossovers, *not* to let you pass.
Now put Sonnenfeld on—"

Jon knocked on the office door to recall Sonnenfeld. He came
inside, took the phone, and received Gideon's special instructions.
After hanging up, he looked at Jon and said, "All right. You can
go. *Why*, I'm not sure. I consider you no more than a criminal!"

"I can sympathize with that, Dr. Sonnenfeld. Good day!"

"You forgot this—" He handed him the decoy vial.

"Oh. Of course. Thank you."

On the way out, he threw it into a trash canister. Then he
looked at his watch and cringed. Fifty-eight minutes had elapsed!
He ran outside and waved to a much-relieved Dick Cromwell,
who had just started the Peugeot.

"Great!" said Dick. "Thought I'd see you next in a paddy-
wagon. Which scenario was it?"

"None of them! We'd probably label it Number 5-B. Anyhow,
it looks like I'll have to get wet on my way to London."

Cromwell's head slumped down. Then he shook it slowly from
side to side.

They reached the Albright a quarter hour before closing. "Hello,
Linda," said Jon. "Meet Dick Cromwell here. The good news is
that *he* won't have to use the phone. The bad news is that *I* will."

"It's been a monotonous day, Professor Weber. I'm *so* glad you
got here to change all that. Where is it this time, the White House
again?"

He nodded and said, "You're positively clairvoyant, my dear!"

"I was really hoping it would be Buckingham Palace."

"Next time!"

Dick Cromwell thought that the scene was a practical joke,
but Jon looked deadly serious when Linda handed him the phone
and he said, "President Bronson? . . . Yes, this is Ernst Becker in
the Promised Land. I'm afraid we'll have to look to the rising

moon . . . I know, I know . . . I've checked everything out. It's doable . . . Oh, yes, Paul Revere is extremely reliable. But he needs help . . . Right . . . Fine . . . I will. And thank you, Mr. President."

"Now, what was *that* all about?" Cromwell demanded.

"C'mon outside. Back in a second, Linda."

"I'm banking on that."

"Ah . . . I'd be eternally grateful if you could hang in here till about 5:15, Linda."

"Only if you'll translate all this for me someday."

"I will. I promise."

Outside, Jon said, "We're killing time until 5:15, when I promised Rast he'd be called."

"What's the Ernst Becker bit?"

"That's my other passport. I forgot to tell you that."

"Oh, I think I have it. The 'rising moon' is the east—Jordan."

"You got it."

"But who's 'Paul Revere'?"

"Rast, of course. You know, 'One if by land, two if by sea . . .' Rast will signal with two flashes, intermittently, from Cape Costigan at midnight."

"And the 'help'?"

"The president is having MacPherson, the secretary of state, flash the green light to his alter ego in Jordan so that their frontier police can help Rast avoid mines. I greased the rails for that yesterday, but it was all on hold until we actually had to go that route."

"Great! Now if only you don't get blown up swimming over there."

"Now, first thing tomorrow morning, you put in a call to Landau at Rehovot and make an appointment for me late in the afternoon. That's in case Gideon checks with him. Late that day, you phone Landau and say I've been held up. Reschedule for the next day. If he or Gideon calls the next day, you have no idea what in blazes happened to me. Got it? You thought I'd be driving over from the publishers in Tel Aviv. That's so Shannon doesn't get suspicious. Once I get to London, I'll call her to say

I'm all right, though I won't say where I am. She's to know nothing, you understand."

"Yes. Yes, of course."

"Okay, It's 5:13. Time to call Rast."

They returned inside, and Jon said, "It pains me to admit it, Linda, but this really *is* the last call."

"Breaks my heart, Dr. Weber. Where to now? The Kremlin?"

"Not this time. ACOR in Amman."

They switched from the Peugeot to the Land Rover and salted a dig of their own into its rear compartment. The lowest stratum was loaded with scuba equipment, the upper layers with cameras, tripods, and photo paraphernalia. There was also a lowest or "bedrock" stratum, where Jon would crawl when they approached possible checkpoints. It was reached only by opening the tailgate, but Cromwell had rigged two hidden slide-bolts on the inside, which would defeat any efforts to open it when latched.

Shadows were lengthening in the early dusk as they drove downward toward the Dead Sea, which is almost thirteen hundred feet below sea level, the lowest point on the earth's surface. The first checkpoint lay about three kilometers ahead.

"Better pull over, Dick," said Jon.

When traffic had passed, Jon opened the tailgate, crawled into the cavity where the spare tire was usually housed, and took on a fetal position. No one was at the checkpoint, and Cromwell turned south along the shore road. Jon pushed himself up in the rear to overcome his cramped position and said, "Open the windows, Dick. Already I'm suffocating."

"Okay. So far, so good, Jon. Not much traffic on the road."

A half hour passed. Little was said. Glib small talk barely disguised the tension they both tasted. The last two days had seemed one long, rotten dream from which he could not extricate himself by waking up, thought Jon. Would he ever be able to shake off the ghastly mortification he suffered at the Shrine of the Book? Yet in view of the dangers ahead, that episode could eventually prove to have been the easy part!

"We're way past Qumran and just about to En Gedi, Jon."

"I'd best hunker down again, then. They have a checkpoint near here."

"Slide the bolts, will you?"

"You bet."

Just after a curve around one of the shore promontories, they came to their first manned checkpoint, and the gates were down across the road. "Here we go," Dick warned.

The Rover braked to a stop. A member of the Israel Defense Force, jaunty beret askew and Uzi at his shoulder, leaned into the window and asked Dick for identification. He supplied it. The IDF trooper scrutinized it closely with his flashlight. "Where are you going this evening?" he asked.

"Masada. I have to do some photography there in the morning."

Another IDF comrade stepped out of the guard shed and peered into the rear compartment, shining a flashlight over the photographic equipment. "Would you step out, please?" he asked.

"Sure." Dick opened the door, got out, stretched his limbs nonchalantly. The two frontier troops rummaged a bit through the photo equipment, and then asked him to open the tailgate.

"Wish I could! Something's sprung the lock mechanism, and I haven't been able to open it for the past couple of weeks. Been meaning to get it fixed. I load everything through the back doors."

One of the guards tugged at the tailgate several times. Jon held his breath, as pull pressure was exerted on the two slide bolts.

"Where will you stay tonight?" the first guard inquired.

"At the Masada youth hostel. It's the only shelter available down there," Cromwell added, with a little chuckle.

The guard flipped on his walkie-talkie and spoke in Hebrew. Dick understood nothing, but Jon heard him calling his base to phone the hostel and determine if they had a reservation in Cromwell's name. While waiting for the reply, Dick asked, "What seems to be the problem, gentlemen?"

"Nothing. This is a frontier area, and we have to make a check, especially at night."

"Oh . . . fine."

"We also got a special border alert from Jerusalem. You don't know a . . ." he paused, looking at his notepad, and continued, "You don't know a Jonathan E. Weber, do you?"

"No."

The radiophone crackled and came to life. "*Ken . . . ken . . . ken,*" the guard responded. Then, turning to Cromwell, he said, "All right. Go ahead."

A wave of relief splashed over Cromwell as he started the Rover and drove on toward Masada. "You can crawl out now, Jon!" he announced. "Just a bit, that is. I think we'll make it."

At Masada, Cromwell checked in at the hostel and lugged some overnight belongings into his cabin. Jon now slid open the bolts on the tailgate and extricated himself from his cramped cocoon. They carried the wet suit and other gear into the cabin, leaving the air tanks and weights in the Rover.

Jon checked his watch and said, "Okay, Dick, it's 8:45 PM. We have a waning moon. It comes up around 10:00, and I want to get wet before then. Now, this place is very near that spa I visited yesterday. Go ask the manager of the hostel if you have swimming rights there, or, if not, where."

Cromwell returned a short while later and said, "They simply use a corridor down to the sea a half mile south of the spa. No charge. And get this: there's even a wadi trail down to the beach there for launching boats!"

"Fabulous! Hadn't banked on it being *that* convenient!"

"Somebody up there likes you, Jonathan!"

"Okay, I'll suit up now."

A half hour later they got into the Rover and drove down the wadi to the beach. Music was playing at the spa, a string of yellow bug lights to the north pinpointing the source. "Nice distraction," Jon observed as he opened the door and prepared to slip into his fins.

"Okay, here I go with the final checklist," said Cromwell. "Ernst Becker passport in waterproof pouch?"

"Check."

"Your *second* fake vial in waterproof belt pouch?"

"Check. Stupid of me to throw the first one away!"

"No one ever claimed you were perfect. The genuine vial in waterproof lead pouch around your neck?"

"Check."

"Once again, what do you do if you're stopped, stripped, and searched?"

"Before they haul me out of the water, I take the real vial and—"

"Yes?" Dick had a big smile on his face.

"I take the real vial and stuff it up . . . ah . . . I put it where the sun doesn't shine." Jon grinned.

"The list says, 'Emergency insertion into posterior terminus of the alimentary canal.'"

"Same difference."

"Submersible metal detector?"

"Check."

"Seventy pound additional weights on shoulders, belt, and lower thighs?"

"Check."

"Are you sure that's enough to compensate for the buoyancy of the Dead Sea?"

"Should be. I want to swim just below the surface—nothing deeper—since I have to check my bearings from time to time."

"Okay, read off the pressure in both air tanks."

"Two thousand pounds in each."

"Will that give you enough bottom time?"

"Ninety minutes' worth. That should be enough to get me into Jordanian waters."

"Okay. Flashlight?"

"Check."

"That's it, Jon. It's 10:10. Time to move out."

"Okay, Dick. Now, tomorrow, don't forget to really do some photography atop Masada, and then head back to Ramallah. Rast will call you there around 1 PM. If I arrived safely and got off to London, he'll say, 'The high-speed film you ordered has arrived.' If not, a code won't be necessary, and he'll have to spell out what happened and what you must do to save my tail . . . *if* it's salvageable."

"I hope to God it's the first alternative. Now, don't forget your sightings: the point you want on Cape Costigan falls in line with the moonrise over those hills there across the Dead Sea."

"Those are the Mountains of Moab."

"And if that metal detector starts whining, for goshsake, *stop* until you use your flashlight to see what's in front of you."

"Right. Ah . . . Dick, I don't want to get mawkish here, but if anything happens to me, tell Shannon why I *had* to do this, why I had to keep it secret from her, and . . . that my last thoughts were of her. She's the most beautiful thing that's ever happened in my life. And then *you* have to carry on the crusade with Glastonbury to prove things, one way or the other. Promise?"

"I promise, Jon. Please take care."

Jon waded into the water, constantly scanning a 180-degree arc in front of him. Dick stepped out of the Rover and did the same for the rear 180 degrees. Mercifully, there seemed to be no witnesses.

Fifteen minutes later, a waning moon started to peep over the eastern horizon of hills. Jon was now a quarter-mile off shore and making rather steady progress, although he was still disturbingly visible in the swatch of moonlight, Cromwell noted, to his dismay. Why didn't he swim with a lower profile?

Dick heard a squeal of brakes behind him. Whipping about, he saw an Israeli jeep parked just behind the Rover, and a white-helmeted frontier guard climbing out. "What are you doing here?" he demanded in Hebrew, then English, Israel's second language.

Cromwell cringed internally but said, calmly, "Just enjoying the moonrise. I hope this isn't some restricted zone."

When asked for identification, Cromwell stood shoreside from the officer so that he would have to face land and not sea while examining it. *Swim on, Jon,* he called silently, *and swim quietly.*

He intentionally took an abnormal amount of time, fishing through various pockets until he found his passport and gave it to the Israeli. Just then, obnoxiously loud rock music blared out from the spa to the north. Cromwell, who loved Bach and hated rock, was grateful for the throb of nonmusic that easily masked any soft splashing in the Dead Sea.

"Where are you staying?" asked the frontier guard.

"Up there," Cromwell pointed, "at the hostel. I was just checking the boat-launching facilities here in case I bring my rig along sometime."

"I thought you were enjoying the moon."

Cromwell laughed. "Both! The two aren't exclusive, are they?"

"All right. But if you ever do take a boat out here, be careful and don't go out too far. We have mines near the international border over there." He pointed uncomfortably close to where Jon was swimming.

"I certainly will. Thanks for the warning."

Cromwell started the Rover and followed the jeep away from the shore, then parked at the hostel. He would spend the next two hours peering at the sea with powerful binoculars, hoping not to see the bright flash of an explosion that would reach his eye sooner than the awful sound.

Jon swam toward the moonlight. Early on, however, he sensed a bad miscalculation. He had not loaded on enough weight for the extraordinary buoyancy of the Dead Sea. No matter how hard he tried to dive, he promptly resurfaced, the back of his wet suit breaking into visibility atop the brackish waters. He kept swimming. What other option was there?

He was now in line with the canal. Looking back, he saw, to his horror, the lights of the Israeli jeep and he hove to, dead in the water. Any spotlight trained on the sea might doom his mission, and he could only wait, motionless, while the issue was decided. But the sound of rock music and the sight of retreating lights on shore heartened him, and he continued swimming, now with maximum thrust on his fins.

Then he realized a second, potentially disastrous mistake: he should not have been able to hear the music, but ought to have been listening to the hum of the metal detector. He quickly flipped it on, tuned it, then continued his swim, the probe of the detector strapped to a shoulder harness and projecting in front of him.

A half hour passed. He continued to aim for the rising wedge of moon and now reached the fields of floating salt bergs, nearly halfway to his target landfall. The hum from the detector continued evenly, no oscillation to indicate the presence of a metallic mine. He had settled into a routine of twenty kick cycles per minute, the briny near-syrup of Dead Sea water compelling such a low rate and slow progress. A scattering of ghostly white salt bergs floated into and out of his way, and Jon had to change his course repeatedly to avoid them.

It must be near midnight, he calculated. The witching hour was the time Rast had said he would start his double flashing. He scanned the horizon of land to the east but saw nothing. By now, though, he must be in Jordanian waters, he thought, which could well be mined also. He increased the volume of the neutral hum of his detector. Still no light on shore.

His legs began to ache. Fun this was not. The whole ordeal was taking on a chimerical cast, a return of the recurring nightmare. He needed something to aim toward, to hope for and head for. He should have told Rast to start his signaling at 11:30 PM. And, of course, there was another possibility: the plan had miscarried, and Rast was not there at all.

Did he see a tiny pinpoint of light? He would know in thirty seconds, the interval between flashes they had specified. *One thousand one, one thousand two, one thousand three*—he counted, until he reached twenty-eight. Clearly, gloriously, and just a little to the left of his heading were two distinct flashes. A half-minute later, the same magnificent sequence. Jon reached down to his belt, pulled out the flashlight, aimed it toward the light source, and flashed twice. As agreed, he was immediately answered by three flashes. Contact!

The final leg to shore still required three-quarters of an hour, but now it was duck soup. The end was in sight, and thus the end was won.

"Lo, Walt!" said Jon, as his feet touched gravelly bottom near shore. "I hope they have ferry service here someday!"

"Welcome to Jordan, you amphibious nut!"

Flanking Rast were two officers of the Royal Jordanian Army. The senior, a captain, shook Jon's hand and said, "The government of the Hashemite Kingdom of Jordan extends you its welcome, Professor Weber—or 'Becker,' that is!"

"Thank you! Grand of you to stage this reception, gentlemen!"

"Ah! It was *most* necessary. Otherwise you would have blown yourself to bits in our mine field here unless Allah had mercy on you! Come, we show you the way."

Jon's third mistake was not to arrange for clothing after his land-fall in Jordan. Wet suits were hardly *de rigueur* on jet planes. Serendipitous was the fact that Rast was nearly his size, and he let Jon borrow one of his suits.

His fourth error was unavoidable. No "Ernst Becker" had ever entered Jordan—at least his passport bore no Jordanian entry stamp—so how could he hope to clear passport control in leaving the country? But with Jordan's foreign minister personally seeing him off at Queen Alia Airport in Amman early the next morning, passport officials were more than cooperative.

TWENTY-FOUR

Glastonbury whisked Jon through customs at Heathrow Airport, and they sped along M-4 to London in a service Jaguar festooned with Scotland Yard's coat-of-arms. Sandy McHugh had flown in from Washington on an earlier jet and now joined them at the University of London Institute of Archaeology in Bloomsbury. Gladwin Dunstable and Tom Paddington were also there, awaiting his arrival. Cordial hellos were exchanged around the conference table, after which Jon turned to Dunstable and said, "Do forgive us for our sudden intrusion into your busy career!"

"Not at all. Glad to be of service," said the ruddy, lanky, flaxen haired archaeological scientist, whose gaunt features melted into a warm smile.

"Were you able to find that bake oven in Pompeii and bring us a sample?"

"I was. It took a bit of doing—the authorities there were just a shade perplexed—but here it is." He reached into his attaché case and put a plastic packet onto the table. "But I do have a question for you, Professor Weber. Why on *earth* did you want me to do this? Oh, I have *some* inkling, of course, but Reginald said you'd give me the full detail."

Jon proceeded to expose the rationale that had led to his assault on the *titulus*, and concluded, "Since only a small part of the original soot you sent Jennings from Pompeii was tested at Weizmann, might the rest conceivably have been used to make ink for the papyrus and the *titulus*? Since carbon from Pompeii would test out to no later than AD 79, it could have served as an admirable pigment base. So I thought that a C-14 test of materials scraped from the *titulus* could be compared with what you just brushed off the

309

same oven. An identical or very similar reading might well prove conclusive."

Frowns around the conference table were hardly what Jon had expected. Dunstable finally broke the silence. "Well, let's see what you have for us by way of quantity."

Jon removed the clear plastic vial from the pouch around his neck and laid it in front of Dunstable and McHugh. They picked it up and examined it closely.

"Careful, gentlemen," said Jon. "This may sound overblown, but the spiritual future of the West could depend on the little grains inside that thing!"

Sandy shook his head a little wistfully and said, "We *may* have enough in your sample for C-14, Jon. But if we do, what would it prove if the results *were* close? It could be a case of pure coincidence."

"What do you mean?"

Dunstable, picking up the argument, said, "Put the case, Professor Weber, that Rama is fully authentic. Your scrapings, then, could test very closely to my soot—age-wise—and still have come from a *totally* different source."

Jon saw that truth in an instant, and he started to feel monstrously foolish, a dolt who had desperately run with the wrong idea, disgracing both himself and his profession. He stood up and paced the room, tapping his right fist into his left open palm. His harrowing adventure in securing wisps of material that might, after all, prove utterly useless added to his sense of futility.

Groping for words, he said, "In other words, gentlemen, this whole ghastly effort of mine was quite probably *worthless?* I risk my life, and surely my reputation, and it's all *in vain?* Can't you at least do *some* sort of comparative analysis? Some other tests, chemical or whatever?"

McHugh was doodling on his pad, but then stopped, looked over to Dunstable, and smiled. The director nodded and said, "Yes. There are other analysis procedures, and they may be *far* more serviceable than radiocarbon in this case."

"Yes indeed, Jon," said Sandy. "I'd think comparative microscopic analysis would be first, followed by PIXE. Do you have facilities for Particle Induced X-ray Emission Analysis here, Dr. Dunstable?"

"We do. And I agree. So if you don't mind, Professor Weber, I'll have our best man, George Lawton, start comparing the two samples optically. Oh, not to worry. I'll tell him they both came from the *Magna Carta,* and that every last particle must be saved. After that procedure, I'd suggest scanning electron microscopy on both samples, and then on to PIXE, and perhaps ESCA."

"ESCA?" Jon inquired.

"Electron Spectroscopy for Chemical Analysis. It brings out some of the elements PIXE doesn't cover. Do you concur, gentlemen?"

Sandy gave Jon a thumbs-up sign.

"Fine! No, excellent," said Jon, saturated with relief.

Dunstable stepped out of the room with the samples and returned in a short time. "Now," he said, "while that's being done, do tell me why you suspect Austin Balfour Jennings, Professor Weber. In the world of archaeology, that's rather like saying your great William Foxwell Albright was a charlatan and a scoundrel."

"I know that. And I can't begin to describe the pain I feel in my very bones at the mere idea. But what about the carbonized wooden handle you never sent him? And the grams of soot that never reached the Weizmann?"

"Thin, thin, thin, Professor Weber. That could have been nothing more than a memory lapse on Jennings's part. And the Weizmann likely specified the amount of soot he was to send."

"I realize that well enough. And I *never* would have done all this if it hadn't been for new information uncovered by Tom Paddington and MI-5. This finally set a *motive* into place, you see. Mr. Glastonbury told me the details by phone in Jerusalem. Why don't you tell him, Reginald? Or you, Tom?"

Glastonbury opened his palms toward Paddington, who responded. "Well, even though I hate to admit it, Reginald certainly did the spade work. He found out, for example, that in his younger years at Oxford, Jennings was not simply gifted in Semitics, but a veritable *genius* in Aramaic linguistics. His teacher,

Professor Giles Weatherby, threw up his hands one day and said, '*Enough!* I can't teach you any more, Austin. Rather, it's high time you teach *me!*' Now, we thought that rather strange in view of Jennings always letting Dr. Weber do the translating in Israel."

"Well, he may have neglected his Aramaic in the meantime," Dunstable objected. "That *was* years ago."

"That may be," said Paddington. "But then the Queen involved herself in this affair. As 'Supreme Head of the Church of England,' she was deeply concerned about what Rama was doing to the Christian faith, particularly since the dig was conducted under a British banner. Reginald and I were called in to Buckingham Palace, and we briefed her on all the information we had to date. She then asked that we use *all* the resources of both Scotland Yard and MI-5, so we sent a small army of intelligence operatives to Oxford and Northern Ireland to fill in the gaps in our Jennings file."

"Oh?" said Dunstable. "What did you find?"

"Little, at first, other than the standard Jennings biography you already know. But then we uncovered fresh data on his *personal* life that exposes a motive for the first time, we think. While he was a teaching fellow at Oxford, he fell in love with an Irish student named Colleen Donnegal, who hailed from Drogheda on the Irish east coast. Evidently she was *quite* a charmer, very much like Shannon, Dr. Weber. In any case, she returned his affections, but drew the line on any further romance."

"Why?" asked Sandy McHugh. "Because he was Protestant and she Catholic?"

"Orange versus green was only part of it. Miss Donnegal was a *novice*, you see, at the Sisters of Salome Convent at Monaghan — that's near the border with Northern Ireland—and she had taken her first vows to be a bride of Christ and not Jennings. The cloister had sent her on scholarship to Oxford to learn Old Testament Hebrew, and she was supposed to return and teach classes at the convent. She did return, and Jennings was heartbroken. He sent her letters, but they were never answered. He later learned she never received them.

"That Christmas, Jennings surmised that she *might* be allowed to spend the holidays with her family at Drogheda, so he lay in wait there. He was right. He saw her leaving home the day after Christmas and confronted her. She was overjoyed to see him again and furious at the nunnery for intercepting her mail. To make a long story short, she returned home to pack her things as if she were returning to the convent, but instead eloped with Jennings to England."

"Well, that's quite romantic," said Dunstable, "but hardly any motive for—"

"There's more," said Paddington. "They lived happily for several years at Oxford, although Mrs. Jennings had a guilt complex because of the way she left the nunnery. She also held firmly to her Catholicism."

"Yes, I picked up that part of it," said Glastonbury. "Her psychiatrist at Oxford was most helpful. But continue, Tom—"

"Just after Shannon was born, she suffered a long postpartum depression. She felt the only way to overcome her conscience pangs at breaking her vows was to make peace with the Monaghan Convent. She wrote the abbess, asking for her forgiveness. The mother superior, in turn, sent her a letter of absolution, but suggested that she return there for a contemplative week, after which they'd formally release her from her vows. Jennings pleaded with her not to go, but the psychiatrist agreed that this *could* be the best possible therapy for her. So, leaving her husband to care for Shannon, she left for Monaghan."

"I'm starting to feel sick," said McHugh. "I think I know how this is going to end—"

"You're right. The abbess turns out to be just a little to the right of Torquemada and the Spanish Inquisition. She'd 'never lost a novice,' she claimed, and wasn't about to start now. She'd release Colleen Jennings from her vows, all right—her *marital* vows. The marriage had no validity, she claimed, since it wasn't performed in the Church. When Colleen objected, she had her afternoon tea laced with laudanum. Colleen started having visions, stayed in the nunnery, and one day they found her hanging in her cell, a belt around her neck."

Grumbles of exclamation boiled up in the group as Paddington continued, "Jennings, of course, was beside himself. He took off a whole semester from Oxford to trace down the truth, and finally learned it from a cook at the convent. He then brought formal charges against the abbess, but the Irish courts permitted canon law to govern the case, and the ecclesiastical court threw it out 'for lack of evidence.' Green versus orange, of course, plus *powerful* intervention by the Irish Catholic church, which felt it had to hush-hush a scandal of this magnitude.

"Now, of course, Jennings was fit to be tied. Over some late-night beers at a pub in Armagh, his hometown, he spilled his awful story to others at the table, who turned out to be militant Protestant Orangemen. Without telling him, they crossed the border one night—Monaghan is just down the road from Armagh—and set fire to the convent, leaving a note to the effect that they were avenging 'the kidnapping and death of Colleen Jennings.' Two aged nuns died in the blaze."

"Oh, no!" said Sandy. "And, of course, here comes the IRA, hot for revenge!"

"Exactly. A week later, a hit squad from the Irish Republican Army slipped across the border, raided the Jennings's homestead at Armagh, and killed his mother and younger brother, wiping out the family—except for Austin Balfour."

"Good Lord!" Dunstable exclaimed. "I do begin to see motive here. But what ever happened to the wicked mother superior?"

"The Church sacked her into retirement," said Glastonbury. "But Jennings probably didn't feel vindicated by that for . . . for losing everything but Shannon."

"Incredible!" said Jon. "Shannon never mentioned any of this to me. She thinks her mother died of some rare form of pneumonia."

"Shannon didn't—doesn't—know these hideous details," said Glastonbury. "'Pneumonia' was the story Jennings passed on to her. He didn't want her to suffer from the true story."

"When did all this happen?" asked Dunstable. "And why didn't we hear about it?"

"In 1974, only a few months after Shannon was born. Why didn't you hear about it? Jennings wasn't famous in those days, and this was 'only another statistic' along that bloody border. Obviously he never revealed it in later interviews, probably blanking it out of his mind—*or* planning a diabolical revenge of his own."

"All right, then," said Dunstable, "let's sum up. Jennings was dealt a horrible card by the Irish Catholics. They killed his wife, mother, and brother, so now he'll have his revenge on them—indeed, all of Christianity—by writing up the Aramaic, which he clearly could do as a linguistic genius, and then hoaxing the rest of it, which he could bring off as an archaeologist. Is that it?"

"That was my conclusion, I regret to say," said Jon.

"Ours too," said Glastonbury.

"Sounds logical to me," said Sandy McHugh.

"Well, I'd be tempted to agree with you, certainly," said Dunstable. "But I find two serious problems with that line of thought. One, I could understand a rabid *anti-Catholicism* on his part, but Rama is aimed at *all* of Christianity, not just Catholicism. And two, he set about his Aramaic mastery long *before* the tragedies of 1974, didn't he?"

Silence blanketed the room, broken only when Dunstable resumed, "So I wonder if we're not jumping to a . . . a very monstrous conclusion here, gentlemen, impugning the character of one of the great scholar archaeologists of our time, a man who has already suffered more than we ever knew."

Again silence shrouded the discussion.

"Well," Glastonbury conceded, "you *do* make sense with those points, Gladwin. It *could* be that we're down the wrong track after all—"

"We're so prone to finding 'culprits,'" said Paddington, "that it hardly ever occurs to us that there may be *no* culprit in a case like this . . . that the finds are, very simply, genuine."

Jon was starting to feel like a worm . . . or worse. He should have been in Dunstable's corner, defending Jennings wherever possible. And here, Judas-like, he seemed to be leading the attack. Talk about erring heroically!

The door of the conference room opened, and Dr. George Lawton walked in, a short wisp of a man in laboratory whites, with overlong strands of brown hair carefully combed across his bald pate. "Excuse me, gentlemen," he said, "but we have some preliminary results of our comparative study."

"Do proceed," Dunstable directed.

"We examined the two samples with standard microscopes, using various light sources and diffractions, and found some rather considerable differences. The carbon granulation from the Pompeii sample is of fairly uniform consistency, whereas the Weber sample has different granulation size in the carbon, as well as admixture of collagen fibers."

Jon tried to save his case. "But my carbon served as pigment for ink and had a binder, so shouldn't we *expect* different granulation? And the collagen fiber must have come from the parchment—"

"Oh, indeed, Dr. Weber, the differences are quite easily explained, and I was merely citing the differences. Now, as to similarities in the samples, we have only two. One isn't very significant, I'm afraid. I refer to the color of the carbon granules: both seem to have a similar degree of 'blackness,' shall we say."

"Bah," Dunstable retorted. "Black is black. Carbon is carbon."

"To be sure," replied Lawton, "though slight color differentials *are* possible in carbon. But the second parallel is more interesting. In both samples, we found particles of a hard or gritty substance that is *not* carbon. They were stained black like the carbon granules, but were much harder."

"What in the world are they?" asked Dunstable.

"We tried to clean several of the particles—rather unsuccessfully—though we did start to see a slight vermilion cast appearing. Perhaps they're grit or sand of some kind."

Jon suddenly brightened and hit the table with a fist. "Ceramics! Could they be fired clay particles, Dr. Lawton? Consider the origin, gentlemen. Do we have bits of that Pompeii oven in both samples?"

"But of course," said Glastonbury, who always managed the first word, or at least the second, if he had been preempted. "Brushing across a ceramic surface *could* have removed such particles, not, Gladwin?"

"Quite possibly. But why would the particles survive in Professor Weber's sample?"

"Well, I doubt if Jenni—" Sandy McHugh stopped and tried to

keep it objective. "I doubt if the perpetrator would have put his ink through a strainer or *filter,* now, would he?"

"He might have," Dunstable replied, "or he might not. But surely this is worth pursuing. I suggest you isolate those non-carbon particles, George, clean them as best you can, and then let us have a look."

"Indeed. Excuse me, gentlemen."

After Lawton returned to his laboratory, Jon suddenly straightened in his chair and said, "I just recalled something, and I hope I'm not too late. Gideon Ben-Yaakov gave me twenty-four hours since yesterday at this time to arrange testing at Rehovot. He'll draw a blank if he checks, and if he goes public with this, all may be lost. May I use your phone, Dr. Dunstable?"

"Certainly."

"Scotland Yard will underwrite the call," said Glastonbury. "Here, use our charge number—"

"And if he isn't cooperative," said Paddington, "MI-5 will contact Mossad in Israel and try to explain things to him."

The overseas operator had the Israel Antiquities Authority within two minutes, but a secretary there explained that Ben-Yaakov had gone for the day. Jon pleaded with her until she released his home phone number, which he then called. The phone rang and rang. No answer. "Please God," Jon sighed, "*don't* let him have gone public with this!"

"Let's try again in ten minutes," said Glastonbury, "and every ten minutes after that."

They tried to manage appropriate small talk during the interims, but the mood around the conference table had all the carefree abandon of a séance. Lawton's potential findings were part of the tension, failure to reach Ben-Yaakov the rest. His home phone continued to ring stubbornly.

Soon the door opened again, and Lawton suggested that the group follow him down the hall to his laboratory. When all had filed inside, he said, "We've separated the non-carbon particulate from the rest of the material and cleaned it as best we could. The microscope to the left is the Pompeii sample; the one to the right is the Weber sample. See for yourselves, gentlemen."

Peering through the eyepiece of the left-hand microscope, Jon saw a brightly illuminated field strewn with jagged boulders of black, dark-brown, and red umber. Then he switched to the right-hand microscope and said, "Those boulders—or rather, granules—look very much like they could be from the same lot, though the *color's* lighter in the Pompeii granules!"

Each, in turn, looked into the tandem microscopes and had to agree, except for Glastonbury, who shook his head and said, "They really don't look the same to me. Sorry, Jonathan. Your lot is *much* darker."

"*Exactly* what we'd expect from granules immersed in carbon pigment," said Lawton.

"Oh! Well, of course!" Glastonbury huffed. "Stupid of me!"

"No, just another sign that you'd best hang it up, Reginald," said a genial Paddington.

"I *knew* you'd say that, Tom. You're *ever* so predictable!"

"Good work, George," said Dunstable. "Do proceed with the next analysis programs."

"When would you estimate the results?" asked Jon.

"I think two days should be sufficient. And I'd welcome your expertise in evaluating our analysis series, Dr. McHugh."

Jon performed some quick calculations. Jennings should not have returned to Israel by then. "Fine," he said. "And thank you, Dr. Lawton."

The phone rang. The operator said, "I have Dr. Ben-Yaakov on the line."

Jon took the phone, covered the mouthpiece, and said, "Pray for me, gentlemen!" Then he spoke: "Hello, Gideon. This is Jon Weber in London . . . Yes, in London . . . Yes, I know I wasn't to leave the country, but I simply *had* to . . . How did I get out of Israel? Tell you later. Now, I'll be returning by the weekend, and I'll report directly to your office on Monday, Okay? We won't have the results for two days yet, but preliminary tests seem to show a common origin for both samples . . . That's right. Do you see the importance, now, of not going public with this? . . . *What?!* You do that and Jennings will *learn!* Then we may *never* have conclusive proof in our lifetimes, or probably ever! . . . Look, Gideon, at this point I don't *care* what laws I've broken. You can throw me in the slammer the moment I see you, but *don't* let the word out. Now, I don't blame you for having gone to the prime minister with this, but *please* call him the moment we hang up and plead for confidentiality, at least for the next week. Can you? . . . *Fabulous*, Gideon! I'm indebted to you . . . Yes, that's a promise! 'Bye."

Then he looked at the others and said, "Well, Mossad won't be necessary after all! Oh, oh, I take that back. Tom, can you get Mossad to clear me at Ben Gurion Airport? I'll be arriving there as 'Ernst Becker,' and with no 'Exit Israel' stamp in my passport!"

"Done," said Paddington, writing himself a memo.

"I hope you don't mind if I haunt your laboratory over the next two days, Dr. Dunstable," said Jon. "There's nowhere else I could possibly be over the next forty-eight hours."

"You're more than welcome, Dr. Weber," he replied. "We'll resume first thing in the morning."

"I'll drive you to Claridge's, Jonathan," said Glastonbury. "We've reserved a suite for you and Dr. McHugh."

They had no sooner unpacked than Jon suddenly said, "*Darn!* I forgot to phone Shannon." A direct-dial call went through quickly enough. Jon fibbed to her that he'd been detained by the editorial work in Tel Aviv, but would return in several days.

"But Jon, where *are* you staying in Tel Aviv? I called your publishers, and they didn't seem to know you were even in town."

"Why'd you want to call me?" he asked, dodging desperately.

"I was lonely. I only wanted to tell you how much I love you."

Jon's eyes filmed. Exit falsehood, enter truth, even if it could cost him dearly. "Darling," he said, "I'm . . . not in Tel Aviv. I'm not even in Israel."

"Where *are* you, then?"

"I can't tell you now, Shannon. All I can plead is . . . that you trust me. I promise to explain everything *very* soon."

"Are you in some kind of *trouble*, Jon? Is anything wrong?"

"No, I'm fine. Please just try to believe me and not worry, Okay?"

There was a long silence.

"*Please*, Shannon. You'll understand very shortly."

"Well . . . all right, but—"

"Tell me, darling, has your father called at all from England?"

"No, I expect him to call tonight."

"All right. Now, this is *very* important. In case he asks about me, or wants to speak to me, just say you don't know where I am at the moment, Okay?"

"Is something wrong with *Papa?*"

"No, no, no," he laughed. "I just . . . have a little surprise for him, that's all. Now, can you be a big girl and play mum?"

"*Well!* Of all the patronizing—"

"Just kidding, little Irish firebrand, just kidding! And I'm not asking you to tell a lie, because you really *don't* know where I am, do you?"

"Oh, yes, I do," she murmured. "Right here in my heart."

"And that, my sweet, is where I hope to stay for the rest of my life. See you soon!"

The next morning, the testing program resumed at the Institute of Archaeology. Dunstable had interrupted all procedures there, so the comparative analysis of the samples could proceed immediately, with excruciating care but at full throttle.

"Electronmicroscopy shows that the noncarbon particles in both samples are indeed ceramic," said Lawton. "We've separated the carbon and the ceramic in both samples, and we'll now analyze all four lots via PIXE and ESCA."

Over the next hours, Jon and Sandy went from computer screen to computer screen. A strong congruence between "Pompeii Ceramic" and "*Titulus* Ceramic" was growing increasingly evident.

"So far, Jonnie, me boy," said Sandy, "it looks as if your little swim mayt have been waarth it after all!"

"Your awful brogue is coming back, Sandy. That's a better sign than any of these tests!"

Late the next day, they all reconvened in the Institute conference room. Gladwin Dunstable summarized the results. "As you know, gentlemen, the carbon comparisons proved similar, though with slight differences easily explained by the one lot having been used in ink. I'm also glad to say that we have enough carbon left from both samples for TAMS testing at Oxford."

"Great!" said Jon.

"But the ceramic comparisons are . . . quite remarkable indeed. PIXE indicates three trace elements as showing up in almost *identical* congruence in both samples." He handed out copies of a graph and said, "This pinpoints the exact relative proportions of strontium, rubidium, and lead in each sample."

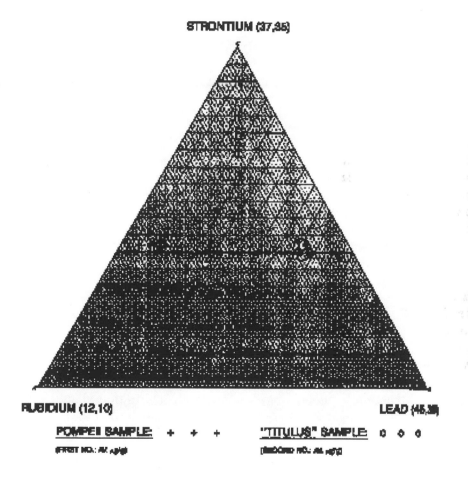

"The ratio points for the Pompeii sample are indicated by cross marks from the three tests conducted," Dunstable explained, "while small circles are the *titulus* scrapings."

Glastonbury studied the illustration and said, "The points certainly fall in the same sectors, don't they? What do the numbers mean?"

"Those are micrograms per gram—units of one-millionth of a gram. Each number is an average for the three tests."

"Looks almost like two fingerprints of the same material," said Paddington.

"An apt comparison, Tom," chortled Glastonbury, "considering your stock in trade. Well, what do you think, Jonathan? You've been rather quiet—"

"Well," Jon replied, "the big question is this: *would* this laboratory be prepared to certify that our two samples came from the same source? If yes, our problems are solved. If not—" He stopped and merely held out his hands.

Lawton wrinkled his brow and looked out the window. "In my opinion, they *do* indeed have a common origin. But if I were haled into court, I'm not sure my opinion would carry the case."

"Why not?" Jon wondered.

"Lampblack from ceramic surfaces was a common source for ancient inks, not?"

"But with identical clay particles?"

"Can we ultimately *prove* that they're identical? Perhaps. Perhaps not."

"And we shouldn't overlook the factor of coincidence," said Paddington. "Even though I'm not Henri Berthoud, try this scenario on for size: conceivably, ink could have been manufactured at Pompeii from a similar ceramic source for soot and—who knows?—exported to Palestine, Pilate actually using it for the *titulus* and—once again—we're back to authenticity."

"I get the picture," said Jon. "And it could be argued, I suppose, that someone *else*, not Jennings, got hold of that soot and did the job if it *is* a forgery."

"*You* were there, Gladwin," chortled Glastonbury. "Maybe *you* did it!"

He laughed, held up his hands, and said, "I'm the one!"

Jon shook his head, took a deep breath, and said, "Well, I was afraid it might come to this. There's really only one ultimate solution to our mystery, gentlemen. I think I'm going to have to try to 'smoke' the truth out of Jennings, so the world won't be left hanging for ages to come. Otherwise, we'll have dogmatic declarations that Rama is authentic, and, oppositely, so many weird theories of fraud, it'll make the Kennedy assassination look like a non-debatable axiom by comparison! You see, if our laboratory evidence is impeachable, the only *final* proof may lie in the mind of Austin Balfour Jennings."

"Fine," said Glastonbury, "but how do you propose to 'smoke' the truth out of him?"

"By confronting him in private and convincing him that I'm on to his scheme, but that I've not yet shared my suspicions with anyone else. I have to put myself in harm's way. At that point, he may try something dangerous, but that would be self-incriminating, and we'd have the truth."

"And if he's innocent?" asked Dunstable.

"I can only plead for his pardon, confessing that my wits have been scrambled to the point of student turning against teacher. Perhaps he may one day forgive me."

They all pondered the plan, as Jon continued. "You see, the shock to the Christian world has been so brutal that I'm not sure 'tiny ceramic particles' will prove that convincing, and this will be debated for centuries to come. So I think our one and only chance at the truth is that face-off, a one-to-one confrontation with Jennings, in which I *may* somehow get him to 'misspeak' himself or admit the truth."

"If he thinks you're the only one who knows," said Glastonbury, "that could be very *dangerous* for you, Jonathan."

"I know," he sighed. "It may not even work. Or Jennings could very well be innocent after all. But do you know of any other way?"

No one responded.

Glastonbury saw "Ernst Becker" off at Heathrow. "Glad you gave in and let our people change your appearance, Jonathan. The

Panama hat and glasses just didn't do the job. That moustache and beard really look distinguished—almost as good as Becker's new passport picture! From now on, whenever you have to fly in or out of Israel undercover, go as Becker and go bearded."

"Hope that won't be necessary much longer. I'm not really cut out for these espionage capers."

"Now, Paddington's arranged for Mossad to meet you at Ben Gurion. They'll whisk you through customs and drive you to Jerusalem."

"Good. I didn't exactly leave my car at the airport, you'll recall! After I've made my peace with Ben-Yaakov, I'll have him drive me to Ramallah. I should get there just in time to welcome Jennings back from Oxford."

"If *only* he didn't return in the meantime! Now Mossad's liaison with MI-5 is Dov Yorkin—looks something like a Jewish Paddington. He'll meet you at Ben Gurion, and he's your contact if you need strategic help. Or in case of physical danger. You and he should rehearse some scenarios on the way to Jerusalem, don't you think?"

"Right."

"And where should I phone you the results of Dunstable's Oxford tests—certainly not Ramallah?"

"No. Better leave a message at the Albright Institute in Jerusalem. I've adopted a secretary there named Linda!"

"Cheerio, then, Jonathan. I have to head for Buckingham Palace to keep the Queen informed. Have a good flight!"

Jon settled into his seat. The starboard jet engine began its escalating whine. The flight attendant had just latched the cabin door when she called to the cockpit, "Oh, oh, we've got a latecomer," and reopened the door. There, filling the doorway, stood a tall figure, who was imperially bald. "The train from Oxford was delayed," he explained and apologized for being late.

"Not at all, Professor Jennings," said the flight attendant. "I'll show you to your seat."

Jon recoiled in horror and instantly pulled *The Times* high about his head. The seat next to him was empty! *Please God*, he implored, silently, *if you have any interest in this affair—*

But no. The attendant stopped next to him and said, "Here's your seat, sir."

Jennings started to sit down, but then changed his mind. "I say, you don't mind if I sit at that row of empties back there, do you? I have some work I want to spread out."

"No problem, sir."

Jon could have sung the "Hallelujah Chorus." But how providential Glastonbury's concern for camouflage. Still, Jennings would have pierced his hirsute façade ten minutes into the flight. Jon hunkered down under blanket and pillows, thanking God that this was an evening flight.

At Ben Gurion, Jon waited until Jennings deplaned before leaving the jet. He would have to stay to his rear from now on. At customs he saw Dick Cromwell waiting to pick up Jennings and blessed Glastonbury once again for his beard. As he loitered behind the column of arriving passengers, a hand tapped his shoulder.

"Dov Yorkin . . . Mossad," said the hand's owner.

"Delighted to meet you, Mr. Yorkin," said Jon. "Jonathan Weber."

"No," Yorkin smiled. "Ernst Becker."

"Sorry! Do you suppose you can drive either of us to Ramallah before *they* get there?" he pointed to Jennings and Cromwell.

"No problem," Yorkin laughed. "We'll use a shortcut."

"And you'll have to explain to Gideon Ben-Yaakov why I wasn't able to see him."

"No problem."

Yorkin and an associate whisked him out of the airport and into a waiting Mercedes. Blue lights flashing into the Israeli night, they burned the kilometers toward Jerusalem, but then avoided the city, using a curving, tire-squealing route over the hills and valleys of Judea. Just when Jon was starting to have second thoughts about Yorkin's route, their Mercedes roared into Ramallah and delivered him to the door of the hotel.

Before Jennings and Cromwell arrived in the Peugeot, he even had time to fall into Shannon's open arms and implore her to keep his absence confidential.

TWENTY-FIVE

So, Austin, how did it go at Oxford?" asked Jon over breakfast the next morning. "You got back earlier than planned—"

"We wound things up more quickly than expected. But the Rama Foundation meeting was no great delight, I'll tell you. Several big contributors are dropping out. However," he chuckled, "several others are signing on. The British Freethinkers Association is pledging us £10,000 annually!"

"That figures!" Shannon tittered.

"What did you do while I was gone, Jonathan? Discover any problem in the evidence we've all overlooked?"

"Precisely that," Jon felt like saying. But he replied, "No. I had to spend quite a bit of time in Tel Aviv with the epitome manuscript."

"Anything wrong?"

"No, just those footnotes in seven languages." He glanced at Shannon, praying she wouldn't betray his trust, even to her own father. She looked at him with eyes of cool sapphire and said nothing. Cromwell, relieved that Jon had survived his harrowing trip to London, was, of course, no problem.

"Well, then, it's off to the dig," said Jennings. "I felt like a fish out of water in England. I suppose I'm a 'dirt archaeologist' in essence. No more, no less."

They drove off to Rama. Sadly, Jon realized it would be their last normal day at the dig. He would confront Jennings late that night.

Long after supper, and just before Jennings retired, Jon knocked on the door and said, "Austin, I have a problem. Would you mind coming up to my room and discussing it with me over a glass of sherry?"

"Not at all. Be up shortly."

327

Bottle and glasses ready, Jon paced his room, tingling with dread at the awful task ahead of him. He held out his hand. It was actually trembling. In the next minutes, he would be indicting a teacher, patron, and friend, a father-figure, and a probable father-in-law-to-be. In the process he would have to lie, deceive, and ensnare to spring the psychological trap, and all with the knowledge that the trap might snap shut, having caught nothing at all. As if prompted from hell itself, Ramallah's favorite jackal chose that moment to start its howling, this time from a declivity just behind the hotel.

There was a knock at the door.

"Come in, Austin."

Pouring sherry for both of them, Jon launched exuberantly into small talk, avoiding the excruciating purpose of their tête-à-tête. They speculated over how the world would receive the epitome. They exchanged plans for the oncoming winter. They talked through a second glass of sherry each.

Jon slowly poured a third—and he intended to pour as many as Jennings could possibly drain—and then he set out on his bitter journey. "Here's my . . . ah . . . problem, Austin," he sighed, looking into the black night outside the window. "All these past months, the name of our game has been 'Find the flaw . . . the chink . . . the blemish . . . that one shred of evidence that doesn't comport with the rest.' *If*, that is, those aren't Jesus's bones. I *think* I may have found it."

"Really? *Smashing*, Jonathan! What in the world is it?"

"Do you recall my asking you what Gladwin Dunstable sent you from Pompeii so you could test the radiocarbon lab at Rehovot?"

"Yes—"

"Well, you told me it was a piece of carbonized wooden handle. Now, please find it in your heart to forgive me, Austin, but I called Dunstable to get more detail on that episode, and he told me no handle was involved. He rather sent you a packet of powder soot or lampblack he'd brushed off one of the bake ovens at Pompeii."

"Oh, dear me, dear me, it certainly *was* that, of course. Stupid memory lapse on my part! Oh yes, I remember now. I *asked* him for something wooden. He said the Pompeii authorities would permit only something like the soot."

"But he said you had *specified* a soot sample. And quite a quantity of it."

Jennings's eyes narrowed. "Unlikely." He shook his head. "Perhaps Dunstable's memory is faulty. But why were you interested in something so insignificant as what Dunstable may have sent me from Pompeii?"

"Well, remember when Henri Berthoud was parading out all his weird scenarios of fraud, the day all of us went paranoid in suspecting each other?"

"Oh yes," Jennings laughed. "I suspected you . . . you suspected Clive . . . Clive suspected me . . . and so on. I think only Shannon was spared because she was too young!"

"Well, we all recognized the *theoretical* possibility that someone on our staff was the perpetrator. Shortly after that, when Montaigne held his press conference and claimed grammatical errors in the Aramaic, it was *you* who—just a little uncharacteristically—kept pressing him on the grammatical question, almost challenging him, as it were, to find something wrong. At the time I didn't notice it, but my memory kept bringing up your performance that day, which suited you perfectly *if* you were the perpetrator."

Jennings smiled. "Come, come, Jonathan! I didn't like how *nebulous* Montaigne was that day, did you? I was only trying to pin him down. In fact, I recall that it was *you* who raised the issue again at the Latin Patriarchate."

"I know that. But my suspicions grew when I learned that you sent only three grams of carbon soot to be tested at Rehovot."

"You mean you called the Weizmann to check on *that?*"

"Yes, I did."

Jennings's jaw dropped. "Great *balls* of fire!" he exclaimed. "You really *do* suspect me, don't you, Jonathan? Look, that was years and years ago. So what if I didn't send all the soot? I simply sent what they required."

Again Jon filled both glasses with sherry. He noticed—and Jennings could not have helped noticing—how the bottle trembled.

"All right, then, Austin," he continued. "What *did* you do with the rest of the soot? Thirty or forty grams' worth?"

"Oh, good Lord, Jonathan! I used it to blacken our faces for a minstrel show here! How in ruddy Hades am I supposed to recall what I did with something like *that*? That long ago?"

"I'll tell you, then. You carefully mixed it with gum arabic and water, and you used the ink to paint the *titulus* parchment, and, perhaps, in different ratios, to write the papyrus too."

Jennings broke out laughing. "Good enough, Jonathan. You've carried your little practical joke far enough. But it's late, and I have to be getting to bed." He saw that Jon was not smiling.

"I'm serious, Austin. I'm deadly serious."

"Well, then, you're a *fool* too!"

"You see, the water would evaporate and not affect radiocarbon dating—if it came to that—and most of the gum gel too. The balance of the material—the carbon residuum—would date beautifully to *before* AD 79—just perfect for your purposes. So any analysis of the ink would register authenticity."

"I can see the strain of all this is getting to be too much for you, Jonathan!" said Jennings, his face darkening. "I won't even begin to explore your motives as a . . . an ingrate and scoundrel, a student viper who'd try to strike the hand of his teacher!"

"Please be sure that this is the most *painful,* the most horribly *difficult* thing I've ever had to do in my life, Austin! The implications here are tearing me apart."

Jennings' mood seemed to soften. "Well, this has shaken all of us. But, put the case that your impossible hypothesis were correct. Why would I *ever* have undertaken anything like this?"

"I don't know yet," Jon lied. "But I'm going to suggest that Glastonbury's panel go over your whole past with a fine-tooth comb. Quite likely, motive enough will be found."

"You mean, you haven't told Glastonbury about these wild speculations of yours?"

"No."

Good. He was swallowing the bait.

"Or anyone else?"

Better. The bait was lodging deeper.

"No. Obviously I had to discuss this with you first."

Jennings thought for some moments, taking a deep sip of wine. Then he put down his glass and said, "Let's continue with your mad scenario. How would you ever, *ever* go about proving that I'd done what you claim I did?"

"I've given that a lot of thought. I have in mind to scrape all the darkest ink off the *titulus*—you know, the 'DAEORVM' letters at the corner—and compare those granules with similar lampblack from Pompeii . . . *if* we can get Dunstable to find the spot where he scraped the first time. If the soot's the same, you're the perpetrator."

Jennings chuckled again. "Such a dreamer you are, Jonathan. Oh, that's a *fine* scheme, all right, and I find only seventeen things wrong with it."

"Such as?"

"Such as the fact that the authorities over at the Shrine of the Book would *never* let you damage this or any other artifacts. You'd be an archaeological outlaw."

"I think they'd cooperate, once they knew the reason for it and how it could break open this mystery."

"Not likely. Have you discussed it with them?"

"No, of course not."

"The second problem is the sampling. You'd never be able to scrape off enough for radiocarbon testing."

"There are other tests—quant and qual, spectrometry, particle analysis."

"And Dunstable, of course, would have no trouble finding that oven?" He was smiling.

"He has a good memory, I understand."

"Have you discussed it with him?"

"Obviously not."

Jennings stood up abruptly and paced the room. Then he stopped and said, "You know, Jonathan, perhaps we've both had too much to drink. I can't believe even in my sodden wits that this conversation is actually taking place. You *really* think I did this? The entire thing?"

Sadly, wearily, Jon nodded.

"Well . . . this is . . . this is just too bizarre for words. Actually you compliment me, sir. I wouldn't know Aramaic well enough to have brought off something like this."

"I know . . . that *is* a problem," Jon again prevaricated. "But who knows? Maybe Glastonbury and Paddington could explore that too. We don't know that much about your Oxford student days."

"Have you suggested that to them?"

"Of course not, Austin! The least I could do was expose my private . . . *horrible* . . . hypothesis to you, and to you alone."

"When do you plan to launch this sensational speculation of yours?"

"I'm going to ask the Shrine authorities for permission to scrape the *titulus* tomorrow morning."

"Fine!" said Jennings. "In fact, I'll drive over there with you. Well, good night, Jonathan. I'll see you in the morning."

He stood up and stalked out of the room, slamming the door behind him.

Jon sat at the table, devastated. Jennings's previous responses had been so in line with his hypothesis. But *why* was his last comment so out-of-line?"

Sleep escaped him that night.

At breakfast the next morning, Jennings called him over to a separate table for privacy. "Well, Jonathan," he opened, "did that all really happen last night . . . our weird conversation? Or was it just a nightmare?"

"It *did* take place, I regret to say." He was finding it difficult to look Jennings in the eye.

"Well, your . . . *disgusting* suspicions of me had one good effect: they drove me back to my files from the Shiloh dig. I spent half the night reading my papers from that era, including correspondence with Dunstable, and I may well be on to something. *Gladwin Dunstable*, it turns out, should be our prime suspect."

"*What?!*"

"It's all coming into focus now. Remember, that was years ago. But now I recall that Dunstable had some unholy interest in Piltdown and other frauds, and he loved to ask me about some of the famous hoaxes in archaeology. Over some late rounds of scotch one night, when I was in my cups, I faintly recall him suggesting how a papyrus might be forged with a fresh batch of 'ancient' ink."

"Why in *blazes* didn't you tell Glastonbury's panel about this?"

"I didn't remember it at the time, Jonathan. It didn't come back to me until I read through that material last night."

"But what possible motive would Dunstable have had for the forgery?"

"How should I know?" Jennings shrugged his shoulders. "Well, unless . . . you know, he *was* a past president of the BFA—"

"What's that?"

"The British Freethinkers Association. Anyway, on—"

"Hold it a minute, Austin," said Jon, as he took a quick gulp of coffee. "Let me sort this out for a moment." Staring out the window, he tried desperately to assimilate the new data. If Dunstable *were* the perpetrator after all, why had he defended Jennings so vigorously in London? He could better have covered his tracks by letting Jennings be suspected instead. But . . . that was *wrong thinking*, he suddenly realized! If Dunstable *were* the forger, he would want to hide the forgery and not have *anyone* suspected, which was virtually his conduct in London.

Glancing back at Jennings, Jon said, "Sorry, Austin! It's just possible that I'm guilty of . . . of a *colossal* error here. But please continue."

"Well, anyhow, on our off days during the Shiloh campaign, Dunstable and I did some surveys down at the Dead Sea, and we stumbled across a cavern shaft south of Qumran on the way to the Wadi Murabba'at. We climbed down inside it and found a burial pit, apparently from the first century. But here's what fascinates me: one of the skeletons there had *a shock of dark hair still attached at the crown of the skull,* I now recall, *just* like our remains."

"That *does* have possibilities, Austin! But why didn't you excavate the burial pit?"

"We didn't own the site. I planned to dig there later on, but never got title to it."

Jennings downed another quick cup of coffee and stared at the hills outside the dining room. "I won't be able to rest until I check out that site and see if, just perhaps, that skeleton is now missing. I'm telling the rest of the staff to dig without me today. Want to come along, Jonathan?"

"Absolutely."

By this time, Jon knew every bend on the Jerusalem-Jericho road. This was his third trip in ten days. They reached the Dead Sea by midmorning. Jennings was at the wheel of the Rover, and he now turned southward along the coastal highway. About three miles below Qumran, he drove westward off the shore road and up a gravel wadi until they reached a sheer rock face and could go no farther.

Jennings studied his map, nodded, and said, "Yes, I think this is it. Let's take our backpacks and move out, Jonathan. It's on foot from here on. With any luck we'll be in and out before the afternoon heat."

They shouldered their packs. Jon followed Jennings up a steep pathway that zigzagged up the pinkish-orange escarpment of Judean hills facing the Dead Sea. Twenty minutes later, Jennings paused and checked his map again. "Yes, this *is* it," he said. "We leave the path here. Follow me."

Jennings now led the way over extremely rough, boulder-strewn terrain. "Are you all right, Jonathan?" he called back.

"Sure! But it's a miracle you ever found that burial pit in *this* wilderness!"

"Well, I will admit that friendly Bedouin helped us. Ah! Should be just over this ridge and down to the hollow beyond."

Ten more minutes of careful climbing brought them to a sloping declivity at the foot of a ruddy granite cliffside that towered a hundred more feet above them. At the base of the cliff, Jennings pointed to a small orifice. "That should be it," he said.

Walking over, he pulled scrub brush and several stones away from the hole to enlarge it. Then he opened his backpack and took out a rope ladder and metal crossbar, part of which doubled as a meter stick. Kneeling down at the edge of the opening, he said, "Here, Jonathan. Shine your torch down inside."

Jon aimed his flashlight and exclaimed, "Wow! That's *some* shaft!"

"That's why I brought the ladder." Jennings now anchored the ladder to the steel bar, which he laid across the ground rock at the orifice. "There," he said, "that'll hold more than five hundred pounds. Now climb down while I hold the light for you. I'll follow after as you hold the light for me."

A little gingerly, Jon gave the rope ladder a practice tug and started climbing down the shaft. The ladder swayed a bit, but seemed strong enough. He climbed down sixteen or seventeen feet from the surface, and then called up, "Okay, I've hit bottom, Austin."

"All right, I'll toss you the torch. Then hold it for me."

Jennings dropped the flashlight. Jon let go of the rope ladder to catch it. That instant, Jennings jerked the ladder up and out of his reach.

"What are you doing, Austin?" Jon called.

There was no response from the top. Jon trained the flashlight a full circle around the base. "I don't see any burial pit here," he said. "Where is it?"

"There isn't any, Jonathan," Jennings replied softly.

"What do you mean?"

"Well . . . I regret to say that the whole business about Dunstable was a fiction. He had nothing to do with Rama. I merely had to . . . ah . . . get you out here."

Jon felt a stab of nausea. But he kept his voice from wavering. "And *you*, of course, had *everything* to do with Rama, right?"

"Right you are, my good friend. From beginning to end, 'twas I, and I alone."

Jon's heart was racing, and he could feel the throb at his temples. "All right, Austin," he called up. "I have two questions, and I'll bet you know what they are."

"Let me guess. *How* did I do it? And *why* did I do it? Is that it?"

"Those are the two!"

"Well, now . . . in answer to the first, I began with a completely authentic archaeological site. All of Rama is genuine except for the cavern finds . . . oh, and the 'Joseph' jar handles. They really were *frightfully* difficult to fabricate, by the way. I practiced etching inscriptions into ceramics with Carborundum drills until I was ready to do the job on authentic first-century jar handles that had no inscription. After using the drill, I finished, of course, with crude tools, so you people would find only 'ancient' workmanship. I then 'aged' the inscriptions by firing them briefly through templates of the lettering. Thermoluminescence, of course, tested the clay nowhere near the incriptions."

"Very clever, Austin. But when did you do all this?"

"Oh, I had two long years to 'salt' the cavern area—1972 and 1973. I was nearby at Shiloh, but I spent most weekends at Rama—alone, obviously. Kensington had assigned title to Oxford and the Rama Foundation—I represented them—so I had no trouble moving on or off the site at will. There were no campaigns at Rama during those years, you'll recall."

"How'd you hit on the cavern?"

"Well, originally it stood exposed along with the upper cavern. I trucked in a first-century sarcophagus, did the inscription, and buried it."

"But how'd you ever get the inscription to have a patina of age similar to the rest of the sarcophagus?"

"Aha! No easy task, I assure you! But you can get patina on limestone by covering it with a wet, salty soil impregnated with iron salts, then exposing it to air, then covering it again for repeated cycles. I did that to the *inside* of the carved lettering, until the color exactly matched the rest of the sarcophagus. But first, of course, I had to have the appropriate skeleton inside, now, didn't I?"

"Right."

"Well, finding first-century bones in Israel is no great chore, as you know, and the set I finally used came from one of the tombs at Qumran, where I dug under de Vaux."

"Why didn't you simply use a set from the Rama cemetery?"

"I tried, believe me. But I couldn't find a male skeleton of exactly the right age. The Qumran bones were close to the mark. But I got the grave linens from the Rama cemetery, a Herodian grave."

"What about the 'crucifixion marks,' so to speak?"

"Aha! I simply laid the spearhead of a first-century Roman

javelin against the rib cage and scored in the imprint with a scalpel, then abraded it with the Carborundum drill. Ditto, the other 'abrasions.' Then, of course, I found a way to add calcareous accretions. I was strong in chemistry during my undergraduate days."

"And the ceramics, of course, were no problem, right?"

"Pottery was the *least* of my problems. I could have brought in a whole collection from the first century. Ditto the coin, ditto the other finds inside and outside the sarcophagus."

"And the *titulus* parchment?"

"You were absolutely on target with your hunch about the Pompeii carbon, Jonathan. I congratulate you! We had some parchment scraps left from the Qumran excavations, which I managed to swipe. Then I mixed up some 'ancient ink' and wrote out the *titulus*—rather brilliantly, if I do say so myself, intentionally making the 'error' that you caught. Didn't that add marvelous credibility?"

"It certainly did. And your different shadings gave the impression of random preservation. But what about the papyrus? How could you ever—"

"The papyrus itself came from one of the minor Dead Sea scrolls that had a ridiculously long blank trailer, so I used part of that. It was all I could do to keep from telling you, 'Don't *bother* testing the papyrus for C-14! Anyone with genius enough to do the Aramaic wouldn't be fool enough to use the wrong paper!' But you finally realized that yourself, I believe."

The weird conversation continued, Jon calling up to the face at the edge of the orifice overhead. For his part, Jennings seemed almost delighted *finally* to be able to reveal his great—if macabre—secret.

"But what about the incredibly accurate Aramaic in Joseph's *ersatz* letter?"

"Well, thank you, Jonathan. Again you surmised the truth. I knew *far* more Aramaic than anyone realized. Well, it's beyond all debate. I know more Aramaic than anyone on earth . . . and certainly more than that fool Montaigne, who blathered about my so-called 'lapses in grammar.' I know, you almost caught me there. I did drop my guard in taking him on, didn't I?"

"You seemed to change character, Austin. You really did. But how did you get Nicodemus's script to look so different?"

"I wrote it with my left hand. I did Joseph's letter with my right."

"Well, even though your whole venture is demonic, Austin, I must say that the papyrus was a masterpiece. I truly believe that if Joseph *had* written such a letter, he'd probably have used your vocables and syntax."

"It *did* take my best efforts, Jonathan. I worked almost a year on that papyrus, and it *is* rural, first-century Aramaic, you know. But I almost lost my patience when it took you and Montaigne so long to get those final phrases translated. I nearly whispered the proper renderings into your ear!"

"But I think your masterstroke was using the cavern rather than some sector at Rama."

"Oh, I *had* to, Jonathan. If I had salted this in one of Clive Brampton's five-meter squares, he'd have noticed the shift in stratification and blown the whistle. This way I could salt the cavern, and then drive in a truckload of mountain surface fill to cover the cavern entrance, letting the winter rains compact it naturally."

"But what if I hadn't discovered the cavern?"

"I'd have 'worked you' closer and closer to it until you did discover it. As it happened, you couldn't possibly have been more cooperative."

"And it was you, of course, who left the darkroom open and the papyrus prints exposed?"

"Of course! How to let the world in on this was really a sticky wicket! But Gideon and his snooping cousin provided *such* a serendipitous solution!"

Jon was silent for some moments. Then he said, "Well, Austin, I have to congratulate you, albeit in a perverse sense. You certainly fooled the entire world, didn't you?"

"Yes, I must admit, it all came off rather nicely, I think."

Hearing Jennings's revelations had held Jon in such morbid thrall that he had given little though to extricating himself from mortal danger. But now he had to seek quick options for himself, he realized with mounting desperation. What did Jennings have in mind? Abandoning him? Killing him? If so, how? A gun? A boulder? Or, conceivably, was he trying to *convert* him?

First, though, he had to ask the second question. "All right, Austin," he called up to that great hairless dome watching him at the mouth of the shaft, "now tell me why you ever did this."

"Well, dear boy, that one has a rather long explanation," he sighed. "You see, I began school as a very dedicated and believing Christian lad. I admired my clergyman father enormously. What a gifted preacher he was! He inspired me to study for the ministry, and so I went to Oxford to do just that. I returned home for Easter holiday that first year. On the morning of Holy Saturday, he was out at the edge of our lawn, fixing the mailbox along the roadside because some car had damaged it. If *only* he'd been facing the opposite direction, he would have escaped. Some driver, who'd had too much to drink the night before, fell asleep at the wheel, veered off the road, and plowed into my father with his car, killing him only partially. After excruciating pain, he died on Easter Sunday."

"How horrible! Tragic! But . . . but what does that have to do with my question?"

"Everything, really. To me, that event shattered any belief in a protecting deity. Such a *tiny* divine intervention would have saved my father that it wouldn't even have passed for a miracle! All God had to do was let the driver go to sleep one *fraction* of a second earlier or later, and the car would have plowed harmlessly into our lawn, hurting no one, least of all, the sodden driver. But there was no divine intervention whatever, obviously. Had God existed, there would have been. Ergo, there is no God."

"That doesn't necessarily follow, Austin."

"I thought it did at the time. I still do, for that matter. But back at Oxford, I immediately switched out of the ministry. In my youthful idealism, I decided then and there that I'd now devote my life to the great task of liberating the world from all religious superstition. I conceived the general outline of Rama at age nineteen, and started mastering Greek and Aramaic as if they were my mother tongues.

"Oh yes, I did try something of a 'shortcut' that required *much* less effort than Rama. After joining the Oxford faculty, I did some

research in Rome and gained access to the *Codex Vaticanus.*
When no one was looking, I took a lemon-based concoction of
mine and added a final line to Mark's Gospel to the effect that
Jesus's body had been stolen." Jennings chuckled, then continued.
"The citric acid was invisible, of course, because I wanted it to
appear as if the *Church* had expunged it."

"Another *problem solved!*" Jon wanted to shout, but first he
asked, "Well, what happened with your maiden voyage into the
world of forgery?"

"Oh, it must have been too sophisticated, I suppose. The dolts
at the Vatican never used ultraviolet on it, apparently."

Jon was about to tell him differently, but why give the wretch
that satisfaction? Instead, he said, "Something doesn't make sense,
Austin. If you opposed *all* 'religious superstition,' why did you
attack Christianity specifically?"

"It's far and away the most formidable system of belief in all the
world and in all of history. Take away that keystone and the other
religions will eventually crumble as well. Yet, Christianity is also the
most *vulnerable* of the lot because of Jesus and His 'Resurrection.'
No Rama could ever disprove Judaism or Islam, you see."

"What about the 'new theology' of a spiritual resurrection?"

"That will satisfy only the intellectuals. Take away Easter and
the bodily Resurrection, and Christianity's doomed. Your John
Updike said it rather well in his *Seven Stanzas at Easter:*

> Make no mistake: if He rose at all
> it was as His body;
> if the cells' dissolution did not reverse, the molecules
>   reknit, the amino acids rekindle,
> the Church will fall."

"That's it? Your father is killed accidentally, and so you dupe
the world?"

"No. There's *much* more, and this quite closely affects the girl
you love—"

Jennings proceeded with the story Jon had already learned
from Glastonbury, but Jon let him finish so he could learn any

fresh details. Jennings's voice wavered as he told it, particularly sections involving the wife he cherished.

"And so there you have it, Jonathan," he concluded. "That wretched abbess imprisons my Colleen, drugs her with laudanum, and kills her—all in the name of the Lord—and the Church slaps her hand! As follow-up, the IRA kills my mother and brother and burns down our homestead—*all in the name of the Lord!* Religious fanaticism simply *has* to be uprooted, Jonathan, no matter what pain it causes. You see, this is the only generation that will be affected. In the God-free world of the future, there will be no pain."

"You have my profound sympathy for all these horrors, Austin. I just wonder how you can take a private tragedy, like yours, and magnify it *exponentially* to make the world suffer with you."

"The suffering will be brief, but so very profitable. It should be very much like childbirth—the pain fades for the joy of a new life. The world *has* to come of age, Jonathan. Religion is an outmoded crutch of the past, and that crutch has impeded progress—scientific and otherwise—from Galileo's time on. And don't tell me the Church has learned from past mistakes. When you have a pope as recent as John Paul II inveighing against birth control in countries like India with its wall-to-wall people, you know that religion is simply suicidal. I'm only helping it along into the grave it rightly deserves."

"I think John Paul was simply *wrong*, Austin, and you're certainly overplaying the science-versus-religion bit. Modern Christianity doesn't stand in the way of any science I know of. You rather have these great, overarching convergences, like the 'Big Bang' theory and a linear universe complementing Genesis very nicely."

"Be that as it may, dear fellow, your own ears have heard the death rattle of religion most recently when those millennialist pilgrim masses descended on Jerusalem, orchestrated into frenzies by their doomsday prophets. *There's* the quintessence of how damaging religion can be to the intellect, and every right-minded person should want to join me in subverting it! And your charismatic congresses here, these people who have the *audacity* to believe God supernaturally intervenes to move their tongues in heavenly ways.

What, pray tell, do you hear? Gibberish, Jonathan, *gibberish*—word salad! If there *were* a God behind that phenomenon, let Him utter some sense . . . say, the formula to defeat cancer, or at least avoid danger. One word in the earphones of that Dutch pilot—'*Stop!*'—would have prevented those two 747s from crashing into each other on the Canary Islands some years ago, saving hundreds of lives."

"We have no argument there, Austin. These are merely fringe elements in the Church. But against the background of world Christianity, you're taking a miniscule percentage and implying it represents the whole. That's like saying all Jews on earth dress in black and wear fur hats, like the Hasidim."

"What I *am* saying is that religion is the mother of fanaticism—religion and insanity *are* next-door neighbors in the brain—and it does devious things to people. A Spanish bus driver leaving Fatima supposedly shuts his eyes and takes his hands off the steering wheel for twenty miles of night driving *as a test of faith!* Or some believers in the Philippines have themselves nailed to crosses on Good Friday! Or a Polish woman receives the bloody stigmata on her hands and feet, 'like Jesus's wounds'!"

"Every institution on earth has its horror stories, Austin, but in America, we—"

"But not in America? You people are the cult capital of the *world!* I don't mean only a Jim Jones who can coax nine hundred of his idiot followers down to Guyana to sip cyanide-flavored Kool-Aid, or those 'made-in-America' religions like the Jehovah's Witnesses or Mormons or what have you. I'm also talking about your faith healers who reject medical science and let people die without antibiotics or insulin—*all in the name of the Lord!* And your vaunted 'mainline' or evangelical churches? You have decay in both wings there. Your liberals have abandoned any gospel for social activism and politics. But your religious New Right are fast following in their footsteps—never abandoning their gospel, of course, but rather cramming it down the throats of the masses with their outrageous use of television and the media."

As Jennings ranted on and on, Jon urgently surveyed his situation.

The shaft was really an old cistern, evidently, and its walls were too smooth to gain any hand- or footholds. Climbing without a ladder would be out of the question. If the shaft had been just a little narrower, he might have tried to shinny up, one foot on each side. He had been a blooming *idiot*, a stupid *imbecile* to have followed Jennings here without first contacting Dov Yorkin, he realized. Instead, he had been so mesmerized by the prospect of ferreting out the truth that he had thrown precaution to the winds. Now he had to gamble everything on one defensive trump, which he'd have to play out very shortly.

He looked up and saw Jennings's large ruddy face still looming over the opening. He had stopped talking, waiting, evidently, for some response. Jon picked up as best he could recall. "Well, Austin, you certainly seem well informed about American religion."

"Oh, I keep a fat file on all your foibles!"

"But again, you're tarring all Christians with the same brush, and that's neither fair nor logi—"

"Look from the present to the past, then, Jonathan! What's Church history but the unholy saga of oppression and wars over the faith—Christians from Venice looting Christians in Constantinople; the Spanish Inquisition burning heretics and Jews; Catholic armies versus Lutheran armies in the 1500s, drenching the countryside in blood; French Protestants getting massacred; witch trials from Joan of Arc to Salem, Massachusetts; and thousands of other grisly events in history—*all in the name of the Lord!* And what are green and orange doing to each other *to this very day* in that cesspool of religious fanaticism called Ireland? Can't you see that what I'm doing is the most humanitarian gesture I could possibly offer the world?"

"No, I don't, Austin! Now, I'll be the first to say that the Church's record is hardly spotless—I'll *surely* grant you that!—but it's due to that nasty item called 'sin' that permeates every institution in society including the Church, so if—"

"Oh, please, Jonathan, spare me a sermon, won't you?"

"Hear me out! I'm only saying it's unfair to blame the Church for all the violence on this planet. History would've been *much* bloodier if there had been no Christianity. It was Christians who insisted on truce days in the Middle Ages, built hospitals to care for the wounded, intervened in quarrels to keep the peace, erected orphanages, shelters for the homeless, and—"

"Yes, yes, yes . . . I know the minor credits, but—"

"That's just it; you've *totally* ignored the credits, Austin! You've forgotten all about the Church's single-handedly keeping Western culture alive during the Dark Ages, civilizing the barbarian invaders of Rome, recopying manuscripts in monastery libraries so that we'd even *have* súch things as books written before Gutenberg. Here you are, one of the world's greatest Semiticists, and you gnaw away at the cultural hand that fed you!"

"Now, see here, Jonathan—"

"No, it's worse than that, Austin. You're trying to *chop* that hand off entirely! Have you forgotten that Christianity is the *alma mater* of Western civilization, the 'nourishing mother' that built the schools and invented the university? That its record, after all, is *far* more positive than you seem to recall? Christianity lay behind many of the greatest accomplishments in the last two thousand years, ranging from basilicas and cathedrals in architecture, to Leonardo and Michelangelo in art, to Johann Sebastian Bach in music. The Church has fostered some of the greatest minds ever to enlighten our world—Augustine, Aquinas, Dante, Luther, Shakespeare, Milton, Newton—"

"We're getting off track, Jonathan," Jennings interposed. "I'm not saying the Church hasn't accomplished some worthy things. Perhaps for that day and age, it was better to have had Christianity than not. What I *am* saying is that we're now into the twenty-first century—the world has 'come of age,' and it's finally time to put the fairy tales aside, or at least regard them for the fantasies they are. We're *alone* in this universe, Jonathan, *alone*. There is no God, and the sooner mankind realizes this, the more responsible we'll become—*must* become. Rather than relying on 'pie-in-the-sky-in-the-great-by-and-by,' as you Yanks put it, it's high time to improve the world solely by our own efforts *now*— not in some mythical eternity. And not by imploring supernatural assistance, which will never arrive . . . cannot arrive."

"You're so very sure of that?"

"Yes I am—no *deus ex machina,* since there's no *deus* in the first place! Evil proves that. When disaster strikes, it's not the great statistics that move me—not the three or four thousand killed in the Italian earthquakes of 1980—but the twenty-five bodies of *children* removed from that *church* east of Naples, when the walls collapsed *during evening Mass*. And it's not that God is anti-Catholic; it's just that God doesn't exist! The sooner we all realize that, the better."

"The existence of evil *doesn't* disprove God's existence, Austin. On the contrary, Christianity offers a solution, a *remedy* for evil. Your view has no remedy whatever. And the Godless world of the future that you envision wouldn't be any paradise, let me tell you. It would probably resemble hell itself! And by the way, whatever happened to your concept of *truth?* How can any shred of your conscience approve such a diabolical fraud? How could you live with yourself after Rama?"

"Oh, I've solved that very simply. Jesus's bones really *are* out there somewhere, Jonathan. We just haven't found them yet and probably never will. Therefore I had to . . . to supply the evidence."

"And what if your premise is flat-out *false?* You'll then have been guilty of tearing the faith out of millions of lives, to say nothing of the suicides, nervous breakdowns, and other catastrophes you've already caused! Now, drop that rope ladder back down here so I can climb out and we can continue this conversation on the way back to Jerusalem."

"Oh, I'm sorry, Jonathan. I really can't do that."

"Why not?"

"Well . . . now you *know* how Rama came to be. The world doesn't. It's really that simple."

"What do you plan to do, imprison me here for the rest of my life? Drop groceries by helicopter?"

"No. I won't put you through that, Jonathan."

"Well?"

There was a long pause. Then, in a soft voice, Jennings replied, "I'm really terribly sorry it had to be you, Jonathan. Now that I've come to . . . to really know you and cherish you more than I thought possible, I wish I'd have trapped von Schwendener of Yale instead. I really *did* want to welcome you into the family. I know Shannon will be crushed. But the *cause,* Jonathan . . . the *cause* is paramount."

"You mean, you'll let me starve to death here?"

"I was thinking of that. But Qumran's nearby. And it's at least possible that someone walking on the highway down there might hear you scream and come to your assistance. Besides, I wouldn't want you to suffer."

"You're going to kill me, then!"

A long silence followed. At last, Jennings said, "Propane really is quite painless, Jonathan. It has only a slight tracking odor. Clive Brampton seemed to have no problem with it at all."

Jon froze in horror. "*What* did you say? *You killed Clive?*"

"I *had* to, Jonathan, although I very much admired him too. You see, Clive had gotten too suspicious about the stratification in front of the cavern at Rama. One day I found him in my office, looking at the manuscript of Kensington's earliest *Rama Survey,* and the sleuth had found reference to *two* exposed cavern mouths northwest of the site. Of course, I had edited this to *one* cavern mouth for the published version, and eliminated all references to the second. Brampton caught it. We had a nasty scene, so I lured him into this very cistern. Regrettably the propane *had* to follow. He cursed me for a little while, but then he passed away. Quite peacefully really."

Bristling with revulsion, Jon struggled for composure. "How did you make it appear that Clive drowned?"

"Well, I winched him back out after he died, gave him artificial respiration to exhaust the propane, and then drove his body to Caesarea. Before dropping it into the Mediterranean, I put a catheter down his throat and filled his lungs with seawater. Then I rowed offshore in a dinghy and dropped the body overboard. What else could it have been but accidental drowning?"

"Why didn't you simply leave him here?"

"His disappearance would have been too suspicious."

Jon thought for a moment, and then asked, "What do you intend in the case of . . . of *my* body?"

"Yours, I think, we'll simply leave here. If you're discovered months or years hence, it will have been a tragic accident, of course. You must have fallen down a hidden shaft."

A cold lump of terror building inside him, Jon said, "You want to foist Rama on the world. But won't there be *enormous* suspicion if one of the two principal investigators simply *disappears?*"

Jennings was silent for some time. "You know, you *do* have a valid point, Jonathan. Hmmmm . . . Well, instead, perhaps I'll return to Jerusalem and call the police, say we got separated, and we'll mount a search party to look for you. You'll be 'found' sometime thereafter, and then there'll be no missing-body mystery. I, of course, will have retrieved the propane canister from the shaft before you're found."

"You're *crazed*, Austin! You realize that, don't you? You're a bloody psychopath! A madman!"

"No, Jonathan. My logic is crystal clear. We all have to make sacrifices for the *cause*. The cause is *everything!* I surrendered *my* life to it. I'm only sorry that you must do so also."

It was now time, high time, to play his trump, Jon realized—to reveal wider knowledge of the plot. This, he had calculated, would be his ultimate insurance against danger. Otherwise, he would surely have called Dov Yorkin and the Mossad.

"Austin, I hate to have to tell you this," Jon called up, "but I've actually trapped you, rather than vice versa."

"And how's that, dear boy?"

"I was lying when I told you I hadn't discussed this with Gideon or Glastonbury or Dunstable. They *all* know. You see, the only way I could worm the truth out of you was to make you *think* I was the only one who knew. But in fact, while you were in England, I was there, too! You see, I've already taken scrapings from the *titulus* exactly where I threatened to, and we compared these with fresh scrapings of soot Dunstable brought back from Pompeii. They *match*, Austin. Ceramic particles from the bake oven showed up in each and give it all away! They have the same ratio of three trace elements—strontium, rubidium, and lead!"

Jennings was silent for some time. Then he began chuckling. "And *how*, pray tell, did you get the Shrine authorities to give you permission to scrape? And *how*, pray tell, did Dunstable so conveniently supply another package of soot?"

"At the Shrine, I scraped first and explained later. I had a horrid phone conversation with Gideon. He warned me not to leave Israel, so I had to smuggle the granules out by swimming across the Dead Sea narrows at night from Masada to Cape Costigan in Jordan. There, Walt Rast and two Jordanian officials met me and put me on a plane to London. Meanwhile, Dunstable had made another trip to Pompeii, found the same bake oven, and brushed the area next to where he had brushed previously. We compared the samples at—"

Jennings was now emitting guffaws of laughter. "Oh, Jonathan, you're *so* creative! Charles Dickens could have learned a thing or two from you, my boy! Attacking the *titulus*? Swimming the *Dead Sea*, no less! I know, I know, a whale swallowed you and spat you up on the other shore, not? Then little green men carried you in relays all the way to Amman, right?"

"No, Austin, this *really* happened!"

Even as he heard himself in the telling, Jon sensed that his own story *did* sound unbelievable. But he forged ahead.

"Listen, Austin, I'm telling you the *truth*. Two days of testing at Dunstable's laboratory showed an *identical* source. Meanwhile, Paddington filled us in on your Irish tragedies, since the Queen had urged an all-out effort by Scotland Yard and MI-5, so he—"

"Oh, but of *course*! Now we'll have a royal reception at Buckingham Palace from the *Queen*, no less!"

"No. Nothing like that."

"*Oho! Oho-ho-ho!*" Jennings chortled in a fit of laughter. "Move over Lewis Carroll, we now have *Jonathan in Wonderland!* Wasn't it Samuel Johnson who said, 'Depend on it, Sir, when a man knows he is about to be hanged, it concentrates his mind wonderfully'? Well, a similar prospect seems to have made you ever so *creative*, Jonathan. But I don't believe a *word* of it! Carry on, now. I'll be with you shortly."

Jennings's head moved away from the opening, and Jon saw only the cobalt sky overhead. Desperately, he combed the walls and floor of the shaft with his flashlight. It seemed to be a natural cistern the Bedouin probably used during the rainy season, since he saw water level marks at the lowest third of the shaft and green scum at his feet. It was also the finest natural prison Jennings could have found, not to say execution chamber.

Fighting to keep a clear mind against the chilling dread that was numbing his extremities, he searched wildly for some plan of deliverance. The situation seemed shot through with unreality. All this could *not* be happening, he told himself, even as his gut cramped in panic.

Again Jennings's bald visage hovered over the opening. "Let me explain propane to you, Jonathan," he said as he tied a rope to a fat white canister of the stuff he had lugged to the edge of the shaft. "This is *so* much better than cyanide, because you can buy it at any sporting supply store as cooking fuel. And it's not as smelly and dangerous as cyanide either. In fact, it's not a poisonous gas at all. But it *is* heavier than air, and it displaces oxygen. So it'll build up gradually at the bottom of the cistern, and you'll die of anoxia—oxygen starvation."

"Where'd you get that canister? I didn't see you bring it along."

"Of course not. After Clive's death, I had it refilled and hid it again in the rocks here, just in case I'd need it a second time. You see, I provided for *every* possible eventuality. That's also why I had to work absolutely alone all these years. Imagine! I suppose you could call it 'the perfect crime,' but for the fact that I'm liberating the world from the shackles of worthless beliefs, which is no crime at all."

"It's *not* the 'perfect crime,' Austin!" Jon cried. "It's hopelessly *flawed!* Do you realize how many people now know what you've been up to? Nine or ten, at the very least! In Israel, that includes Gideon Ben-Yaakov, Dick Cromwell—he's the one who drove me down to the Dead Sea—and Dov Yorkin of Mossad. In Jordan, there's Walter Rast. In England, we have Glastonbury, Paddington, Dunstable, Sandy McHugh, and others, including the Queen."

"Oh, dear me. What about your White House and President Bronson?" Jennings sneered.

"The president and the State Department half know. They arranged for Jordan's cooperation when I swam the Dead Sea."

"And how about the United Nations?" Jennings taunted. "Nice attempt, Jonathan!"

"You're a *fool,* Austin! I'm telling you the *truth!* Another murder on your hands will only make things worse for you!"

Jennings ignored him and said, "I'm turning the spigot on full now, Jonathan. It shouldn't take very long. If you want to go quickly, simply lie down at the bottom of the cistern. If you must have your last thoughts, then stand up!"

"I was on the *same plane* with you from England, Austin! And I can prove it. *You came on late and they had to open the door for you!* I was disguised in a beard and moustache!"

Jennings was silent for some long moments. Then he laughed and called down, "I almost believed you, Jonathan! But you obviously learned that from Dick Cromwell, because that's the first thing I told him at Ben Gurion!"

"*No,* Austin! I was *there!* It's the bloody truth!!"

"Oh, shut up and don't be tedious!" Jennings huffed. "Don't make this more difficult than it has to be!"

Jon now heard an awful hissing and watched Jennings lower the bulky white canister, playing out his rope, a grimace of determination warping his features.

Again Jennings called down, "I want you to know that I *do* regret losing you as a friend, a colleague, and a son-in-law, Jonathan. And I'll grant you the courtesy of not standing here to watch you die. I don't think I could stomach that. After I've secured the canister, I'll go back to Qumran and ask if anyone's seen you there. I need to establish an alibi, of course."

An invisible jet stream of gas was whistling from the spigot. The canister stopped five feet over his head when Jennings tied the rope to the steel crossbar.

"*Stop it, Austin!*" Jon screamed. "You'll *never* get away with this! *You'll see!*"

Jennings shook his head sadly and muttered, "Why do they always say that?" He looked down at Jon for several moments, nodded, and said, "Good-bye, Jonathan!" Then he stood up, shouldered his backpack, ignored Jon's shouts, and walked down the mountain path to the waiting Land Rover.

Late in the day, after he had duly inquired at the tourist cafeteria and gift shop at Qumran, Jennings returned to the cistern, this time taking along the portable air pump and hose they should have used when first entering the cavern at Rama. Lugging a heavy twelve-volt battery up the steep pathway left him breathless, but it would provide power for the last item on his meticulous checklist.

Leaning over the orifice of the cistern, he shined a flashlight down inside the shaft. Jon lay sprawled across the mossy floor, his legs stiffened in a step position, and his arms and hands submerged in the green, rocky slime. There was no breathing, no movement of the rib cage. He was dead.

Jennings tugged the propane canister up and out of the shaft. He then dropped plastic flex hose almost to the floor of the cistern and connected the pump to his battery terminals. The motor whirred into life, sucking propane out of the cistern and dissipating it into the air. During the half hour he calculated the pump should run, Jennings carefully staged the circumstances of Jon's "accidental" death. Using a camp spade, he dug a steep slide next to the opening, where, obviously, the poor man had lost his footing and slid into the shaft. He also enlarged the orifice so that a sliding victim would easily slip through. Several large rocks were conveniently situated near the rim, on which he might have struck his head. To give him the appropriate wound, Jennings took a large stone, aimed it over Jon's head at the base of the shaft, and let it fall. Training his light on the corpse, he saw that it had gashed the back of his skull. "Well done," he said.

He looked at his watch. Forty minutes had passed. He turned off the pump and packed his things. Before leaving, he carefully scrutinized the entire site to make sure he had left *nothing* behind.

One last time he went to the lip of the opening and peered downward. "Rest in peace, Jonathan," he said. "Rest eternal grant to him, O Lord, and let light perpetual shine upon him."

He shouldered his backpack and made two trips to lug the battery, compressor, canister, and tools down to the Rover. Unexpectedly he was nagged by a small ethical problem. Why had he used the traditional words of the Anglican liturgy in a prayer over Jon's dead body? Oh well, he consoled himself, he must have done it for Jon, who had still believed. He himself was beyond all that nonsense.

TWENTY-SIX

Returning to Ramallah that night, Jennings appeared highly agitated when he asked Shannon and Dick Cromwell whether Jon had somehow returned there in the meantime. No, they replied. He then picked up the phone and called the Jerusalem police to report Jon missing.

The next morning, authorities mounted a massive search effort along the western shore of the Dead Sea. Several helicopters from the Israel Defense Force were fluttering over the pinkish-beige escarpment above Qumran, in radio contact with search parties on the ground. Jennings, Shannon, and Dick led the central search column, Jennings pointing out where they had been surveying when Jon had wandered away with the words, "I'm going to climb that ridge and check the other side."

But a search of the other side revealed nothing. The first day's effort turned up no clue whatever, because Jennings had intentionally started the search a mile too far northward. Shannon was beside herself with dread. "I'll *die* if anything's happened to him, Papa," she cried. "I'll just *die!*"

"There, there." He stroked her hair. "Don't worry, my child. I'm sure we'll find him."

Cromwell, meanwhile, was torn between exposing Jennings for the monster he seemed to be, or, as he almost felt Jon urging him, *not* to blow their cover just yet. When Gideon Ben-Yaakov and Dov Yorkin had first arrived at Qumran, it was all he could do to intercept them and plead that they play the role with him. "You've *got* to!" he whispered, so Jennings wouldn't overhear. "It's exactly the way Jon would want it."

"I say we should arrest him *now*," said Gideon. "We've been led around by the nose long enough."

"You do that, and we may *never* be able to find Jon!"

"He's right," Yorkin conceded.

"One more day, then," Gideon agreed. "We arrest at sundown tomorrow."

By lunchtime the following day, they had found nothing. "Maybe we should head farther south," Jennings suggested. But a unit of the IDF had already anticipated him and was searching along the very ridge that led to the cistern. Twenty minutes later, all cell phones crackled with the news, "We've found him!"

The search parties converged on the site. When Jennings's group arrived, Dick Cromwell asked the officer in charge, "Where is he?"

The officer pointed down the shaft.

"Why haven't you pulled him out?"

"Well, because he's dead. And we didn't want to move him before the photographer arrived."

Shannon shrieked, then buried her head against her father's chest and sobbed convulsively. Meanwhile, the photographer stepped out of a helicopter and began his work.

"Give me a line," the officer commanded when the photography was completed. He tied the rope under his arms and across his chest. "Now lower me down—slowly. I'll send him up first the same way."

Six of the soldiers dug their heels into the ground at the edge of the opening, slowly playing out the rope. Horror hung in the air. Shannon wept uncontrollably, while everyone else stood mute and somber. Gideon shook his head and tapped the ground impatiently with his boot. Dick clenched his fists, ready to smash Jennings in the face. Jennings himself feigned shock and sorrow.

"Okay, hoist away!" came a voice from the pit. "But slowly, slowly."

The six troops started tugging in unison. After a seemingly endless wait, Jon's bloodied head appeared over the edge. His eyes were open, which only added to the horror. They removed the rope from his shoulders. Suddenly his corpse raised its right arm slightly, pointed at Jennings, and said thickly. "Arrest 'im . . . for murderin' Brampton . . . me too . . . almost."

Shannon shrieked again and collapsed. Jennings stood rock still and gasped, his skin first white then livid. Cromwell dashed to Jon's side and shouted, "*Water! Give him water!*"

They held a canteen to Jon's lips as he slowly slurped, then gulped, the life-giving fluid. A medic swabbed the dirt off the wound at the back of his head and applied antiseptic and bandages.

Meanwhile, Yorkin had stepped up to Jennings and said, "Extend your arms, sir." Jennings did so, limply. Yorkin slapped handcuffs onto his wrists.

They laid a stretcher on the ground next to Jon. "No, gimme a little time," he protested. "I . . . think I can walk."

"You'll *ride!*" Cromwell commanded. "Congratulations, you magnificent fool! What do we have here, a resurrection?"

"Somethin' like it. Tell ya later."

They stopped at the cafeteria rest house at Qumran. Gideon Ben-Yaakov asked the few tourists inside please to leave the premises "due to an emergency," and then they brought Jon into the air-conditioned lunch room. "Would you like a cold beer?" Gideon asked him.

Jon held up three fingers. Ben-Yaakov promptly placed three ice-cold bottles of Maccabee Beer in front of him. Disdaining a glass, Jon sucked the first bottle dry, almost without stopping. He was into his second when Ben-Yaakov suddenly realized that this was hardly the beverage for someone who had not had liquids for two days. "You might get sloshed in your condition, Jon," he said, removing the bottles and replacing them with a huge pitcher of water. Jon drained two glasses before saying another word.

Jennings was under guard at the back of the room, his turgid face aimed only at the floor. Shannon looked at him wild-eyed and distraught, a corrosive emotional mix swirling inside her—endless gratitude that Jon was alive, worry over his wounds, but horror that her father was somehow implicated in all this.

Jon poured himself another glass and said, "First off, how can I ever thank all of you for . . . for finding me and saving my life?"

Applause and cheers filled the room.

"You look like you saved your own, Jon!" said Cromwell. "Now tell us what happened."

Jon told it all in full detail and noticed sadly how Shannon looked at her father from time to time in shock, then in horrified disgust.

"So Jennings left me with that hideous canister of propane hissing over my head, out of reach," he continued, "and I started to smell the ghastly stuff. I tried jumping as high as I could, but only teased the bottom of the canister. I took off my shirt and swatted it, but it only dangled around the sides of the shaft and kept hissing.

"Then—luckily—I recalled how propane is used—for burning in camp stoves. Great! If I could only *light* the stuff, it would burn off rather than gassing me. At that point, I would have given anything to have had a match on me, but I don't smoke. I knew I had to hurry, too, or lighting that gas would have blown out a crater where the cistern used to be. All I had with me was a flashlight. If I'd had a coil of wire, I could maybe have used the batteries to create a spark, but I didn't. I opened the flashlight and dumped the batteries, because I thought of another way to generate spark. I took the open edge of the flashlight and scraped it across some rocky outcroppings in the side of the cistern . . . Nothing." He paused and gulped down another glass of ice water.

"If you don't finish this, Jon," said Cromwell, "we'll take that pitcher away."

"Okay." Jon smiled. "By now the gas was probably up to my chest, and I started to feel giddy, dizzy, lightheaded. I looked up and prayed. I think I said, 'God, it's in Your hands. If I die, there are others out there who *should* be able to expose this fraud. But they don't have all the facts, and the faith will be mortally wounded. And so *let that dark stone over there be flint, and then let it spark. For Christ's sake—literally!'*"

"Good Lord!" Gideon exclaimed. "What happened then?"

"Well, the good Lord came through. I turned myself toward the wall of the cistern, hunkered against it for an explosion, closed my eyes, and started striking that flintlike rock with the open edge of the flashlight. The first strike did nothing. Neither did the second. Nor the third. I very nearly gave up. But then I thought that maybe the gas hadn't reached that level yet, so I waited a bit, then tried again. Nothing! I tried *again*. There was a colossal *WHOOOMPP!* along with blazing light and searing heat. My shirt was on fire. I whipped around and madly rubbed the fire out on the cistern wall. I could smell my singed hair. After that, I almost passed out because the explosion had used up a lot of the oxygen. But thank God we have the heaviest air on earth at the Dead Sea, and soon I could breathe again. Then I looked up and saw this . . . this beautiful, *beautiful* plume of heavenly blue flame burning out of that canister spigot!"

Laughter and another round of applause rocked the room.

"So I had *that* problem licked," Jon continued. "My next worry, though, was this: what if Jennings should return and see that flame? He'd have switched to cyanide, I'm sure. Waiting there was pure horror, I'll tell you. But when the flame *finally* burned out, it was the most beautiful sight since sunset on the Mediterranean!

"Then, of course, I had to play dead. I sprawled myself across the floor of the cistern just minutes before Jennings returned. He used an air compressor to suck what he thought was propane out of the cistern, while I, of course, couldn't move a muscle. Finally he gave me the Church's blessing. *You bloody hypocrite, Austin!*" he yelled across the room. "And then he left."

"But what about your head wound?" Yorkin inquired.

"Oh, I almost forgot. Jennings dropped this huge rock on me. Luckily most of it hit the ground next to my head or I'd have been killed then instead."

"What about the murder of Clive Brampton?" asked Yorkin.

While Jon described the gassing and the fake drowning, he saw repugnant horror on the faces of Shannon and Cromwell. They could no longer even look at Jennings for sheer revulsion.

Finally Gideon asked, "Could you, perhaps, tell us now how Jennings faked everything at Rama?"

Jon shook his head. "Too long a story. I'm still a little flaky. Tell you tomorrow in Jerusalem, all right?"

"Yes. Yes, of course!"

"Ah, one request, if you don't mind," said Jon, tiring visibly. "The world has a . . . has a right to know, of course. But please, *please* let's communicate the truth in as orderly a fashion as we can. Otherwise, we'll only be opening a Pandora's box of rumors across the earth."

"Yes, that's *very* important," Gideon agreed. He then stood up and announced, "In the name of the government of Israel, I must demand *absolute* confidentiality from *all* of you until formal announcement is made in the very near future. Is that *clearly* understood?"

The assent was unanimous.

As they got up to leave, Jon told Ben-Yaakov, "You're one heck of a good guy, Gideon. Sorry I had to give you such a rough time."

"No, it's just the reverse, Jon," he chuckled. "Forgive me for thinking you were a vandal, a smuggler, an outlaw, and a maniac!"

"What else *could* you think?"

Every stratum in Israel seemed to hum with activity over the next two days. While Jon recuperated, the Israel Antiquities Authority alerted the world media to send representatives to "a final press conference regarding the Rama excavations" in Jerusalem four days hence. In custody, meanwhile, Jennings was examined by a panel of psychiatrists and pronounced fit to stand trial, even though afflicted with a compulsive neurosis on religious matters. Cromwell phoned the publishers in Tel Aviv to hold off any printing of the epitome. Shannon was distraught and uncommunicative, so profoundly shocked and dazed by what her father had done that it seemed to bury the joy of Jon's rescue. Naomi, however, put fresh flowers on Clive Brampton's grave, promising his spirit that someday she would personally kill Austin Balfour Jennings if she could, since Israel had no death penalty.

The final press conference that would ever be associated with Rama took place on the last Thursday in November, coincidentally, the American Thanksgiving Day. But, then, Rama had an old habit of desecrating holy days and intruding into holidays. The 3,500-seat National Convention Center in West Jerusalem was filled to capacity. A forest of microphones loomed up in front of the podium, and television cameras commanded most of the aisles. The chief of the Jerusalem Fire Department was apoplectic.

Three men sat at the green table on the dais—Gideon, Jon, and Austin Balfour Jennings. Behind Jennings stood two uniformed police guards. At 10:05 AM, Gideon opened the conference. "I bid you all welcome, on behalf of the Israel Antiquities Authority. This will be the final press conference concerning the Rama excavation, since we are pleased to announce that all controversies regarding it have now been resolved. Let me say in advance that nearly all of the archaeology and the artifacts at Rama are *absolutely* authentic, and must *not* be impugned because of what has now proven to be *fraud* at the cavern area."

A tremendous commotion filled the auditorium. Gideon rapped for order, then continued, "What is clearly the greatest hoax in history has been perpetrated by Professor Austin Balfour Jennings at my extreme right. That deception was finally discovered, largely through the dedicated efforts of Professor Jonathan E. Weber, at the center." He now recounted the crisis that Jon had survived at the Dead Sea, after which he said, "Professor Weber, perhaps you'd be kind enough to tell the world what is fraudulent and what is genuine at the cavern area."

Jon leaned toward his microphone and said, "Shortly we'll be passing out a complete summary of our findings. But, to put it briefly—" He went on to give a précis of Jennings's frauds. He concluded, "Finally, he buried the entrance to the cavern with local surface materials, and almost a quarter-century of rains settled the area enough to resemble undisturbed ground."

Most eyes in the auditorium were fixed on Jennings. He sat before his microphone, chin on the palm of his left hand, registering no detectable emotion. He merely stared blankly toward the rear of the auditorium.

"You may well wonder," Jon continued, "why we have Dr. Jennings on the platform here. He is, after all, under indictment for murder in addition to fraud. By his own admission, he put to death our excellent colleague, Dr. Clive Brampton."

A thunder of commotion welled up. Again Gideon rapped for order. Jon resumed, "Dr. Jennings told us of his profound regret over what he had done. No 'plea-bargaining' of any kind was involved, I can assure you. He has volunteered to supply all remaining details in the fullest possible confession, so that the world may know the truth, once and for all, and we need not be subjected to theories and vagaries for centuries to come. And so, Professor Jennings, you have the floor. What else can you tell us, also about your motives?"

For some moments, Jennings said nothing. Then he slowly shook his head and said, into the open microphone: "I . . . I can't bring it off, Jonathan. I . . . I really *wanted* to, you know. That was a marvelous idea you had—to use Clive's drowning as part of our plot, and then to *stage* a 'murder attempt' on my part as you hid in that hole near the Dead Sea . . . but especially to give out the story that I forged it all! Look, I'd do *anything* to cover up the truth about Rama. Like Father Montaigne, I was *almost* ready to sacrifice my professional reputation for Jesus and claim I did it all. But *you* get off scot-free in this scenario of yours, while *I* have to pay the price—life imprisonment for 'murder,' so-called! It's not fair, Jonathan, and I won't perjure myself any longer."

Turning back to the audience, he exclaimed, "Rama is *not* a fraud, ladies and gentlemen. Everything is *authentic* there! Jesus's bones *have* been discovered, I deeply regret to say. But *truth* comes before *everything* else!"

General pandemonium broke out in the auditorium. Some reporters made a dash for telephones.

"Turn off that maniac's microphone," Gideon hissed to a technician.

"Whoever leaves this auditorium now is a *fool!*" Jon announced. "This is only a last, desperate subterfuge on the part of a psychotic *liar!* We were foolish to believe any regrets on his part. Once again, he's trying to take us all for idiots!"

As the auditorium quieted down, Jon took an inventory of the damage done by Jennings's demonic genius. He quickly realized that the only *material* link to the truth that existed were Dunstable's carbon and ceramic particles. He had called to say that the Oxford accelerator found "virtually identical" amounts of C-14 in them . . . always the "virtually." Because of that adverb,

Jon knew, the fanatics who feed on religion or religion-debunking, the marginal minds, and the conspiracy theorists would have a field day for centuries to come. Perhaps even believers, now, could never be sure. They would only be "virtually" sure that the bones were not Jesus's.

Jon glanced at Jennings, who still stared straight ahead, the trace of a smile tugging back the corners of his ample mouth. The hall had hushed to a vast silence, awaiting Jon's response. He was preparing to launch into a dissertation on ceramic particles when suddenly he remembered something better—*far* better. He made a lunge for his attaché case. "I never thought it would come to this, ladies and gentlemen," he announced, "and not since my ordeal at the Dead Sea did I think to check. But while I was in the cistern and Jennings was ranting overhead, I did have the sense to turn on the little microcassette recorder I always carry with me for personal memos. I've no idea if the batteries were fresh enough, but let me try—"

He tried to rewind the mechanism, but the cassette wheels barely turned. "O God," he whispered. "I wonder if I got *any* of it!"

Schmuel Sanderson, the AP stringer in Jerusalem, leaped up to the dais. "I owe you one, Professor Weber," he said. "I've got the same brand recorder. Here, try mine. I just put in fresh batteries this morning."

Jon thanked him, switched the cassette, and rewound it. Then he pressed the "play" button and held it up to the microphone. "MUST CHECK WITH LINDA AT THE ALBRIGHT—" filled all speakers in the hall. He pushed the stop button and announced, sheepishly, "That's a memo—*not* the right spot." He pushed "forward" again for some moments, and then "play."

Again Jon's voice came through loud and clear: "AND YOU, OF COURSE, HAD EVERYTHING TO DO WITH RAMA, RIGHT?" Jennings's voice now boomed across the entire auditorium: "RIGHT YOU ARE, MY GOOD FRIEND. FROM BEGINNING TO END, 'TWAS I, AND I ALONE—"

Jon had it, and, as he would soon learn, he had it all! For the next fifteen minutes, the hall sat in stunned silence as the awful drama played itself out.

At the end, Jon extracted the cassette and handed the recorder back to Sanderson. Then he took the dead batteries out of his own recorder and set them on the green table in front of him. "Thanks, fellas," he said to the two type AA penlight batteries. "You gave your all. But, then, you also saved one huge chunk of civilization. Good old coppertops!"

TWENTY-SEVEN

The auditorium broke into pandemonium. The pages who were passing out the releases were mobbed. Phone lines, e-mail, cable, telex, radio, shortwave, TV satellite transmissions, and the mails out of Israel were jammed with accounts of the Rama exposure, and it commanded the world's headlines for days afterward.

"EASTER AT THANKSGIVING!" bannered the *Chicago Tribune,* and church bells started ringing across the world the moment the news broke. The Sunday following—the first Sunday in Advent—marked the beginning of a new church year, and clergy across the world were quick to note the happy coincidence as they tried to preach to jammed congregations, though both shepherd and flock were often so overcome with emotion that they took to hymns and prayers instead. The long, long nightmare of uncertainty was over at last, the resurrection of the Resurrection a cause for global joy.

While the Christian world celebrated over the next months, however, Jonathan Weber suffered. It was not the closing of the Rama excavations—they were completed in any case—or the dozen manuscript volumes of now nearly useless scholarly tomes attesting to "the virtual authenticity" of Rama that troubled him, but the woman in whom he had *not* confided his suspicions of her father. In the weeks following her father's arrest, Shannon seemed shattered by the riptide of horror that had flooded her life so instantaneously. In a single hour she had had to learn the grisly details of her mother's death; that the father whom she loved and endlessly admired was a record-shattering liar, deceiver, and scoundrel, who had murdered one of her closest friends in behalf of his insane scheme; that her father's crimes had also affected millions of innocents; and that the man she loved so exuberantly had withheld the truth from her, then died a terrible death, but then returned to life. The human psyche can stand only so much.

The Israeli court trying Jennings understood as much, and both prosecution and defense tried to spare Shannon as much as legally possible. Jon bore the brunt of it all as chief witness for the prosecution, and the world had not watched an Israeli trial so intensely since that of Adolf Eichmann. The prosecution, in fact, had insisted that the extraordinary law passed by the Knesset, permitting the death penalty for Eichmann, really ought to apply to Austin Balfour Jennings as well, since he also had committed "crimes against humanity." Although there was considerable support for that view, Jennings came off with life imprisonment. He would spend the rest of his days in his cell, deeply immersed in Semitics studies and writing a dictionary of rural Aramaic, which he dedicated "To the Memory of Clive F. Brampton." The scholarly world was pleased, deeming it a "compensation for crime," though some critics wondered if Jennings were not preparing tools for another forger in the twenty-second century!

The day after Jennings's sentencing, Jon returned to Ramallah and found this letter in a sealed envelope slid under his bedroom door:

Jonathan,

I'm finally able to see things in better perspective. At last, for example, I can try to see your point of view in withholding the truth about Papa from me. But you were wrong in assuming that it would have been difficult for a daughter to keep such a confidence from the father she loved. Didn't I keep silent about your absence when my father returned from England—because of the man I loved? And that was not, as you thought, because of the "surprise" you had in store for him. Some "surprise" indeed!

Not that I condone what Papa did. He has disgraced the name of Jennings for centuries to come. You were loving and chivalrous in offering to "solve that little problem" for me by changing my name in marriage. But when a man and a woman pledge

themselves to each other, they should be able to trust each other.
You were unable to do that.

I want to start a new life for myself, Jon. I will have left Israel
by the time you read this, and if I never set foot here again, it
will be too soon. To me this is strictly the Unholy Land. I am
not returning to Oxford, so please don't try to find me there, or
anywhere else. I loved you, Jon . . . more than life itself. I sup-
pose I'll always remember our love, but I'm no longer in love
with you.

> *Good-bye,*
> *Shannon*

The rash of phone calls Jon made to the international airlines at
Ben Gurion proved futile. By now, Shannon would be landing . . .
where? England?

The shock was fierce and brutal. He sat at his bedroom desk,
reading and rereading Shannon's letter, as if a new reading might
somehow change something. Great tears flooded his eyes. Had a
jackal outside howled at that moment, he would have strangled
the animal with his bare hands.

The days and weeks following were laced with loneliness and
pain. The only glimmer of gladness was his success in dodging the
press. Every other magazine in the world, it seemed, wanted "*the*
inside story" on how he had come to suspect and then unmask
Jennings.

Jon hid out in Galilee for a while, until he could stand it no
longer. Each time he looked at the blue Sea of Galilee, he felt
another searing stab of recollection and then grief. Shannon was
everywhere: along the beaches, behind the waterfall at Panias, in
a becalmed sailboat on the lake, in the glorious hotel at Tiberias.
Love was a fearful equalizer: what it gave in joy and ecstasy, it
took back in heartbreak and agony.

Cromwell, who was helping him close the dig, was the one con-
fidant with whom he could bare his heart. Dick thought it "easily
possible" that Shannon might change her mind, but the Jerusalem
psychiatrist who had helped Noel Nottingham pointed out that

the traumas she had suffered could well have upset all her previous emotional attachments.

"*La donna e mobile*," said Jon, trying to wax philosophical. Too keenly he remembered his first great love in college, who had simply flown out of his life one day, without so much as a good-bye kiss. Was history repeating itself?

Even though he *knew* it would only add torture to his grief, Jon could not help himself. He opened the booklet of love poems Shannon had sent him months earlier and read them over and over again. He easily memorized his favorite:

> *I long to wake*
> *in the shelter and comfort*
> *of your strong protective arms.*

> *I await the day*
> *when our union will be complete,*
> *and our souls together for all time.*

"For all time?" he whispered, over a new stab of sadness.

> *I breathe for you,*
> *and because of you I live*
> *more fully than ever imagined.*

> *I want to capture your heart*
> *and hold it prisoner*
> *within my soul eternally.*

"Is eternity so short?" he asked his empty room.

Just before Christmas, he phoned Glastonbury and asked if he could try to locate Shannon for him, "as a personal favor." The odds, after all, were strong that she had gone to Britain. Glastonbury had a surprisingly difficult time of it, but he finally identified her whereabouts as Drogheda in Ireland. Evidently, Shannon was trying to discover her roots. Jon wanted to fly there at once, but Glastonbury wisely counseled against it. "She needs time to recover, Jonathan," he said. "Come on the scene too soon, and you'll ruin any chance to win her back."

The following spring, the last field- and paperwork had been done in closing Rama. Jon embraced Achmed Sa'ad and Ibrahim for the last time, asking them to extend his thanks to the Arab labor force for having worked so diligently. Cromwell had left for the States a week earlier. During his last morning in Jerusalem, Jon bade good-bye to Nikos Papadimitriou at the Rockefeller, and even Claude Montaigne at the École Biblique.

"See," the little Frenchman said, "I *told* you it was a forgery, no?" His eyes twinkled happily.

"*Vous avez raison, mon cher Père!*" affirmed Jon. He embraced him and took his leave.

He thought of paying Jennings a final visit in prison, but then vetoed the idea. Someday, perhaps.

His last official act was to witness the reburial of the Christlike remains at the Qumran cemetery, from which Jennings had removed them. His last visit was to Clive Brampton's grave.

Gideon Ben-Yaakov and Naomi Sharon saw him off at Ben Gurion Airport. "Thanks, Gideon," said Jon. "Thanks for being such a prince despite all the flak I sent your way!"

"No! Thanks to you in behalf of archaeology, Jon. We should be able to handle fraud much better in the future. We've learned a few things."

Naomi threw her arms around Jon and wept. But they were tears of joy. "Tell him, Gideon," she squealed.

Gideon beamed and said, "Naomi . . . has consented to be my wife."

Jon exploded with surprise. "*Delighted* for both of you! Now, *that's* a match made in heaven! May you parent a whole dynasty of diggers!"

"This summer!" Naomi exclaimed. "If you come back for the wedding, we'll make you the best man, Jonathan. Won't we, Gideon?"

"Absolutely!"

It was the nicest *bon voyage* he could have received, Jon mused, as his 747 took off for the States. His sabbatical was over. At two years, it surely had been a *long* one.

Easter came late that year. It would be the first Festival of the Resurrection since the Rama exposure, and the Christian world was preparing for the most exuberant celebration ever.

"Shannon is checking her roots," Jon mused. "I ought to get back to mine." He recalled how he had surprised his parents two Christmases earlier. This time he would do it for Easter.

Déjà vu. The same flight brought him to St. Louis, the same highway to Hannibal. Only this time, Missouri 61 was rimmed in a green bursting with wildflowers, rather than snow and ice. The 11 AM service at St. John overflowed with jubilant worshipers. Again Jon donned sunglasses and hunkered into the last pew, next to a phalanx of new parents with howling babies.

This time the figure in the wheat-colored alb who mounted the pulpit had a spring in his step and a smile on his face. His father also delivered what was probably the finest sermon of his life, trying hard not to refer to his own son too proudly or too often.

At the close, the Reverend Erhard Weber waxed eloquent:

"Why did God permit something like Rama to happen?" you may well ask. Since I don't advise the Almighty, I can't really say. But the old adage "You never appreciate anything unless it's taken away from you" surely applies here. Christians across the entire world, who almost lost the very heart of their faith, are now cherishing it as never before. We see a new wave in all denominations and in all lands. We see massive outpourings for worship, and not just on Easter Sunday. We also see a great movement toward Christian unity now sweeping the Church. Just last week, Pope Benedict XVI invited all those scholars and church leaders who had worked so hard in Jerusalem to come to Rome and lay plans for a great ecumenical council—Vatican III—which will aim for much greater unity in Christendom.

And so, once again, God has taken human plans for evil and turned them into blessings. This Easter, we have a Deliverer again—not a deceiver. We have the assurance of life after death—not just dissolution and dust. We have the resurrection of the body and the life everlasting! Amen!

"*Amen!*" the congregation responded, in most *un*-Lutheran fashion. His father closed the Bible and stepped down from the pulpit. But suddenly he returned, smiled, and shouted, "*He is risen!*"

"*He is risen indeed!*" the congregation replied, in the classic Easter response.

Although he had heard the phrases hundreds of times since childhood and Sunday school, they never carried as much meaning for Jonathan Paul Weber as at that moment.

His eyes were too blurred to notice a figure who walked over from the other side of the sanctuary, and now crowded into the pew next to him. "Why don't you take off those silly glasses and let the people see one of God's greatest heroes, Jon," she whispered. "Or shall I get someone else to introduce me to your parents?"

Shannon had never looked more beautiful. She was radiant with the new spring, the new Easter for both of their lives. Jon clasped her to himself in a delirium flooded by torrents of total joy. Later would come any questions about how she came to be there. For now, heaven had descended to earth.

"Such carrying on—in church, no less!" someone whispered. But the rest of the congregation was singing the final hymn, triumphantly:

> Lives again our glorious King!
> Where, O Death, is now thy sting?
> Once He died our souls to save;
> Where the victory, O grave?

ABOUT THE AUTHOR

Paul L. Maier is a best-selling author of both fiction and non-fiction. A professor of ancient history at Western Michigan University, he graduated from Harvard (M.A.) and Concordia Seminary (M.Div.), before he took his Ph.D. *summa cum laude* at the University of Basel, the first American ever to do so. He has several million copies of his books in print—in twelve languages. His popular novels include *A Skeleton in God's Closet, More Than a Skeleton, Pontius Pilate,* and *The Flames of Rome.* He also penned the best-selling trilogy of books on the life of Jesus and earliest Christianity, now included in one volume, *In the Fullness of Time.* His translations of the first-century Jewish historian Josephus and the father of church history, Eusebius, are widely used. His children's book, *The Very First Christmas,* received the Gold Medallion Award in 1999, and was followed by *The Very First Easter* and *The Very First Christians.* Dr. Maier travels and lectures widely, appearing frequently in national radio, television, and newspaper interviews. He and his wife, Joan, have four daughters.

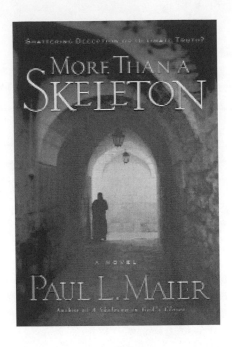

W hat if Jesus returned for an interim appearance before His final coming? And in a manner least expected? Once again, Dr. Jonathan Weber must determine the truth at all costs.

Joshua Ben-Yosef attracts a huge following. He speaks more than a dozen languages—fluently and without accent. His words ripple with wisdom and authority. And the crowds that follow him are enthralled as he heals the sick, gives sight to the blind, casts out demons, and even raises the dead.

More Than a Skeleton, from the #1 best-selling author of *A Skeleton in God's Closet*, pulls the reader into a world where all assumptions about Christ's return seem to be fulfilled in a mysterious figure who is . . . much more than a skeleton.

ISBN: 1-5955-4003-2

Made in the USA
San Bernardino, CA
15 June 2013